modern publicity volume 54

world advertising review 1985

edited by Philip Kleinman

Cassell

Holt, Rinehart
and Winston

Edited by Philip Kleinman
Designed by Langley Iddins

Typeset by Central Southern Typesetters, Eastbourne, UK
Artwork by Southern Flair Ltd, Eastbourne, UK
Reproduction by Colourscan, Singapore
Printed and bound by Canale S.p.A., Turin, Italy

British Library Cataloguing in Publication Data

World Advertising Review 1985: Modern
Publicity Volume 54
1. Commerical art—Periodicals
I. Kleinman, Philip
659.12 NC997.A1

UK ISBN 0-304-31113-8
US ISBN 0-03-007003-1

contents

The diamond jubilee of a new book

This first edition of *World Advertising Review* also marks its diamond jubilee. The paradox is simply explained. Despite the change of title, this is the 60th volume in a line which stretches back, through previous name changes, to 1924. In that year the magazine *The Studio* published a special number called *Posters and Their Designers.* A similar volume was published the following year under the title *Art and Publicity*. Both were so well received that Geoffrey Holme, proprietor of *The Studio,* decided there should be an annual devoted to the best in advertising art. This appeared from 1926 to 1929 under the title of *Posters and Publicity*. In 1930 it was renamed *Modern Publicity*, as which it was to survive through 53 editions.

But words change their meaning, and the title appropriate in the 1930s is no longer so in the 1980s, when 'publicity' has come to have in English a specialised meaning quite different from 'advertising'. To avoid any ambiguity, especially for the sake of new readers, it was felt necessary to find a new title. While we were changing the name it also seemed right to emphasise the book's main distinguishing feature, which is of course its internationality. Hence *World Advertising Review*.

If the title is new, the editorial policy remains, however, precisely what it has been since 1983, that is to make this annual a showcase for the brightest ideas conceived in all countries in the field of printed advertising. The text again attempts to explain the relevance of those ideas to the marketing conditions in which the advertisers and agencies concerned have to work.

Now some comments on the contents of the 1985 *Review*. Last year's *Modern Publicity*, it will be remembered, promised to turn the spotlight in successive editions on different countries, including some of the smaller advertising markets which might otherwise go inadequately represented. The promise holds good for *World Advertising Review*. Last year particular attention was devoted to India; this time around Italy, Norway and the Netherlands are much better represented than previously.

Norway is well represented in several of the 22 sections into which the book is divided, including Public Service and Political, which this year is one of the most interesting categories. It is noteworthy that some of the most striking designs in the section are in black and white. Among them are British campaigns for Oxfam (Fletcher Shelton Delaney), the National Society for the Prevention of Cruelty to Children (Saatchi & Saatchi Compton), the Spastics Society (Benton & Bowles) and the Greater London Council (Boase Massimi Pollitt). Another impactful black and white ad is that by MPM, of Brazil, for Alcoholics Anonymous, showing a man crucified on a wine glass. Excellent colour ads in the same section are contributed by two Oslo agencies, Heltberg and Ogilvy & Mather, about respectively road safety and health information.

Several agencies make their appearance for the first time in this edition (considering it as 60th of a series rather than first to bear the new name). Worthy of mention are the new French agency Boulet Dru Dupuy Petit, represented by visually impactful campaigns for Hertz and French Railways as well as others, and the small Milan agency STZ (Suter Tschirren Zucchini) which has a well developed sense of humour. This can be seen from its work for Bidone vacuum cleaners, Sisal carpets and Vortice convection heaters – unlikely subjects, you might have thought, for jokes.

At one time banks and financial institutions would have beeen seen as the least likely subjects of all for advertising humour. No more. A glance at the Financial section will show that the trend, noticeable in previous years, towards using humour as a means of humanising the image of the bank has gained yet more ground. Particularly engaging are the caricatures used by Ted Bates 3 in Stockholm, for Götabanken, and Grey, Düsseldorf, for the Norddeutsche Landesbank.

As well as new agencies and new campaigns it is a pleasure to include fresh examples of some long-running campaigns already chosen for previous annuals. The ads by Collett Dickenson Pearce for Benson & Hedges are the most obvious case in point. The campaign has not ceased to amuse, though it is outdone in surrealism by some other ads such as Ally & Gargano's for Karastan carpets and the Kasugai poster, reproduced on this edition's dust jacket, for Sistiene women's clothes.

A highly innovative campaign, launched shortly before selection for this *Review* ended, is that created for Volvo by TBWA, London and published internationally in upmarket newspapers and business journals. The campaign, represented in the Corporate section by the first ad to have appeared, takes the form of moral fables illustrated by well known artists and with no direct praise of the advertiser.

The stories, with morals such as the need to be prepared for change and the triumph of far-sighted prudence over short-sighted greed, can be – and Volvo no doubt hopes will be – taken as applying to the company, but they do not have to be. The first in the series was written by a copywriter, but TBWA has been approaching well known non-advertising authors to contribute. The campaign has had a mixed reception, going down less well in the United States, the land of the hard sell, than in the United Kingdom, where advertising has become to a much larger extent a branch of the entertainment industry.

It will be interesting to see whether other agencies follow TBWA's lead in turning printed advertising, or a small part of it, into a kind of literary and artistic sponsorship. Next year's edition of *World Advertising Review* may have the answer. As to whether such a style of advertising will do anything for the clients, well that's another question entirely. But if any evidence is forthcoming the text of next year's *Review* will report it.

Philip Kleinman

ABERDEEN CABLE
GAVE US £350,000.
NUTRASWEET
GAVE US £1 MILLION.
COMPAQ GAVE US £1 MIL LION.
PLAYER'S
GAVE US £2 MILLION.
AIR CANADA GAVE US £1·3 MILLION.
KIMBERLY CLARK GAVE
US £1·4 MILLION.
PHILIPS GAVE US £3·5 MILLION.
JOHN WEST
GAVE US £1·3 MILLION.
GUINNESS WORLDWIDE GAVE US £3 MILLION.
GUINNESS U.K. GAVE US £7 MILLION.
P.C.L. GAVE US £500,000.
CAMPARI GAVE
US £1 MILLION.
PHILIPS
GAVE US £2 MILLION.
W. H. SMITH CABLE
GAVE US £500,000.
BEECHAM GAVE
US £1·6 MILLION.
PRICE WATERHOUSE GAVE US £250,000.
RALEIGH GAVE US THE BOOT.
Well, you can't win 'em all. Witness our 1984.
To our credit, we added umpteen new bits of business. To our chagrin, Raleigh got on their bike.
(We lost a couple of others, too.)
All told, however, we put on business worth more than £30 million.
Which goes nicely with the £14m we added in 1983. And the £15½ million we acquired in '82.
If you care to contact our chairman, Peter Warren, he can tell you the facts behind these figures.
Initially, we can reveal this: O&M.
Ogilvy & Mather. Brettenham House, Lancaster Place, London WC2E 7EZ. Telephone: 01-836 2466

1

ABC1's had some rather primitive ideas about the microwave oven.

Superstition, hearsay, ignorance, fear and tall tales were rife.

"Microwaves," we were informed, "have these deadly invisible ultra-thermic gamma rays. A woman in Lithuania once zapped...."

"Not only that," interrupted someone else, "but for three hundred notes all you can cook with them is baked bloody potatoes."

So we took a few double page spreads in the women's magazines to show housewives what the Philips microwave could really do.

It poached, browned, roasted and seared.

Simmered; stir-fried and steamed.

It dried herbs, chambreed claret, and, believe it or not, even rustled up a quick sloe jelly.

And after all that our £300 Philips ultra-thermic Gamma Ray Baked Potato Zapper did something even more remarkable. It sold out.

OGILVY & MATHER

Brettenham House, Lancaster Place, London WC2E 7EZ. Tel: 01-836 2466.

2

1, 2, 3
United Kingdom
Agency: Ogilvy & Mather, London

Negative headlines are well known to be risky, though copywriters are often keen on them. O & M seems to have done itself no harm by accentuating the negative. The body copy in the 'idiot' ad explains that only one person, out of 100,000 who commented, disliked the agency's picture of a baby at its mother's breast (published in last year's edition of this book) aimed at arousing interest in the Canned Food Advisory Service. The visual in the 'boot' ad offsets the headline by showing symbols of the many new clients which did not follow the example of Raleigh in firing O & M. The third ad indulges in fantasy to make the serious point that the Philips microwave oven has been a commercial success. Agencies like to imply, as here, that such success is due to advertising, even when they do not actually say so.

4, 5
Japan
Agency: Kasugai, Nagoya City

Each year Kasugai produces a series of posters designed simply to show off its creative imagination. These are two of the best.

3

4

5

6, 7
Spain
Agency: McCann-Erickson, Madrid

Two pages from a brochure which uses attractive, though not entirely unfamiliar, surrealistic images to illustrate the product areas in which the agency claims expertise. Clients and brands mentioned in the brochure include Kodak, Paper Mate, Nestlé and Flora margarine.

8
Netherlands
Agency: Ted Bates, Amsterdam

'Everyone wants to be the brown egg, but how do you get to be it?' asks the headline. Copy explains that when people have the choice between a white and a brown egg, they'll almost certainly go for the brown one even though it tastes no different. Bates, says the ad, gives the same kind of added value to each product it handles by creating for it a Unique Selling Personality. The Unique Selling Proposition (as defined years ago by Bates's Rosser Reeves in the US) is apparently no longer enough.

9
United Kingdom
Agency: Young & Rubicam, London

Y & R capitalises here on the fame of one of its longest-running campaigns, or rather series of campaigns – for Smirnoff vodka. The point made in the left-hand half of the ad is that advertising makes a big difference between otherwise identical products, a point no ad agency is likely to find fault with. The two ads within the right-hand half are one of Y & R's oldest for the brand and one which featured in Modern Publicity 1983. Both won praise, but the older one ('Accountancy was my life until I discovered Smirnoff') was much more of a trendsetter than its successors.

6

7

8

9

10
United States
Agency: Hutchins/Y & R, Rochester, New York State

Pictured as a military commander is Rob Wilson, the agency's manager of consumer accounts. The military metaphor is often used in marketing but rarely given the visual back-up it gets here.

11
Italy
Agency: Young & Rubicam, Milan

'If you are satisfied with your agency, telephone Y & R', says this cheeky ad. Copy explains that one of the secrets of success is never to be satisfied, for no situation cannot be improved. What makes the ad particularly cheeky is that it was produced after a period during which Y & R was not thought greatly to have distinguished itself creatively. However, the ad is one of the first fruits of the arrival of a new creative director, Gavino Sanna, formerly at Benton & Bowles.

12
Netherlands
Agency: Marketwinning Ayer, Wierden

'The consumer likes gooseflesh' says the headline. Image and heading are explained in the body copy which says consumers like to feel emotion. The copy refers to Ayer's worldwide philosophy of Human Contact, putting as much emphasis on people as on the products advertised.

13
Italy
Agency: FCA/Sabbatini Baldoni Panzeri, Milan

A page from a launch brochure for a new Italian agency, affiliated to FCA of Paris. The headline refers, as the picture makes clear, to the power struggle 'in many big agencies' and its 'influence on the final product'. The new shop promises, of course, to be different. The cover of the brochure bears a quotation fictitiously attributed to Woody Allen: 'If there is a God, does he realise there are 26 different types of aspirin?'

10

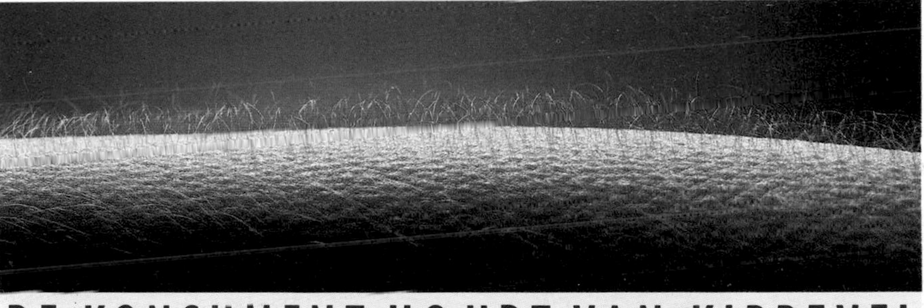

12

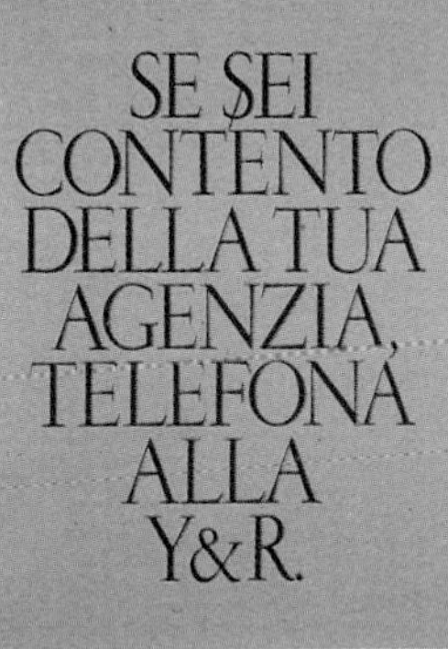

11

13

14
Haig whisky
Japan
Agency: Dentsu, Tokyo

'More delicious than work' is the headline. The sexual innuendo is unmistakable. In the West the feminist lobby would be outraged. But the picture is pretty.

14

15

15
Cutty Sark whisky
France
Agency: Young & Rubicam, Paris

One of a series of pleasing verbal-cum-visual puns (though very few puns find their way into this book). The headline here is 'Whisky dry' and the Cutty Sark ship is indeed high and dry.

16
Doble-V whisky
Spain
Agency: McCann-Erickson, Madrid

The agency has picked up the hint in the brand name of Hiram Walker's Double-V whisky. The image is a double one, with the furniture reflected in surrealistic style. The copy line tells the reader that the whisky 'is where you are'. One seeks in vain for any connection between that line and the visual theme.

16

17
Seagram's V.O. Canadian whisky
United States
Agency: Ogilvy & Mather, New York

The agency's objective was to prop up the declining fortunes of the brand by making V.O. 'a more relevant brand choice for the young adult population' while hanging on to its existing older market. The solution was to focus on an attitude said to be shared by the two groups, 'the work ethic inherent in the return to traditional values being witnessed nationwide.' Hence the 'reward' theme, illustrated in a series of human interest pictures.

For over fifteen years Robert Koralja, Andrew Koralja and Joseph Koralja have helped to keep Jersey City safe, safe, safe.
So they each received a bottle of V.O.

17

18
Johnnie Walker whisky
Switzerland
Agency: Young & Rubicam, Bern

Y & R's Swiss office keeps coming up with ingenious uses of the Johnnie Walker symbol (see the previous two editions of this book). Here is another one.

18

19
Johnnie Walker Red Label whisky
United Kingdom
Agency: Young & Rubicam, London

Advertising in international media by the same agency for the same brand is far more strait-laced than this UK campaign, which takes the aspirational element in other Red Label ads and parodies it.

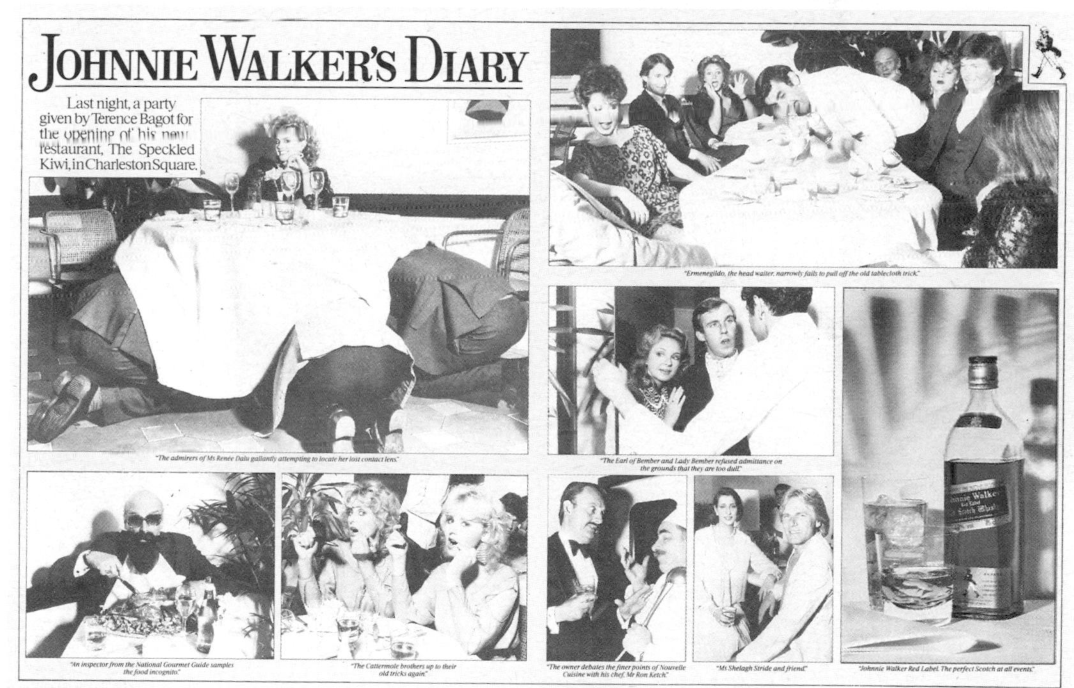

19

20

21

REMY MARTIN
"Just checking."
REMY MARTIN FINE CHAMPAGNE COGNAC. DISTILLED ONLY FROM GRAPES GROWN IN COGNAC'S TWO FINEST CRUS.

22

20
Hennessy Cognac
United Kingdom
Agency: Leagas Delaney Partnership, London

The brand is dubbed Very Special, and the visual treatment manages also to be special. The pictures look very different from other people's booze advertising.

21
Hine Cognac
United Kingdom
Agency: Dorland Advertising, London

A captivating picture. The fantasy element could easily have been overdone. But, with cognac the price it is in Britain, an unsubtle execution would have been counter-productive.

22
Rémy Martin VSOP Cognac
United Kingdom
Agency: SSC&B: Lintas, London

A pre-Christmas ad which manages to put a clever new twist into the hackneyed Christmas wrapping theme.

23

23
Plymouth Gin
United Kingdom
Agency: Lowe Howard-Spink
Campbell-Ewald, London

One of a witty series of ads which prove that good work can be done on comparatively small accounts. But then, a small brand can afford to take risks, such as addressing those who wish to learn to be gentlemen, which bigger brands might not.

24
United States
Gordon's Gin
Agency: Grey Advertising, New York

Quite a different approach from FCB's much admired British advertising for the same product (see no. 25). This uses the human touch, obviously aimed at yuppies (young urban professionals).

24

25
Gordon's Gin
United Kingdom
Agency: Foote Cone & Belding, London

FCB's previous work on Gordon's proved that a pack shot could be a thing of beauty. In this campaign featuring different kinds of cocktail the green bottle moves away from centre stage, but the show is still eye-catching.

25

26
Smirnoff vodka
United Kingdom
Agency: Young & Rubicam, London

The latest phase in Y & R's Smirnoff advertising, of which it feels justifiably proud (see its self-promotion ad in the previous section) marks a return to fantasy, though of a different kind from the first phase 15 years ago.

26

27
Vladivar vodka
United Kingdom
Agency: Kirkwood & Partners, London

Vladivar, number two brand in the UK to Smirnoff, has consistently over many years stuck to the same humorous advertising theme, making fun of the Russians. The latest campaign, jokier than ever, may well have pleased the young women known to be important consumers of vodka. The copy tells of the female agent who discovered the operations of a Soviet spy ring using a fake hairdressing salon to extract electronically from the heads of workers at the Vladivar distillery in Warrington the secrets of the brand's formula. Yes, the humour is somewhat juvenile.

27

28, 29
Martini
West Germany
Agency: McCann-Erickson, Frankfurt

What these two Martini ads, for the Rosso and Extra Dry varieties of the drink, have in common – apart from their fantasy character – is the outstretched female arm, with the rest of the female unseen. Women, one supposes, are the target readers, though the fantasy figures are male. The heading on the 'chess' ad is 'Classical opening', and on the 'green man' ad 'It's something about the suit'. The pay-off line on both is 'Martini, ice-cold encounter of the stimulating kind.'

28

29

30

30
Martini Extra Dry
United Kingdom
Agency: McCann-Erickson, London

The drinks tray as a water lily. This is fantasy of a different, tenderer kind than the German Martini ads. The agency calls this particular ad not 'Water lily', however, but 'Goldfish'. Yes, if you look carefully, you can see it.

31
Campari
International
Agency: B Communications, Milan

Sexy, yes. But very pretty, too. One of a series of attractively photographed pack shots.

31

32
Suntory Twilight Cocktails Book
Japan
Agency: Dentsu, Tokyo

A somewhat bizarre mixture of Japanese and Western artistic styles characterises this spread from a booklet on the making of cocktails put out by Suntory, the giant Japanese drinks firm.

32

33a, 33b
Amaretto di Saronno
France
Agency: Roux Séguéla Cayzac & Goudard, Paris

'Make love to me, long drink.' Well, the sex sell cannot get much more blatant than that. The pay-off line on this two-page ad, 'To be consumed in moderation', is presumably meant as a joke.

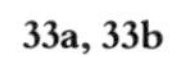

33a

Fais-moi
l'amour
long
drink.
A consommer avec modération.

33b

34
Taranagi Kiwi-Fruit Cocktail
South Africa
Agency: Campbell-Ewald, Cape Town

The packaging design for Taranagi, by the Janice Ashby Design Studio of Cape Town, won a gold Clio award in 1984. This ad, which positions the product as a versatile, stylish mixer, relies on the simple but effective visual device of showing a gradually emptying bottle as it explains the uses to which the drink can be put.

34

35
Banks's Ale
United Kingdom
Agency: TBWA, London

'Oldfangled, Unspoilt by progress', Banks's sticks to the style it has laid down for itself. This picture owes something to the influence of the cartoonist Heath Robinson.

36
Tetley Bitter beer
United Kingdom
Agency: Kirkwood & Partners, London

The brand is the biggest-selling beer in the North of England, and this poster campaign reflects that market position. It also reflects a movement among advertising creatives generally to draw the consumer's attention to the medium as well as the message.

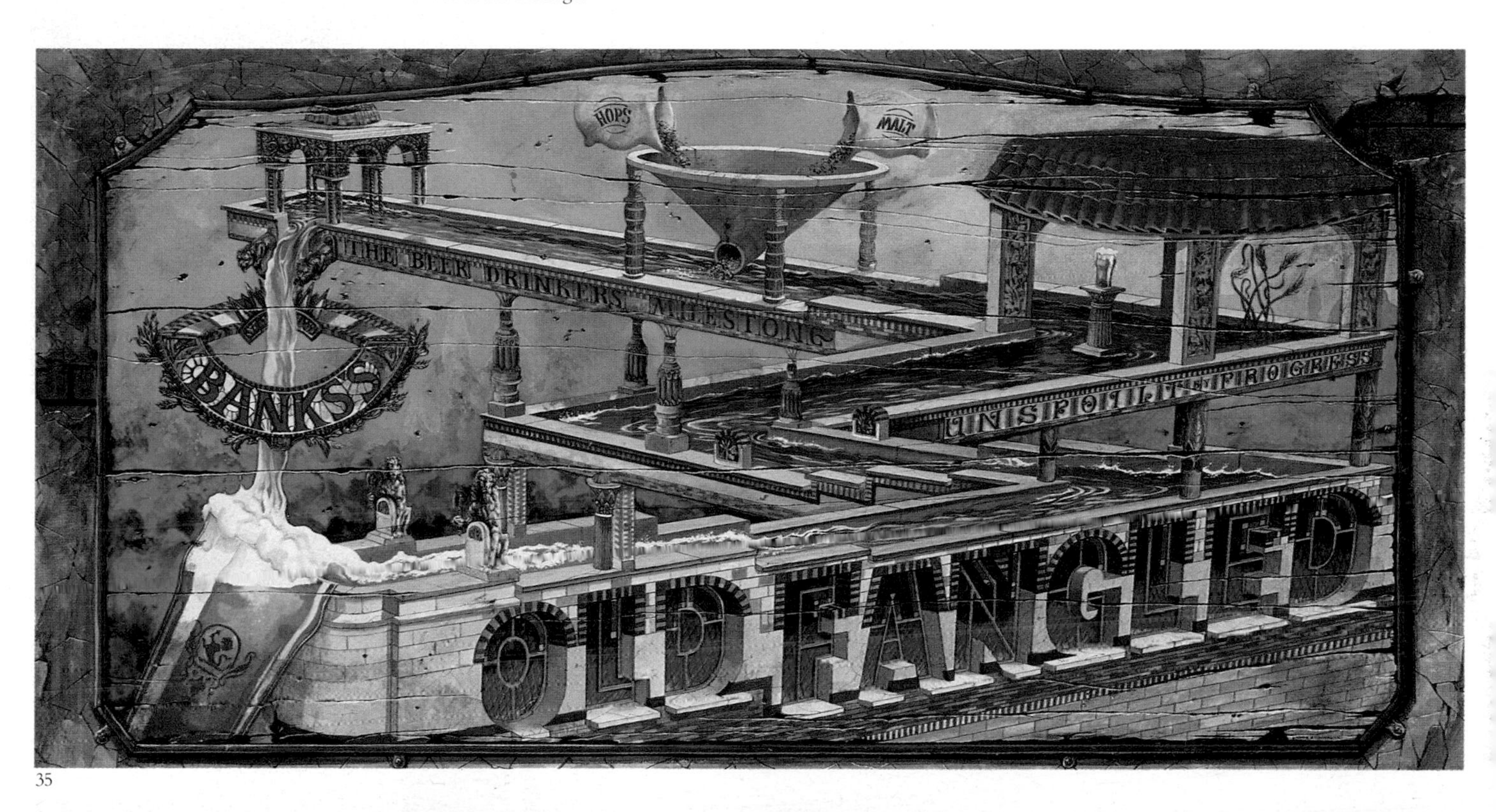

35

36

WHICH OF THESE OLYMPIC IDEAS MAKES SENSE?
THE PODIUM SPECIALLY MADE FOR THE DEAD HEAT.
THE ATHLETE SPECIALLY MADE FOR THE TRIPLE JUMP.
COME BACK
THE PISTOL SPECIALLY MADE FOR THE FALSE START.
THE BIRD-HOUSE SPECIALLY MADE FOR THE CLAY PIGEONS.
THE BATON SPECIALLY MADE FOR THE FUMBLED CHANGEOVER.
THE TARGET SPECIALLY MADE FOR THE HAMMER THROWER.
THE SPIKES SPECIALLY MADE FOR THE CLUMSY RUNNER.
THE WATER-WINGS SPECIALLY MADE FOR THE BUTTERFLY STROKE.
Long Life
THE BEER SPECIALLY BREWED FOR THE CAN.
ON
THE LIGHT SWITCH SPECIALLY MADE FOR THE WEIGHTLIFTER.
THE OLYMPIC TORCH SPECIALLY MADE FOR THE SMOKELESS ZONE.
THE SWIMSUIT SPECIALLY MADE FOR THE HIGH DIVER.

37

39
Allied Breweries take-home beers
United Kingdom
Agency: Kirkwood & Partners, London

Imported brews have become fashionable in UK beer marketing. This trade ad amusingly draws attention to Allied's range of 22 different beers.

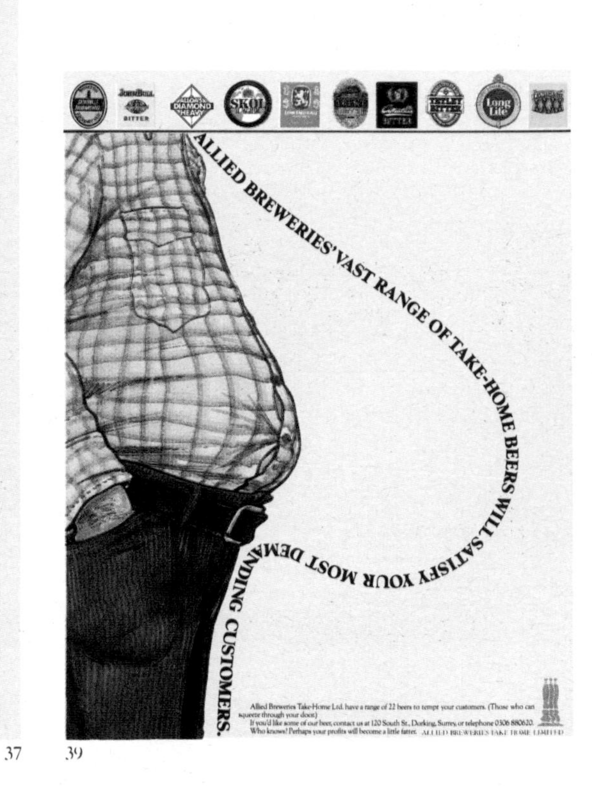

ALLIED BREWERIES' VAST RANGE OF TAKE-HOME BEERS WILL SATISFY YOUR MOST DEMANDING CUSTOMERS.

39

37
Long Life beer
United Kingdom
Agency: Kirkwood & Partners, London

Long Life is Britain's oldest canned beer and has sold for 28 years on the promise 'Specially brewed for the can'. This is one of a series of humorous ads featuring that promise as the only sensible idea among a number of absurd ones.

38
Loburg beer
Belgium
Agency: McCann-Erickson, Brussels

'A beer, a style', says the headline. The style projected is one of youthful bourgeois elegance, rather different from the associations of many other beers.

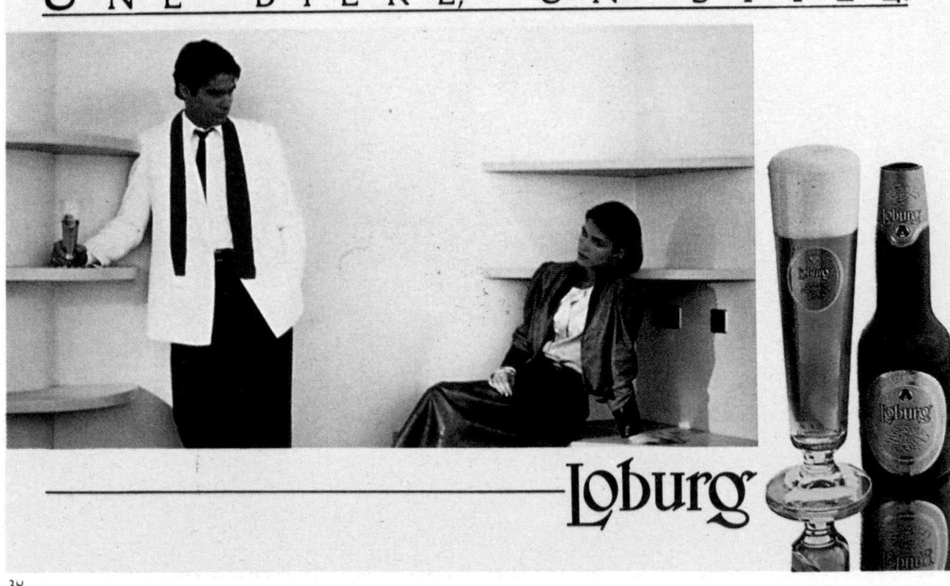

UNE BIERE, UN STYLE.

38

40
Kirin Beer
Hong Kong
Agency: SSC&B: Lintas, Hong Kong

This ad supposedly has a Japanese look. It is said to be aimed at Hong Kong's 'trendsetters'.

41
Kirin beer
Japan
Agency: Dentsu, Tokyo

This is the launch ad for a beer sold in an unusual new container.

40

41

42
Babycham
United Kingdom
Agency: Saatchi & Saatchi Compton, London

Babycham is a perry drunk mainly by young girls. This poster, launching the canned version of the product, attempts to appeal to their romanticism in a way which is intended to be rather more than a joke. The misty quality of the photography is supposed to help play on these feminine emotions.

42

43
Cockburn's Special Reserve Port
United Kingdom
Agency: J. Walter Thompson, London

Another piece of British whimsy in the same vein as Lowe's campaign for Plymouth Gin. Most port-drinkers are probably of an age and class to appreciate this kind of rather old-fashioned joke.

INSTEAD OF going down with his ship, Admiral Sir Miles Peacock (pronounced *Peaco'*) went down with laryngitis. Or so it seemed.
But the truth of the matter lay in the Admiral's admirable *reserve:* A chap couldn't possibly address a young lady *without first making the acquaintance of her parents.* And since the latter were resting in peace three hundred fathoms below, Sir Miles contemplated his naval prospects in silence until, after eight days, they came across one bottle of Cockburn's (pronounced *Co'burn's*) Special Reserve port bobbing up and down amongst the jetsam.
"Port to starboard, my dear!" bellowed Sir Miles, seizing both the bottle and, indeed, the opportunity for a little conversation simultaneously.
Alas, the poor girl didn't know which way to look.

THAT FAMOUS BRITISH RESERVE.
Miles out of port.

43

44
French wines
Denmark
Agency: McCann-Erickson, Copenhagen

'Be a little bit French tonight' is the headline on this ad, which eschews human interest in favour of logo-designer's tricks.

VÆR EN LILLE SMULE FRANSK I AFTEN.
Gør denne aften til noget særligt. Tag en eller to flasker god fransk vin med hjem.
Der er noget højtideligt over at åbne en flaske god fransk vin. Et symbol på samvær. På at netop dette øjeblik skal nydes fuldt ud. Og netop evnen til at få det bedste ud af livets gode sider, er en kunst, som franskmændene mestrer til perfektion.
Prøv selv i aften. Ud over selve øjeblikket kan du nyde verdens bedste vinlovgivning: Appellation Contrôlée på etiketten betyder, at vinen er godkendt efter lovens strengeste kriterier. V.D.Q.S. er signalet om, at du står med en kvalitetsvin fra et af de utallige frodige, franske vindistrikter. Og Vin de Pays eller Vin de Table betyder, at du har valgt den vin, som man nyder i Frankrig til hverdag.
Vær en lille smule fransk i aften. Gør denne aften til noget særligt. Der er lagt så meget kærlighed i hver eneste flaske fransk vin, at du sagtens kan dele den med andre.
Og fransk vin koster ikke mere af den grund.
Fransk vin. Du fortjener det.
1

44

45
Sanraku wines
Japan
Agency: Dentsu, Tokyo

'Wine is make-up for the emotions', says the headline. The image of the beautiful model is fused with that of the traditional Japanese craft of origami (paper folding) in an intriguing – though, to a Western eye, irrelevant – manner.

46
Veuve du Vernay wine
United Kingdom
Agency: Foote Cone & Belding, London

The attraction of the series to which this ad belongs lies in the headlines celebrating inconsequential anniversaries. Note that the bottle, as photographed, bears a family resemblance to the Gordon's Gin bottle, with its beads of moisture, made famous by the same agency.

47
French wines
United Kingdom
Agency: Aspect Advertising, London

This poster links up with a TV campaign in which the talents of the mime Marcel Marceau are used to sell the products of his native country.

ワインは気持のお化粧です。
メルシャンボナンジュ。

45

46

47

48

There's one inescapable truth about any road accident. The heavier the car that runs into you the more damage it does.

It seems obvious doesn't it.

Yet there are companies that persist in building cars like tanks.

Surely a more intelligent thing to do is to build cars that are as strong as possible yet are as light as is practicable.

Count yourself lucky if an Audi runs into you.

That's the principle we follow at Audi.

Take the Audi 100. It has elasto polypropylene in non-stress areas; boot linings and wheel arches.

The windows and windscreen are of lightweight laminated glass. Inner door frames are aluminium. Soundproofing is sandwiched foam. Even the jack is aluminium.

In all, there's a weight saving over comparable cars of about 3 cwt.

But there's another reason the Audi is, in our view, a safer car.

It's easier to stop. Being lighter, the brakes do not have to work as hard to bring the car to a halt.

It's more manoeuverable. An Audi may even be able to avoid an accident in the first place.

But what if you were in the Audi when you ran into trouble, how safe would you be then?

You'd have a crumple zone in front, that's bigger than that of an 'S' class Mercedes.

You'd have a steel sub-frame that exceeds all the German safety laws by up to 300%.

You'd have self-stabilising steering in front of you and dual-circuit disc brakes beneath you.

In fact the only thing better than having an Audi run into you, is you being in an Audi to start with■

49

The concept of power, mobility, grip and control on each corner of a moving body, is far from being an idea on which Audi have sole copyright. Nature's reproduction line runs off perfect models each and every day.

The challenge was, how to find a way of giving today's driver the very same sensations?

Audi looked first at how far the car had gone, then considered where it ought to go.

When four-wheel braking was introduced to Grand Prix racing in 1914, it pushed car technology a long way forward.

Everyone now takes it for granted that all four wheels of a car are used to brake it. So surely shouldn't it follow that all four wheels ought to drive it?

One advantage of four-wheel drive is obvious. It's taken heavy, lumbering vehicles over every kind of terrain in virtually every country in the world.

Because, irrespective of load, the traction developed by a vehicle with four-wheel drive is up to twice as great as with any car with just two-wheel drive. But it also carries with it a drawback.

Traditionally the transfer case positioned behind the engine and the gearbox unit, took up space, added weight, and wasted power through the movement of bearings, gears and oil.

In March 1980 tradition was not only broken, but shattered. Many thousands of hours of research and even more thousands of Deutchmarks investment, paid off.

With a car featuring a unique system of permanent four-wheel drive.

A car with a lightweight, economical, transfer differential in a conventional gearbox.

A car capable of staying superglued to the road at 135 mph.

The Audi quattro.

As you'd expect, the quattro delivers up to twice the traction when compared with a two-wheel drive car.

But not just on ice or in snow.

Its even distribution of power means lesser demands on tyre adhesion even on a dry road.

There is no longer any need to maintain speed for fear of losing traction, even on steep gradients in wet or snow covered conditions.

Being set up for slight understeer, its cornering radius increases if speed is excessive, and is tightened as the throttle closes.

You can accelerate out of corners faster, with the confidence of complete control and stability.

(However, just be aware that you can only brake as quickly as you can accelerate.)

And the back bar motoring correspondent's claim that, "You won't need brakes, you'll run out of petrol first," for once isn't true.

Audi introduced their four wheel drive car based on an original idea by someone else.

In our own tests, when an identical four-wheel drive Audi was converted to front-wheel drive, there was only 2.5% more fuel saved when both were driven at a constant 100 kph and 130 kph. Taken up to a constant 160 kph, there was a fuel saving of only 1%.

So yes, compared with a two-wheel drive car on a perfect surface, an Audi quattro appears to use a marginal amount more fuel.

But remember this: with every car, otherwise identical engines can vary in consumption by plus or minus 5%.

Six cylinder engines can use more than a four.

Most automatic transmissions are thirstier than a manual gearbox.

By comparison, the additional consumption of the four-wheel drive Audi is so minimal it's virtually impossible to measure.

Given that, it's not surprising Audi has put so much faith in its performance. So much so, that for 1985 permanent four-wheel drive will be available in every model group.

A leading motoring journalist wrote that driving one "was like being welded to the road."

Welded to the road it may be. Riveted to the spot it isn't.

We only wish we could take all the credit■

quattro

50

48
Audi Quattro
West Germany
Agency: Team/BBDO, Düsseldorf

The headline wishes readers 'A good start to the New Year'. The snow-covered rear of the car pushes home the double meaning. One of a series of cleverly photographed close-ups of different portions of the Quattro's anatomy.

49
Audi 100
United Kingdom
Agency: Bartle Bogle Hegarty, London

The point of this award-winning picture is that, as the copy explains, the car is made of strong but lightweight materials, which is claimed to make braking easier than in other, comparable vehicles. The Agency's print advertising for Audi does not include the German tag line 'Vorspung durch Technik' (leadership through technology) which infuriatingly it insists on using (mispronounced by a voiceover and without translation) in its TV commercials. The agency says this is effective in ramming home the car's German origin, held to be a marketing advantage in the UK.

50
Audi Quattro
United Kingdom
Agency: Bartle Bogle Hegarty, London

The copy compares the four-wheel drive of the Quattro with 'Nature's production line' which confers power and control on each corner of a moving body. But, even without the words, the four paw-marks would make the point instantly.

51a, 51b
Renault 5 TSE
France
Agency: Publicis, Paris

One pair among a number of paired posters produced by Publicis to announce the launch of the new version of the Renault 5. 'Farewell, cruel world', sobs the old model. 'Hello, it's me, the Renault Super-five', exclaims the new one.

52, 53
Fiat Panda
Italy
Agency: Benton & Bowles, Milan

Two illustrations of 'This incredible Panda world.' One bears the headline 'To carry a snack for all the gang you need a Panda.' The other has the oriental couple saying 'Our ox is in love and will not work.' Pay-off line of the series is 'Panda puts freedom in motion.' As with Davidson Pearce's UK campaign for Panda, featured in last year's edition, the fantasy humour underlines the serious selling point of the car's versatility.

51a

51b

52

53

54
Volvo 740
United Kingdom
Agency: Abbott Mead Vickers/SMS, London

For advertising people the most interesting thing about this picture is the identity of the man lying under the car. He is David Abbott, a partner in the agency that bears his name and one of London's best known copywriters. He is indeed the writer of the ad though he is not named in it.

IF THE WELDING ISN'T STRONG ENOUGH, THE CAR WILL FALL ON THE WRITER.
That's me, lying rather nervously under the new Volvo 740.
For years I've been writing in advertisements that each spot weld in a Volvo is strong enough to support the weight of the entire car.
Someone decided I should put my body where my mouth is. So we suspended the car and I crawled underneath.
Of course the Volvo lived up to its reputation and I lived to tell the tale.
But the real point of the story is this; the Volvo 740 may have a different body shape, a fast and frugal new engine, a new interior and a new suspension system, but in one respect it's just like the Volvos of yore.
It's so well built you can bet your life on it.
I know. I just did.
NEW VOLVO 740 RANGE STARTS AT £9,249. 2.3 LITRE ENGINES. CARBURETTOR AND INJECTED VERSIONS AVAILABLE. PRICES INCLUDE CAR TAX AND VAT (DELIVERY AND NUMBER PLATES EXTRA). CORRECT AT TIME OF GOING TO PRESS. CUSTOMER INFORMATION TELEPHONE: HIGH WYCOMBE (0494) 33444.
To: Volvo, Springfield House, Mill Avenue, Bristol BS1 4SA.
Mr/Mrs/Miss
Address
Postcode
THE NEW VOLVO 740. FROM £9249.

54

55

55
Opel Corsa TR
Spain
Agency: McCann-Erickson, Madrid

'Get out of the ordinary' is the sense of the headline over the car seen driving out of a poster. In fact there is not much in the model to distinguish it from all the other ordinary cars. The agency is making a brave attempt to give an ordinary family saloon a fun image.

56
Volkswagen Polo
United Kingdom
Agency: Doyle Dane Bernbach, London

The striking picture is based on a true story and illustrates the protection given by the car's 'rigid steel safety cell'. Since this is an advertisement and not a magazine article, we are not, of course, told how many other makes of car would have survived such an accident equally well.

This man went to hospital.
A127 BWV
This man walked home.

56

but joining the ranks of 'les Gee-Bees', as the French like to label Britons who hurtle lemming-like in pursuit of the sun along the autoroutes to the Mediterannean each summer, is an adventure spiced with an element of hazard.

Few things are more blissfully satisfying, to those who appreciate a good car and the joy of driving it over long distances on uncrowded roads, than the sheer fun and anticipation of disgorging from a Channel ferry with the delicious piquancy of holiday freedom stretching ahead.

Keep in mind, however, a cautionary tale when planning a continental motoring holiday. A British driver, thrown temporarily off guard by a refuelling stop, pulled out of a filling station forecourt onto the wrong side of the road. In the acrimonious aftermath of the resulting collision, the unfortunate miscreant lambasted the other motorist for being where he should not have been. During the confusion which followed, the chilling truth dawned, adding severe embarrassment to the errant driver's guilt.

An innocent abroad, caught out on his first experience of continental driving? Not a bit of it. This was a highly experienced driver, familiar with motoring on the right hand side of the road on frequent foreign business trips, and newly returned from a holiday in France … driving on the right as he incautiously pulled out of the first filling station back on home soil.

There is no special mystique about driving on the other side of the road. Driving long distances with your right hand shoulder unfamiliarly hugging the kerb is not the prime danger zone. Strangely enough, stopping is the hazard, or at least, setting off again after a stop. Think doubly hard after every pull-off, however brief.

It is a bizarre but useful habit to adopt a family policy of reminding the driver to pull out onto the correct side of the road after a halt for a meal, refuelling, overnight rest or merely leg-stretching break from the road. A chorus of 'drive on the right!' from the back, as key goes into ignition, can prove an amusing responsibility for youngsters as well as helping to keep the driver alert.

The other main danger ignored by many British motorists embarking upon a once-a-year continental motoring trip is that of under-estimating distances, and failing to appreciate the fatigue felt … being pummelled for too many hours by the noise and vibration of a car – however luxurious and refined at today's high cruising speeds.

Spain is not a day's drive from the northern French coast unless you have ambitions to be a lone assailant on a 24-hours endurance race. Plan for an absolute maximum of 500 miles a day, preferably 300, stopping at least once every three hours for a light meal or non-alcoholic drink, or simply to stretch your limbs.

Before embarking on a cross-Channel trip, have the car serviced and either ask your garage to supply – or hire from one of the motoring organisations – a kit of essential spares. A warning triangle, for use in the event of any unexpected emergency, and a first-aid kit are mandatory in several continental countries, so carry both.

It is a little known rule of French law that all motorists – including visiting foreign tourists – must carry a complete set of spare bulbs for all the car's lights, so don't be caught out by that one. EEC agreements on motor insurance mean that you can now legally cross the Channel without taking additional insurance, but it would be very unwise to do so. The agreements only allow for the minimum cover as it exists in each country, and a green card from your insurers is still necessary to ensure comprehensive cover while abroad.

A full British driving licence is acceptable in most European countries. For Italy … official … licence, and for Spain you need an International Driving Permit and bail bonds. All are obtainable from AA and RAC offices in this country before you go.

If anyone aged under 20, or who has held a full driving licence for less than a year, drives in France, the car must be equipped with a rear sticker showing that the vehicle is restricted to a maximum speed of 90 kilometres per hour.

Three more legal points: you must carry with you either the vehicle registration document, or a photocopy; the car should bear a GB plate near the rear registration plate; and most European countries require front seat belts to be worn and ban young children from travelling in front. Age limits vary from 10 to 14 years, depending on the country.

Throughout most of Europe, a general driving rule is to give way to traffic approaching from the right. Beware of trams in city centres, which usually take priority over other vehicles. Take care, also, to give way to ambulances, fire engines or military vehicles, even when you apparently have right of way.

The notorious old French system of 'priorite a droite', which encouraged elderly battered Deux Chevaux to hurtle out of rural side roads in the path of main road traffic, has largely been abandoned, but be prepared for the occasional ancient farmer to behave as though it still exists.

Prominently posted yellow diamond signs slashed by a black diagonal line at the approach to junctions inform you that you do *not* have right of way and must give priority to other traffic.

On mountain roads, be prepared to give way to large lorries and coaches, which often automatically have priority over other traffic. Downhill traffic should always give way to ascending vehicles on alpine roads.

At roundabouts in France, it has long been the practice for vehicles entering the junction to have priority, illogically, over those already negotiating it. That rule recently changed, but beware. Old driving habits die particularly hard in France.

The temptations of higher speed limits abroad are heady but potentially costly. Germany remains the only country where you can still legally enjoy the delight of driving your car flat out, unfettered by … of punitive action if you … by the local law enf… where, maximum spe… but most are at arour… the French: 130 kilome… top limit on toll-payin… they someti… between toll points! – and 110 kph on other motorway class roads.

Unfortunately, ignorance of the law is never a legitimate excuse, merely a partial mitigation. That may be hard on an ignorantly errant driver in Britain, unwittingly caught out infringing one of the thousands of individual regulations affecting motor traffic on home territory. It is even tougher to remain constantly on the right side of obscure continental legislation.

Already this year, for example, the Italian authorities have been imposing fines on a number of visiting British motorists whose cars negligently lacked a passenger door mirror. Such a mirror, providing a rearward view along the left hand side of the car, is a legal requirement in Italy where, of course, that side of a vehicle normally accommodates the driving seat.

An odd little quirk in French law, introduced last summer, imposes a lower than normal speed limit in wet weather. When it rains on French roads, you are legally obliged to comply with … which are 10 kilometres an hour less than whatever is shown as the signposted limit for that particular stretch of road.

The normal 130 kph maximum speed limit on the toll autoroutes – which translates to just over 80 miles per hour – is cut by 20 kph in rain to 110 kph, or 68 miles per hour. Unlike Britain's advisory reduced speed limits which frequently appear on motorway overhead gantries in heavy rain, the French rain limits are mandatory.

The wet weather speed reduction is arguably sensible, but its introduction was an emotive response to a horrific, widely publicised coach crash on a rain-swept autoroute in the middle of the night two years ago, which claimed the lives of 53 people, most of them children.

Norway has a curious little cameo of a law which prohibits smoking while at the wheel in urban areas. In Austria and Germany, you must carry a first-aid kit. Resist the temptation to sound your horn in Vienna, since local regulations forbid it.

Switzerland has a memorable oddity of a law which condemns the washing of cars in the street on a Sunday. Should you venture into Yugoslavia, you are required to … certificate listing any visible … car, and must obtain … vary enormously … pump prices, … rates, fluc… widely … quickly outdate … price comparisons. But as a general guide, Andorra and Luxembourg are usually distinctly lower than the rest, while prices are normally reasonable in Germany, Austria, Belgium, Holland, Sweden and Switzerland. In France, Spain and Italy, petrol is dear, although the high cost of Italian petrol can be offset by vouchers available to visiting tourists. Portugal has the most expensive fill up price of them all.

It is one of the supreme pleasures of driving in north America that petrol is so cheap there – approximately two-thirds the price of ours. The disgruntling blight on United States motoring, however, is the sleepy Federal top speed limit of 55 mph.

Ignore it at your peril. In many States, drivers widely flaunt it, but it tends to be efficiently – though patchily – enforced. Beware, too, the soporific effect of such leisurely cruising on long journeys, which can be a particular hazard for Europeans accustomed to higher cruising speeds in cars without the comfort aid of cruise control.

On-the-spot fines for speeding … are common throughout much of mainland Europe, and can be heavy, around 600 francs, not far short of £60, is a normal penalty for a simple speeding offence in France, and the gendarmes demand local currency.

Your credit card will not do ▷

FURTHER INFORMATION FROM VOLKSWAGEN SALES ENQUIRIES, YEOMANS DRIVE, BLAKELANDS, MILTON KEYNES MK14 5AN. TELEPHONE: (0908) 679121. EXPORT AND FLEET SALES, 95 BAKER STREET, LONDON W1M 1FB. TELEPHONE: 01-486 8411.

57

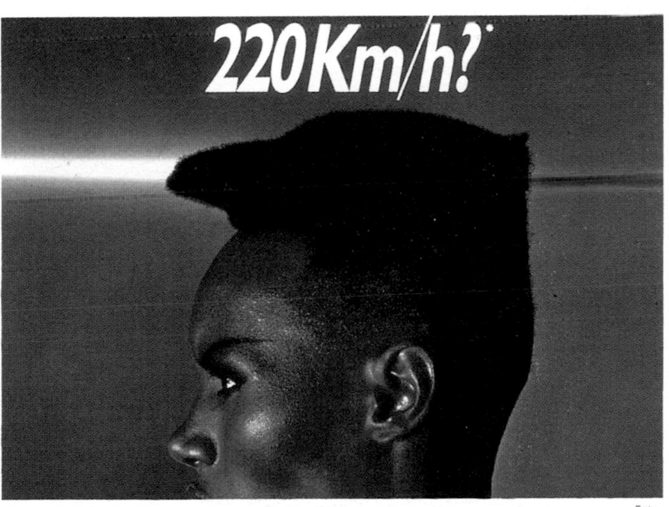

58a

C'est démon!

CX GTI Turbo

58b

57
Volkswagen Golf GTi
United Kingdom
Agency: Doyle Dane Bernbach, London

What a clever use of space. The long copy, looking like editorial matter, also reads like it. It consists of a series of tips for British motorists going abroad without a single word about the Golf.

58a, 58b
Citroën CX GT1
France
Agency: Roux Séguéla Cayzac Goudard, Paris

The over-exposed Grace Jones, seen in last year's edition in a Japanese ad for Toyota, is used here in a sequence of two pages to promote another car. '220 kilometres an hour?' say the words, 'It's fiendish.' It's certainly a different way of picturing a fast car.

59
Ford cars
United Kingdom
Agency: Ogilvy & Mather, London

This press ad to promote the whole Ford range was used in conjunction with a TV commercial which also put the emphasis on the company's technological heritage. The pictorial mini-history includes the famous Model T of 1908 and one of the planes built by Ford in a later decade. The most interesting information in the right-hand panel is that Ford designed the computer systems at the US Space Administration's mission control centre.

60
Ford Mercury Lynx
United States
Agency: Young & Rubicam, Detroit

'Go by the numbers', the reader is told, and the most important numbers are here supplied, including price, petrol consumption, size and turning circle. Effective simplicity that was probably a lot less easy to achieve than it looks.

61
BSL tankers
France
Agency: GMC/Brains Ayer, Paris

To promote interest in the BSL tanker exhibited at the 1984 Paris Motor Show, the agency devised this poster depicting the vehicle as a space shuttle. Copies were mailed to clients, prospects and the press.

62
Pirelli tyres
United Kingdom
Agency: McCormick Publicis, London

Exactly how the giant serpent is supposed to represent the product's road-gripping qualities is not clear. But it is a memorable picture.

63
Goodyear Grand Prix-S
United Kingdom
Agency: Lowe Howard-Spink Campbell-Ewald, London

Comparing a tyre to a lifebelt is another simple but effective visual device. Like the same agency's TV advertising for the product, the ad uses the words of Sir Robert Mark, London's former police chief.

64
Honda CBX motorcycle
Netherlands
Agency: Team, Rotterdam

The priest does not need six gears to make his way, the copy tells us, but he recognises beauty of design when he sees it.

59

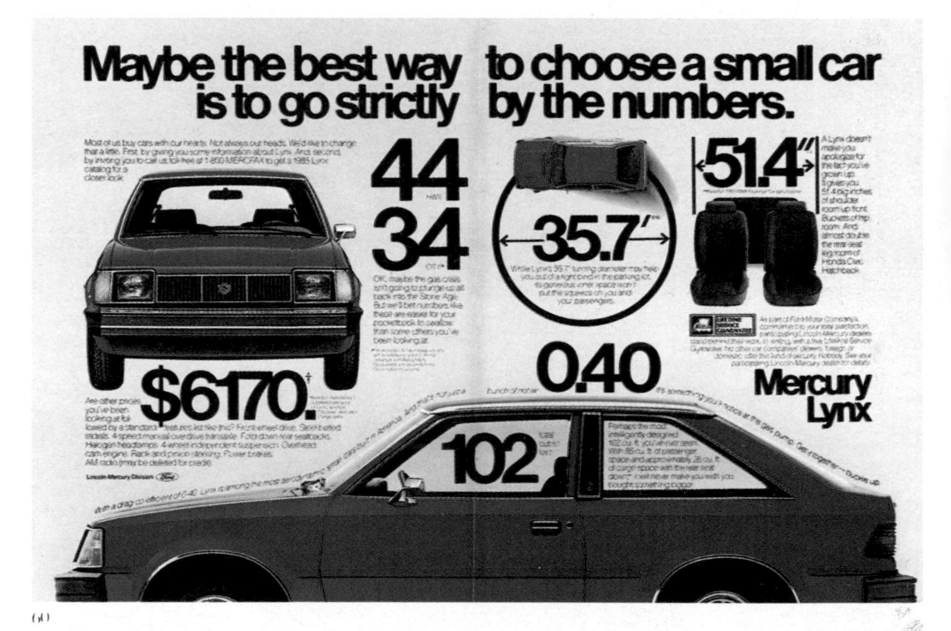

60

61

62

"Make no mistake they can both save lives in bad weather."

Robert Mark
Sir Robert Mark

"Storms are just as much a hazard to motorists as they are to shipping.

So when Goodyear told me that they had developed a tyre that made driving safer in bad weather, I was interested.

But before I agreed to say a word in favour of their Grand Prix-S, I demanded that Goodyear prove their claims.

Using an underground camera, they showed me how their tyre put more tread on the road than even its closest rivals.

And using their test track, they demonstrated how this extra grip enabled a car to handle more surely and pull up more sharply, particularly in wet conditions.

Having seen all the evidence at first hand, I am convinced the Grand Prix-S can be a lifesaver in bad weather.

I'm even more convinced that it is a major contribution to road safety."

GOODYEAR
Grand Prix-S
A major contribution to road safety.

63

Sapristie, de wereld verandert toch ook op een goede manier. Normaal gesproken zal onze pastor zijn weg door het leven niet met 6 versnellingen afleggen. Maar hij herkent schoonheid in de schepping. Ook al is het een bonk techniek. En één-weg koppelingen of hydraulische kleppenstellers komen in zijn boek niet voor. Tòch is het geen Wonder dat hij een Honda ziet staan.

En dat hadden Honda-rijders hem wel kunnen voorspellen.

HONDA
HONDA NEDERLAND
Divisie Honda Benelux N.V.
Nikkelstraat 17 – 2984 AM Ridderkerk
Telefoon 01804-23333

64

65, 66, 67
Hertz car-hire
France
Agency: Boulet Dru Dupuy Petit, Paris

An imaginative, if hyperbolic, campaign designed to illustrate the theme that Hertz takes the risk out of car-rental. The vultures (headline: 'With Hertz things won't degenerate into Hitchcockery') make in a negative way the point that Hertz cars do not break down. The naked man ('With Hertz you won't end up in your underpants') is meant to make clear that there are no hidden charges. The motorist marking his route with pebbles ('With Hertz you won't play at Hansel and Gretel') is accompanied by copy explaining that the company computer supplies every customer with a precise and detailed itinerary.

68
Shell petrol
France
Agency: Publicis, Paris

In 1984's sharply competitive petrol market Shell turned to the soft sell. One pair of posters juxtaposed a heart with the company emblem. In the pair photographed here the emblem replaces the letter A in the French 'j'aime', meaning 'I love.'

69
Shell Top Motor Oil
Netherlands
Agency: Ogilvy & Mather, Amsterdam

'What gets Porsche moving?' is the headline, and copy tells us that the German car-manufacturer uses TMO on all its vehicles. It's a clever way of making the gooey stuff look interesting.

70
Shell Super Diesel T motor oil
Norway
Agency: Ogilvy & Mather, Oslo

The picture communicates its message immediately. The humour – comparing motor oil to brandy – is rare in advertising for this kind of product.

71
Europ Assistance
France
Agency: Publicis, Paris

Europ Assistance is an international service offering subscribers protection against all sorts of risks, including falling ill on holiday. In Europe, however, it is best known for arranging repair facilities for motorists. The heading on this poster reads 'Ask us for the moon', in other words ask for everything you can think of. Of course, pedants may object that what the moon-stranded family shown would ask for is not the moon but the earth. But why spoil a good joke by being too logical?

65

66

67

68

WAT BEWEEGT PORSCHE?

Porsche levert er al zijn auto's mee af, Niki Lauda en Alain Prost smeren er hun race-wagen mee en voor veel autofabrikanten is het dé kwaliteitsnorm.

TMO, de Top Motor Olie van Shell, wordt algemeen beschouwd als de beste motor-olie ter wereld. Vanwaar die uitgesproken voorkeur? Omdat het ècht wat uit maakt. Omdat TMO echt de levensduur van de motor verlengt. Omdat TMO echt het olieverbruik verlaagt en echt brandstofbesparend werkt (gemiddeld 3%).

Omdat TMO echt bestand is tegen extreem zware belasting. En daar zijn zeker niet alleen de Porsches en de race-wagens van deze wereld gevoelig voor.

Iedere auto is gebaat bij de onovertroffen eigenschappen van Shell TMO. Dus ook de uwe.

TMO. ALGEMEEN BESCHOUWD ALS DE BESTE OLIE TER WERELD.

69

LAGRET PÅ FAT.
TAPPET AV A/S NORSKE SHELL.

Shells nye olje – SUPER DIESEL T er utviklet for å møte dieselmotorens spesielle krav.
Velger du SUPER DIESEL T får du en olje som:
- løser sotproblemene med oljefortykning som følge
- tåler høyere temperaturer
- tåler høyere mekaniske belastninger
- gir større korrosjons-beskyttelse

SHELL SUPER DIESEL T er ideell for alle diesel personbiler og en nødvendighet for turbo diesler.

SHELL SUPER DIESEL T. DEN NYE SUPEROLJEN FOR PERSONDIESLER.

70

71

ALEXON'S
CHRISTMAS
WRAPPING
by
TERENCE
DONOVAN

72

LESS IS MORE.

A
PHOTOGRAPHIC
PROFILE
FOR ALEXON
BY
B. LATEGAN.

73

72, 73, 74
Alexon women's clothes
United Kingdom
Agency: Saatchi & Saatchi Compton, London

Alexon was a fashion house with an old-fashioned, middle class image. The agency's aim was to brush up and glamorise that image, which it did with the help of first class photographers. Richard Avedon did a series of pictures of Alexon's African collection. Terence Donovan's is the delightful juxtaposition of nude and suit. Barry Lategan's 'Less is more' picture has the stylistic distinctiveness of a painting.

75
Sistiene women's clothes
Japan
Agency: Kasugai, Nagoya City

Kasugai and its creative director, Shozo Murase, set a high standard of visual imagination. Look back at the same firm's work in the first section.

76

76
Gloria Vanderbilt women's clothes
United States
Agency: Doyle Dane Bernbach, New York

One of a long series of ads for clothes and footwear, all featuring in different ways the shadow of the mysterious man. Slogan: 'Let the adventure begin.'

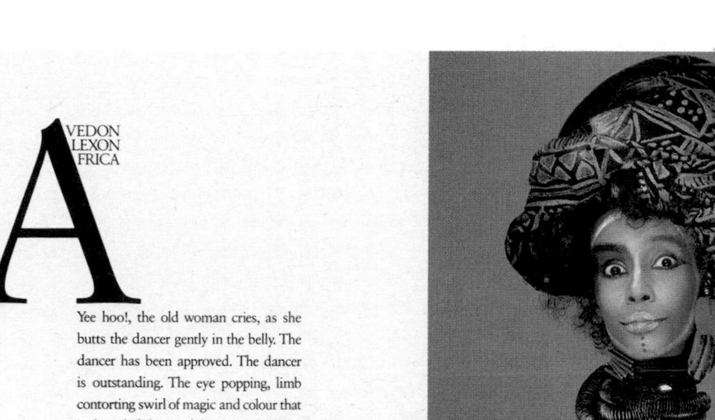

A
VEDON
LEXON
FRICA
Yee hoo!, the old woman cries, as she butts the dancer gently in the belly. The dancer has been approved. The dancer is outstanding. The eye popping, limb contorting swirl of magic and colour that is the tribal dance of the Nomads of the Niger has reached its mesmeric climax. In a great white egg of a studio somewhere on New York's East Side, Richard Avedon the photographer who Truman Capote has called "The man with gifted eyes," breathes the tingling magic of the Wodaabe tribe into Alexon's African collection. Colours and primitive pattern woven into cloth, woven into clothes bring Alexon screeching into the now.

74

75

77
Rodier women's clothes
France
Agency: Boulet Dru Dupuy Petit, Paris

One of a series of ads showing a Rodier-dressed girl at the centre of attention. The series catchline (printed here vertically) is 'They give themselves confidence with Rodier.' The heroine of this particular ad is saying 'Has someone lost a hand?' The heavy sexual innuendo might not go down so well in some other countries.

77

78
New Man clothes
United Kingdom
Agency: Aspect Advertising, London

Aspect has used outside illustrators for some of its graphically unusual ads for New Man. This one is illustrated by John Davis, joint creative director of the agency.

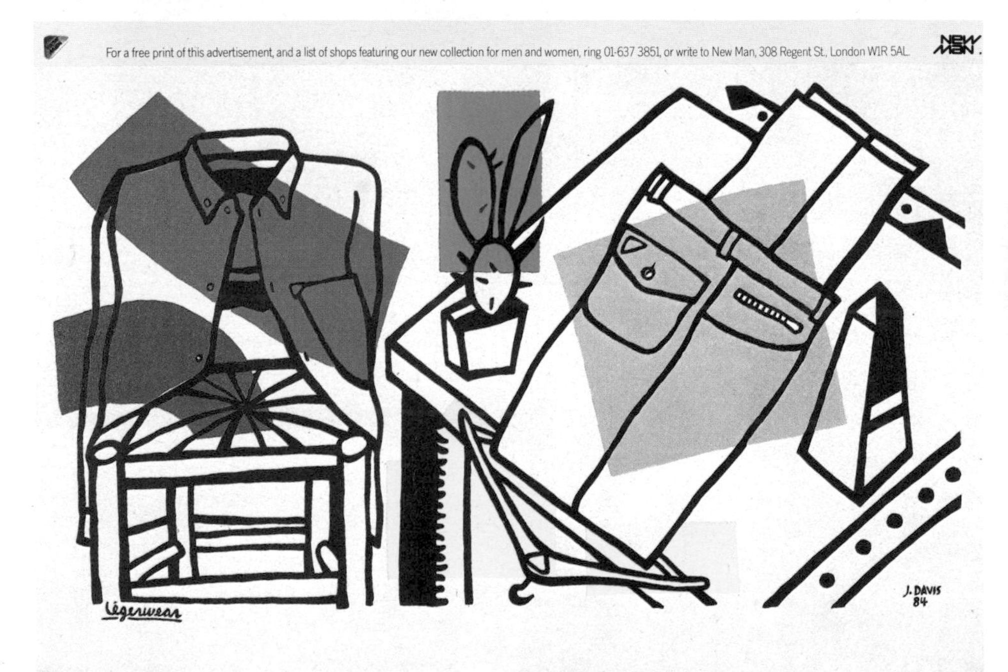

78

79
Wrangler jeans
United Kingdom
Agency: Collett Dickenson Pearce & Partners, London

Notice the denim texture and the stitching of the house plant, telephone and walls as well as the jeans. Not as compelling, perhaps, as the jeans-dressed foetus in the Wrangler ad by Dupuy Saatchi, Paris, featured in last year's edition, but cute all the same.

79

80
Lois jeans
France
Agency: Grey, Paris

Part of an award-winning campaign, excellently photographed. The copy line, 'On her (or his) skin was marked Lois' is the same on all the ads, but not all are as erotic in flavour as this one.

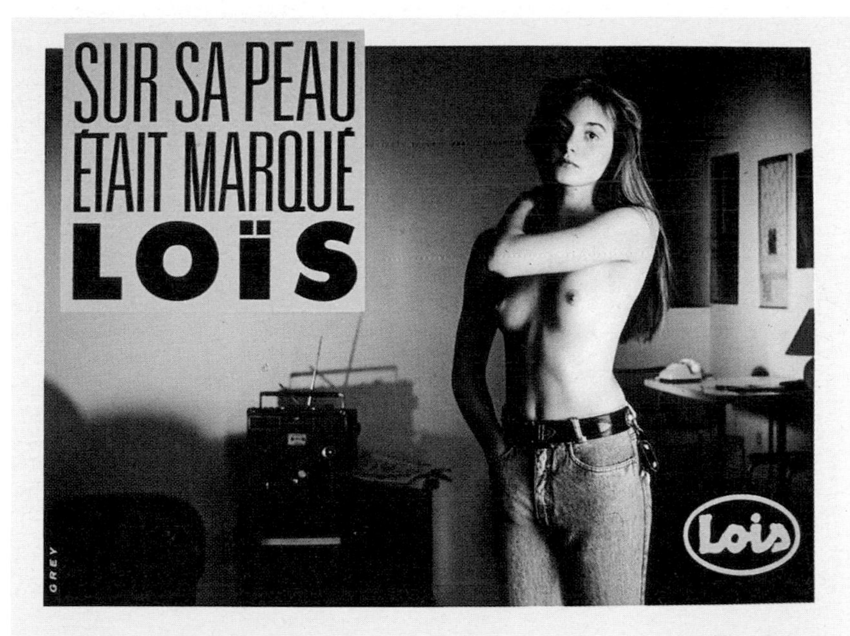

80

81
Maverick jeans
Argentina
Agency: SSC&B: Lintas, Buenos Aires

The Argentine jeans market is big but highly fragmented, with many foreign brands. The declared aim of this campaign is to associate the qualities of the original jeans, as made in the North American West, with an up-to-date range. Caption is 'The legend of today'. The combination of two styles of illustration, representing old and new, is unusual but does not quite gel.

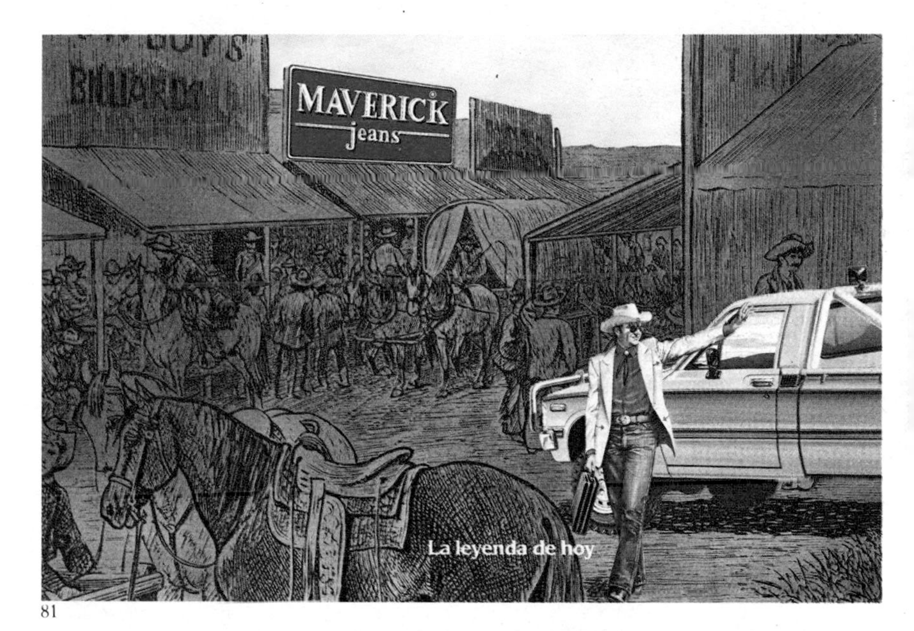

81

82
FU's jeans and baggy trousers
India
Agency: Enterprise Advertising, Bombay

Joie de vivre is the keynote of this ad. Nothing wrong with a touch of youthful, even comical, exuberance in a message addressed to youthful consumers.

82

83
Woollen garments
Netherlands
Agency: Young & Rubicam, Amsterdam

This ad, from a fashion series, is headed 'Wool will walk.' Notice that the coat is on a hanger apparently hooked over the top of the ad. Like the British poster for Tetley beer this illustrates an inclination on the part of some advertising creatives to draw attention to the medium as well as the message.

84
Welcomme knitting wool
France
Agency: Boulet Dru Dupuy Petit, Paris

'A Welcomme is worn like a perfume' says the headline. The ad, with its sensual pose, is very much in the style of perfume advertising.

85, 86
Woollen garments
France
Agency: Publicis, Paris

The agency's intention is to make the Woolmark logo a symbol of the good life. The logo is therefore linked both visually and verbally in this campaign with a variety of desirable situations. Thus we have 'Woolmark of tenderness' (the poolside scene) and 'Woolmark of seduction' (with the logo on the booze bottle).

87, 88
Eiser tights (Fianna and Friz brands)
Finland
Agency: Liikemainonta-McCann, Helsinki

Eiser tights were relaunched with a range of new brand names and new packaging as well as advertising aimed at creating a modern, exciting image. The copy line on both the ads shown here is 'Genuine. Confidence starts from quality.'

83

84

85

86

87

88

89
Pingouin tights
France
Agency: Boulet Dru Dupuy Petit, Paris

One of a series of joky ads which, unusually for this category, feature men as well as women. The headline has a double meaning, 'Charm which walks (or works).'

90
Jim underpants
Spain
Agency: Tandem DDB Campmany Guasch, Barcelona

In the 1983 edition of this book an ad by Toronto agency Raymond Lee & Associates, showed a strip of paper rolling upwards to reveal the ski underwear of two men and a woman. Here the idea is the same but the execution wittier.

91
Romano shoes
India
Agency: Enterprise Advertising, Bombay

The advertiser, Sterling Shoes, designs bags and belts to go with its footwear. A series of colourful ads to launch the new range puts the emphasis on the ensembles rather than on the shoes.

92
K Shoes
United Kingdom
Agency: Abbott Mead Vickers/SMS, London

Most of the ads in this series have depicted women in conventionally masculine roles. This one follows a different tack to get across the 'Times are changing' theme.

89

90

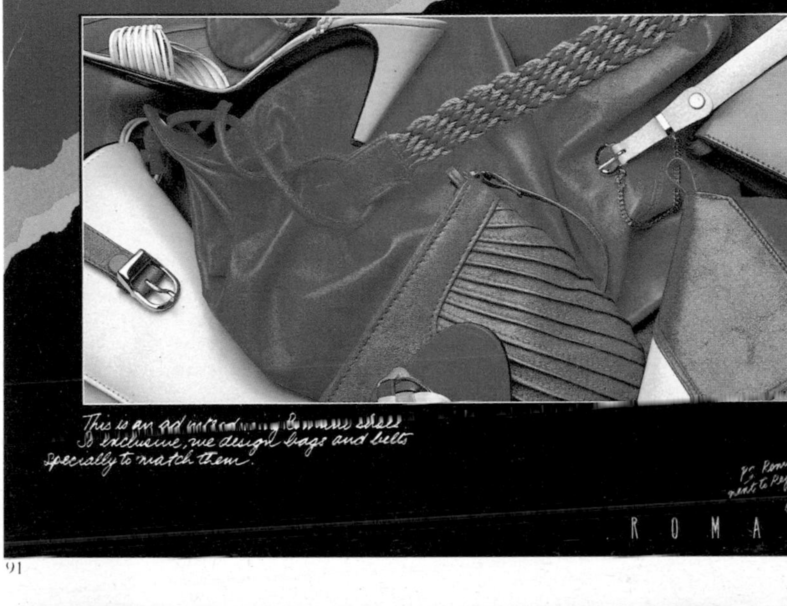

91

92

93, 94
New Balance sports shoes
United Kingdom
Agency: TBWA, London

In one of these two ads a simple yet effective visual device is used to back up the claim of design superiority in the manufacturer's football boots. The other ad uses a less simple, and perhaps less effective, device to emphasise that New Balance takes anatomical differences into account in designing sports shoes for women.

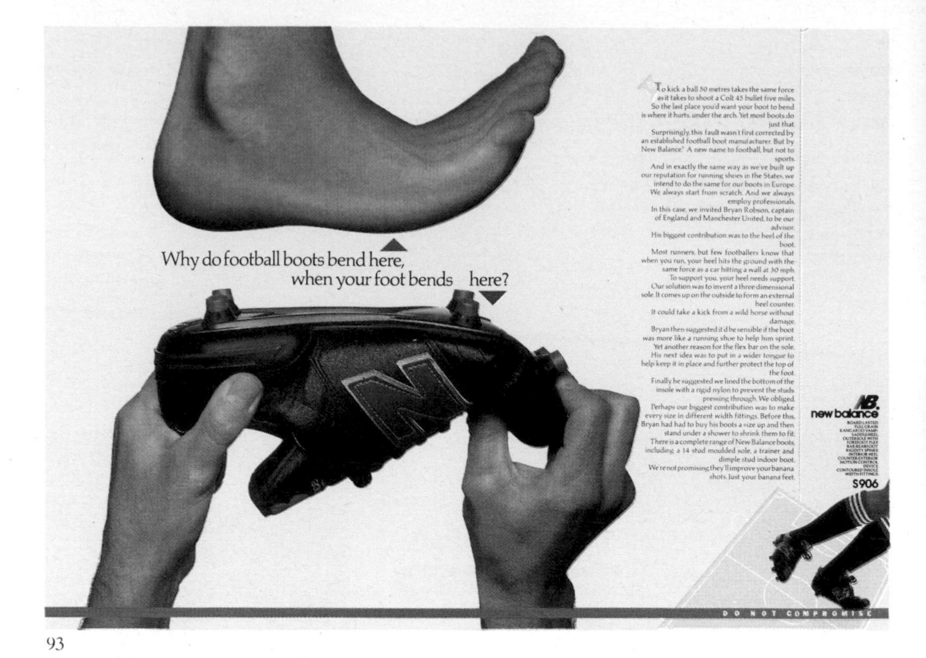

93

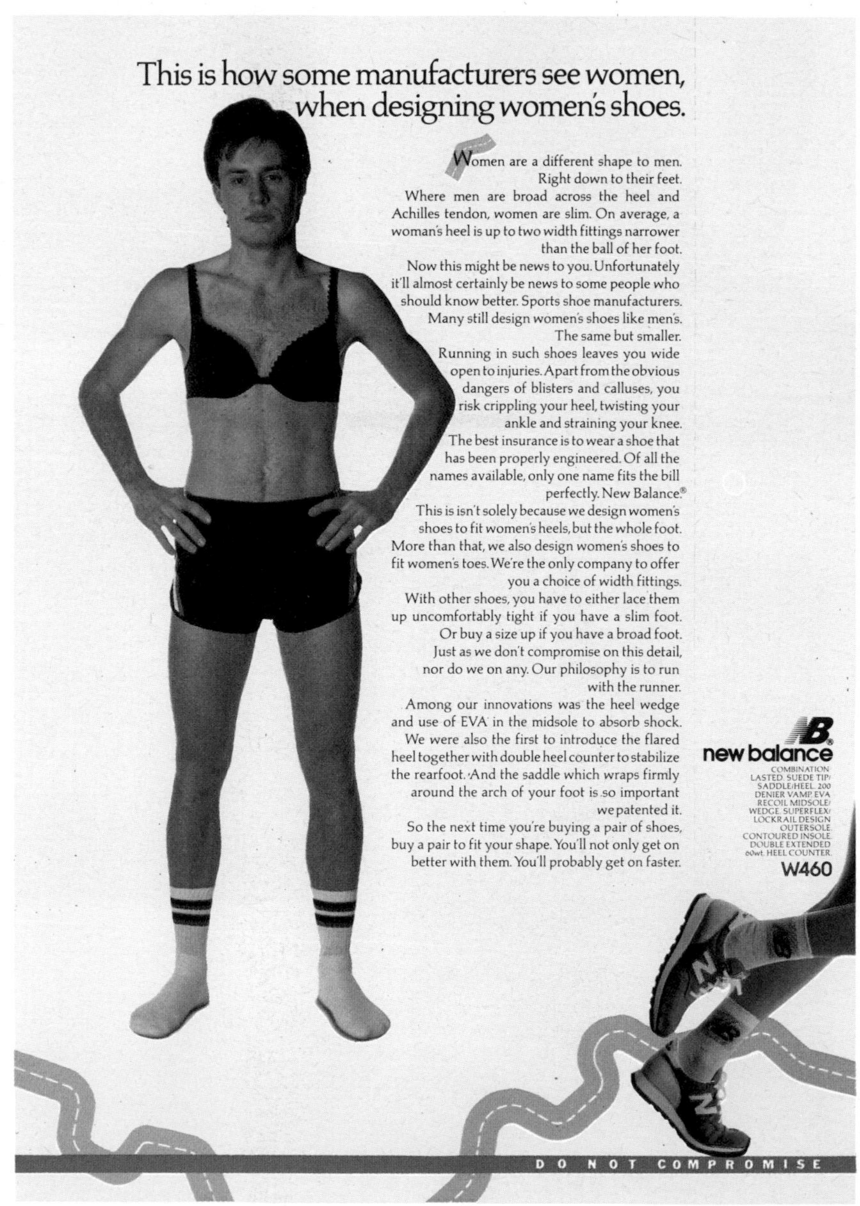

94

95
Adidas sports shoes
Norway
Agency: Myres/Lintas, Oslo

'Swimming is the only Olympic event we do not have a shoe for' says the headline. The ad appeared while the 1984 Olympic Games were on. A nice piece of visual inventiveness.

96
Adidas sports shoes
Spain
Agency: Bassat Ogilvy & Mather, Barcelona

The silver trophy makes the point at once. But to remove any doubt the headline reads 'Let it always go out to win.'

97
Nordica ski boots
Italy
Agency: Publinter Ayer, Milan

In 1984 Nordica claimed to have increased its share of the world market for ski boots from 26 to 28 per cent. This, then, is market leader advertising, meant to reinforce the product's already strong reputation. 'The higher up the more Nordica' say the words. The eagle is intended to back up the double meaning of high altitude and high quality.

95

96

97

„Ladylike verzeiht mir jeden Fehler."

Ladylike ist eine Speicher-Schreibmaschinen-Serie mit Korrekturspeicher, der Fehler tipp, tipp, tipp, mühelos beseitigt.

Jeder macht mal einen Schreibfehler. Umständliche Korrekturen sind die Folge.

Ladylike hat einen Korrekturspeicher. Damit lassen sich Fehler, bis zu vier Zeilen rückwirkend, mit einem Tastendruck korrigieren.

Ladylike hat aber noch einiges mehr zu bieten. Z.B. umfangreiche Speichermöglichkeiten für Routinearbeiten.

Die Kapazität läßt sich bei allen Ladylike Speicher-Schreibmaschinen der Xerox 600 Serie beliebig ausbauen. So lassen sich Routinebriefe, Verträge, Anreden, Grußformeln etc. speichern und jederzeit bequem abrufen. Ein Fingerdruck auf die entsprechende Sensortaste reicht. Den Rest macht Ladylike. Fehlerfrei.

Wenn Sie mehr über Ladylike wissen wollen, senden Sie uns den Coupon. Damit machen auch Sie bestimmt keinen Fehler.

Ladylike. Die Lady unter den Schreibmaschinen.

Abtrennen und absenden an: Rank Xerox GmbH, Abt. MKO 31, Postfach 110 950, 4000 Düsseldorf 11. Ich möchte Ladylike kennenlernen. Geben Sie mir nähere Informationen.

Name:
Firma:
Straße:
PLZ/Ort:
Position:

RANK XEROX®

98
Rank Xerox Ladylike electronic typewriter
West Germany
Agency: Heye Needham & Partner, Düsseldorf

Coming late to the typewriter market, Rank Xerox and its agency decided on an aggressive style, designed to make its presence quickly felt. It was also decided to address advertising direct to the users, i.e. secretaries, rather than the purchasers. Hence the brand name, Ladylike, and the secretaries' mouths talking about the machine. 'Ladylike forgives me every mistake' says the headline on this ad, which explains the machine's memory and correction facilities.

99
IBM typewriters
United States
Agency: Doyle Dane Bernbach, New York

Like the German ad for the Rank Xerox typewriter, this is addressed specifically to secretaries. It is one of a series featuring letters of type. Here Y stands for 'you', the secretaries.

100, 101
Commodore computers
West Germany
Agency: J. Walter Thompson, Frankfurt

Commodore claims leadership of the West German micro-computer market, with 70 per cent of home machines. The aim of this campaign, to improve unaided recall of the brand name, is said to have been triumphantly achieved. Each ad in a long series appeals to a different professional or interest group, with a heading of the form 'Why the . . . needs a Commodore computer.' In the red pencil ad it's the 'purchasing manager' who is addressed and who is said to be looking for value for money in buying a computer as well as everything else. The other ad explains why 'the inventor' needs a Commodore.

102, 103
IBM computers
West Germany
Agency: GGK, Düsseldorf

Two examples from a delightful series of humorous illustrations by René Fehr done for GGK's Düsseldorf office while Michael Schirner was still creative director. (He has since left to start his own agency, KKG!) The space satellite picture is prefaced with the words, on a previous page, 'Our speediest colleague'. Copy explains that this is Roger 2, the satellite. The other picture is prefaced 'What is getting lighter and lighter'. In a couple of images the illustrator has summed up the history of computers.

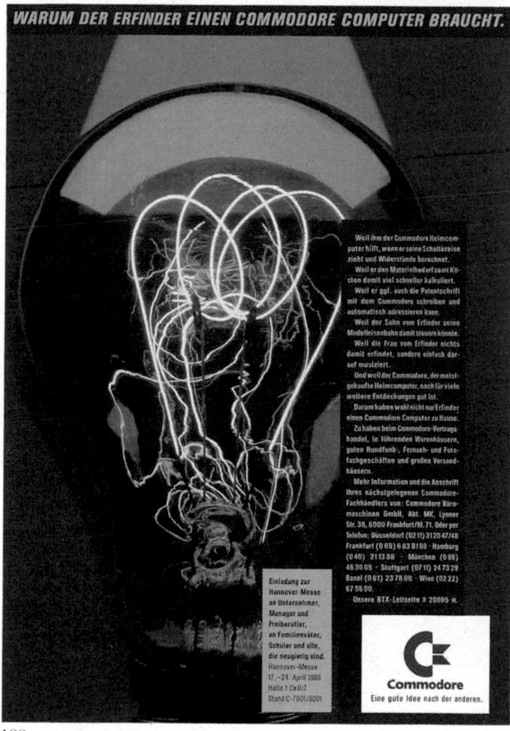

100

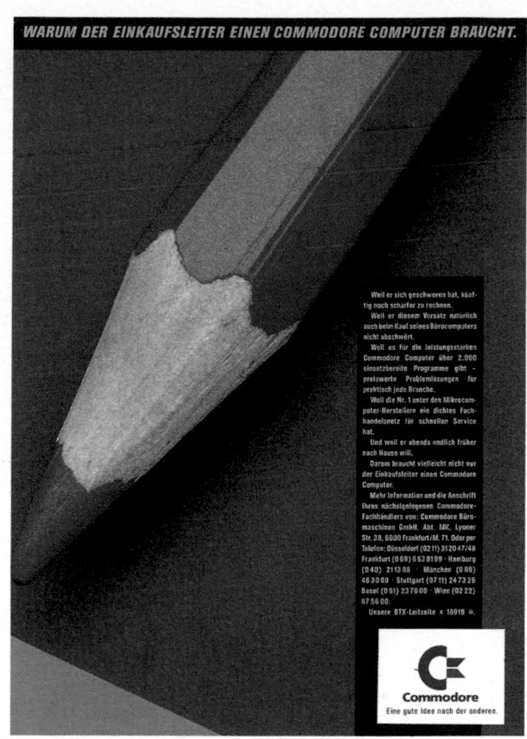

101

102

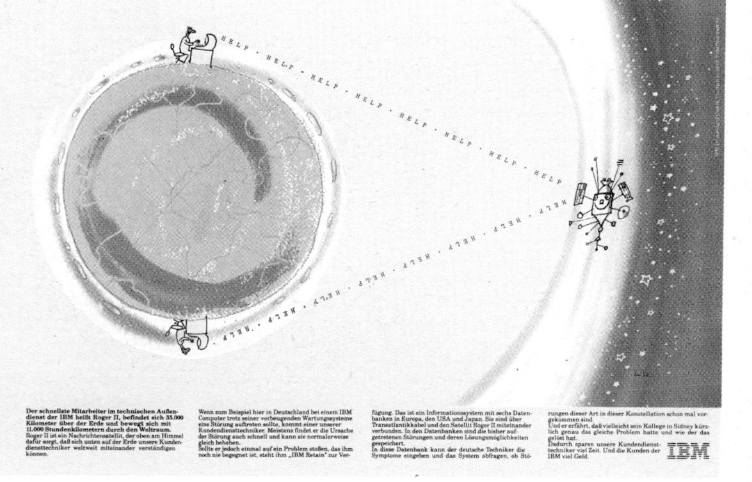

103

104
Digital computers
Most European countries
Agency: Benton & Bowles, London

Digital Equipment Corporation, the world's second biggest computer manufacturer, has a relatively low level of awareness among managers in Europe. Its product range is made to be compatible with other major brands. Hence the barrier-free theme of this campaign.

105
NCR computers
West Germany
Agency: Die Crew, Stuttgart

Human interest is the aim of this campaign by the new Stuttgart agency Die Crew for 'the personal computer with a heart'. 'Welcome, my best friend' is the unusual headline on this ad, showing the product being delivered to a horticulturist.

106
IBM small computers
United States
Agency: Doyle Dane Bernbach, New York

One of a series which, like the Commodore ads by JWT in Germany, shows emblems of various fields where computers can be helpful. Copy here refers to fund-raising by the New York Philharmonic Orchestra.

107
Nelco Corona personal computer
India
Agency: Enterprise Advertising, Bombay

A cheeky one, this. As the copy says, IBM has used a Charlie Chaplin lookalike to advertise its computers all over the world. IBM's is the market leader of personal computers but several machines, including Corona 'are not only IBM PC-compatibles but are superior to it in terms of performance capabilities.'

108
Honeywell computers
Italy
Agency: RSCG Mezzano Costantini Mignani, Milan

'You need Honeywell, Honeywell needs you', says the heading. Copy refers to the usefulness of computers to local government authorities, symbolised by the towers.

109
Honeywell computers
United Kingdom
Agency: Gold Greenlees Trott, London

What a simple but clever idea to use paper clips, staples, pencils etc. to spell out the message that computerless offices waste time and money.

104

105

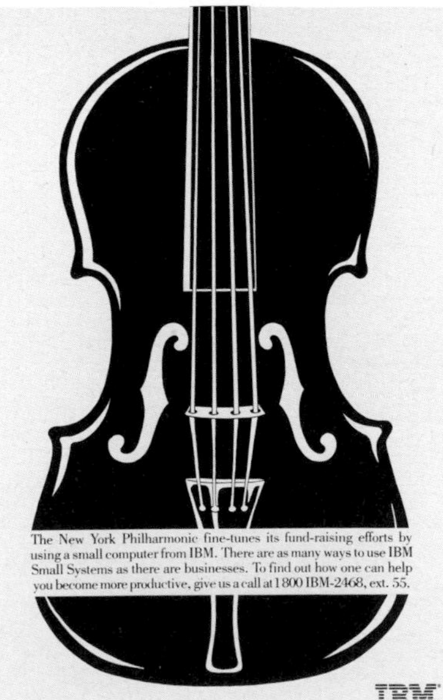

106

107

VOI AVETE BISOGNO DI HONEYWELL
HONEYWELL HA BISOGNO DI VOI.
Queste torri sono prese d'assalto.
Le amministrazioni locali assolvono a funzioni sempre più complesse, il rapporto centro-periferia diventa sempre più articolato e il pubblico si aspetta un servizio che resti qualitativamente buono.
Honeywell è l'alleato ideale di Comuni, Provincie, Regioni, Università, U.S.L. e di tutti quegli enti la cui attività, per essere pienamente funzionale, necessita di un alto grado di razionalizzazione.
Oggi i microcomputers e i grandi sistemi Honeywell, con i loro programmi applicativi, affrontano e risolvono i problemi specifici dei singoli enti.
Siete stati proprio voi col vostro lavoro a insegnare a Honeywell come fare per difendere le vostre torri: eccoci al vostro fianco.
Conoscere e risolvere insieme.
Honeywell
Honeywell Information Systems Italia
Per informazioni scrivere a Honeywell I.S.I. Sviluppo Commerciale, Via

108

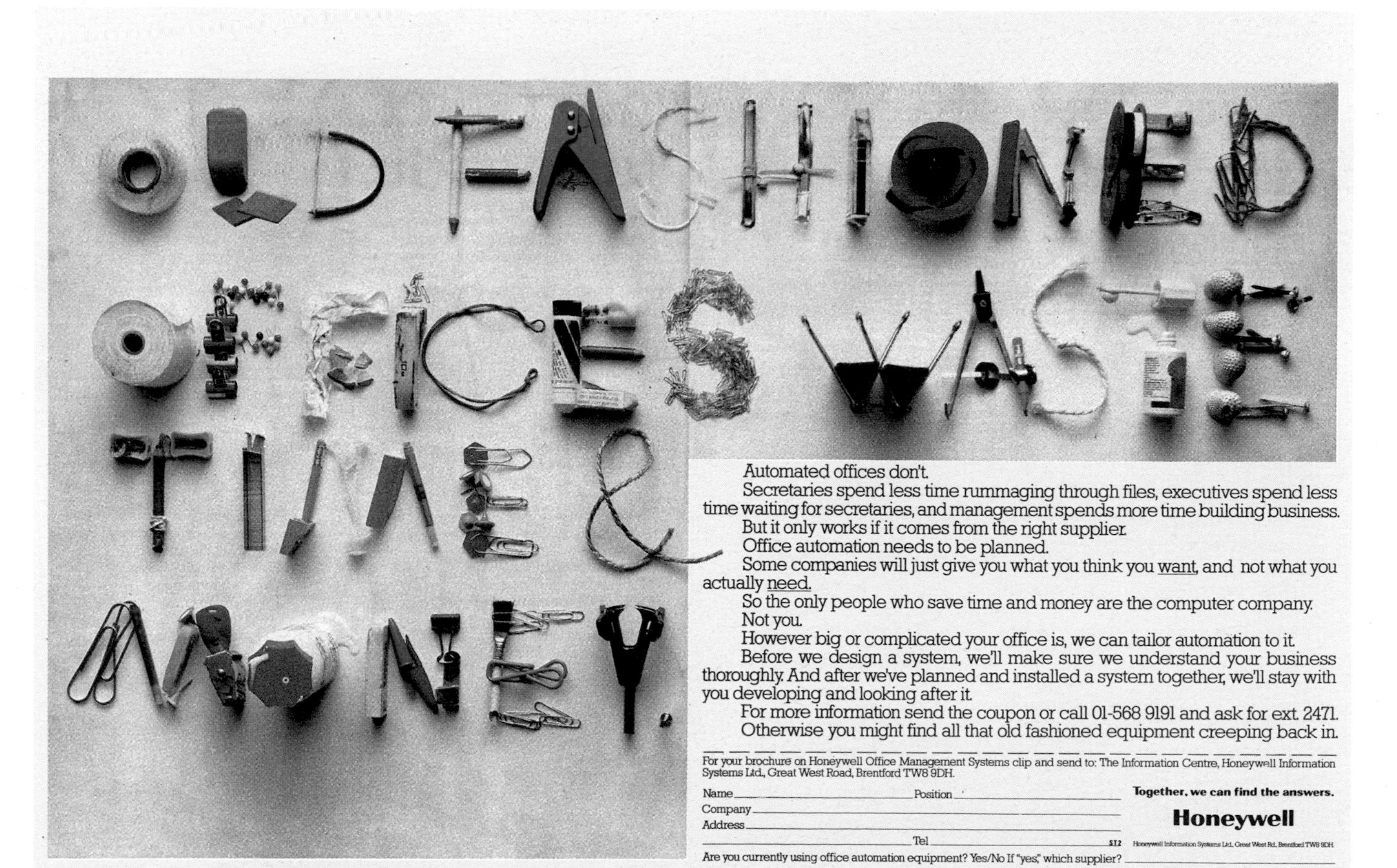
OLD FASHIONED OFFICES WASTE TIME & MONEY.
Automated offices don't.
Secretaries spend less time rummaging through files, executives spend less time waiting for secretaries, and management spends more time building business.
But it only works if it comes from the right supplier.
Office automation needs to be planned.
Some companies will just give you what you think you want, and not what you actually need.
So the only people who save time and money are the computer company.
Not you.
However big or complicated your office is, we can tailor automation to it.
Before we design a system, we'll make sure we understand your business thoroughly. And after we've planned and installed a system together, we'll stay with you developing and looking after it.
For more information send the coupon or call 01-568 9191 and ask for ext. 2471.
Otherwise you might find all that old fashioned equipment creeping back in.
For your brochure on Honeywell Office Management Systems clip and send to: The Information Centre, Honeywell Information Systems Ltd., Great West Road, Brentford TW8 9DH.
Name Position
Company
Address
Tel
S12
Are you currently using office automation equipment? Yes/No If "yes," which supplier?
Together, we can find the answers.
Honeywell
Honeywell Information Systems Ltd., Great West Rd., Brentford TW8 9DH.

109

110
BBC Micro computer
United Kingdom
Agency: Aspect Advertising, London

Nothing spurious about the human interest of this picture. Copy explains that the machine acts as a teacher, encouraging handicapped children to persevere with their exercises, saving the cost of a physiotherapist. The BBC Micro, now found in many British schools, is made by Acorn Computers, originally in association with a BBC television course on computing.

111
Sharp PC5000 personal computer
United Kingdom
Agency: Ayer Barker, London

The machine can be carried in a small case but can be connected via telephone with 'your own office computer'. Hence the office in a briefcase.

112
Philips Elephant computer
Singapore
Agency: SSC&B: Lintas, Singapore

Looking for a selling proposition, though perhaps not a unique one, the agency hit on the clear video display which eliminates the eye strain caused by 'most ordinary computer screens'. The visual makes the point before you even read the copy.

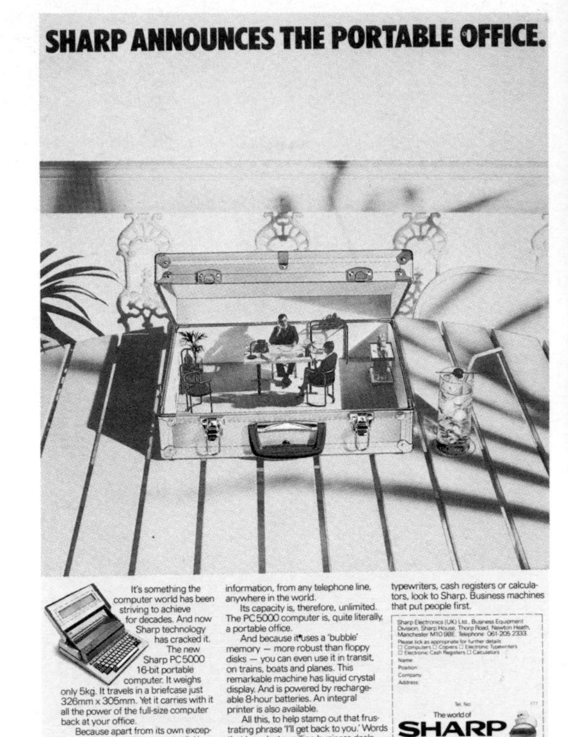

111

Two years ago, Britain couldn't afford to treat children like this.

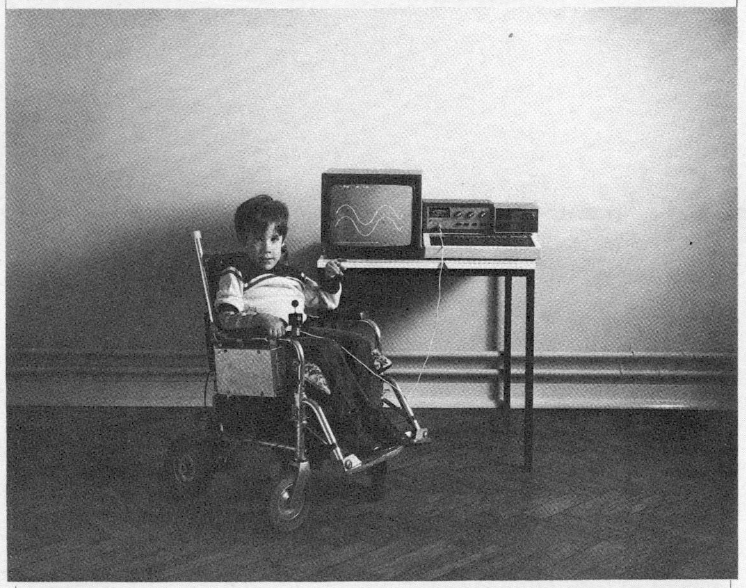

Matthew is five years old and suffers from a rare muscular disorder.

He's connected to a microcomputer. But to him, it's more like a sports coach.

As he tries to control his muscles, it responds. And as he gains control, it encourages him to continue making headway by setting him increasingly higher goals.

With this system, physically handicapped children have overcome the tedium of doing their exercises and actually started to enjoy them.

It was conceived by an imaginative physiotherapist from Huntingdon Health Authority. She knew nothing about computers, but had all the right instincts.

She had an inkling that microcomputers could help children to persevere in their exercises. And she realised that, with the plummeting cost of technology, computers were becoming widely used in primary and secondary schools.

This meant she would be able to treat her young patients during the course of their normal routine. And without any heavy financial burden on the Health Service.

She collaborated with a team of experts. And they focused their thoughts on the BBC Microcomputer.

In their own words, it was the only computer for the job. For one thing, availability would rarely be a problem. Because the BBC Micro now accounts for over 80% of the computers being ordered under the current D.O.I. scheme to introduce micros to primary schools.

Equally important, it readily accepts specialised and even unorthodox equipment. Indeed, adaptability to fulfil many roles is at the very core of its design.

That is why, besides being used in many homes, it is performing diverse roles in offices, hospitals and research laboratories.

Perhaps what is most encouraging, though, is what the physiotherapist has demonstrated. The BBC Micro is open to ideas from people in all walks of life.

(All suggestions about new and unusual applications are welcomed by the External Projects Director at the address below.)

The £399 BBC Micro. No other computer in its price range is at home in so many situations.

>The BBC Micro

For local stockists, ring 01-200 0200. The BBC Microcomputer System is designed, produced and distributed by Acorn Computers Ltd., 4 Fulbourn Road, Cherry Hinton, Cambridge CB1 4JN. Tel: 0223 245200. Physiotherapy equipment by Aleph One Ltd., Cambridge.

110

112

113
ICL Distributed Computer Systems
United Kingdom
Agency: J. Walter Thompson, London

The trench warfare picture illustrates what the copy calls 'the classic example of a breakdown in communication'. ICL systems consist of machines which can be used either as personal computers or for communication with others in the company, sharing information contained in each.

113

114

114
Alice children's computer
France
Agency: Boulet Dru Dupuy Petit, Paris

'A computer for all levels' says the headline. Copy explains that the product, jointly created by Matra and the publisher Hachette, will enable youngsters to progress from elementary to advanced computing skills.

115
Data General computer systems
United States
Agency: Foote Cone & Belding, New York

'The choice of a computer system may be the most crucial decision a corporation can make' says the copy. And the picture dramatises the point.

115

Are you investing in a load of old bull?

If you're not in constant touch with the Stock Exchange, the answer could, alas, be yes.

Share prices yo-yo by the minute; no two authorities can agree on the underlying trends.

Bull turns bear, and vice versa, faster than you can say "bewildered financial zoologist".

(If you think we exaggerate, check the record for Friday May 4th, when the Thirty Index opened on a record high, but the bull market was dead by lunchtime.)

Ending up as the victim of someone else's killing can be murder on your profits.

But, short of spending all day on the phone to your stockbroker, how do you stay informed?

A DESK-TOP STOCK EXCHANGE.

Buy, rent or otherwise acquire an Apricot computer. Apricot owners can call upon Communique, a unique package of financial and business services.

Services stockbrokers use, like Extel Priceline and Datastream.

Bringing you continuous updates on 3,200 UK stocks and 47,000 share prices from around the world.

As well as keeping an eye on your portfolio, so you always know exactly what you're worth.

THE LOWDOWN ON 1,000,000 FIRMS.

Do you ever need to check on a company's performance, executives or public statements?

Communiqué gives you entreé to Dun & Bradstreet, Key British Enterprises, Pergamon Infoline, Data-Star, Textline and Eurolex.

Which, in layman's terms, means inside information on all 950,000 companies registered in the UK, and many abroad.

Plus every story published during the last five years by the FT, the Dow Jones News Service and more than 100 influential international journals.

(Simply punch in key words, say, 'fibre optics' and 'Czechoslovakia,' and the stories will be on your desk in minutes.)

ACTING ON INFORMATION.

Because you need to act fast, our package includes many other valuable services.

Prestel, which has everything from the time of the next New York flight, to whether your favourite hotel is fully booked.

Micromail, a speed-of-light mail system for talking to mailbox users worldwide. Telex, to reach the rest.

Of course you may not need all these services, in which case simply select the ones you want.

Previously, subscribing to even a few of them would have meant a room full of terminals, screens and operators.

Now all you need is a desk.

Adding Communiqué to your Apricot costs a mere £395+VAT. A derisory sum considering what you already risk.

Seeing profits (to quote Shakespeare) "exit with a bear behind".

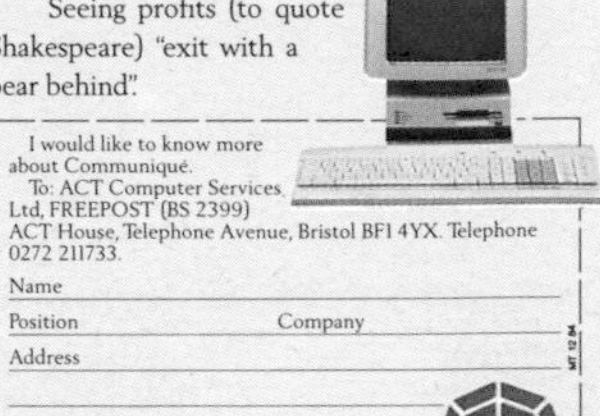

I would like to know more about Communiqué.
To: ACT Computer Services Ltd, FREEPOST (BS 2399)
ACT House, Telephone Avenue, Bristol BF1 4YX. Telephone 0272 211733.

Name
Position Company
Address
Tel

THE ANSWER IS
Apricot WITH Communiqué

116

Warning: these games show no mercy.

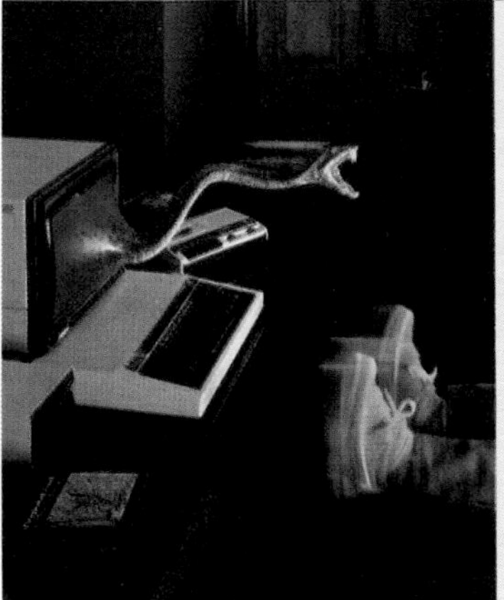

Acornsoft have now unleashed eight more merciless games onto unsuspecting BBC micro owners.

Ranging from 'Gateway to Karos,' where putting a foot wrong could mean instant death. To the relentless antics of Drogna which could have you dying with laughter.

Gateway to Karos.

An adventure game in which you'll need all your patience and ingenuity just to stay alive. Your objective is to find the Talisman of Khoronz but, whichever path you choose, you'll be beset by treachery. Serpents lie in wait and magical phenomenona are in abundance. Should you find the Talisman, you've still to find your way back.

Kingdom of Hamil.

As the rightful heir to the Kingdom of Hamil, you are in the unusual position of having to prove your claim to the throne. Evil people are trying to prevent you accomplishing your task by any means. An adventure game fraught with many dangers, puzzles and problems.

Tetrapod.

You're in an arena littered with dormant lizards, killer bees and other hostile creatures with whom you'll have to do battle to survive. But beware of your own laser bullets, as they bounce off the arena walls.

Drogna.

A game for two people – preferably with devious minds. There are two vaults containing diamonds and your job is to collect and transfer them to your home base. While your opponent is out collecting you could sneak in and steal his loot . . . but keep an eye out for him doing the same to you.

Crazy Tracer.

An arcade style game where you're in charge of a paint roller. Guide your roller around a maze of rectangles while evading monsters who are committed to destroying it. Gain extra rollers and bonus points by painting different objects. But you'll have to avoid running out of paint.

Volcano.

Mount Crona has erupted after 150 years of silence. And your mission as an Emergency Rescue Helicopter Pilot is to save sightseers stranded on the slopes. Time is of the essence as the lava approaches the sightseers. But you'll have to take time to evade – or shoot – the boulders being hurled from the volcano.

Carousel.

A re-creation of the fairground shooting gallery – with a difference. Shoot down all the ducks, owls and rabbits before you run out of ammunition. Watch out for the low-flying ducks. If you fail to shoot these, they'll steal your bullets and reduce your chances of success.

Meteor Mission.

On an alien planet are six stranded astronauts. Launch your capsule from the Mothership and by avoiding – or shooting – meteors and alien craft, pick up the astronauts one at a time and return them to the Mothership.

All games – with the exception of Gateway to Karos which is currently only available on cassette – can be bought direct in either cassette or disc form. You will find all these programs at your local Acorn stockist. To find out where they are simply call 01-200 0200. Credit card holders, phone 01-200 0200, anytime. Or 0933 79300, during office hours.

Alternatively, you can order the games by sending off the coupon below to: Acornsoft, c/o Vector Marketing, Denington Estate, Wellingborough, Northants NN8 2RL. Please allow 28 days for delivery.

To: Acornsoft, c/o Vector Marketing, Denington Estate, Wellingborough, Northants NN8 2RL.
Please send me the following software games:

PROGRAM	QUANTITY	DISC/CASSETTE
Gateway to Karos		
Kingdom of Hamil		
Tetrapod		
Drogna		
Crazy Tracer		
Volcano		
Carousel		
Meteor Mission		
TOTAL		

Price Cassette: £9.95; Disc: £11.50
I enclose PO/Cheque payable to Acornsoft Ltd. Or charge my credit charge.
Card Number:
Name
Address
Postcode
Signature
Registered No. 1524763 VAT No. 215 8023 85

ACORNSOFT

117

FAIRE
QUE
L'ENTREPRISE
RESPIRE.
Burroughs
AVEC VOUS, AVANT TOUT.

118

116
Apricot Communiqué service
United Kingdom
Agency: Collett Dickenson Pearce & Partners, London

Owners or renters of an Apricot computer are invited in this ad to use Communiqué, 'a unique package of financial and business services', giving access to many data-bases. The intriguing series of pictures shows a bull market on the Stock Exchange being transformed into a bear market within hours. The Communiqué service keeps the subscribers in constant touch with share prices.

117
Acornsoft computer games
United Kingdom
Agency: Aspect Advertising, London

Ad for eight new games designed for the Acorn-made BBC Micro. Among them a game called 'Gateway to Karos' in which 'serpents lie in wait and magical phenomena are in abundance'.

118
Burroughs Linc
France
Agency: Boulet Dru Dupuy Petit, Paris

Linc is defined as Burroughs' fourth generation computer language. Copy says it helps users cut down the time they need to devote to their computer system. Hence the heading 'Enabling the company to breathe'.

119
Comshare System W software
United Kingdom
Agency: Leagas Delaney Partnership, London

Copy, describing 'a computer software program designed to help companies examine all their financial options', declares that 'Deng Xiaoping might seem an unlikely capitalist.' Since the Chinese strongman was denounced by his enemies not so many years ago as a 'capitalist-roader', that's not so unlikely as the copywriter may think.

120
British Telecom telex service
United Kingdom
Agency: KMP Partnership, London

An attempt to brush up the image of the telex, perceived by business people as antiquated. Copy puts the emphasis on the Telex Plus service which enables a message to be sent automatically to up to 100 destinations. The violent image, relying on the fact that for years telex has been faster than a speeding bullet, is part of the attempt to make users look at the service with fresh eyes.

119

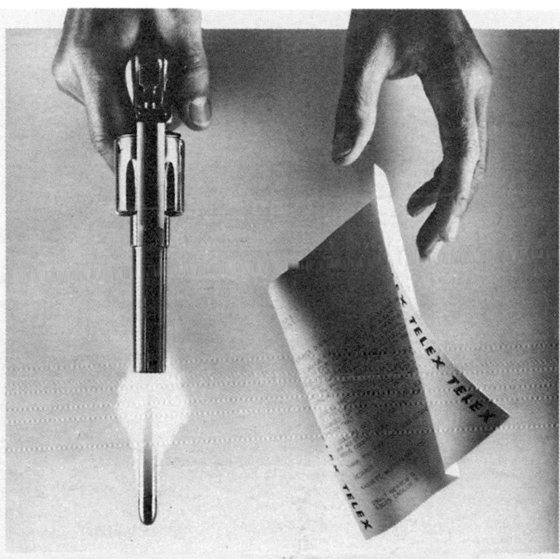

120

121
Xerox 3890 copier
Japan
Agency: Dentsu, Tokyo

'Flexible and changing', the words of the headline, are allegedly the attributes shared by the machine and by Sarunosuke Ichikawa, the famous kabuki actor shown here. He is always developing new techniques of expression.

122
IBM copier
United States
Agency: Doyle Dane Bernbach, New York

The invisible copier (because people do not notice it when it is working properly). A strong selling message and, since copiers are really not much fun to look at, not such a silly picture as you may at first think.

121

This is what every copier should look like.

When a copier is working properly, few people notice.

Which is why an IBM Model 60 Copier tends to become invisible.

It works so well, people take it for granted.

An IBM computer inside helps keep it running smoothly. So you get consistently high quality copies. And many easy-to-use features.

Including a job-interrupt feature, which allows small jobs to interrupt big ones.

And all of this for a price that's less than that of any other copier in its class.*

So if you're interested in buying a copier that doesn't cost a small fortune, give some serious thought to the IBM Model 60 Copier.

You might even buy it sight unseen.

IBM

IBM Series III Model 60
Write today to IBM,
DRM, Dept. 2G, 400 Parson's Pond Drive,
Franklin Lakes, New Jersey 07417.
☐ Please send me a free brochure.
☐ Please have an IBM representative call me.
NAME
TITLE
COMPANY
STREET ADDRESS
CITY
STATE ZIP
BUSINESS PHONE
The Invisible Copier

Call *IBM Direct* 1 800 IBM-2468 Ext. 2.

*Copier/duplicators rated at 70 copies per minute as of 4/1/84, with reduction, automatic document feed and collator.

122

123
Rank Xerox Marathon copier
Netherlands
Agency: Young & Rubicam, Amsterdam

'Will it be a relay race or the Marathon?' asks the headline. The relay race refers to the passing of paper from hand to hand when you don't have a Rank Xerox Marathon. The spring-heeled runner actually has no relevance to the story but makes an interesting picture.

Wordt 't een estafette
of de Marathon?
Hoe meer papier er binnen uw organisatie van hand tot hand gaat, des te groter is de kans op storingen bij het kopieerapparaat.
Tussen het afdrukken, vergaren en sorteren door, kunnen uw medewerkers menige steek laten vallen. Met 'n Xerox Marathon® 1075+ is dat praktisch uitgesloten. Ontworpen op betrouwbaarheid, gaat deze copier door, waar andere 't opgeven.
1075
MEER MOGELIJKHEDEN DOOR MODULAIRE OPBOUW.
Eén Xerox Marathon® 1075+ zet alle decentrale copiers in de schaduw. Zowel qua mogelijkheden en werktempo, als wat de verhouding prijs/prestatie betreft.
Dit apparaat is namelijk leverbaar in verschillende configuraties. U kiest een Automatische Originelenverwisselaar en een opvangbak voor gestaffelde sets als u in recordtijd rapporten wilt vermenigvuldigen. Kant en klaar bijeen geniet en desgewenst automatisch voorzien van een kartonnen voor en/of achterkant.
Of u kiest voor een Originelen Doorvoersysteem, waar u één of twee 20-vaks vergaareenheden op aan kunt sluiten.
Het Originelen Doorvoersysteem is ook voorzien van een continu doorvoersysteem voor kettingformulieren.
BEDIENINGSGEMAK EN VEELZIJDIGHEID.
Elke Xerox Marathon® 1075+ communiceert met u. Een beeldvenster vertelt in glasheldер Nederlands hoe u het apparaat stap voor stap bedient en een beeldscherm laat zien hoe onverhoedse storingen in een mum van tijd te verhelpen.
U maakt enkelzijdige afdrukken of dubbelzijdige afdrukken. Ook dubbelzijdige afdrukken van twee enkelzijdige originelen.
Verkleinen kunt u via vier vaste factoren, of in stappen van 1% tot 65% van het origineel. Raakt de hoofdpapierlade leeg, dan schakelt het apparaat automatisch over op de hulppapierlade.
Terwijl afdruk na afdruk elektronisch op kwaliteit wordt gecontroleerd. In een tempo van 70 per minuut.
ELEKTRONISCHE KOSTENBEHEERSING.
Voor vergaande kostenbeheersing rust u het apparaat uit met een Auditron. Een elektronisch tellersysteem voor registratie van afdrukken per afdeling of per project.
Ook kunt u de Auditron gebruiken om middels geheime codenummers het aantal gebruikers van de machine te beperken.
BLIJVENDE KWALITEIT.
Door een veelheid aan ingebouwde software vergen service-beurten aan de Xerox Marathon® 1075+ een minimum aan tijd. Een waarborg voor blijvende kwaliteit.
Rank Xerox® kwaliteit. Streng bewaakt door het grootste servicenet van Nederland. Extra bevorderd door de levering van Xerox papier en verbruiksartikelen, die uw apparatuur optimaal laten functioneren.
De Xerox Marathon® 1075+:
het enige alternatief voor decentraal kopiëren.
Voor een demonstratie belt u 03404-62060. Of u stuurt de bon in.
Xerox Marathon copiers gaan door, waar andere het opgeven.
RANK XEROX

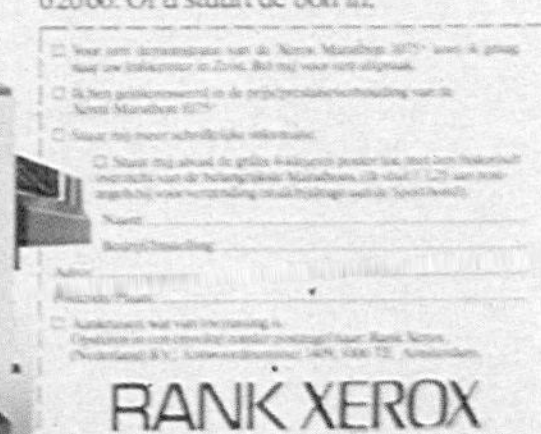

123

124
Rank Xerox 1055 copier
France
Agency: Young & Rubicam, Paris

'The new copier which folds large-format sheets' has its capability strikingly emphasised by this comical creation.

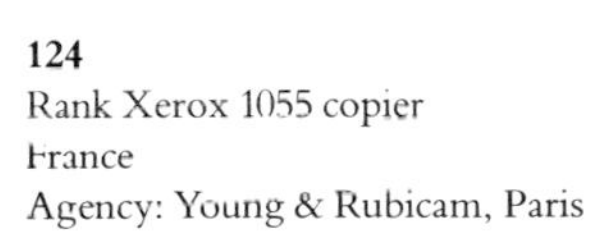

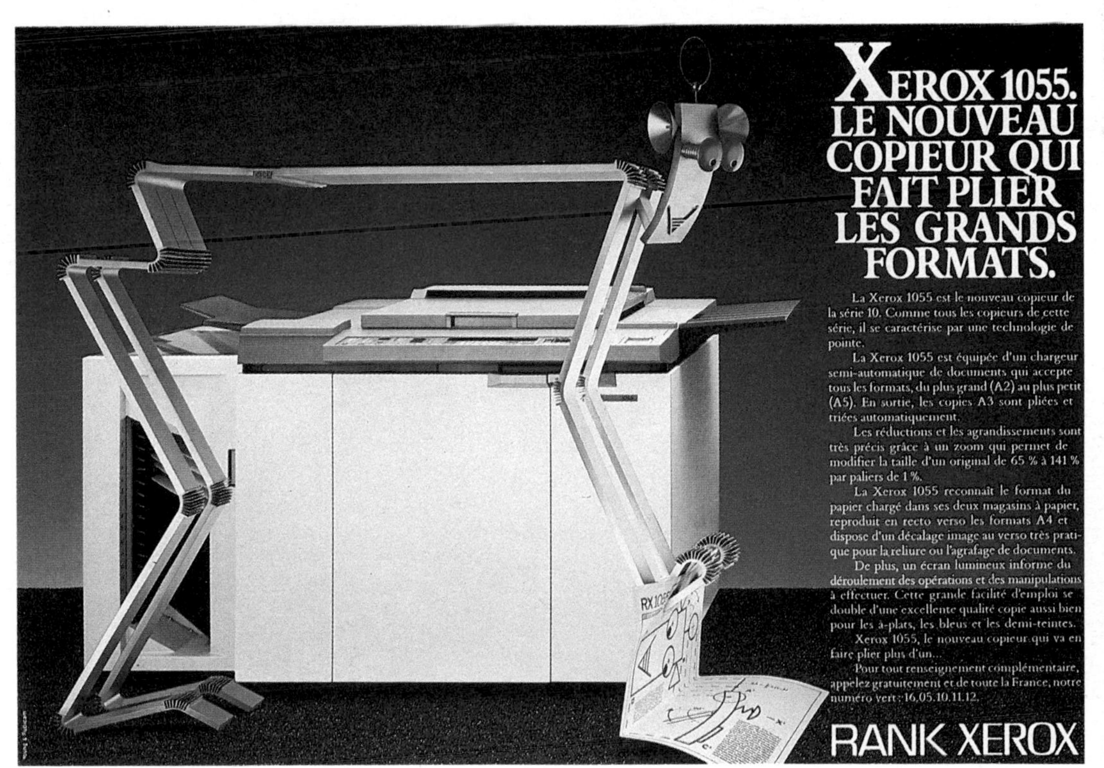

XEROX 1055.
LE NOUVEAU COPIEUR QUI FAIT PLIER LES GRANDS FORMATS.
La Xerox 1055 est le nouveau copieur de la série 10. Comme tous les copieurs de cette série, il se caractérise par une technologie de pointe.
La Xerox 1055 est équipée d'un chargeur semi-automatique de documents qui accepte tous les formats, du plus grand (A2) au plus petit (A5). En sortie, les copies A3 sont pliées et triées automatiquement.
Les réductions et les agrandissements sont très précis grâce à un zoom qui permet de modifier la taille d'un original de 65 % à 141 % par paliers de 1 %.
La Xerox 1055 reconnaît le format du papier chargé dans ses deux magasins à papier, reproduit en recto verso les formats A4 et dispose d'un décalage image au verso très pratique pour la reliure ou l'agrafage de documents.
De plus, un écran lumineux informe du déroulement des opérations et des manipulations à effectuer. Cette grande facilité d'emploi se double d'une excellente qualité copie aussi bien pour les à-plats, les bleus et les demi-teintes.
Xerox 1055, le nouveau copieur qui va en faire plier plus d'un...
Pour tout renseignement complémentaire, appelez gratuitement et de toute la France, notre numéro vert: 16.05.10.11.12.
RANK XEROX

124

125

Voor IBM is de nachtrust van'n secretaresse even belangrijk als de maanreis van Armstrong.

Waar een secretaresse vroeger alleen ten koste van veel overwerk aan toekwam, doet ze nu in 'n handomdraai.
Zij werkt met 'n IBM systeem. De NASA doet dat ook.
Die zou zonder hulp van zeer geavanceerde elektronische navigatiemiddelen moeite hebben gehad om Armstrong op de meter nauwkeurig op de maan te krijgen.
Wat IBM voor de NASA betekent, betekent IBM nu ook voor meer aardse projecten.
'n Secretaresse kan daar over meepraten.
Haar baas ook. Hij stelt hoge eisen aan de papieren uitvoer van zijn kantoor.
Zorgvuldigheid, representativiteit, uniformiteit en snelheid zijn woorden die bij hem hoog genoteerd staan.
IBM Visietekst bijvoorbeeld speelt voor de volle honderd procent op zijn eisen in.
Teksten kunnen tot op het moment van verspreiding ingrijpend gewijzigd worden.
Over de juiste spelling hoeft niemand zich ook meer druk te maken.
Secretaresses hebben er een briljant geheugen bij.
In het Visietekst systeem zitten 150.000 Nederlandse woorden opgeslagen. Wordt 'n woord verkeerd gespeld, dan licht het duidelijk op.
De kaartenbak van vroeger heeft het veld geruimd. Er ligt geen letter informatie meer begraven in 't archief.
Alle gegevens staan nu op diskette. Een druk op de knop en ze komen boven water.
Hoeveel klanten zijn er in Zutphen? Hoeveel huizen zijn er in 't 2de kwartaal verkocht?
Cijfermateriaal kan ook rekenkundig bewerkt worden: optellen, aftrekken, vermenigvuldigen en delen.
Knelpunt dat informatie blijft liggen nadat het getypt is, behoort ook tot het verleden.
Interne post, PTT, telex (weer overtypen), en koeriersdiensten kunnen worden omzeild. Nadat een document getypt is, hoeft het papier zich niet meer te verplaatsen.
Alleen de informatie verplaatst zich. Van het ene Visietekst systeem naar het andere.
Of naar daarvoor geprogrammeerde computers.
Via de normale telefoonlijnen.
Als u onderstaande bon invult krijgt u meer informatie.
Daarna is het misschien een prima idee om u te laten demonstreren hoe IBM Visietekst bij u ogenblikkelijk rendabel gemaakt kan worden.
Zend deze bon in 'n ongefrankeerde envelop naar:
IBM Nederland N.V.,
Verkoop Informatie Centrum,
Antwoordnummer 10060,
2700 VB Zoetermeer.
Naam:
Bedrijf:
Functie:
Adres:
Plaats:
IBM
meer dan'n produkt

126

HEUTE KOMMT THOMSON
MIT DER ELEKTRONIK VON MORGEN.

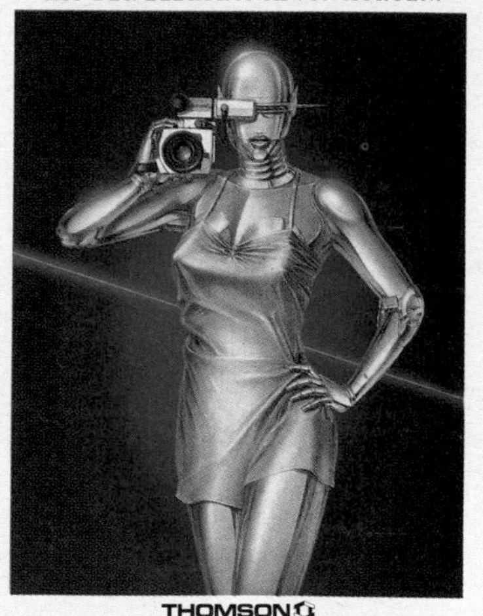

THOMSON
EUROPAS DIALOG MIT DER ZUKUNFT.

127

125
Sony
Netherlands
Agency: KSM, Haarlem

This science-fiction-style picture bears the headline 'Thinking about the future is essential in communication.' Copy talks about the development of information technology and Sony's part in it.

126
IBM
Netherlands
Agency: KVH/GGK, Amsterdam

'For IBM', says the headline, 'the secretary's night's sleep is as important as Armstrong's journey to the moon.' Copy talks both about IBM's involvement in the American space exploration programme and about the company's labour-saving office equipment.

127
Thomson-Electronic
West Germany
Agency: Heye Needham & Partner, Düsseldorf

Like the Dutch ad for Sony, this uses a futuristic theme. 'Thomson comes today with the electronics of tomorrow' says the headline over the alluring female robot. The pay-off line is 'Europe's dialogue with the future'. Thomson-Brandt, of France, is indeed one of Europe's biggest electronic concerns, and its products were already well known in Germany under subsidiary brand names such as Nordmende and Telefunken. This ad is part of the company's effort to launch the Thomson brand name into the German leisure electronics market.

128
Northern Telecom
United States
Agency: J. Walter Thompson, Chicago

Other ads in JWT's campaign for this client have focused on the contrast between modern and ancient information technologies. This ad is designed specifically to create awareness of Northern Telecom's presence in the US marketplace. Notice the microchips on the underside of the map of the country.

129
Siemens India
India
Agency: Lintas, Bombay

Copy takes the company's Vertix 1, a 'universal X-ray unit that works off an ordinary 15-amp socket', as an example of 'international technology being specifically tailored to meet the needs of Indian industry'.

130a, 130b, 130c
Volvo
International
Agency: TBWA, London

The agency approached several well known writers to compose fables for this unusual corporate campaign. The story in the first of the series was written, however, by Chris Martin, who was creative director of TBWA, London until his recent departure to become a partner in his own agency. Here it is, with an illustration by artist David Hockney. It tells of the race between two princes to be first to finish building a castle. One paid his workers little. The other, the winner, treated his labour force well. The reader is not told, but is expected to see, the analogy with Volvo's labour relations policy.

128

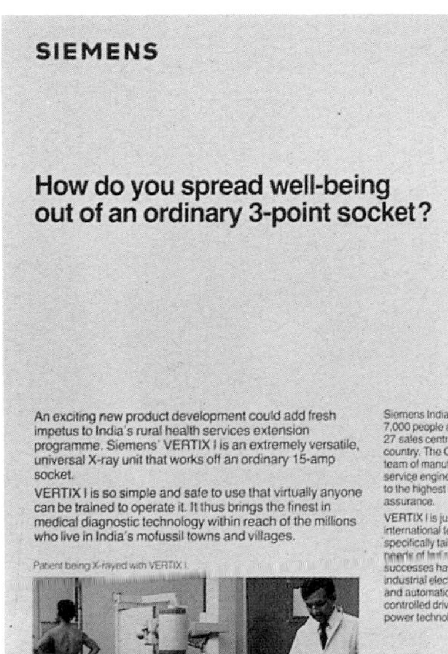

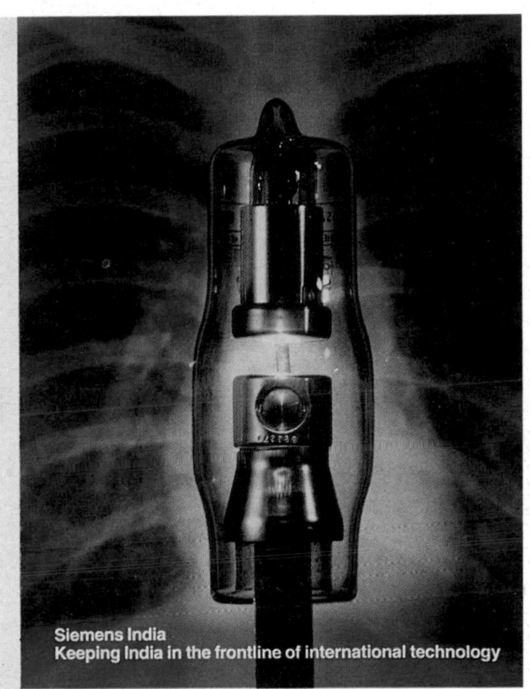

129

130a

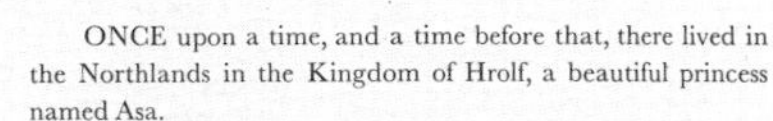

The Castle Race

by Christopher Martin
illustrated by David Hockney

ONCE upon a time, and a time before that, there lived in the Northlands in the Kingdom of Hrolf, a beautiful princess named Asa.

She had many suitors from all parts, but two noble princes, Agnay and Volund, were far more persistent and determined than the rest.

Unable to decide between them, Asa sought her father's advice. 'Both are princes,' she said, 'both fine horse-men and one as handsome as the other. How shall I choose?'

At this, King Hrolf summoned the two princes to his court. 'Guarding the northern and southern entrances to my Kingdom are two identical hills,' he said. 'Take one hill each and on it build a castle fit for a princess. Whoever shall finish first will marry Princess Asa. But one thing. You must complete the task for no more money than this.' And so saying the King gave each prince one thousand crowns in gold (a modest fortune in those days). The two princes began at once, though with rather different attitudes of mind.

Prince Agnay reasoned thus: 'It is a race,' he said, 'so speed is of the essence. I will engage many labourers who will have to work for low wages. We will use local stone because it is convenient and cheap, if a little difficult to work. We won't waste time with proper scaffolding, we will sleep rough and eat what wild berries can be found on the hill.'

Prince Volund was of a different mind: 'Building castles is long, laborious and often dangerous work,' he said. 'I will engage only enough men that I can pay fair wages. We will

130b

haul stone from across the mountains because it is easier to work. We must cut down pine forests as scaffolding and to make proper shelters for the men, and we will engage full-time hunters to keep us well supplied with deer and wild boar.'

'Furthermore,' said Prince Volund, 'every man who helps me build this castle shall have a part ownership of it, which will entitle him and his family to seek refuge here in times of trouble.'

At the end of the first summer, King Hrolf came to view the progress. Agnay's castle was half complete, but poor Volund had only just begun. The people laughed at Volund. 'It will doubtless be a very fine castle when it's finished,' they mocked. 'What a pity there will be no princess to live in it.' King Hrolf wasn't so sure.

Then winter came. And as you know, winters in the Northlands are very severe. Cold hands found Agnay's stone even harder to work. Accidents, caused by the lack of scaffolding, trebled. The berries disappeared from the hillside, and where there had been grass for a bed, now there was snow.

Mumblings and grumblings became visible discontent, and one by one Agnay's men downed what tools they had and asked, 'Why should we work under these conditions?' Volund's labourers knew they would gain lifelong security for their families from the finished castle. They went to Volund and said, 'Because we are so far behind in the race, we have looked around and found ways of being more efficient.'

And so it was that as Agnay fell into disarray, Volund went from strength to strength. And, as you will have guessed by now, one summer and winter later he not only finished first, but had built by far the most beautiful castle.

At the wedding, which by all accounts was a splendour in itself, King Hrolf took Volund to one side. 'I have gained more than a son,' he said.

'In this part of the Northlands, the lessons that you have taught will never be forgotten.'

VOLVO

130c

131

131
Tinplate manufacturers
West Germany
Agency: Lintas, Hamburg

'I was a can' says the nail pictured here, and copy explains that millions of empty cans are recycled, thus conserving precious raw materials. The ad, paid for by the Tinplate Information Centre, supported by four manufacturers – Dillinger, Hoesch, Otto Wolf and Rosselstein – is linked to a series catchlined 'Tinplate classics'.

132
RAG
West Germany
Agency: Team/BBDO, Düsseldorf

RAG stands for Ruhrkohle Aktiengesellschaft, or Ruhr Coal Company. The ad shown here was the first in a corporate campaign using the RAG logo as the hook on which to hang a series of statements about little known aspects of this well known company. The headline says 'Ruhr Coal is getting ever younger.' Copy explains that RAG is West Germany's biggest provider of apprenticeships. Other ads show the logo made up not of men, but microprocessor chips (to illustrate technological sophistication) and oil (because coal is used to produce petroleum).

Die Ruhrkohle wird immer jünger.
Fur junge Leute ist die Ruhrkohle AG eine der großen Hoffnungen auf eine berufliche Zukunft. Die RAG ist der größte industrielle Ausbilder der Bundesrepublik.
Zur Zeit werden über 11.000 junge Mitarbeiter bei uns ausgebildet: in 18 Berufen. Vom Energieanlagen-Elektroniker über den Bergmechaniker bis zum Meß- und Regeltechniker.
Das Ergebnis unserer aktiven Ausbildungspolitik: eine junge, qualifizierte Mannschaft. Jeder vierte Mitarbeiter der RAG ist jünger als 26. Die Energie unserer jungen Mitarbeiter ist so zukunftsreich wie die Ruhrkohle selbst. Und die Ruhrkohle reicht noch weit bis ins nächste Jahrtausend.
RAG
DIE RUHRKOHLE.

132

How to punctuate

By Russell Baker

International Paper asked Russell Baker, winner of the Pulitzer Prize for his book, Growing Up, and for his essays in The New York Times (the latest collection in book form is called The Rescue of Miss Yaskell and Other Pipe Dreams), to help you make better use of punctuation, one of the printed word's most valuable tools.

When you write, you make a sound in the reader's head. It can be a dull mumble — that's why so much government prose makes you sleepy — or it can be a joyful noise, a sly whisper, a throb of passion.

Listen to a voice trembling in a haunted room:

"And the silken, sad, uncertain rustling of each purple curtain thrilled me — filled me with fantastic terrors never felt before . . ."

That's Edgar Allan Poe, a master. Few of us can make paper speak as vividly as Poe could, but even beginners will write better once they start listening to the sound their writing makes.

One of the most important tools for making paper speak in your own voice is punctuation.

When speaking aloud, you punctuate constantly — with body language. Your listener hears commas, dashes, question marks, exclamation points, quotation marks as you shout, whisper, pause, wave your arms, roll your eyes, wrinkle your brow.

In writing, punctuation plays the role of body language. It helps readers hear you the way you want to be heard.

"My tools of the trade should be your tools, too. Good use of punctuation can help you build a more solid, more readable sentence."

"Gee, Dad, have I got to learn all them rules?"

Don't let the rules scare you. For they aren't hard and fast. Think of them as guidelines.

Am I saying, "Go ahead and punctuate as you please"? Absolutely not. Use your own common sense, remembering that you can't expect readers to work to decipher what you're trying to say.

There are two basic systems of punctuation:

1. The loose or open system, which tries to capture the way body language punctuates talk.

2. The tight, closed structural system, which hews closely to the sentence's grammatical structure.

Most writers use a little of both. In any case, we use much less punctuation than they used 200 or even 50 years ago. (Glance into Edward Gibbon's "Decline and Fall of the Roman Empire," first published in 1776, for an example of the tight structural system at its most elegant.)

No matter which system you prefer, be warned: punctuation marks cannot save a sentence that is badly put together. If you have to struggle over commas, semicolons and dashes, you've probably built a sentence that's never going to fly, no matter how you tinker with it. Throw it away and build a new one to a simpler design. The better your sentence, the easier it is to punctuate.

Choosing the right tool

There are 30 main punctuation marks, but you'll need fewer than a dozen for most writing.

I can't show you in this small space how they all work, so I'll stick to the ten most important — and even then can only hit highlights. For more details, check your dictionary or a good grammar.

Comma [,]

This is the most widely used mark of all. It's also the toughest and most controversial. I've seen aging editors almost come to blows over the comma. If you can handle it without sweating, the others will be easy. Here's my policy:

1. Use a comma after a long introductory phrase or clause: *After stealing the crown jewels from the Tower of London, I went home for tea.*

2. If the introductory material is short, forget the comma: *After the theft I went home for tea.*

3. But use it if the sentence would be confusing without it, like this: *The day before I'd robbed the Bank of England.*

4. Use a comma to separate elements in a series: *I robbed the Denver Mint, the Bank of England, the Tower of London and my piggy bank.*

Notice there is no comma before *and* in the series. This is common style nowadays, but some publishers use a comma there, too.

5. Use a comma to separate independent clauses that are joined by a conjunction like and, but, for, or, nor, because or so: *I shall return the crown jewels, for they are too heavy to wear.*

6. Use a comma to set off a mildly parenthetical word grouping that isn't essential to the sentence: *Girls, who have always interested me, usually differ from boys.*

Do not use commas if the word grouping is essential to the sentence's meaning: *Girls who interest me know how to tango.*

7. Use a comma in direct address: *Your majesty, please hand over the crown.*

8. And between proper names and titles: *Montague Sneed, Director of Scotland Yard, was assigned the case.*

9. And to separate elements of geographical address: *Director Sneed comes from Chicago, Illinois, and now lives in London, England.*

Generally speaking, use a comma where you'd pause briefly in speech. For a long pause or completion of thought, use a period.

If you confuse the comma with the period, you'll get a run-on sentence: *The Bank of England is located in London, I rushed right over to rob it.*

Semicolon [;]

A more sophisticated mark than the comma, the semicolon separates two main clauses, but it keeps those two thoughts more tightly linked than a period can: *I steal crown jewels; she steals hearts.*

Dash [—] and Parentheses [( )]

Warning! Use sparingly. The dash SHOUTS. Parentheses whisper. Shout too often, people stop listening; whisper too much, people become suspicious of you.

The dash creates a dramatic pause to prepare for an expression needing strong emphasis: *I'll marry you — if you'll rob Topkapi with me.*

Parentheses help you pause quietly to drop in some chatty information not vital to your story: *Despite Betty's daring spirit ("I love robbing your piggy bank," she often said), she was a terrible dancer.*

?()!!

"Punctuation puts body language on the printed page. Show bewilderment with a question mark, a whisper with parentheses, emphasis with an exclamation point."

Quotation marks [" "]

These tell the reader you're reciting the exact words someone said or wrote: *Betty said, "I can't tango."* Or: *"I can't tango," Betty said.*

Notice the comma comes before the quote marks in the first example, but comes inside them in the second. Not logical? Never mind. Do it that way anyhow.

Colon [:]

A colon is a tip-off to get ready for what's next: a list, a long quotation or an explanation. This article is riddled with colons. Too many, maybe, but the message is: "Stay on your toes; it's coming at you."

Apostrophe [']

The big headache is with possessive nouns. If the noun is singular, add 's: *I hated Betty's tango.*

If the noun is plural, simply add an apostrophe after the s: *Those are the girls' coats.*

The same applies for singular nouns ending in s, like Dickens: *This is Dickens's best book.*

And in plural: *This is the Dickenses' cottage.*

The possessive pronouns *hers* and *its* have no apostrophe.

If you write *it's*, you are saying *it is.*

Keep cool

You know about ending a sentence with a period (.) or a question mark (?). Do it. Sure, you can also end with an exclamation point (!), but must you? Usually it just makes you sound breathless and silly. Make your writing generate its own excitement. Filling the paper with !!!! won't make up for what your writing has failed to do.

Too many exclamation points make me think the writer is talking about the panic in his own head.

Don't sound panicky. End with a period. I am serious. A period. Understand?

Well . . . sometimes a question mark is okay.

Russell Baker

Today, the printed word is more vital than ever. Now there is more need than ever for all of us to *read* better, *write* better and *communicate* better.

International Paper offers this series in the hope that, even in a small way, we can help.

If you'd like to share this article and all the others in the series with others — students, employees, family — we'll gladly send you reprints. So far we've sent out over 20,000,000 in response to requests from people everywhere. Write: "Power of the Printed Word," International Paper Company, Dept. 13V, P.O. Box 954, Madison Square Station, New York, NY 10010. © 1984 INTERNATIONAL PAPER COMPANY

INTERNATIONAL PAPER COMPANY
We believe in the power of the printed word.

133

133
International Paper
United States
Agency: Ogilvy & Mather, New York

The advertiser's problem was that its customers, publishers of books, magazines and newspapers, regarded it as simply a commodity supplier. It wanted to position itself as a partner in the future of publishing. The strategy adopted was to help build future readership for publishers' products by encouraging young people to take more interest in the printed word. O & M's solution is to use long and informative – but enticing – copy, bylined by people who command respect among the young.

ARCO
We're making tracks for the Olympics.
For example, we're refurbishing the Los Angeles Coliseum and rebuilding its track so it's a world-class environment for the world-class athletes who will compete there in the 1984 Los Angeles Olympics.
And we're building seven practice tracks at schools in and around Los Angeles. Tracks that will give our Olympic hopefuls the finest training facilities available. Facilities that will also be available for our future Olympic hopefuls.
But there's a lot more to do. For example, it costs $15.50 a day to support just one athlete at the Olympic training center in Colorado Springs. So, the U.S. Olympic effort needs your help, too. With donations which will help pay for equipment, travel, coaching, lodging, meals, and sports medicine. Donations which will ensure that we field the best U.S. Olympic team ever assembled.
Send your tax-deductible contribution to the U.S. Olympic Committee –Southern California, P.O. Box 54010, Terminal Annex, Los Angeles, CA 90059. And join with us in supporting the 1984 Olympic Team. They need our help. And they deserve it!

ARCO
Atlantic Richfield Company
We're putting our energy into America.

134

Want to see water where it almost never rains?

Borg-Warner submersible pumps help bring vital irrigation water 5000 feet, almost a mile, straight up from beneath arid desert sands. That's today's Borg-Warner. Diversified for financial stability. A company worth watching.

Watch Borg-Warner

For an annual report call 312-322-8680.

135

134
Atlantic Richfield Company
United States
Agency: Foote Cone & Belding/Honig, Los Angeles

The Olympic stadium inside the running shoe is there to draw attention to the message that Arco refurbished the Los Angeles Coliseum for the 1984 Olympics.

135
Borg-Warner
United States
Agency: Foote Cone & Belding, Chicago

The eyeball-to-eyeball picture of a camel draws attention to the fact that, among its many activities, the company supplies equipment to pump water from beneath the desert.

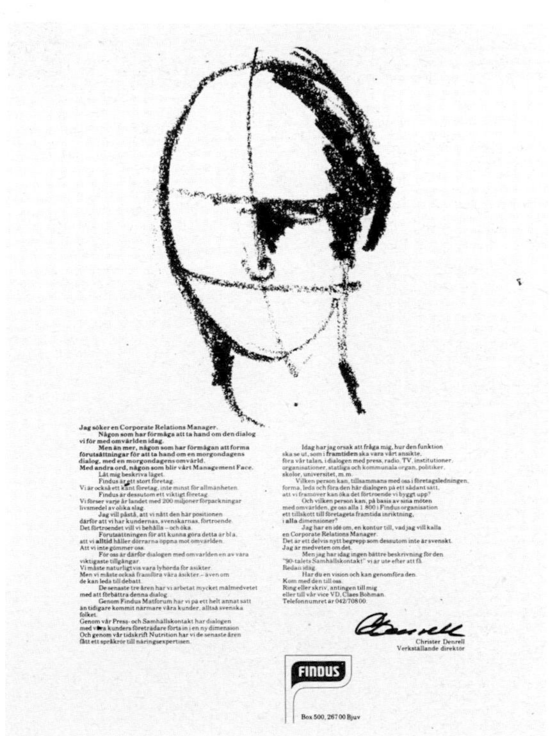

136

136
Findus
Sweden
Agency: Ted Bates, Helsingborg

Classified recruitment ads are not infrequently designed to bolster the advertiser's reputation as well. This large-space newspaper classified ad, for a Corporate Relations Manager, actually devotes most of its copy to describing the company's important position in the Swedish food market. Signed by the boss, Christopher Denrell, it invites applications from people who can help Findus improve its reputation for reliability.

137
Drug manufacturers
India
Agency: Jaisons Advertising, Bombay

That old visual cliché, the globe, is here combined with the symbol for a pill to emphasise the export performance of members of the Indian Drug Manufacturers Association. Copy combats the 'strange myth' that things made outside India are of better quality.

138
American Telephone & Telegraph
United States
Agency: N. W. Ayer, New York

One ad in a campaign run at the time AT&T was divesting itself of its local telephone operations in the US. The purpose was to inform a select readership about the new structure of the company and its various fields of activity. This particular ad emphasised its pre-eminence in statistical quality control. Pay-off line in this, as in all other ads in the campaign, 'We're reaching out in new directions.'

139a, 139b, 139c
Skandia Insurance Company
Sweden
Agency: SSC&B: Lintas, Stockholm

Three out of a series of eight ads which, step by step, completed the company's symbol. Each of the first six ads described a different aspect of Skandia's business. The last had a general report on its progress. Reproduced here are ads number 3, 7 and 8 of the series, with the respective captions 'Who can be 130 years old and still young?', 'We manage our customers money as if it were our own' and 'What have we done with your money?'

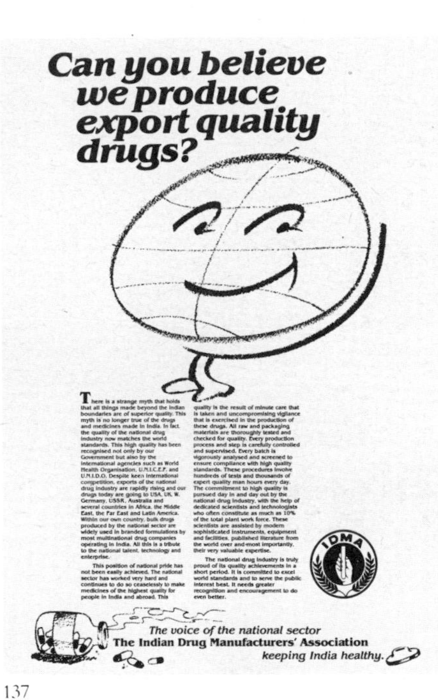

137

138

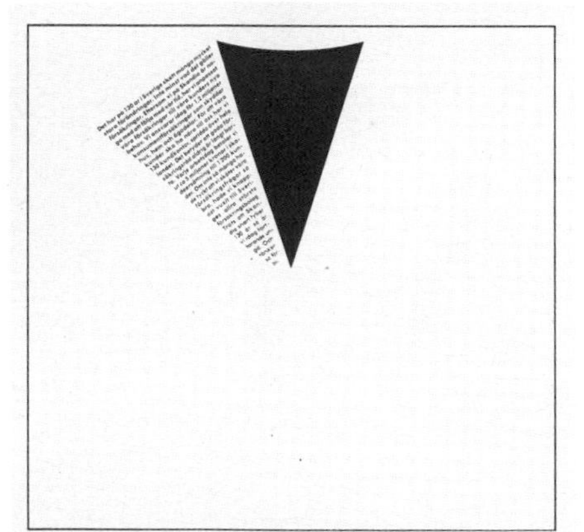

139a

139b

139c

1965

A routine press conference in London, and an off-the-cuff remark by Shell UK's top geologist. Within minutes his comments are on every Editor's desk in Fleet Street, and by morning, being repeated the length and breadth of the country. While the sceptics scoff, the politicians pray. If what has been hinted at is indeed true, it will alter the economic and political fortunes of Britain for decades to come. Out in the North Sea, it is reported, Shell expects to strike oil.

1966

The financial markets of London buzz with anticipation following Shell's discreet announcement of 'a significant gas discovery' 32 miles off the coast of East Anglia. Within two years Shell and other companies are bringing North Sea gas ashore, and with it a dramatic revival for the British gas industry. Plans are made for completely converting the National Grid to natural gas.

1967

Armed with the latest seismic data, two geologists from Shell set up a small office in a tiny flat, over a bookshop, in the centre of Aberdeen. It seems as good a place as any from which to tackle their awesome task. They have been instructed to begin exploration of the vast and hostile waters of the northern parts of the North Sea.

1971

At the northernmost offshore well yet drilled in the world, a veil of secrecy descends over Shell's activities. Communications with the mainland are suddenly coded through 'scrambler' phones. Information is rushed to Shell's scientists for prompt analysis. Until, as abruptly as they began, the exploration team cease all activity, seal the well, and are clearly seen making off for entirely new locations. A simple manoeuvre to ensure that nobody guesses what they have found.

1972

Shell proudly announce the discovery of what will prove to be a giant oil and gas find for Britain, the Brent Field.

1974

The latest analysis of the Brent Field shows that the possible reserves of oil and natural gas liquids are double the original estimate. With Britain's oil deficit still around £3.8 billion, the news is welcome indeed.

1976

The very high ratio of gas and gas liquids to oil being produced at Brent leads to a daring new scheme. A pipeline 278 miles long is to be laid on the seabed, to bring ashore the gas and gas liquids for separation. It will be the longest, and deepest, offshore pipeline ever built and is yet another challenge for British industry. Much of the technology required for North Sea development must be capable of operating in waves of up to 100 feet high, and in gusts of wind up to 100 miles per hour. In this instance, underwater cameras, side-scan sonars and computer systems are needed that will operate 600 feet beneath the sea.

1978

The scheme is a success. Now it will be possible to bring the gas and gas liquids ashore for further use. The gas will be extracted and fed into the National Grid.

It would be possible to split the remainder into ethane, butane, propane and natural gasoline – important resources for industry.

To do so, a highly advanced plant, costing many millions of pounds, will have to be specially built.

1980

Work begins on the £400 million Gas Liquids Plant being built by Shell at Mossmorran, and on the 138 mile pipeline that will feed it. Soon Mossmorran will be the largest construction site in Europe.

1982

Oil production from Brent approaches 310,000 barrels per day. This vast quantity helps transform Britain's oil deficit of yester-year into a surplus of around £4.4 billion.

1984

A VIP gathering to witness the opening of the new Mossmorran plant. Distinguished speakers touch on one or two environmental aspects of the plant, such as how it has been built tucked into the contours of the land so as to be as unobtrusive as possible. Also mentioned are the industrial aspects, such as how the hydrocarbons being produced will ultimately be used in the manufacturing of a thousand and one household items, from lipsticks to records.

But above all, it is noted that the opening of Mossmorran marks the culmination of the twenty years in which Shell, and the countless number of smaller British companies that have worked for her, have invested thousands of millions of pounds and great skill and ingenuity in the North Sea.

With excitement, we all look forward to the next twenty years.

IT SEEMED AS GOOD A PLACE AS ANY
TO START LOOKING FOR NORTH SEA OIL.

YOU CAN BE SURE OF SHELL

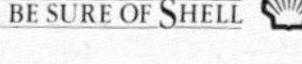

140

140
Shell
United Kingdom
Agency: Ogilvy & Mather, London

The ad tells the story of 20 years of North Sea oil exploration and extraction. In the early days two Shell geologists set up an office over a bookshop in Aberdeen, the one shown. The story leads up to the 1984 opening of the Mossmorran fractionation plant, built so as not to be an eyesore. Shell corporate advertising is aimed at reducing the cynicism with which the public views Big Oil.

一九八四年
八月三十一日(金)—九月五日(水)
松屋銀座八階大催場
最終日五時閉場　入場無料
主催—日本デザインコミッティー
コミッショナー—永井一正

出品者
井上嗣也
岩倉榮利
北岡節男
金相珍
サイトウマコト
瀬口英徳
the air
高松伸
戸田正寿
日比野克彦
副田高行
藤江和子
森田正樹
八束はじめ
山本清
ヤマザキミノリ

デザインニューウェーブ'84日本

MATSUYA GINZA

DESIGN KAZUMASA NAGAI

142

141
Design New Wave '84 Japan exhibition
Japan
Studio: Nippon Design Centre, Tokyo

Poster designed for the Japan Design Committee by Kazumasa Nagai.

142
1985 World Cup Marathon
Japan
Agency: Dentsu, Tokyo

The ideogram for 'run' is written twice on this poster for the marathon in Hiroshima. Each brush stroke represents a running man.

143
Sankai Juku dance troupe
International
Studio: Takayuki Itoh Design Office, Tokyo

The dance troupe's international tour was sponsored by Mitsubishi Motors, whose logo is tucked away discreetly at the foot of the poster.

ETERNAL VOYAGE
山海塾
SANKAIJUKU
DANCE OVER THE UNIVERSE
MITSUBISHI MOTORS SUPPLY VEHICLES FOR SANKAIJUKU'S WORLD TOUR

143

IN SHAFTESBURY AVE.
LAST FRIDAY NIGHT,
THERE WERE
9 MURDERS, 13 FIGHTS,
3 SUICIDES,
6 NAKED WOMEN,
1 TORTURE, 40 THIEVES,
PETER PAN
AND SEVERAL FAIRIES.

THE LONDON THEATRE. ACT ON IT.

144

144
London theatres
United Kingdom
Agency: Saatchi & Saatchi Compton, London

Ads without pictures do not normally get into this book, but this one has visual, as well as verbal, charm because of its typography. For those who do not know, Shaftesbury Avenue, where the 'murders' etc. took place, is where many of London's theatres are located.

145

145
Ninth Festival of Asian Arts
Hong Kong
Studio: SS Design, Hong Kong

An amusing idea which one can well imagine being used to advertise entirely different things. Clothing, perhaps?

146
New York Philharmonic concert
India
Agency: Enterprise Advertising, Bombay

This is as much an ad for cigarettes as for a concert. The poster has the colour, and bears the brand name, of Charms cigarettes, made by the Vazir Sultan Tobacco Company, co-sponsor of the concert in Bombay. It even has the statutory health warning at the bottom. 'The spirit of freedom' is the brand slogan, but the agency has cleverly made it fit the occasion, with musical notes turning into birds and flying away.

TIME AND TALENTS CLUB CONCERTS COMMITTEE
AND
THE VAZIR SULTAN TOBACCO COMPANY
PRESENT
NEW YORK PHILHARMONIC
WITH
Zubin Mehta
IN AID OF MEDICAL, EDUCATIONAL AND SOCIAL RELIEF
SHANMUKHANANDA HALL, BOMBAY
17TH AND 18TH SEPTEMBER,1984

Come, celebrate the spirit of freedom.

CHARMS

NEW YORK PHILHARMONIC TOUR OF ASIA 1984 SPONSORED BY CITIBANK N.A.
CIGARETTE SMOKING IS INJURIOUS TO HEALTH

146

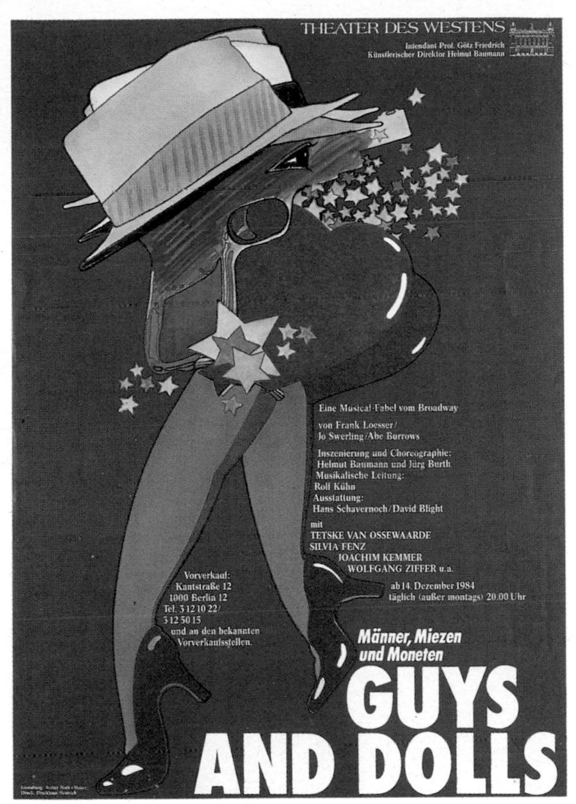

147

147
Guys and Dolls
West Berlin
Studio: Noth & Hauer, Berlin

The spirit of the musical conveyed as concisely as possible in this poster for the Theater des Westens.

148

148
Berlin Film Festival
West Germany
Studio: Noth & Hauer, Berlin

Each year Noth & Hauer come up with fresh combinations of the same design elements in their Festival posters. This is up to their usual standard.

149

149
Government Building Agency exhibition
Netherlands
Studio: Samenwerkende Ontwerpers, Amsterdam

RGD are the initials of the Dutch Government Building Agency, or Rijksgebouwendienst. The exhibits shown cast shadows in the form of the letters. The sense of the headline is 'Building for the State.'

Nu behöver du inte ha en svåger i banken.

Vi förstår att ett uttryck som "svåger i banken" kan myntas.

Ibland hör man ju talas om "den eller den" som fått ett fint lån i "den eller den" banken trots att det egentligen var helt omöjligt att få lån.

Men hos oss på Götabanken har du ingen nytta av en svåger. Vi anser nämligen att *ditt sparande* ska vara avgörande för vad vi kan erbjuda dig utöver det vanliga.

Tänk efter: Om du handlar väldigt mycket i en affär kan du få mängdrabatt och handlar du tillräckligt ofta får du säkert andra fördelar. Köper du årskort på en idrottsarena får du bästa plats, samtidigt som du betalar mindre per gång. Totalt sett ger du företaget mer i inkomst och då är det naturligt att du får vissa förmåner.

Precis så tänker vi på Götabanken också.

Har du ensam eller tillsammans med din familj ett samlat sparande på minst 40.000 kronor i Götabanken kan du vara säker på att du får förtur till lån.

Dessutom får du också andra förmåner som resevaluta utan expeditionsavgift, ett speciellt resekort med kostnadsfri reseolycksfallsförsäkring m m.

Och det bästa är att du får en egen bankman som tar hand om dig och din familjs bankaffärer.

Götabanken

DIE NORDDEUTSCHE ART, DURCH DIE BRILLE DES KUNDEN ZU SEHEN.

Man spricht von der „Vogelschau" und der „Froschperspektive", wenn man sagen will, daß die Welt ganz unterschiedlich wirken kann, je nachdem, von wo aus man sie sieht.

Im Geschäftsleben ist das ebenso. Jede Branche hat ihre eigene Sicht. Das liegt schon daran, daß sich im Verhalten zwischen Wettbewerbern und im Umgang mit den Kunden mit der Zeit Spielregeln bilden, an die sich jeder zu halten hat, der erfolgreich sein möchte.

Auf diese Tatsache haben wir uns eingestellt. Für uns ist es deshalb selbstverständlich, mit allen Regeln bestens vertraut zu sein. Unsere Mitarbeiter sind es gewohnt, Finanzierungsprobleme aus der Sicht Ihres Marktes zu sehen. Denn je besser wir Ihre Ansichten verstehen, um so größer sind die Aussichten, Ihnen mit Finanzierungsrat und Kreditierungstat zur Seite zu stehen.

Stellen Sie uns auf die Probe. Wir wären nicht die Nummer 1 in Norddeutschland geworden, wenn wir uns immer nur den eigenen Kopf zerbrochen hätten.

NORD/LB
Georgsplatz 1
3000 Hannover 1
Tel. 0511/103-0
Telex 9216-20
Btx *21030#

NORD/LB
NORD/LB-Zentrum
3300 Braunschweig
Tel. 0531/487-1
Telex 952540
Btx *953300#

NORD/LB
Luxembourg
26, Route d'Arlon
L-1140 Luxembourg
Tel. 00352/4723911
Telex 048/2263

NORD/LB
London
20, Ironmonger Lane
London EC 2V 8EY
Tel. 00441/6001721
Telex 051/884882

Zentralbank der niedersächsischen Sparkassen.

NORD/LB
NORDDEUTSCHE LANDESBANK
GIROZENTRALE

150
Götabanken
Sweden
Agency: Ted Bates 3, Stockholm

Götabanken is the first Swedish bank to have offered wealthier customers the services of a 'personal banker'. Hence the message of the headline, 'Now you don't need to have a brother-in-law in the bank'. The illustration, one of a striking series by Magnus Andersson, is presumably to be understood as showing the closeness of the customer and his personal banker. Or is it his brother-in-law?

151, 152, 153
Norddeutsche Landesbank
West Germany
Agency: Grey, Düsseldorf

Like Bates's Swedish campaign this one uses funny illustrations to make serious points. The point of the two men sharing the same pair of spectacles is in fact almost the same as that of the Swedes sharing the same suit. Headline reads: 'The Norddeutsche way, seeing through the client's spectacles.' The illustration is by Goffin. The other two pictures, by André François, are headed respectively 'The Norddeutsche way, showing composure' (the chessmen) and 'The Norddeutsche way, thinking before rather than after.'

154
Amro Bank
Netherlands
Agency: FHV/BBDO, Amsterdam

This ad eschews symbols and shows foreign locations directly and recognisably to underline its message that, if customers run out of money abroad, they can telephone a special number wherever they are to get Amro Bank travellers' cheques. The headline says 'Our financial aid posts abroad'.

155
Sparebanken
Norway
Agency: Foote Cone & Belding, Oslo

'Don't let your bonus go up in smoke' is the message in this ad for the leading Norwegian savings bank. Copy explains the new bonus system.

156
NatWest Bonus Saver Account
United Kingdom
Agency: J. Walter Thompson, London

Artistically not a great picture. But a strong simple visual device gets over the message that saving with the National Westminster Bank is a good way of enabling the customer to have a holiday.

152

153

155

154

156

157
National Westminster Bank
United Kingdom
Agency: J. Walter Thompson, London

Unlike the Norddeutsche Landesbank and Götabanken, NatWest had no need of an illustrator to make the visual joke seen here. Nature is the joker. The rare Chinese dog photographed, as copy explains, is priced at about £1,500. A dog-breeder who needed a loan to buy one, and got the money from NatWest, named the animal after the bank.

We weren't sure what it was either, but we still gave Mrs. Snelling a personal loan to buy it.

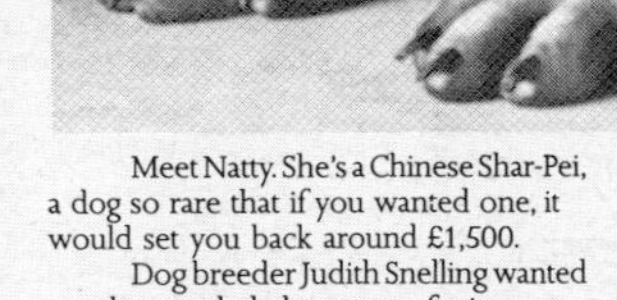

Meet Natty. She's a Chinese Shar-Pei, a dog so rare that if you wanted one, it would set you back around £1,500.

Dog breeder Judith Snelling wanted one, but needed a loan to pay for it.

So she applied to her local NatWest, and although we'd never even heard of a Shar-Pei, we gave her a Personal Loan on the spot.

Which delighted her so much that she actually named her new dog after us.

But Natty is only one of many unusual things we've helped pay for.

In fact, the chances are that whatever you've got your eye on, you could get a NatWest Personal Loan (£200-£5,000) to pay for it.

Just fill in an application form at your local NatWest, or post it to us. There's usually no need to see the manager, and you don't even have to be a NatWest customer when you apply.

So why not follow Mrs. Snelling's lead, and send for an application form today?

Written credit details available from any NatWest branch, by phoning 01-200 0200, or from: National Westminster Bank PLC, FREEPOST, Poole, Dorset BH14 0BR.

Name

Address

Branch where account held (if applicable).

Applicants must be 18 years or older.

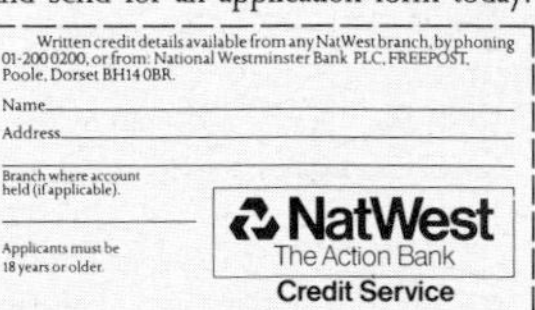

National Westminster Bank PLC, 41 Lothbury, London EC2P 2BP.

157

158
First Interstate Bancorp
United States
Agency: Foote Cone & Belding/Honig, Los Angeles

This ad is addressed not to customers but to bankers, more precisely owners of small banks. They are told they can avoid take-over by becoming franchisees of the First Interstate network. The alligator represents the bigger banks which have been doing the take-overs. A fine picture but not, perhaps, one that would inspire confidence among bank customers.

Guess what's happened to more than 50 of Florida's banks.

They've been swallowed up. In fact, over the past two years, more than 50 of Florida's banks have been merged or acquired.

Just as easily, you, too, could fall prey to a merger or acquisition. But there is an alternative that can afford you a way not only to survive, but to thrive.

That alternative is a franchise with First Interstate Bancorp.

Franchising:
the profitable partnership.

As a franchisee of First Interstate Bancorp, you'll have access to the resources of the 7th largest banking organization in the nation with assets of over $44 billion. Together with our franchisees, we have over 1,000 full-service banking offices in 14 states, making us one of the largest retail banking systems in the country.

In addition to size and strength, you'll gain benefits that only a large bank can offer. For example, you'll be able to realize savings on a wide range of items, from forms and checks to computer hardware and software. Plus, you'll have access to specialized services such as mortgage banking, discount brokerage, international trading, and data processing.

Most importantly, you'll still retain local ownership, management independence, and control of your bank.

Franchising:
the proven alternative.

Our success in the marketplace has been proven time and time again. Currently, First Interstate Bancorp has franchise agreements in 7 states, including Colorado, Hawaii, Alaska, Montana, Wyoming, Wisconsin and New Mexico.

Operations in these states represent a total of 22 banks with 73 offices. By the end of 1984, their combined assets will total $2.6 billion.

Find out more about how you can become part of the First Interstate Bancorp's successful franchise program by calling John Dean, President, First Interstate System, Inc. (213) 614-3043.

Consider franchising. It could make your tomorrow a whole lot easier.

First Interstate Bancorp

158

159
Banco Exterior de España
Spain
Agency: McCann-Erickson, Madrid

One of a series of prettily laid-out ads illustrating the bank's international connections with symbols of other countries – stamps, coins, pottery or, here, musical instruments.

159

160
Alliance Building Society
United Kingdom
Agency; TBWA, London

The most interestingly original feature of this magazine campaign is the explicit statement that the advertiser has chosen to save the high price of TV commercials. The question logically arises of why it does not save even more money by not advertising at all. But readers are obviously not expected to pursue the argument that far.

160

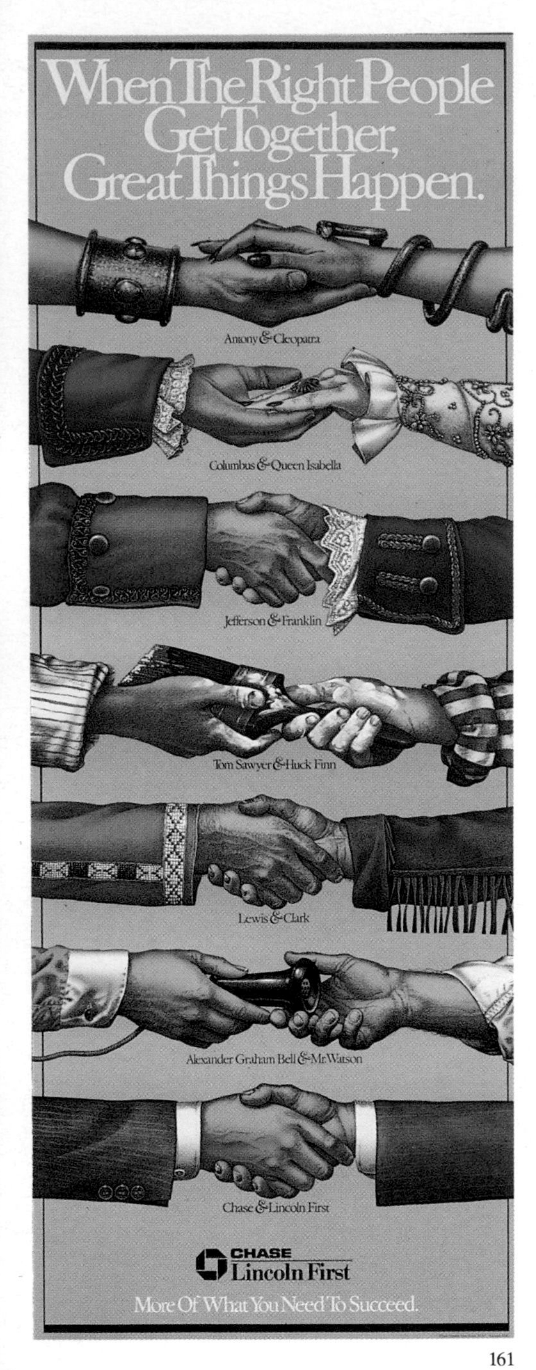

161

161
Chase Lincoln First
United States
Agency: Hutchins/Y & R, Rochester, New York State

One poster in a series which tries to present the tie-up between two banking organisations in a favourable light, comparing it with other successful partnerships in history. Actually Lincoln First, an upstate New York bank, was taken over by Chase Manhattan, so not much partnership was involved, though the locally well established Lincoln name was retained.

162

162
Investors In Industry Group
United Kingdom
Agency: Doyle Dane Bernbach, London

A distinctive style of illustration, by Jeff Fisher. Copy talks of 3i's 'creative' abilities, an adjective much in use in advertising agencies but which one suspects no financier would ever have used if speaking for himself.

163
ICFC
United Kingdom
Agency: Doyle Dane Bernbach, London

Another joke illustration which makes a serious point. ICFC (Industrial and Commercial Finance Corporation), part of the Investors in Industry group, specialises in helping small companies – in this case to take over a much bigger manufacturer.

163

164
Alex Lawrie
United Kingdom
Agency: Gold Greenlees Trott, London

The advertiser is a factoring company which specialises in collecting money owing to other firms, thus freeing them to get on with acquiring more debtors. This is the most striking of a series making the point that businessmen cannot afford the time to chase after slow payers.

One thing's for sure. It won't be going anywhere.
Because you can't chase new business if you're busy chasing old invoices. So why not leave it to Alex Lawrie?
We collect payments, send reminders, even prepare statements.
How does it work? Simple. You send your invoices to us, (or direct to your customers), and we see they're paid, in a friendly business-like manner.
We can ease your cash flow too, by sending you up to 80% of the invoices' value, the very next day.
(And that includes those your customers are already sitting on.)
To Alex Lawrie, Beaumont House, Beaumont Rd., Banbury, Oxon. OX16 7RN. Tel: (0295) 4567. Please send me details of how Alex Lawrie can help my business.
NAME
POSITION
COMPANY
ADDRESS
TEL
We'll make time for you to make money. Alex Lawrie
That's not all. We offer simple invoice discounting, supply export factoring, and we can even run credit rating checks on potential customers.
In short, a whole range of services to save you time.
And time is money. So the quicker you clip the coupon, the quicker you'll start making more of it.
WHAT HAPPENS TO YOUR BUSINESS WHILE YOU'RE CHASING OLD INVOICES?
SULLIVAN & GRAHAM
TOTAL AMOUNT DUE
SULLIVAN

164

165
Diners Club
Hong Kong
Agency: SSC&B: Lintas, Hong Kong

Unlike the girl in the Eurocard ad, this holidaymaker is obviously not staying at home. Notice the image of the card reflected in her goggles.

166
Eurocard
West Germany
Agency: Young & Rubicam, Frankfurt

A curious choice of location to make the point that, if you go away on holiday, the Eurocard will help you pay for travel, hotels and restaurants. The headline says that with a card 'wherever you are you'll still be on top.' Using a stay-at-home to illustrate a holiday theme is certainly original.

167
Legal & General
United Kingdom
Agency: Kirkwood & Partners, London

This is a trade ad for the insurance company addressed to brokers and bringing to their attention a booklet specifying rates payable for personal protection policies by people in many different occupations. But not professional stuntmen. Another eye-catching picture which, like Y & R's German ad for Eurocard, is at odds with the message in the body copy.

165

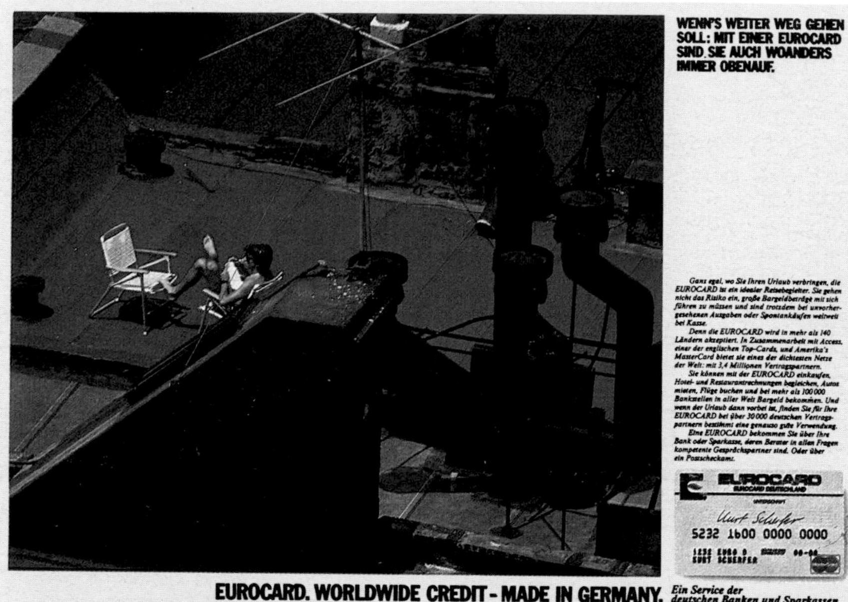

166

167

168
Albany Life Assurance
United Kingdom
Agency: Lowe Howard-Spink
Campbell-Ewald, London

Visual and verbal messages work together perfectly here, even though they are both in a sense negative. But insurance is about the negative side of life.

169
Connecticut General Life Insurance Company
United States
Agency: Doyle Dane Bernbach, New York

Connecticut General, part of the CIGNA group, tells businessmen in this ad of ways in which it is trying to supervise the cost of medical treatment for their employees. Costs won't be contained by providing bigger bandages, says the copy. The picture says it too.

168

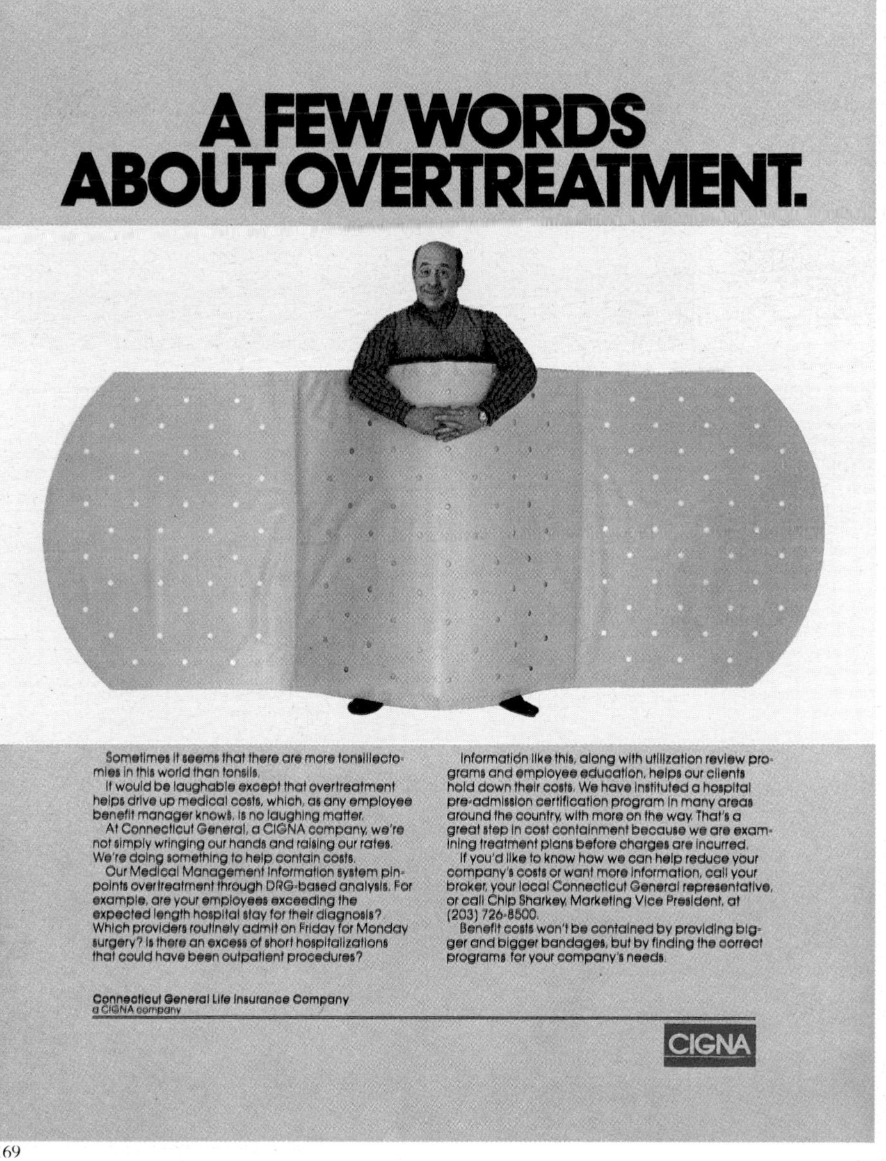

169

170
Bovril cubes
United Kingdom
Agency: Ogilvy & Mather, London

The aim of what the agency calls its 'big cube' campaign is to get across the rich, and supposedly superior, flavour of the product, a beef extract used in cooking. Other pictures in the series show a cube hanging on a butcher's meat hook and a cube being auctioned at a cattle fair.

171
Sharwood's sauces
United Kingdom
Agency: Wight Collins Rutherford Scott, London

The Chinese character made of spare ribs means 'aromatic', as a tiny footnote explains. Long copy includes cooking hints as well as a little history, but it's the picture that really counts. For once a food photograph that arouses curiosity as well as appetite.

170

From Sharwood's, three new sauces for spare ribs. Naturally, we've followed the original recipes to the letter.

Over 1000 years ago, in a corner of Northern China, someone first had the idea of cooking ribs of pork over an open flame. Char Sui cookery was born.

Like all simple ideas it caught on and spread. Char Sui – literally 'burnt fork' – is what we in the West call barbecueing. But if the world has successfully copied the cooking technique, it has found it much harder to re-create the authentic Char Sui sauces.

Barbecue sauces abound in the shops, but not one of them can match the piquancy you'd experience in Hong Kong, Canton or Peking.

At least, until now.

Because Sharwood's have created a range of sauces made to the exacting standards set down by the classic Char Sui recipes.

A CONTRAST OF FLAVOURS.

The three sauces have their own distinctive flavours, but in each you'll experience the classic Chinese concept of contrast.

In one, ginger is contrasted with honey; in another, orange is contrasted with sherry and juniper.

Hoi Sin, which is the definitive spare rib sauce, pits simple ingredients, like vinegar and sugar, against exotic ones, like ginger, fennel, cinnamon and cloves.

As the recipe demands, we roast and press sesame seeds to give the sauce a hint of nuttiness. And we blend in Szechuan pepper – a rare and expensive berry – to add an aroma like bitter orange.

What we don't add to any of the sauces are artificial flavourings and preservatives.

The Chinese don't, so Sharwood's don't.

CHINESE BARBECUE SPARE RIBS.

16 spare ribs
½ jar of SHARWOOD'S BARBECUE SAUCE

METHOD: Put the spare ribs on a sheet of aluminium foil. Brush the

spare ribs generously on both sides with the barbecue sauce. Wrap the foil around the ribs and place it in a moderate oven (375°F or Gas Mark 5).

After one hour, open the foil and let the ribs cook for a further 15 minutes in a hotter oven (425°F or Gas Mark 7) basting and turning the ribs until the sauce evaporates and becomes a delicious and thick glaze. Remove from the oven. Serves four.

RIBS AND RICE.

In Chinese restaurants, spare ribs are usually served as a starter – but there's nothing to stop you turning them into a meal. You'll find that spare ribs go very well with boiled rice, especially if you add a little extra sauce to keep the rice moist.

If you're feeling more adventurous, try Sharwood's Special Chinese Rice. It's full of interesting surprises: mushrooms, shrimps, peas, onions, even water chestnuts. All seasoned with a characteristic blend of Chinese spices.

A FEW MORE RECIPE IDEAS.

Once you've discovered how simple it is to cook spare ribs, you might want to try Sharwood's barbecue sauces with beef, lamb, or any kind of poultry.

Just cook the meat in the same way as you did the ribs, inside the aluminium foil. Or if you prefer, simply grill the meat and spoon on the sauces at the table.

And by all means experiment. There's no end to the creative possibilities with these, and Sharwood's other Chinese foods. If you'd like some ideas, send for our full colour Chinese recipe booklet.

Simply write, enclosing a first class stamp, to: *The Chinese Kitchen, (BBAC), J A Sharwood & Co Ltd, London NW10 6NU.*

ABOVE: The letter we've so deliciously created out of the ribs means 'aromatic' – the taste that is the hallmark of Chinese Char Sui cookery.

171

172
Heinz Tomato Ketchup
Belgium
Agency: Young & Rubicam, Brussels

'Born for each other' is the caption on this neat piece of branding. Not everyone, however, would agree that ketchup is the thing to go with a juicy chop.

172

173
Birds Eye vegetables
United Kingdom
Agency: McCann-Erickson, London

Look carefully. Every element in the picture of the Country Club house consists of vegetables or scraps of vegetables. An amusing piece of artwork.

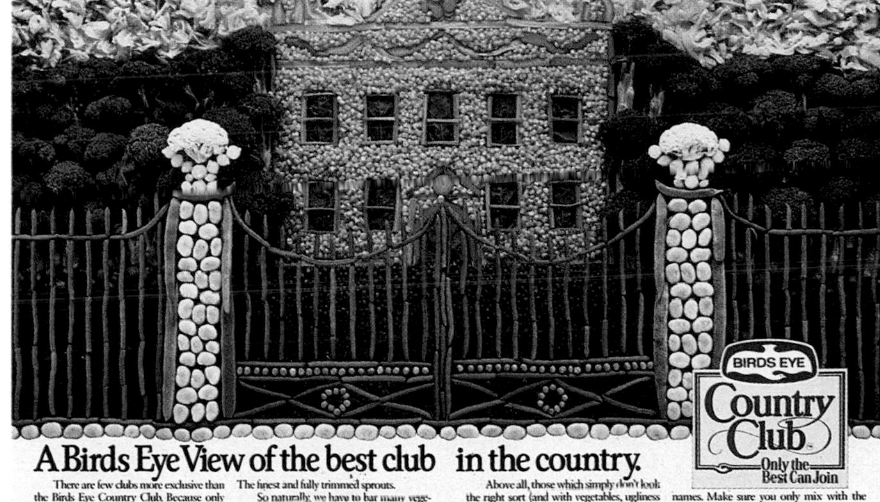

173

174
Hettema Zonen potatoes
Netherlands
Agency: Weda Erkend, Leeuwarden

This trade ad, by a company which specialises in developing new varieties of potato, tells growers that 'You too can reach the top. With Hettema.'

OOK U KUNT DE TOP BEREIKEN.
MET HETTEMA.

HETTEMA ZONEN
Met Hettema oogst u succes

174

175
Heinz Baked Beans
United Kingdom
Agency: Young & Rubicam, London

The simple but well executed picture of a can-opener gives point to the question implied in the headline. The answer is supplied, of course, in the pack shot down below and also in the copy, which refers to the approval expressed for baked beans in Audrey Eyton's book *The F Plan Diet*. (F stands for fibre.)

176
Eggs
Netherlands
Agency: ACT, Amsterdam

'The magic box . . . and the doubled-up egg trick' is how the two topmost pictures are captioned. Underneath are shown examples of doubled-up omelettes. Pay-off line: 'Everyone can do magic with an egg.'

177, 178, 179
Voiello pasta
Italy
Agency: RSCG Mezzano Costantini Mignani, Milan

Three of a large number of visually witty ads for a small, expensive brand which advertises exclusively in magazines. The campaign won top place in a reader popularity poll held by one magazine. The Olympic torch, made up of pasta pieces is captioned 'The 1988 Olympic Games in Naples?' (The advertiser is based in the city.) The cockerel ad bears the words 'Naples. Which other cuisine in the world could give more taste to the Feathers than to the birds?' (Feathers is the name of the type of pasta shown.) The third ad says that 'the honour of being stained with Bucatini (another type of pasta) is reserved for beautiful ties only.'

175

177

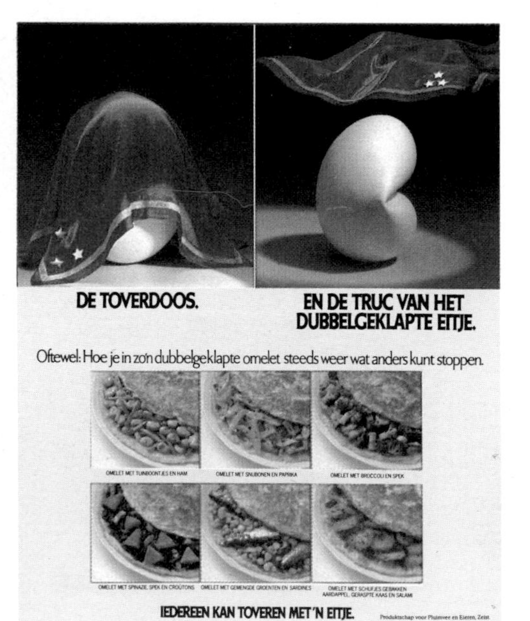

176

178

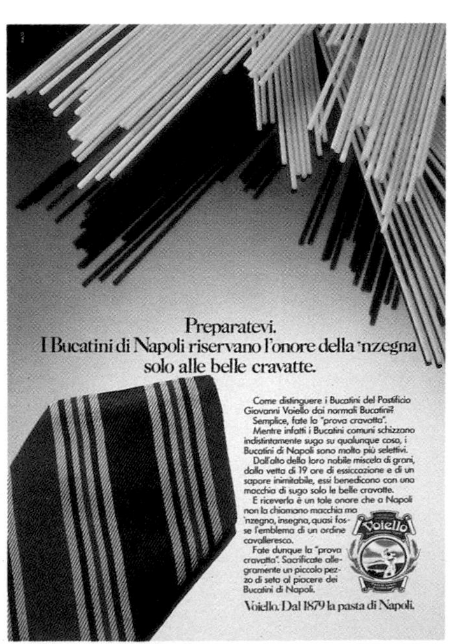

179

·FAR AND AWAY THE BEST BANANA·

180

La vérité toute nue sur les fruits.
Seul un fruit dévêtu, révèle vraiment ce qu'il offre (par 100 g).
VITAMINES
MINERAUX
VALEUR NUTRITIVE
Bananes Chiquita. Les chouchous de Mère Nature.

181

VISPGRÄDDE.
OCH LITE FANTASI!

182

180
Fyffes bananas
United Kingdom
Agency: Marsteller Little & Strodl, London

Purely a branding exercise is how the agency describes this poster for Fyffes. Marsteller, a Young & Rubicam subsidiary, is playing the same kind of visual game here for Fyffes that Y & R Brussels has been doing for Chiquita.

181
Chiquita bananas
Belgium
Agency: Young & Rubicam, Brussels

'The naked truth about fruit' says the headline, and the tables below it compare the nutritional value of bananas favourably with that of apples and oranges. A Chiquita ad from the same agency in last year's edition showed a banana road, along which people were cycling. Another recent ad showed an apple changing into a banana. This picture is simpler but wittier.

182
Del Monte canned fruit and cream
Sweden
Agency: McCann-Erickson, Stockholm

A joint effort by two advertisers, Del Monte and Arla Dairies. Heading: 'Del Monte. Whipped cream. And a little fantasy.'

183
Calvé peanut butter
Netherlands
Agency: J. Walter Thompson, Amsterdam

The brand has been extremely successful, and the little boy with the crooked cap is said to have become a national celebrity with enormous fan mail. The headline: 'My mother thinks I'm mad about it because it contains so many vitamins. Stupid, eh?' Pay-off line: 'Children just know what's good.'

184
Apéricube cheese
France
Agency: Young & Rubicam, Paris

The neo-cubist style of the illustration is inspired by the shape of the product, cheese marketed in small cubes to accompany apéritifs. The headline is a pun on the well known French song 'Boire un petit coup c'est agréable' (To have a little drink is pleasurable) with the word 'cube' replacing 'coup'.

185
Jif peanut butter
United States
Agency: Grey Advertising, New York

Like the Dutch ad by JWT for Calvé, Grey goes for cute kid appeal. And you can't get much cuter than this little girl and her family of toys.

186
Kiri cream cheese
France
Agency: Young & Rubicam, Paris

Another cute kid to set beside the Dutch and American peanut butter eaters. The caption, complete with childish misspellings, reads: 'When I grow up I'll be a Kiri seller and I'll eat it all myself.'

183

185

184

186

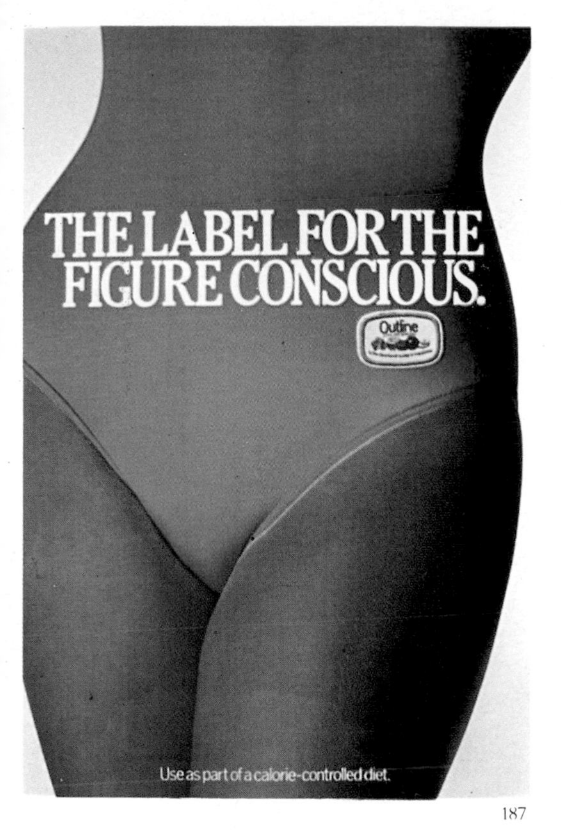

THE LABEL FOR THE FIGURE CONSCIOUS.
Outline
Use as part of a calorie-controlled diet.

187

187
Outline margarine
United Kingdom
Agency: McCann-Erickson, London

A neat bit of branding. Outline is a slimmers' product, and this ad is calculated to catch the eye of any woman slimmer.

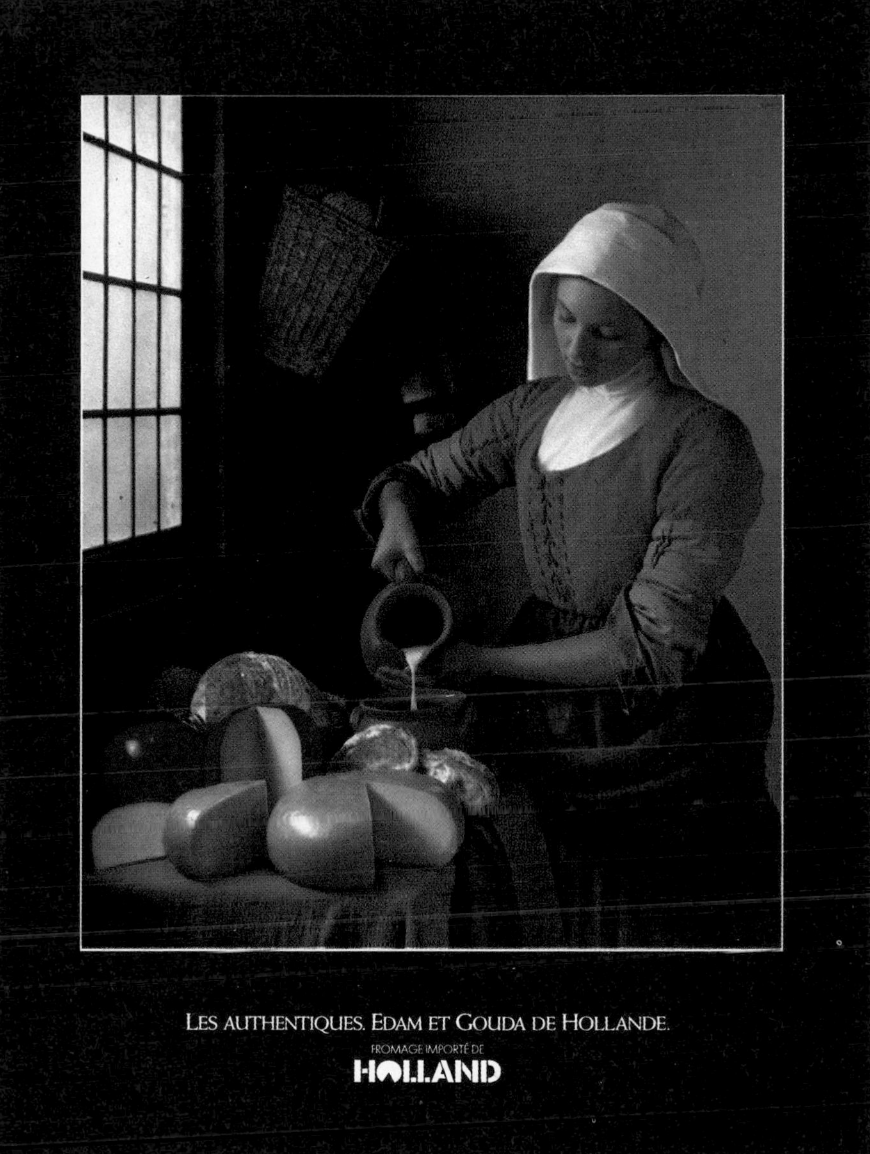

LES AUTHENTIQUES. EDAM ET GOUDA DE HOLLANDE.
FROMAGE IMPORTÉ DE
HOLLAND

188

188
Dutch cheeses
Canada
Agency: McCann-Erickson, Toronto

One of a series of photographs designed to look like oil paintings by Dutch masters. The idea is to communicate an impression of craftsmanship as well as of authentic Dutchness.

Déroulez jeunesse.
Le petit suisse, c'est idéal pour les enfants,
notamment pour les bébés qui passent
du biberon à la cuiller.
Parce que c'est toujours du lait,
mais du lait plus onctueux, plus épais.
vous amenez progressivement vos enfants
à manger des aliments solides.
Et si le petit suisse a beaucoup d'autres
qualités, c'est que pour le faire,
il faut trois fois son volume de lait.
Il est très riche en éléments nutritifs.
aussi possède-t-il ce dont l'enfant
a besoin pour sa croissance:
beaucoup de calcium, de protéines
et des vitamines A et D.
Le petit suisse, c'est l'aliment
parfait pour aider votre enfant à grandir.
Alors déroulez le petit suisse.
Petit suisse gervais.

189

189
Gervais petit suisse
France
Agency: Young & Rubicam, Paris

Copy explains that the petit suisse, a kind of cream cheese which comes in the shape of little cylinders, is ideal for babies being weaned. The headline, 'Unroll youth' is a play on words, relating to both the way the product is unwrapped and to the development of the infant.

190
St. Ivel Shape soft cheese
United Kingdom
Agency: Bartle Bogle Hegarty, London

Like the McCanns ad for Outline, this is addressed to the figure-conscious, but it uses a very different approach. Instead of focusing on the desired goal (the slim body) it engages the reader's attention with a surprisingly large amount of neatly pictorial information about different kinds of bread and how to use them. A stopper for the growing number of health food fanatics.

190

191
Jordans Original Crunchy Bars
United Kingdom
Agency: TBWA, London

Like the McCanns ad for Birds Eye vegetables, this uses the product to play a visual game. The relevance of the F, formed by the bars, is that it immediately communicates to health food buyers, aware of the big-selling book *The F Plan Diet,* that the product is high in fibre. Now, why didn't Y & R think of using baked beans to form an F?

Health and efficiency, a plan by Jordans ◆

On busy days when you really have to put your back into it, don't turn your back on your body.

Our Original Crunchy Bars are high in fibre, making digestion faster, more efficient. Other bars use dried skimmed milk, caramel and emulsifiers. Our bars contain no artificial additives, preservatives or colouring. We use sesame and sunflower seeds, hazelnuts, bran and wheatgerm. Efficiency means output in relation to input. Wholefood energy is all we put in our bars, for your body to take out. All this means that we're the healthiest, bar none.

People Maintenance ◆ Jordans

191

192
Motta snacks
Italy
Agency: Foote Cone & Belding, Milan

'The shop window of good things' says the caption. A pleasing way of presenting what is basically a simple pack shot.

192

193
Kit Kat chocolate bar
United Kingdom
Agency: J. Walter Thompson, London

A very distinctive pack shot, this one. One detects, nonetheless, the influence of the long-running UK campaign for Benson & Hedges cigarettes by Collett Dickenson Pearce. This is surrealistic in the B & H manner and, like the B & H ads, enlists the reader's interest by not spelling out the brand name in full. Even the slogan 'Have a break, have a Kit Kat' has been cut in half.

193

194
Penguin chocolate bars
United Kingdom
Agency: Saatchi & Saatchi Compton, London

The point of this poster was to back up a promotion in which special packs contained an extra bar. There is no originality in depicting real penguins to sell the product of the same name. The manufacturer, United Biscuits, has been doing it for years. Nevertheless this particular picture is delightful.

194

195
Smarties
United Kingdom
Agency: J. Walter Thompson, London

Yes, the puzzle can be solved, and quite easily with the help of a little lateral thinking. Nothing like getting the readers, as well as the copywriter, to play games if you want to keep their attention.

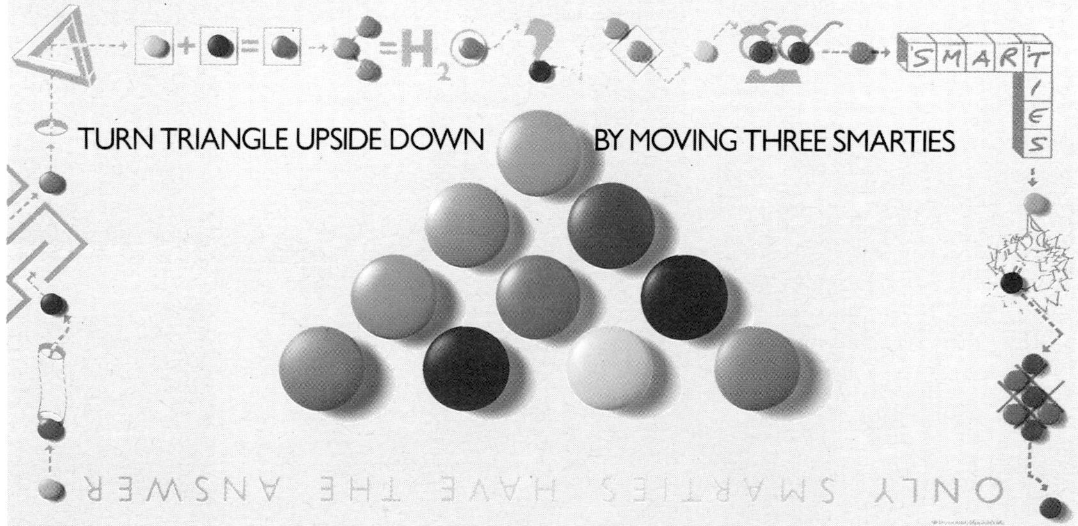

195

196
Reese's Pieces
United States
Agency: Doyle Dane Bernbach, New York

For these peanut-flavoured sweets Doyle Dane set out, like JWT for Smarties, to give youngsters something to have fun with. This is one of a series of ads which ran in comic books. In each the monster character from outer space uses a gibberish word which is translated for the benefit of earthlings.

197
Nescafé (Gold Label)
Norway
Agency: Heltberg Creative Service, Oslo

Like JWT's Dutch ad (201), this poster depicts coffee beans rather than the granules which actually come in the Nescafé jar. To reinforce the notion of pure coffee it puts a jar in the tray of an old-fashioned coffee-grinder. Essentially it says exactly the same as the Dutch ad despite the different choice of visual terms.

198
Kanis & Gunnink coffee
Netherlands
Agency: PPGH Moussault, Amsterdam

'Our coffee needs no biscuits' says the headline. It's a different, and witty, way of claiming quality.

199
Colombian coffee
United States
Agency: Doyle Dane Bernbach, New York

Now here we don't see a single bean. Perhaps that is because the National Federation of Coffee Growers of Colombia, unlike Nescafé, is not trying to sell instant coffee granules. In this case the idea of quality is conveyed not through the product but the cup you would serve it in – if you could afford such a classy bit of crockery.

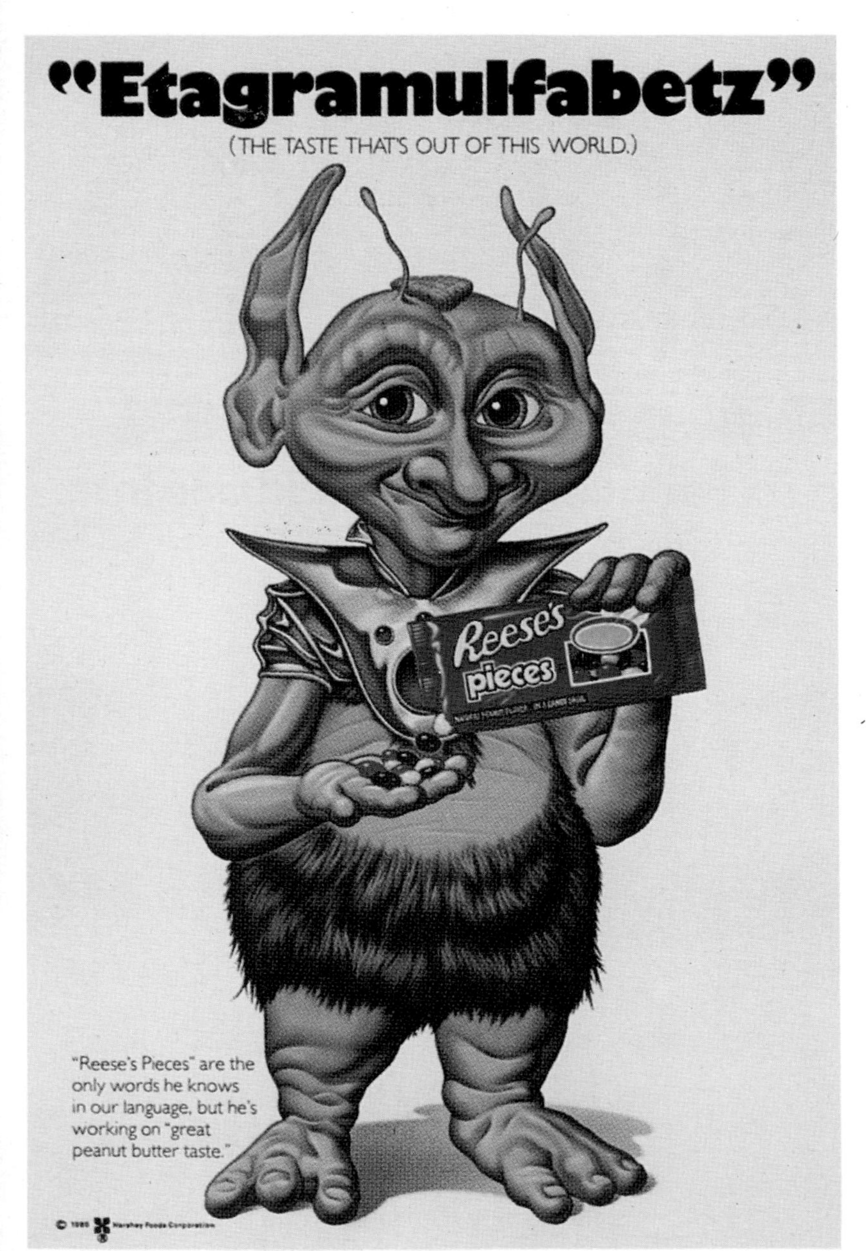

196

197

198

Luckily, the Colombian Coffee
hadn't been poured.

The richest coffee in the world.

199

200
Milk
Sweden
Agency: Ted Bates 1, Stockholm

This point-of-sale poster in food stores was backed with a booklet giving milk-based recipes for a variety of soups. The booklet also featured the image of the man made of foodstuffs. Headline: 'Soup begins with milk.'

201
Nescafé (Gold Label)
Netherlands
Agency: J. Walter Thompson, Amsterdam

The idea behind the extra-long jar pictured in this trade ad is given in the copy which explains that an ordinary 200 gram jar of Nescafé granules contains as many coffee beans as would fill a jar nearly three times as big. The headline says 'Isn't Nescafé's success a little transparent?' Consumers, it is claimed, can see what a lot of pure coffee they are getting.

200

201

202
Milk
United Kingdom
Agency: Harrison McCann, London

The 'pinta' (pint of milk) glows on the doorstep. An ad from a campaign created for the Dairy Council for Northern Ireland and seen only in that province.

203
Ferrarelle mineral water
Italy
Agency: Michele Rizzi e Associati, Milan

One of an amusing series of ads which all put the same questions – 'flat, gassy or Ferrarelle?' – but illustrated with different images of paucity or excess.

204
Evian mineral water
United Kingdom
Agency: TBWA, London

The missing word in the caption is presumably 'pink', since that is the colour of the dancing figure in the foreground, and 'in the pink' also means fit and healthy. It's the deliberately crude and smudgy style of the illustration which makes the impact, however.

205
Lucozade
United Kingdom
Agency: Ogilvy & Mather, London

The product was traditionally sold as a drink for convalescents unable to eat properly. O & M has repositioned it as an energy-boosting soft drink for all, not just invalids. The traffic lights poster uses the amber colour of Lucozade to support the energy-giving message. It was printed in solid colours with a silk-screen process.

HOME IS WHERE THE PINTA IS.
PUT FRESH MILK ST.

202

LISCIA?

203

204

205

206
Sunkist lemon drink
France
Agency: DDB2, Paris

'San Francisco, quench our thirst' says the headline on this sexy pack shot. The product is described as 'canned California', which is where the lemons come from. DDB2 is part of the Doyle Dane Bernbach group.

206

207
Coca-Cola
Japan
Agency: Dentsu, Tokyo

Headline: 'New thoughts about taking a break'. The famous American logo looks somewhat odd in this traditional Japanese rural scene.

207

208, 209
Schweppes
West Germany
Agency: GGK, Düsseldorf

Several of the earlier ads from this inventive series were seen in last year's edition. Here are two more. You do not need to know German to see the joke. Some of the earlier items in the 'Schweppes Encyclopedia' are available in booklet form for fans of the campaign.

ENZYKLOPÄDIE DES SCHWEPPENS. FOLGE 57

Schwepposkop (grch.), (das), Gerät, das es möglich macht, Schweppes aus nächster Nähe in Originalgröße zu sehen. Dieses sog. Nahsehen entwickelt sich immer mehr als Alternative zum Fernsehen, weil man dabei ein herrliches ⟶ *Schweppsorama* genießen kann. Versuchsanordnung: linkes Auge Schweppes Bitter Lemon, rechtes Auge Schweppes Bitter Grapefruit. ⟶ *Schweppeduum mobile.*

Schwepposkop

SCHWEPPES. DIE GESCHMACKVOLLE ERFRISCHUNG FÜR GENIESSER.
HABEN SIE HEUTE SCHON GESCHWEPPT?

208

ENZYKLOPÄDIE DES SCHWEPPENS. FOLGE 56

Schweppernich, Klemens Wenzel, Fürst von, Vorsitzender des Wiener Kongresses (1814 - 1815), an dem unter anderem sein Gegenspieler ⟶ *Charles Maurice de Schweppeyrand* (Frankreich) sowie ⟶ *Viscount*

Europa 1815

Schweppereagh (Großbritannien) und ⟶ *Fürst Schweppenberg* (Preußen) teilnahmen und Europa in Schweppes-Verkaufsgebiete aufteilten. (Der Kongreß schweppt.) ⟶ *Maria Schweppesia.*

SCHWEPPES. DIE GESCHMACKVOLLE ERFRISCHUNG FÜR GENIESSER.
HABEN SIE HEUTE SCHON GESCHWEPPT?

209

Karastan Rug Mills, a Division of Fieldcrest Mills, Inc.
Some of us have more finely developed nesting instincts than others.

INVEST IN Karastan

210

Assassinio sul tappeto occidentale. Si pensa a un delitto passionale. Gli indizi sono scarsi. L'assassino ha usato un tipico coltello orientale, mentre la vittima era sdraiata su un tappeto occidentale in pura lana vergine che ha destato non poca meraviglia. Il tappeto Prelude era marchiato Sisal, ma quest'ultima sembra completamente estranea all'accaduto. Per l'identikit del tappeto occidentale telefonate a: 0523/41341. Vi indirizzeranno al più vicino punto vendita.

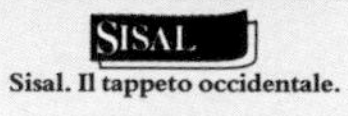
SISAL
Sisal. Il tappeto occidentale.

211

210
Karastan carpets
United States
Agency: Ally & Gargano, New York

This ad has a fashionably surrealistic look about it, but the image is making a perfectly logical point about the warmth and comfort of the product. Not the kind of picture you can easily forget. Volume sales of the carpets increased by 26 per cent in 1984, three times as much as the category as a whole.

211
Sisal carpets
Italy
Agency: STZ, Milan

No headline, but the copy starts with the words 'Murder on the occidental carpet', obviously an allusion to the Orient Express. The joky caption goes on to say that the victim, apparently of a crime of passion, was stretched out on a pure wool carpet 'which aroused not a little wonderment.'

212
Woollen carpets
Netherlands
Agency: Young & Rubicam, Amsterdam

The woollen map gives visual expression to the information that by 1986 carpet manufacturers in all West European countries will be using the Woolmark on their products. Headline: 'Are we getting yet another united Europe?'

213
Behr Headline furniture
West Germany
Agency: Marsteller, Frankfurt

One of a series of lifestyle ads in which pieces of furniture are integrated into human interest situations. This particular situation is captioned 'Cupboards with unlimited possibilities' (the German includes an untranslatable pun). Copy talks about the exciting new colours and shapes of the Headline range. Before this campaign the advertiser had a somewhat conservative image. The account is no longer with the agency, which closed as part of the deal which set up the Havas Conseil Marsteller network.

214
Dunlopillo beds
United Kingdom
Agency: TBWA, London

An interesting example both of the negative approach and of refusing to show the product. But the picture is compelling enough to make you read the copy and learn that, because too many people sleep on the wrong type of bed and suffer accordingly, the advertiser has introduced a system 'that allows you to combine mattresses and divans in hundreds of different ways' for maximum comfort.

212

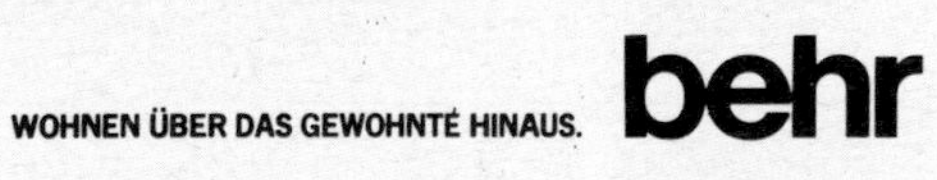

213

214

215
Kaldewei baths
West Germany
Agency: Hildmann Simon Rempen & Schmitz/SMS, Düsseldorf

Not just a sex sell. What you can see is 'the bathtub with the two better halves'. Copy explains that it is built to fit the back comfortably whichever way you face.

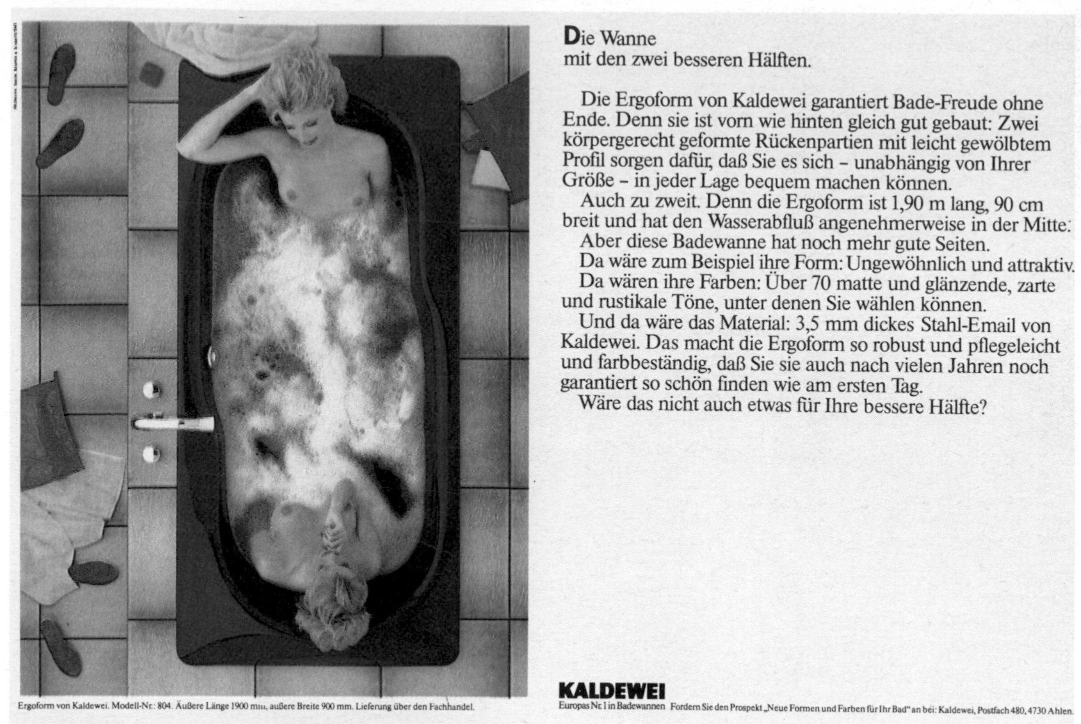

Die Wanne
mit den zwei besseren Hälften.
Die Ergoform von Kaldewei garantiert Bade-Freude ohne Ende. Denn sie ist vorn wie hinten gleich gut gebaut: Zwei körpergerecht geformte Rückenpartien mit leicht gewölbtem Profil sorgen dafür, daß Sie es sich – unabhängig von Ihrer Größe – in jeder Lage bequem machen können.
Auch zu zweit. Denn die Ergoform ist 1,90 m lang, 90 cm breit und hat den Wasserabfluß angenehmerweise in der Mitte.
Aber diese Badewanne hat noch mehr gute Seiten.
Da wäre zum Beispiel ihre Form: Ungewöhnlich und attraktiv.
Da wären ihre Farben: Über 70 matte und glänzende, zarte und rustikale Töne, unter denen Sie wählen können.
Und da wäre das Material: 3,5 mm dickes Stahl-Email von Kaldewei. Das macht die Ergoform so robust und pflegeleicht und farbbeständig, daß Sie sie auch nach vielen Jahren noch garantiert so schön finden wie am ersten Tag.
Wäre das nicht auch etwas für Ihre bessere Hälfte?
KALDEWEI
Europas Nr. 1 in Badewannen Fordern Sie den Prospekt „Neue Formen und Farben für Ihr Bad" an bei: Kaldewei, Postfach 480, 4730 Ahlen.
Ergoform von Kaldewei. Modell-Nr.: 804. Äußere Länge 1900 mm, außere Breite 900 mm. Lieferung über den Fachhandel.

215

FA PIU' BELLA FIGURA UN PICASSO, UN TIZIANO O UN LIGABUE?

MARAZZI
Una casa diventa la tua casa.

216

216
Marazzi tiles
Italy
Agency: Benton & Bowles, Milan

The headline is the stopper in this picture of a tiled wall. 'Would a Picasso, a Titian or a Ligabue look nicest?' it asks. Copy suggests that there is no reason not to hang a picture on a wall tiled with colourful ceramics from the wide Marazzi range.

217
Saraband bedroom furnishings
Australia
Agency: Dalziell Harper & Grey, Melbourne

One of a series of deliberately cheeky ads created for the 'young at heart'. The strategy is appropriate to an advertiser struggling to increase its market share against two bigger, entrenched competitors.

WHAT WILL YOU WEAR TO BED TONIGHT?
BACCARAT by Saraband.
A bold, exciting design that will have you waking up early, just to see how good you look. In mocca, dusty rose or silver. And available in quilt covers, pillow cases, sheets, bedspreads, comforter sets, curtains and fabric by the metre.
Baccarat is just one of the refreshing new season's designs in Saraband's 1985 catalogue.
Along with a stunning new range of bedroom colours, designs and ideas, it explains how Saraband can deliver the quality of the expensive brands at only a fraction of the cost. Quality you can actually feel.
Ask your retailer for a free copy of our catalogue. Or write to Saraband, P.O. Box 252, Reservoir, Victoria, 3073.
SARABAND
ISN'T IT TIME YOU WOKE UP TO SARABAND?

217

416 αγώνες πρωταθλήματος, 47 αγώνες κυπέλλου,
16.213 ώρες προπόνησης, μέσα σε 16 χρόνια...

**Η ομάδα ανανεώθηκε 3 φορές.
Το δάπεδο καμμία. Είναι ΣΕΛΜΑΝ.**

Κάθε δάπεδο άπό παρκέτο ΣΕΛΜΑΝ, διακρίνεται γιά τήν άντοχή του στήν καθημερινή χρήση όποιουδήποτε χώρου γιά πάρα πολλά χρόνια, τήν άκρίβεια τών προδιαγραφών του καί τήν όμορφιά του.
Τά παρκέτα ΣΕΛΜΑΝ, έχουν άψογη έφαρμογή, στεγνώνονται μέ τίς πιό σύγχρονες μεθόδους καί παράγονται σέ 3 τύπους:
Λωρίδες, 'Ανγκλέ καί Κλασσικό, μέ γλώσσα καί λούκι (σόκορο) καί άπό τίς 4 πλευρές καί σέ διάφορες διαστάσεις.
Προσφέρονται σέ 3 είδη: Τροπικά, Δρύϊνα καί Πεύκης.
Τά παρκέτα ΣΕΛΜΑΝ είναι σχολαστικά διαλεγμένα άπό ξυλεία πρώτης ποιότητας, μέ μεγάλη ποικιλία χρωματισμών καί «δένουν» ώραιότατα μέ κάθε είδους έπίπλωση, δίνοντας νέα διάσταση στό χώρο. Καί τό σπουδαιότερο: Τό σήμα τής ΣΕΛΜΑΝ έγγυάται τήν άναλλοίωτη ποιότητά τους καί τό ύψηλό έπίπεδο τών προδιαγραφών τους.
Καί άν συγκρίνετε τό κόστος τών παρκέτων ΣΕΛΜΑΝ μέ άλλα ύλικά, ύπολογίζοντας καί τήν άντοχή τους στό χρόνο, σίγουρα θά έκπλαγείτε εύχάριστα.

**Παρκέτα ΣΕΛΜΑΝ
Αξίζουν περισσότερο
απ'όσο κοστίζουν**

ΣΕΛΜΑΝ, ΕΛΛΗΝΟΕΛΒΕΤΙΚΗ ΒΙΟΜΗΧΑΝΙΑ ΕΠΕΞΕΡΓΑΣΙΑΣ ΞΥΛΟΥ Α.Ε.
ΒΟΥΚΟΥΡΕΣΤΙΟΥ 32, 106 71 'Αθήνα Τηλ.: 3602211-19, 3619937 20, 3647770-71

218

218
Shelman parquet flooring
Greece
Agency: Ted Bates, Athens

The message is simple: membership of the basketball team changed completely three times over, but the floor stayed the same. Basketball is Greece's second most popular sport and, according to the agency, proved a strong attention-getter in introducing the product to architects and prospective house-owners as well as the traditional target group of builders.

219
Pressalit toilet seats
Denmark
Agency: NP/Grey, Arhus

One way of endowing these mundane objects with a little glamour is to put them on a pedestal. The cleaning woman saves this treatment from being too hopelessly pretentious.

220
Cera bathroom fittings
India
Agency: Shilpi Advertising, Bombay

The manufacturer, Madhusudan Ceramics, turned a disadvantage – the fact that, unlike its competitors, it does not make glazed tiles – into an advantage by promoting the idea of colour contrasts in the bathroom. People do not choose furniture to match the walls of their other rooms, says the copy, 'so why do it in your bathroom?'

Danish design
- for a most practical purpose.

- the finest seat in house
Everlasting colours · Easy mounting · Easy cleaning

219

Why blend into the background

When you can come out with flying colours

By matching the colour of your sanitaryware to your bathroom walls, you are pushing them into the background.
Now you have the option of using sanitaryware that contrasts beautifully with your walls. Cera–sanitaryware that comes in 30 marvellous shades, to give your bathroom endless mindblowing combinations.
Cera-sanitaryware to colour your fancies.

VITREOUS

'Ankur Building'

Mirzapur Road
Ahmedabad 380 001

220

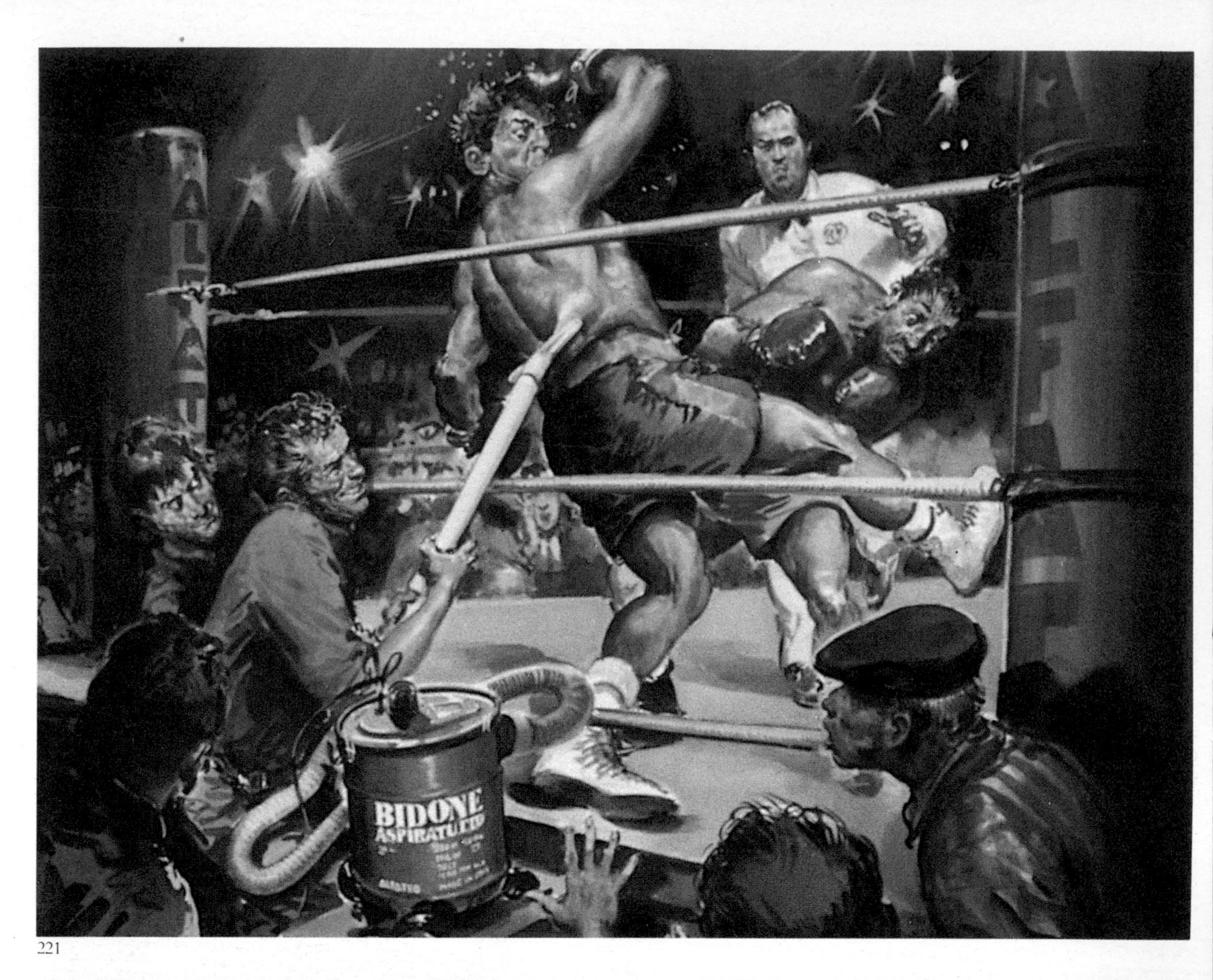
BIDONE
ASPIRATUTTO

221

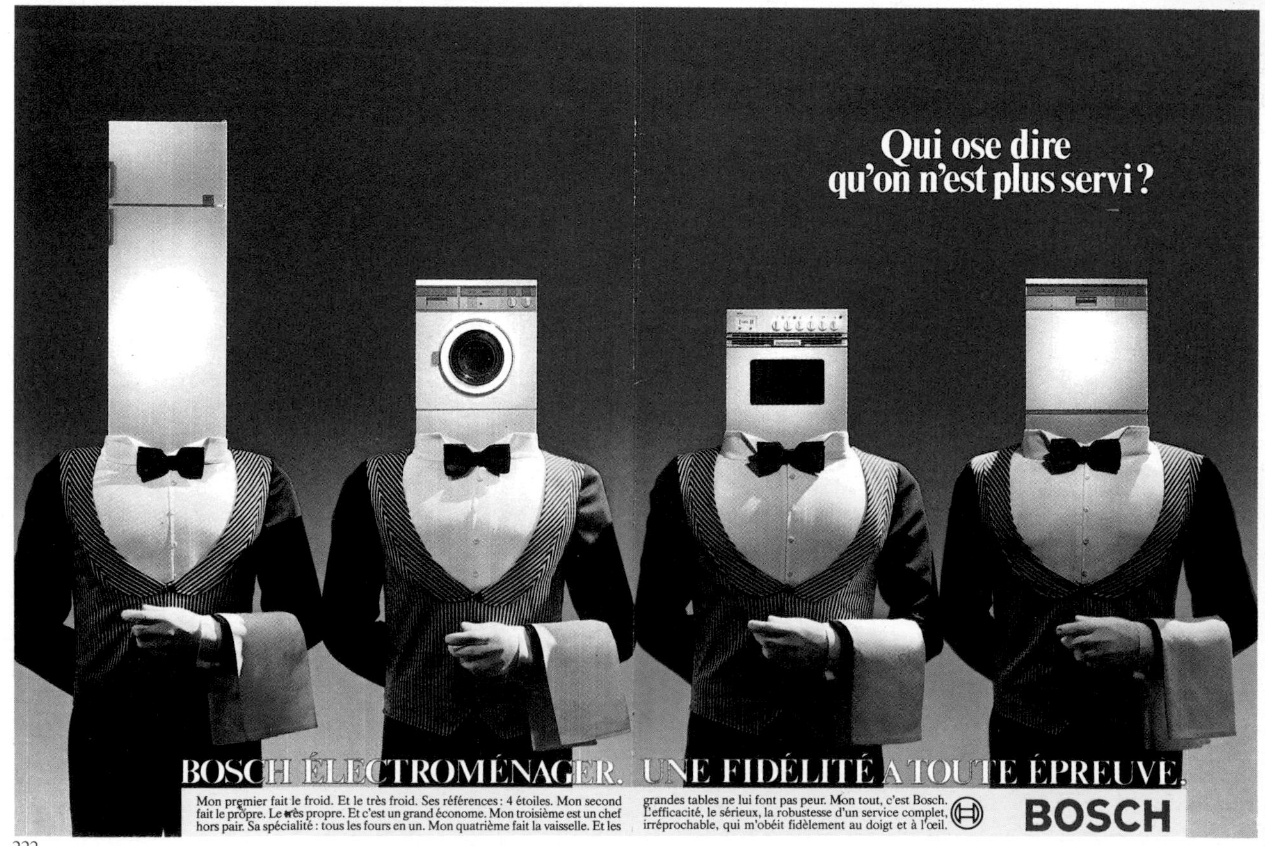
Qui ose dire
qu'on n'est plus servi ?
BOSCH ÉLECTROMÉNAGER. UNE FIDÉLITÉ A TOUTE ÉPREUVE.
Mon premier fait le froid. Et le très froid. Ses références : 4 étoiles. Mon second fait le propre. Le très propre. Et c'est un grand économe. Mon troisième est un chef hors pair. Sa spécialité : tous les fours en un. Mon quatrième fait la vaisselle. Et les grandes tables ne lui font pas peur. Mon tout, c'est Bosch. L'efficacité, le sérieux, la robustesse d'un service complet, irréprochable, qui m'obéit fidèlement au doigt et à l'œil.
BOSCH

222

221
Bidone vacuum cleaner
Italy
Agency: STZ, Milan

One of a long-running series of humorous ads for a product which, starting from nothing about seven years ago, is now claimed to be brand leader. Television advertising ties in closely with the press campaign, the commercials consisting, unusually, of sequences of still illustrations. The picture here is extracted from such a film.

222
Bosch domestic appliances
France
Agency: Delrieu Duprat, Paris

A different way from that adopted in the Italian ad for Candy of showing a whole range of products, but equally ingenious. Headline: 'Who dares to say one cannot get service any more?'

223
Candy domestic appliances
Italy
Agency: B Communications, Milan

The unusual visual neatly encapsulates the message that appliances in the new Candy range are made to go with each other and with the 'most exclusive' kitchen fittings. Headline: 'Things beautiful and efficient.'

224
Vortice convector heater
Italy
Agency: STZ, Milan

Very funny! Unfortunately most Italian magazine publishers do not share the sense of humour of Fritz Tschirren, STZ's Swiss creative director (and the T in its name). The ad ran only once in one publication and was rejected by others as too sexploitative. Copy reads: 'At last you can transform your wife into a *Playboy* pin-up without making her catch cold.'

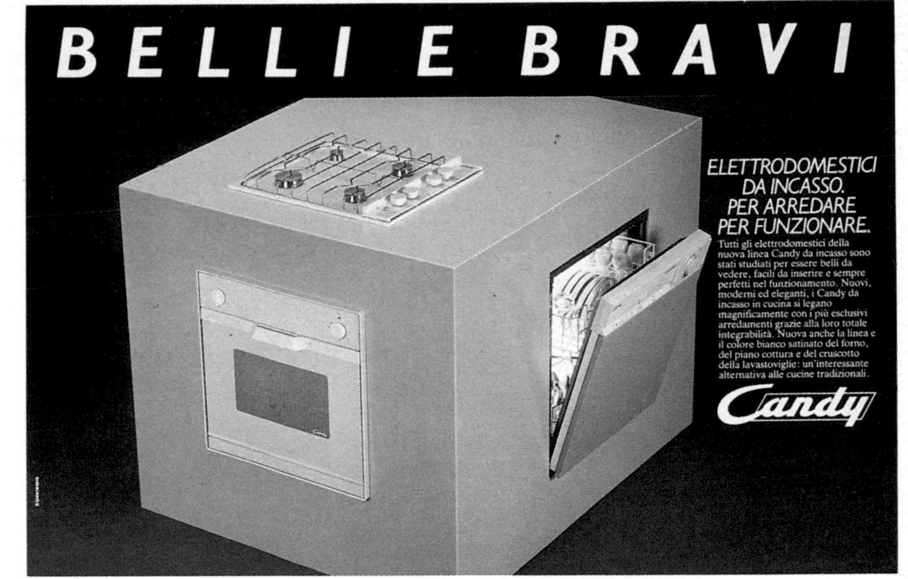

BELLI E BRAVI
ELETTRODOMESTICI DA INCASSO.
PER ARREDARE PER FUNZIONARE.
Tutti gli elettrodomestici della nuova linea Candy da incasso sono stati studiati per essere belli da vedere, facili da inserire e sempre perfetti nel funzionamento. Nuovi, moderni ed eleganti, i Candy da incasso in cucina si legano magnificamente con i più esclusivi arredamenti grazie alla loro totale integrabilità. Nuova anche la linea e il colore bianco satinato del forno, del piano cottura e del cruscotto della lavastoviglie: un'interessante alternativa alle cucine tradizionali.
Candy

223

Finalmente potete trasformare vostra moglie in una modella di Playboy, senza farle prendere il raffreddore. Il termoconvettore della Vortice riscalda gli ambienti in soli 20 minuti.

Viviamo in tempi difficili. Nessuno crede più a niente e a nessuno. E figuriamoci alla pubblicità. Cosa significa per esempio "riscalda in 20 minuti"? Significa che riscalda in 20 minuti da 13° a 20° un ambiente "intermedio" di 39 m3 con temperatura esterna di + 6° e un coefficiente medio di dispersione K 2,6. Il termostato fa sì che la temperatura rimanga a 20°. A1000 o 2000 Watt. Il termoconvettore può anche essere installato a muro: diventa così un pannello radiante. Lo trovate presso i negozi di materiale elettrico e di elettrodomestici.

STZ

Elettrosociali S.p.A.
20067 Zoate (MI)

224

225
New World Option 3 cooker
United Kingdom
Agency: TBWA, London

A play on words reflected in a play on images. Copy claims the Option 3 is 'the only gas cooker that can fit flush to your cabinetry at the sides and on top.'

225

226
Seiko pocket colour TV receiver
Japan
Agency: Dentsu, Tokyo

Science fiction, a popular source of inspiration among advertising creatives everywhere, provides the style of this ad, headed 'What does this TV intend to do on earth?' The pretty girl is supposed to be an extra-terrestrial being, even if that's not the way she looks to you.

226

227
JVC VideoMovie
United Kingdom
Agency: Lowe Howard-Spink Campbell-Ewald, London

Two ads here for the price of one. What you can see is a trade ad incorporating a double-page-spread consumer magazine ad, complete with fold down the middle. The trade ad gets over, even more strongly than the original did, the smallness of the camcorder, actual size of which was shown in the magazine ad.

227

228
Sony Trinitron TV receiver
United Kingdom
Agency: Boase Massimi Pollitt Partnership, London

The press version of a TV campaign in which a man is seen growing from childhood to old age seated on a sofa in front of a TV set which does not wear out. The press ad plumps intelligently for one image to make the same point rather than imitating a sequence of moving pictures. Copy says 'Most settees aren't built to last like Sony Trinitrons.'

228

229
Technics hi-fi set
Netherlands
Agency: Ted Bates, Amsterdam

'A passion for the slim' is the headline on this stylish picture, containing a 'super-slim' hi-fi set. Illustration, by Dick Prins, is combined with photography of the product.

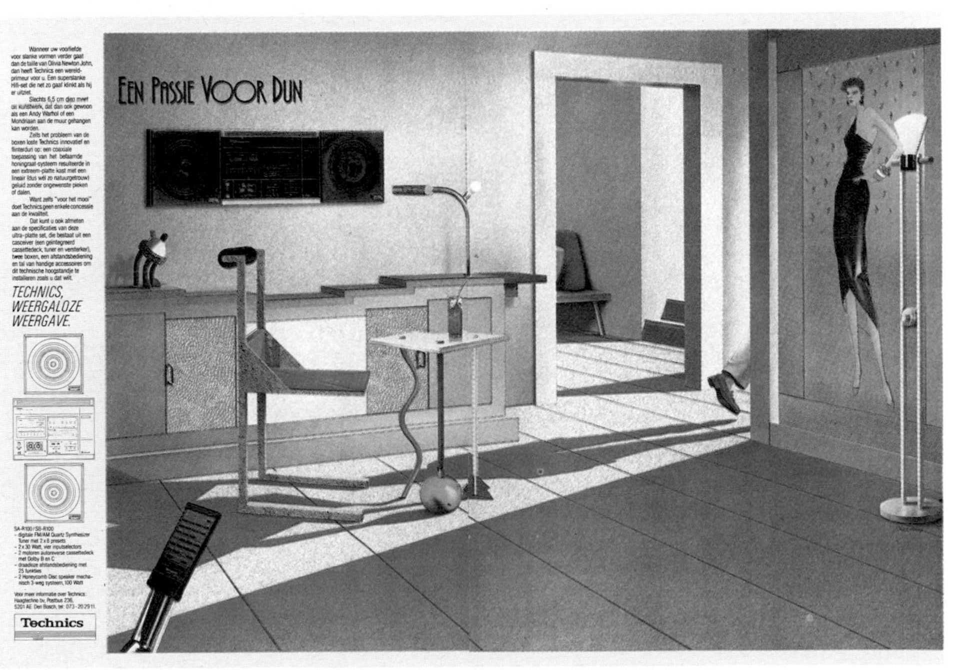

229

230
Panasonic portable videoset
Netherlands
Agency: Ted Bates, Amsterdam

'New from Panasonic. The lightest VHS portable videoset in the world.' That's the headline, but you do not need to understand the language to see at once what point is being made. Unfortunately no details are available about the precise method used to make the sandcastle.

231
BASF video cassettes
Netherlands
Agency: Young & Rubicam, Amsterdam

No complicated technical claims here. Just a bit of fanciful imagery. And a memorable, if not quite logical, English-language slogan.

232
Wharfedale loudspeakers
United Kingdom
Agency: Saatchi & Saatchi Compton, London

This intriguing picture is not of a Wharfedale loudspeaker but of a Gibson Flying V electric guitar. One of a series of pictures making the same point about accuracy of sound reproduction.

Nieuw van Panasonic.
De lichtste VHS portable videoset ter wereld.

3600 Gram. De hele videoset, camera plus recorder weegt niet meer dan een pasgeboren baby.

Dat is zo licht dat u er moeiteloos uren mee langs het strand wandelt, vakanties voor het nageslacht vastlegt, hele sportwedstrijden opneemt, noem maar op.

Wat u opneemt is altijd perfect van beeldkwaliteit. Ook als het beeld-voor-beeld-, stilstaand beeld-, of slow-motion weergave is.

Zelfs op de plaats waar verschillende opnamen in elkaar overgaan zijn de beelden absoluut streep- en trillingsvrij.

Vanaf de camera, de WV-PA2 met Auto-Focus, kunt u alle bandloopfunkties bedienen.

En daarmee is het niet alleen de lichtste set, maar ook één met de meeste mogelijkheden.

Completeert u de recorder NV-180E met de bijbehorende tuner VW-ET180 EO (niet afgebeeld), dan beschikt u over een combinatie die niets onderdoet voor de allerduurste huiskamer video.

Voor een videoset met zoveel mogelijkheden moet u beslist naar de Panasonic dealer om de set te zien, te voelen, vast te houden. Echt, u zou er zo mee weg willen lopen!

Voor meer informatie over Panasonic: Haagtechno bv, Postbus 236, 5201 AE Den Bosch, telefoon 073 - 202911.

Panasonic
PANASONIC, VOOR TOPPRESTATIES

230

BASF ONDERZOCHT DIEPGAAND DE MARKT VAN AUDIO- EN VIDEOCASSETT ES EN KWAM DAARBIJ TOT BELANGWEKKENDE ONTDEK
KINGEN TROK DAARUIT DE CONCLUSIE DAT HAAR IMAGE NIET BETER VERWO ORD EN IN BEELD GEBRACHT KAN WORDEN DAN DAT OP
DEZE PAGINA GEBEURT. FLY BASF BINNENKORT OP TV, IN RTV-, FAMILIE-, OPI NIE-, JONGEREN EN SPECIAL INTEREST BLADEN BASF
FLY BASF

231

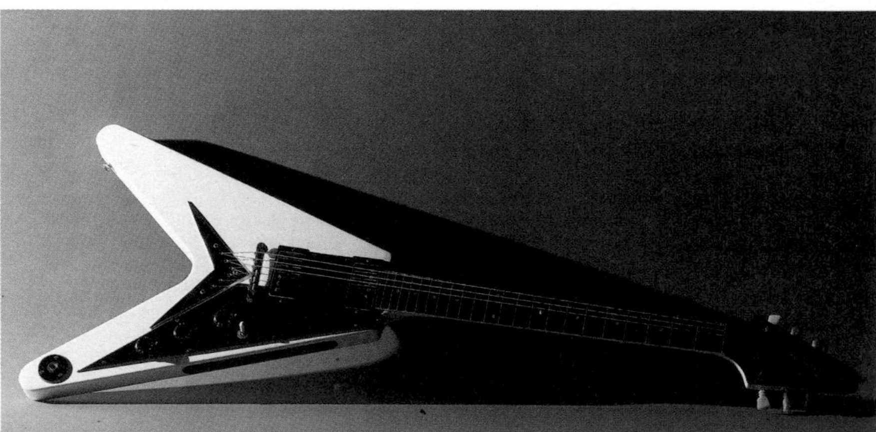

If you can't tell whether it's a Gibso n or a Fender, it isn't a Wharfedale.

We don't believe that electric guitars should sound the same on your speakers, when they don't in real life.

So we have now developed a whole armoury of techniques to remove every trace of distortion. Even the tiny traces that could mask or blur the distinctive sound of this Gibson Flying V.

Such attention to accuracy has made us the leaders in modern loudspeaker design.

By using laser beams to produce dynamic holograms of a speaker cone in action.

By using cumulative resonance spectra which is a three dimensional plotting of the sounds a speaker shouldn't be making.

And by evolving these two techniques into something even more sophisticated, a scanned laser plot.

Not surprisingly, our research calls for new ways of making speaker components. So we make most of them ourselves.

The result of our efforts is not only better sounding speakers, but also better value than you'll find elsewhere.

Whether you choose from our six Laser models, our four TSR-2's, or one of our Mach series (like the Mach 5 shown here).

Each of our Mach series is ten times as efficient as ordinary speakers.

So both you and your neighbours will be able to hear the world's most famous makes of instruments, when you listen to Britain's most famous make of speakers.

Wharfedale Loudspeakers. Highfield Road, Idle, Bradford, Yorkshire. Telephone (0274) 611131.

232

233
Polaroid video cassettes
United States
Agency: Ogilvy & Mather, New York

The cliché image of Father Christmas is given new meaning in this ad which explains that Polaroid tape cleans the recorder heads as it plays. Copy tells readers not to 'let dirty heads spoil your Yuletide fun'.

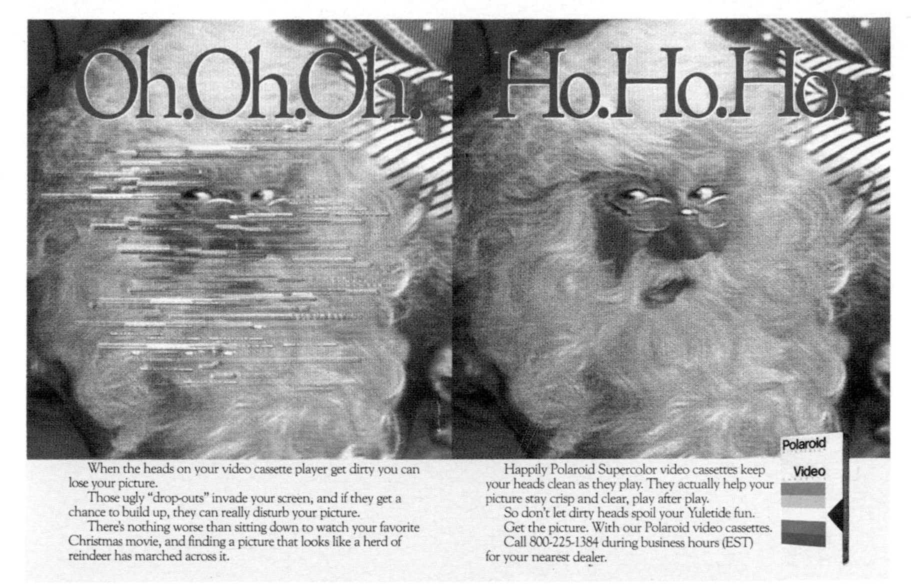

Oh.Oh.Oh.
Ho.Ho.Ho.
When the heads on your video cassette player get dirty you can lose your picture.
Those ugly "drop-outs" invade your screen, and if they get a chance to build up, they can really disturb your picture.
There's nothing worse than sitting down to watch your favorite Christmas movie, and finding a picture that looks like a herd of reindeer has marched across it.
Happily Polaroid Supercolor video cassettes keep your heads clean as they play. They actually help your picture stay crisp and clear, play after play.
So don't let dirty heads spoil your Yuletide fun.
Get the picture. With our Polaroid video cassettes.
Call 800-225-1384 during business hours (EST) for your nearest dealer.
Polaroid
Video

233

234
Sharp radio-cassette recorder
United Kingdom
Agency: Ayer Barker, London

The radio as lipstick emphasises the range of colours in which the product is available. The ad is obviously aimed in particular at style-conscious women.

234

235
JVC car stereo
United Kingdom
Agency: Lowe Howard-Spink Campbell-Ewald, London

Reminiscent, this one, of David Ogilvy's classic line 'At 60 miles an hour the loudest noise in this new Rolls Royce comes from the electric clock.' Except that here, of course, the engine is understood to be very noisy, so the hi-fi system must be capable of even greater loudness.

235

236
Sony UCX audio tapes
United Kingdom
Agency: Boase Massimi Pollitt Partnership, London

What a clever idea to communicate the idea of audio distortion by visually distorting a page of rock music reviews. This ad is certainly a stopper. Of course, as with all negative copy approaches, it has to be hoped that readers will remember to associate the fault depicted with the competition and not with the advertiser's product.

237
Instapure water filter
United States
Agency: Doyle Dane Bernbach, Los Angeles

The disturbing image draws attention to the ad's message that unfiltered tap water tastes of chlorine. The target readers are the middle and upper income groups with gourmet pretensions.

238, 239
I Guzzini electric lighting
Italy
Agency: STZ, Milan

No bold headlines spoil the pictures or indeed tell you what they are advertising. You have to look at the words underneath. The witty copy of the shop window ad begins by quoting an American physicist who commented on how boring life would be if we lived in a two-dimensional world. Even in a three-dimensional one, bad lighting can flatten what we see. Good lighting confers a 'theatrical quality' on everyday reality. The other ad begins 'And God said let there be light' and goes on to declare that common mortals should be equally concerned about the lighting they use.

236

237

Illuminare, parte XVIII. Il fisico americano James A. Coleman ha scritto: "Dovremmo ringraziare la sorte che non ci fa vivere in un mondo bidimensionale.

La vita sarebbe veramente piatta, perché ogni persona e ogni cosa sarebbero piatte... Ancor peggio: le persone sarebbero solo ombre viventi di se stesse!"

Tuttavia, anche in un mondo a tre dimensioni, un uso maldestro dell'illuminazione può appiattire e banalizzare la scena.

Una buona regia luminosa, invece, rende più plastici i volumi e le forme, distribuisce nell'ambiente diversi gradi di luce e ombra, trasforma gli oggetti in affascinanti sculture, conferisce spessore teatrale al mondo d'ogni giorno.

Nella foto vedete una vetrina illuminata da downlights, spots regolabili, orientabili, scorrevoli.

Cambiate tutto questo con un'illuminazione casuale, e addio magia. Ma anche la nostra casa, il nostro arredamento, il nostro modo di vivere hanno bisogno di essere valorizzati con una adeguata "qualità teatrale".

Per saperne di più, scrivete a: iGuzzini Illuminazione s.p.a., P.O. Box 39-59, 62019 Recanati.

Riceverete in omaggio il "Trattato di illuminotecnica", un testo che piacerebbe anche al professor Coleman.

iGuzzini
Industria Illuminotecnica

Illuminare, parte X. "Dio disse: sia la luce! E la luce fu. Dio vide che la luce era cosa buona e separò la luce dalle tenebre" (Genesi).

Sembra, dunque, che Dio si sia convinto della buona qualità della luce soltanto dopo averla "accesa". E noi, comuni mortali, non dovremmo essere più dubbiosi di Lui sulla qualità delle luci per le nostre case, gli uffici, le vie, le vetrine?

L'uomo di oggi è un gran consumatore di luci. Ma spesso lo è in modo convenzionale, acritico, distratto.

La buona luce è molto di più che semplice radiazione elettromagnetica. È arredamento, cultura, tecnologia, qualità della visione, regia luminosa.

La buona luce personalizza l'ambiente, protegge la vista, non fa spreco di corrente, rende più vivibile il nostro habitat. Ed è così importante che ha bisogno di seri specialisti: come l'industria iGuzzini, che non si limita a produrre apparecchi decorativi ma fa dell'illuminazione una vera e propria "arte della ragione".

Per una visione completa del problema, scrivete a: iGuzzini Illuminazione s.p.a., P.O. Box 39-59, 62019 Recanati.

Riceverete in omaggio il "Trattato di illuminotecnica", moderna bibbia per chi desideri una luce migliore.

iGuzzini
Industria Illuminotecnica

240
Osram electric lighting
West Germany
Agency: GGK, Düsseldorf

One of many visually delightful ads in this campaign, already sampled in last year's edition. This one shows a marine organism magnified fiftyfold by a microscope using an Osram mercury bulb. The campaign slogan is 'bright as broad daylight'.

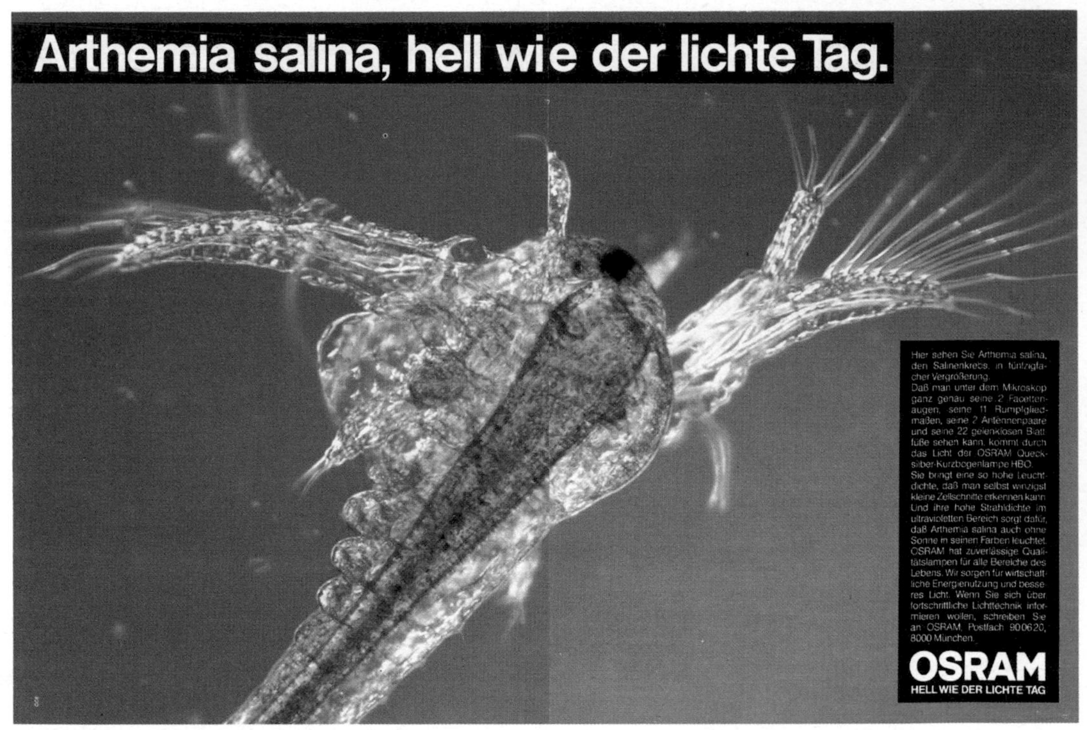

240

241
Eswa and Termostan underfloor heating
Norway
Agency: McCann-Erickson, Oslo

'Only children know when dolls are cold' says the headline on this appealing, if sentimental, ad from a campaign aimed at people building or renovating their homes. Eswa underfloor elements and Termostan underfloor cables are presented as the most comfortable and economic forms of electrical heating.

241

242

243

242
Bontempi electronic organ
Italy
Agency: Publicis, Milan

A Folon illustration, immediately recognisable as such. The headline says 'Discover that you know how to play.' The rest is left to the illustrator.

243
Duracell batteries
United Kingdom
Agency: Dorland Advertising, London

The clock is Big Ben. It does not run on batteries, even Duracell ones, which sell on longevity. But the product claim is well enough known for the giant battery to be understood as not just a joke.

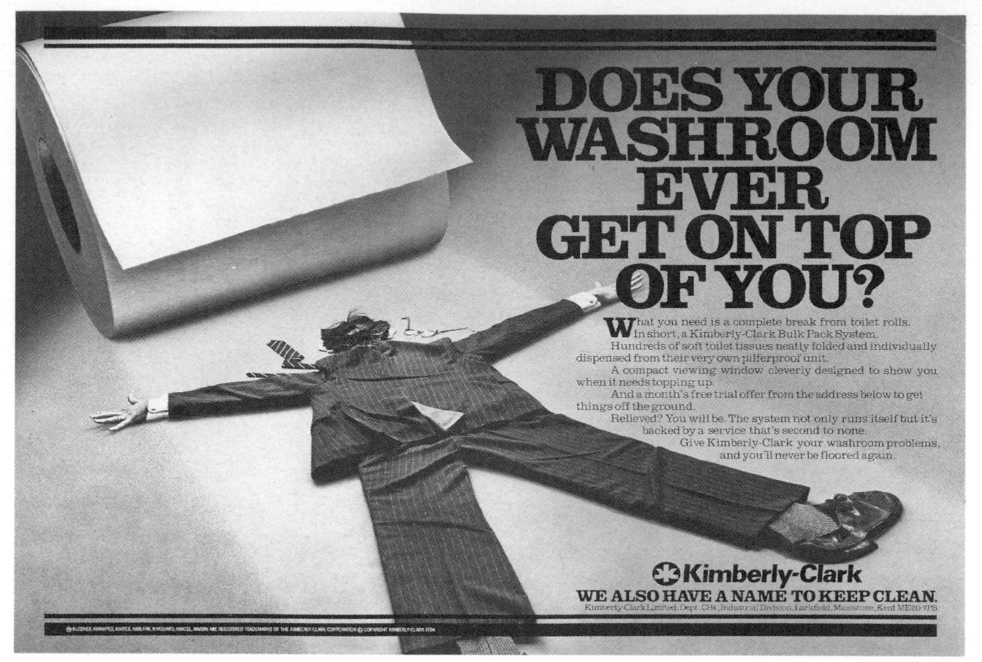

244

244
Kimberly-Clark toilet tissues
United Kingdom
Agency: Fletcher Shelton Delaney, London

A striking image, even if it is the visual expression of a play on words. The product promoted is a 'Bulk Pack' system of toilet tissues for work-place washrooms, to replace toilet rolls which are easily stolen.

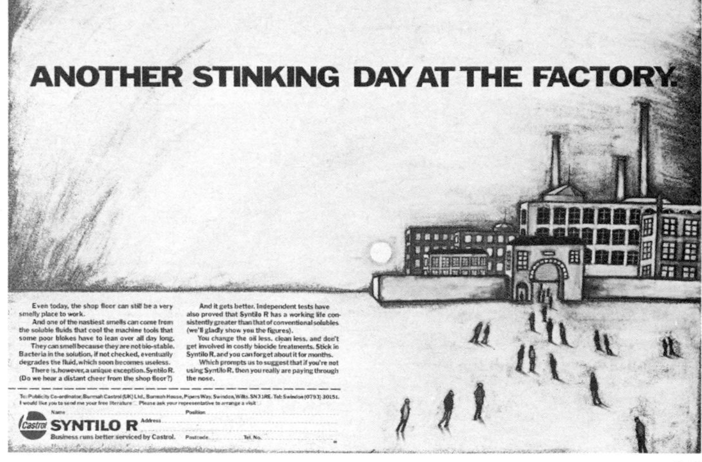

245

245
Castrol Syntilo R
United Kingdom
Agency: Dorland Advertising, London

The English painter L. S. Lowry, who is famous for his industrial landscapes, provides the artistic inspiration for this ad for a sweet-smelling, long-lasting coolant.

246

246
Vortice ventilation and heating
Italy
Agency: STZ, Milan

'What use is a ceiling fan in winter?' asks the headline. The picture poses the same question. Body copy supplies the answer, namely that it drives warm air downwards, thus achieving a more homogeneous temperature in the workplace and a consequent saving in heating costs of up to 30 per cent.

247
Swarttouw stevedores
International
Agency: McCann-Erickson,
Amsterdam

The Frans Swarttouw company operates three bulk goods' terminals in the port of Rotterdam. As the copy says, for such a firm 'there is nothing more important than well motivated personnel', so that is what the ad is selling – the men rather than their equipment.

EXCEPTIONAL MEN AT AN EXCEPTIONAL MOMENT.

'First the work, then the photo', these Swarttouw specialists declared. And our 822 other employees would say the same.

For an international bulk goods stevedore, located in the heart of Europe, there is nothing more important than well motivated personnel. Because they, plus excellent equipment, produce the highest quality of work – and ensure client satisfaction.

As a result of thorough training and practical experience, every individual on the Frans Swarttouw payroll is a genuine specialist. Their trademark is reliability and accuracy: whether they are salesmen, client representatives, members of the central planning department, or working in the shifts in one of our three terminals.

Together they create the best basis for providing fast, efficient service – according to client specifications.

FRANS SWARTTOUW

P.O. Box 54143,
3008 JC Rotterdam, Holland.
Tel. 3110 297722
Telex: 28932

247

248
ESAB robot welders
Netherlands
Agency: Young & Rubicam,
Amsterdam

This ad, boosting Swedish industrial products in general and ESAB welding equipment in particular, plays on – and at the same time makes fun of – Dutch feelings of national pride. The headline says 'Belgian welders are more intelligent than Dutch ones, believe the Swedes', and the picture shows a Belgian (reading an Antwerp newspaper) seated beside his ESAB robot. Copy explains that, though the Dutch may look down on their Belgian neighbours, Belgium has made greater progress in installing automatic welding equipment.

(op ± 0,2 millimeter nauwkeurig) dezelfde bewegingen te herhalen en doorlopend lassen te maken van hoge kwaliteit.

ESAB maakt ook off-shore lasapparatuur, een enigszins misleidende benaming voor heavy-duty apparatuur die ook in woestijnen onmisbare diensten bewijst. Daarnaast brengt ESAB voor de doe-het-zelver draagbare, maar kwalitatief éven perfekte lasapparaten.

Wij realiseren ons dat sommige mensen schrikken bij het horen van woorden als automatisering en robotisering. Toch is de ESAB technologie in de eerste plaats het logische resultaat van een [illegible] denkproces waarin de uiteindelijke gebruiker centraal staat.

Of 't nu gaat om kantoormeubilair, prefabwoningen of verpakkingen, Zweedse produkten zijn altijd te herkennen aan de bijna spreekwoordelijke degelijkheid, de technologische geavanceerdheid en de gebruiksvriendelijke vormgeving.

Als u meer gedetailleerde informatie wenst over Zweedse produkten en ESAB in het bijzonder, stuur dan onderstaande bon op.

Binnen enkele dagen liggen de brochures op uw bureau.

ESAB

Belgische lassers zijn intelligenter dan Hollandse, zo menen de Zweden.

Nederlanders plegen altijd wat lacherig en laatdunkend te doen wanneer 't gesprek op onze Zuiderburen komt. Misplaatste superioriteitsgevoelens als u 't ons vraagt.

Het 'achterlijke' België is bijvoorbeeld veel verder met het automatiseren en robotiseren van het lassen dan Nederland. Daar zijn wel enkele – zwakke – excuses voor te vinden.

Nederland heeft vrijwel geen opleidingen voor gerobotiseerd lassen. Onze meeste decision-makers hebben nog te weinig ervaring met dit onderwerp.

Terwijl de Belgen drommels goed beseffen dat ESAB lasautomaten en lasrobots een belangrijke bijdrage leveren aan produktiviteitsverhoging, zich snel terugverdienen en werk afleveren van hoog kwalitatief niveau.

In 1904 vond Oscar Kjellberg, de oprichter van ESAB, de beklede laselectrode uit. Sindsdien heeft ESAB, door een permanent research- en ontwikkelingsprogramma, zijn toppositie in de internationale lastechnologie weten te behouden.

Ongeveer één op de twee robot-lasinstallaties is van ESAB (wereldwijd!).

Voor 't MIG/MAG lassen ontwikkelde ESAB een serie halfautomaten met een balans-arm die het gewicht van de laskabel vermindert en daardoor het laswerk gemakkelijker en accurater maakt.

In moderne industrie-sectoren zoals lucht- en ruimtevaart, nucleaire industrie en off-shore waar met aluminium, titanium, inconel, roestvaststaal, enz. wordt gewerkt is geavanceerde lastechnologie een absolute voorwaarde.

ESAB konstrueerde de PULS-ARC machine voor [illegible] booglassen. De PULS-ARC klaart de moeilijkste lasklussen, geeft 'n betere controle op het eindresultaat en is bij uitstek geschikt om aan een robot gekoppeld te worden.

In 'n continu produktieproces is de robot, beter dan de lasser, in staat zeer snel en uiterst precies

Stuur mij vrijblijvend uitgebreide informatie over
☐ ESAB ☐ Andere Zweedse industrieën, te weten ______
Naam: ______
Bedrijf: ______
Functie: ______
Adres: ______
Postcode/Plaats: ______
Deze coupon in een ongefrankeerde envelop sturen aan: Zweedse Handelsdelegatie,
Antwoordnummer 18427, 2500 WL 's-Gravenhage. ES 2

Zweden zijn niet gauw tevreden.

248

249
Unichema oleochemicals
Western Europe, Far East and Australasia
Agency: Ayer Barker, London

Part of a campaign run in leading international chemical industry journals to explain the suitability of Unichema materials for products ranging from cosmetics to cars and tyres. Here we have what would look like a typical women's magazine ad if it were not for the unfamiliar (to women's magazine readers) name on the pot of cream.

THE NAME FOR OLEOCHEMICAL QUALITY.

For the cosmetics and toiletries industry, Unichema oleochemicals provide an abundant, natural source of non-toxic, biodegradable ingredients.

PRISORINE isostearic acid and PRICERINE glycerine are important raw materials for cosmetic formulations, while high quality Unichema esters and alkanolamides – manufactured from captively produced fatty acids – form the base for many famous cosmetic brands.

For bath oils, body lotions, nail varnish removers, skin preparations and anti-perspirants, the emolliency of Unichema ESTOL esters makes them ideal constituents.

Other ESTOL esters act as consistency modifiers and emulsifiers in cosmetic creams.

With neutral odour and excellent colour, the ESTOL range is the standard choice for high-quality preparations.

The same range offers phthalate and acetate esters as solvents and carriers for perfumes and fragrances.

And if you're looking for an excellent base for toilet soaps ask about our PRISAVON soap noodles.

In cosmetics and toiletries, as in textiles, leather processing, plastics, rubber and lubricants, Unichema is your guarantee of oleochemical quality.

As the world's leading supplier of oleochemicals, with manufacturing bases in both hemispheres and an international network of sales offices and agents, Unichema ensures the oleochemicals you require are readily available and of consistently high quality.

Unichema works with you in your industry. Researching. Evaluating. Improving. And guaranteeing your supply.

Just contact any Unichema sales office.

Unichema International, PO Box 2
2800 AA Gouda, The Netherlands.
The Netherlands: Tel: (01820) 42911. Telex: 20661.
Federal Republic of Germany: Tel: (02822) 721. Telex: 08 125 113.
United Kingdom: Tel: (051) 645 2020. Telex: 629408.
France: Tel: (01) 563 0863. Telex: 643217.
Australia: Tel: (03) 647 9311. Telex: AA 30130.
Malaysia: Tel: (03) 302115. Telex: MA 39535.
USA: Tel: (201) 599-0670. TWX: 753224.

Unichema International
Dynamic in Oleochemicals

249

250

252

253

250
Filter mask
Japan
Agency: Dentsu, Tokyo

A graphic demonstration of how dirty a worker can get. But fortunately his mouth and nose were protected by a filter mask made by the Sumitomo 3M company. Headline: 'Thank you for your hard work, masked industrial worker.'

251
Portucel packaging
Portugal
Agency: McCann-Erickson/Hora, Lisbon

Portucel, copy tells us, offers protection and safety to suit any product. The headline says 'Packaging Protection.' The somewhat mundane message is made interesting by the image of the packed bubble.

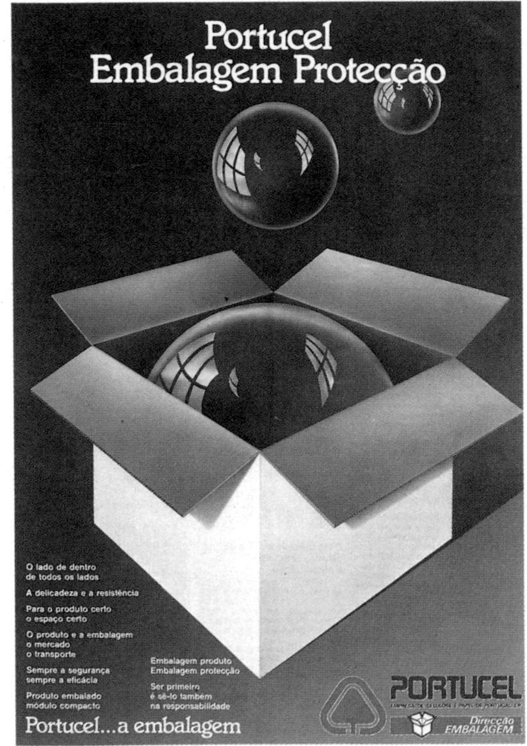

251

252
Gujarat industrial locations
India
Agency: Shilpi Advertising, Ahmedabad

A knocking ad, one of several which decry the claims advanced by other Indian States. This concentrates on the alleged peacefulness of labour in Gujarat, contrasted with the unrest which elsewhere 'can turn an entrepreneur into a pawn'. It's eye-catching for any businessman, but one wonders whether the positive message will come over as strongly as the negative one.

253
Solel Boneh International
International
Studio: Shosh & Yona, Tel Aviv

The old visual clichés, like the globe, can still have new twists put in them, as on the cover of this brochure for the Israel-based Solel Boneh construction group.

254
Mobil OPPalyte packaging film
United States
Agency: Hutchins/Y & R, Rochester, New York State

What better spokesperson for a new wrap, asks the agency, than a mummy with wrapping that has lasted for thousands of years? Going by the expression on its face, however, this particular mummy does not seem all that old.

Every few thousand years or so,
a great wrap comes along.
OPPalyte from Mobil.
Worth the wait!
But don't wait any longer.
Learn more about OPPalyte.
Mobil Chemical
Your Packaging Consultants

254

255
Rotherham Enterprise Zone
United Kingdom
Agency: Ayer Barker, London

Last year's edition included an ad for the same client by Roles and Parker, an agency specialising in industrial advertising, which has since been absorbed into Ayer Barker. To illustrate the success story of a fish farm opened in the Rotherham development area, South Yorkshire, what more appropriate image than a fish-hook in the shape of the town's logo?

255

256
AEG power supply systems
United Kingdom
Agency: Young & Rubicam, London

An eerie image makes the point that hospitals, as well as other places, can ensure uninterrupted electric power with AEG equipment. A similar image, though the message is quite different, will be found in a New York Y & R ad (about the dangers of alcohol) in the Public Service section.

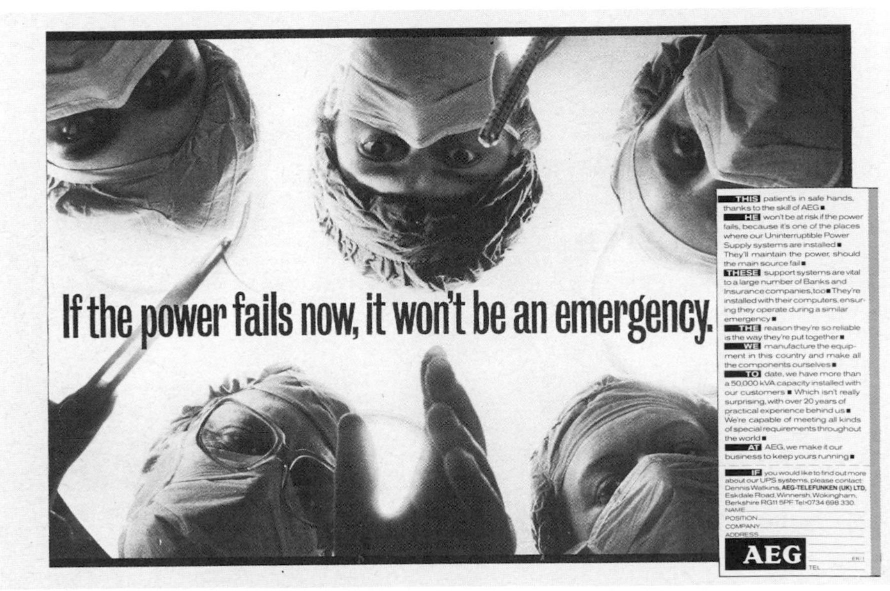

256

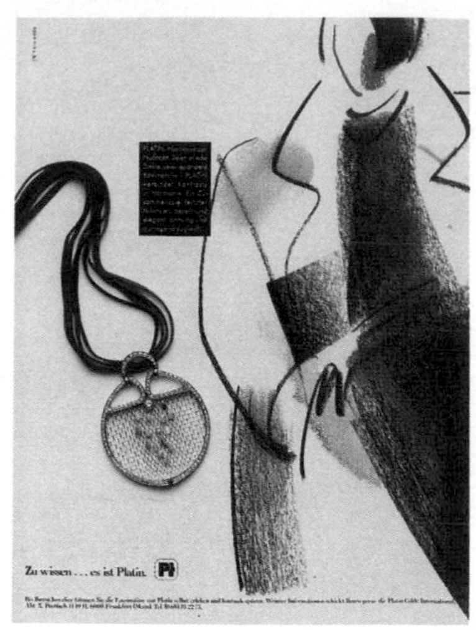

257

258

257, 258
Platinum jewellery
West Germany
Agency: J. Walter Thompson, Frankfurt

Two ads from a distinctive series financed by the International Platinum Guild and the Rustenburg Platinum Mines. The campaign aim is to communicate, through the artistic quality of the graphics, the high value of the jewellery. It was conceived against a background in which gold jewellery has on average declined in purity. On the other hand platinum jewellery alloys are 95 per cent pure platinum. The ad showing a couple tells us the metal's durability makes it the symbol of lasting relationships. The other says it harmonises with other precious metals and stones.

259

259
'Diamond Desires'
United States
Agency: N. W. Ayer, New York

To promote diamond sales during the Christmas 1984 shopping period Ayer created a sequence of eight pages featuring 50 pieces of jewellery by different manufacturers. This photograph, by Albert Watson, filled the first page of the collection, catchlined 'Diamond Desires'.

260
Gold jewellery
United States
Agency: Doyle Dane Bernbach, New York

'Nothing else feels like real gold', declares the copy, though one may question how real 18 carat gold is, and that is what is being advertised. What makes this ad special is not the sexy situation but the way the picture appears encrusted with gold lettering.

261
Pearls
Japan
Agency: Dentsu, Tokyo

'The power to manipulate your line of vision' says the headline on this pretty picture. Another example of the Japanese fondness for non-Japanese models.

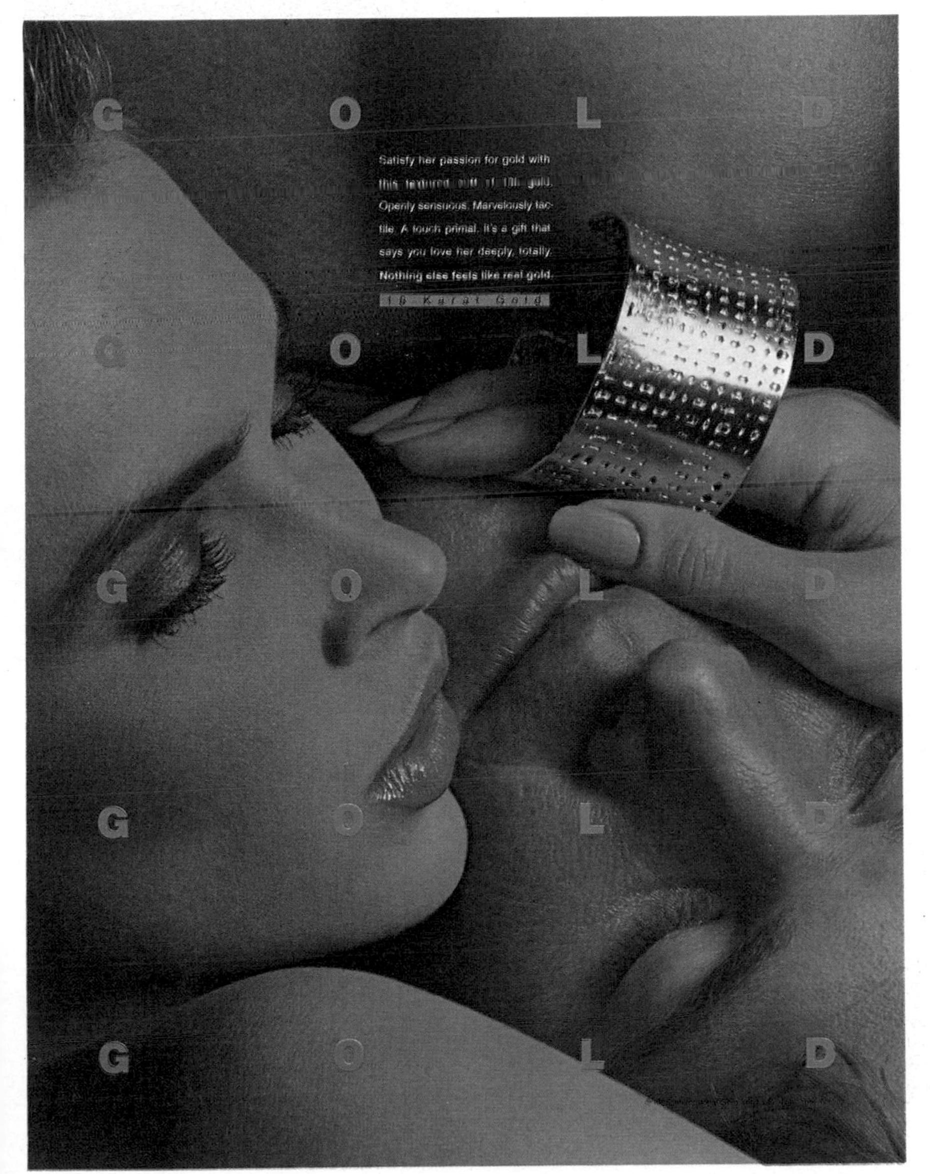

260

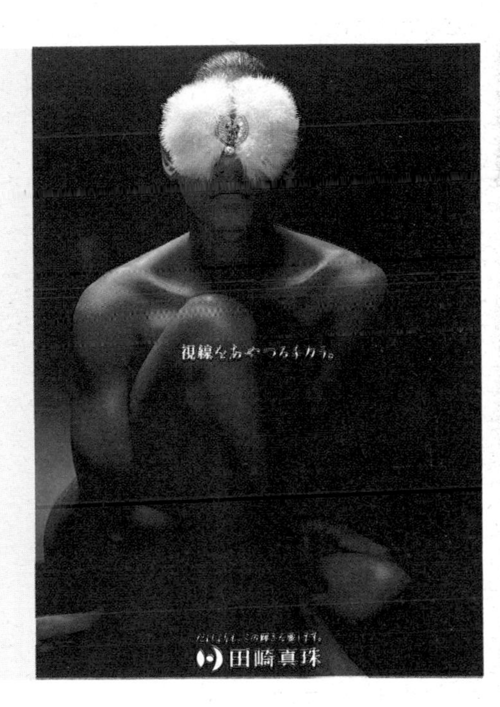

261

262
Timex watches
France
Agency: DDB2, Paris

This is not so much a sexy as a joky ad, with the zero of the price crossed out and the legend 'a zero adds nothing'. It's one way of trying to make cheapness appear smart – or at least not something to be ashamed of.

263
Diamonds for men
United States
Agency: N.W. Ayer, New York

The fastest-growing category of diamond jewellery, research shows, is gifts for men, of which three-quarters are bought by women. Each ad in Ayer's 'From a woman to a man' series depicts a man's surprised delight at receiving such a gift. The romantic tenderness of the picture contrasts with the explicit eroticism of J. Walter Thompson's French campaign (a sample of which appeared in last year's edition) on the same theme.

264
Tissot watches
United Kingdom
Agency: Travis Dale & Partners, London

This ad neatly hits two birds with one stone. Or rather conveys two messages – slimness and expensiveness – with one image. The agency is a subsidiary of Collett Dickenson Pearce & Partners.

265
Lamborghini watches
France
Agency: Soprano, Paris

Now here expensiveness, not cheapness, is the theme, as would be expected of products sold under the upmarket Lamborghini name. The ad cleverly manages to kill one bird with two stones – the visual as well as verbal allusion to Leonardo da Vinci's notebooks and the sketches of the Lamborghini car as Leonardo might have drawn them.

266
Swatch watches
International
Agency: McCann-Erickson, Zürich

Swatch, manufactured by a subsidiary of Asuag-SSIH, Switzerland's biggest watchmaking group, is a marketing success story and one of the things which saved the industry from ruin after the inroads made by Far East producers. The Swatch, with its low price and fun advertising, is positioned as a fashion accessory for young trend-setters.

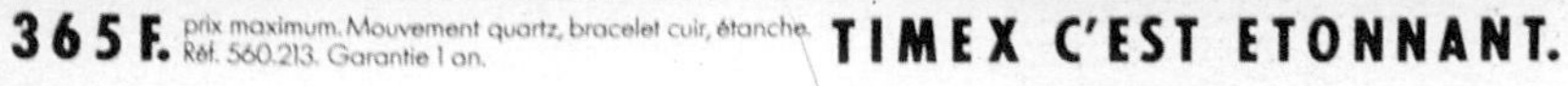

262

263

Chances of somebody buying you one are even slimmer.

TISSOT
SWISS WATCHES

264

i VINCI di
Lamborghini®

MONTRES · PARFUMS · MAROQUINERIE · BAGAGES
DISTRIBUTEURS : PROJET 112 PARIS (FRANCE ET BENELUX) - L. VIGNANDO S.A. GENEVE (SUISSE)

265

SWITCH TO SWATCH.™

THE CRAZY NEW WAVE IN SWISS WATCHES.

Swatch. On one hand, it's very Swiss. Water-resistant. Shock-resistant. With precise Swiss quartz technology. On the other hand, it rocks the boat. With outrageous colors. Up-to-the-minute styles. And prices under $35. So why not get two or three? Watch out for them at fine stores everywhere.

swatch™ QUARTZ

266

MEDIA DEPT.
Media adopt a low profile having overlooked The Mail on Sunday's value in reaching ABC1s.
The Mail on Sunday is the most cost effective national Sunday newspaper for reaching ABC1 adults. Source: NRS (JICNARS) January – June 1984.

267

MEDIA DEPT.
When the media chief told Petherick to adopt a more youthful profile, he really meant him to book The Mail on Sunday.
The Mail on Sunday has more readers between the ages of 25 and 34 than any other quality Sunday newspaper. Source: NRS (JICNARS) January – June 1984.

268

267, 268
The Mail on Sunday
United Kingdom
Agency: Saatchi & Saatchi Compton, London

For a trade paper campaign, aimed at advertising agency media buyers, this is outstanding. And though the jokes might be lost on non-specialists, they are calculated to make the target readers pay attention. And to ask themselves whether they are making sufficient use of the newspaper.

269a, 269b
Working Woman
United Kingdom
Agency: Aspect Advertising, London

Working Woman, a new British magazine, is written for career women. Its launch followed a teaser campaign featuring the poster showing three men. When the magazine came out so did the second poster in which one of the men's faces was revealed as the mask on a woman. A third poster, in which another male mask was dropped, coincided with publication of the second issue of the monthly.

270
People magazine
United States
Agency: Young & Rubicam, New York

The ad answers its own question. The children of the post-war baby boom now form the largest segment of the American adult population, earning almost half of the nation's personal income. Of the 23 million weekly readers of People 69 per cent 'are Boomers', therefore the magazine enables advertisers to 'influence the people who are influencing America'.

269a

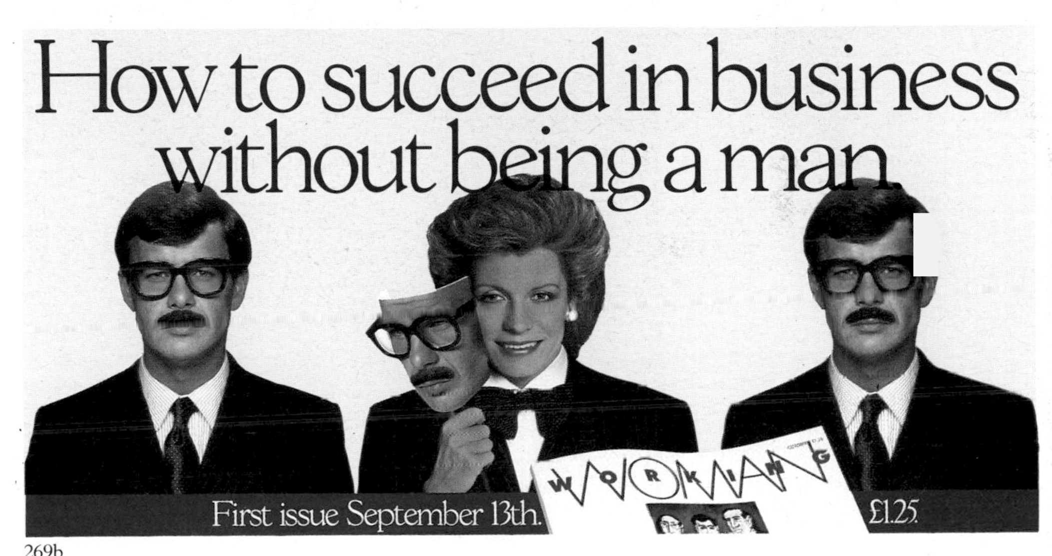

269b

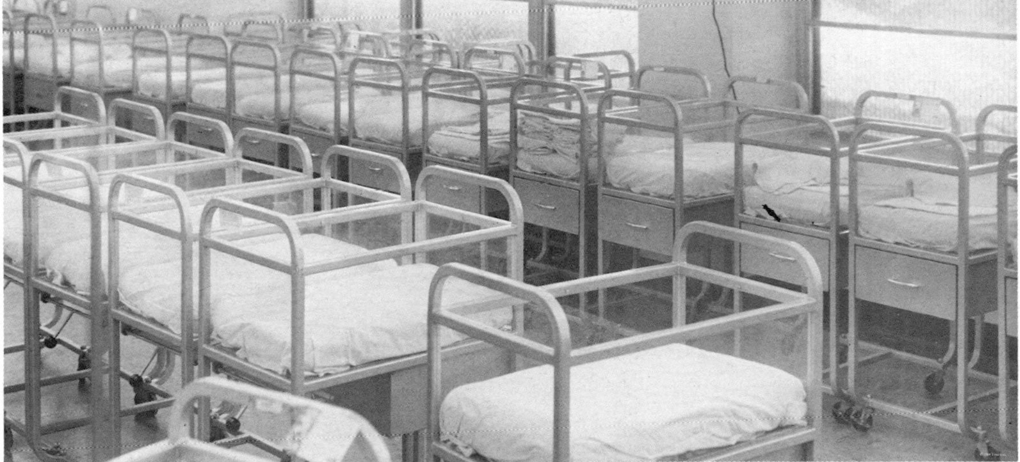

270

271
Europeo magazine
Italy
Agency: CPV Kenyon & Eckhardt, Milan

The ad, headlined 'We give you a minute to guess who it is', is from a campaign to relaunch the weekly magazine *Europeo*. The face, as is revealed in the last few lines of the body copy, is that of former Italian Prime Minister Giovanni Spadolini. Pay-off line: 'Europeo, to get a closer view of things.'

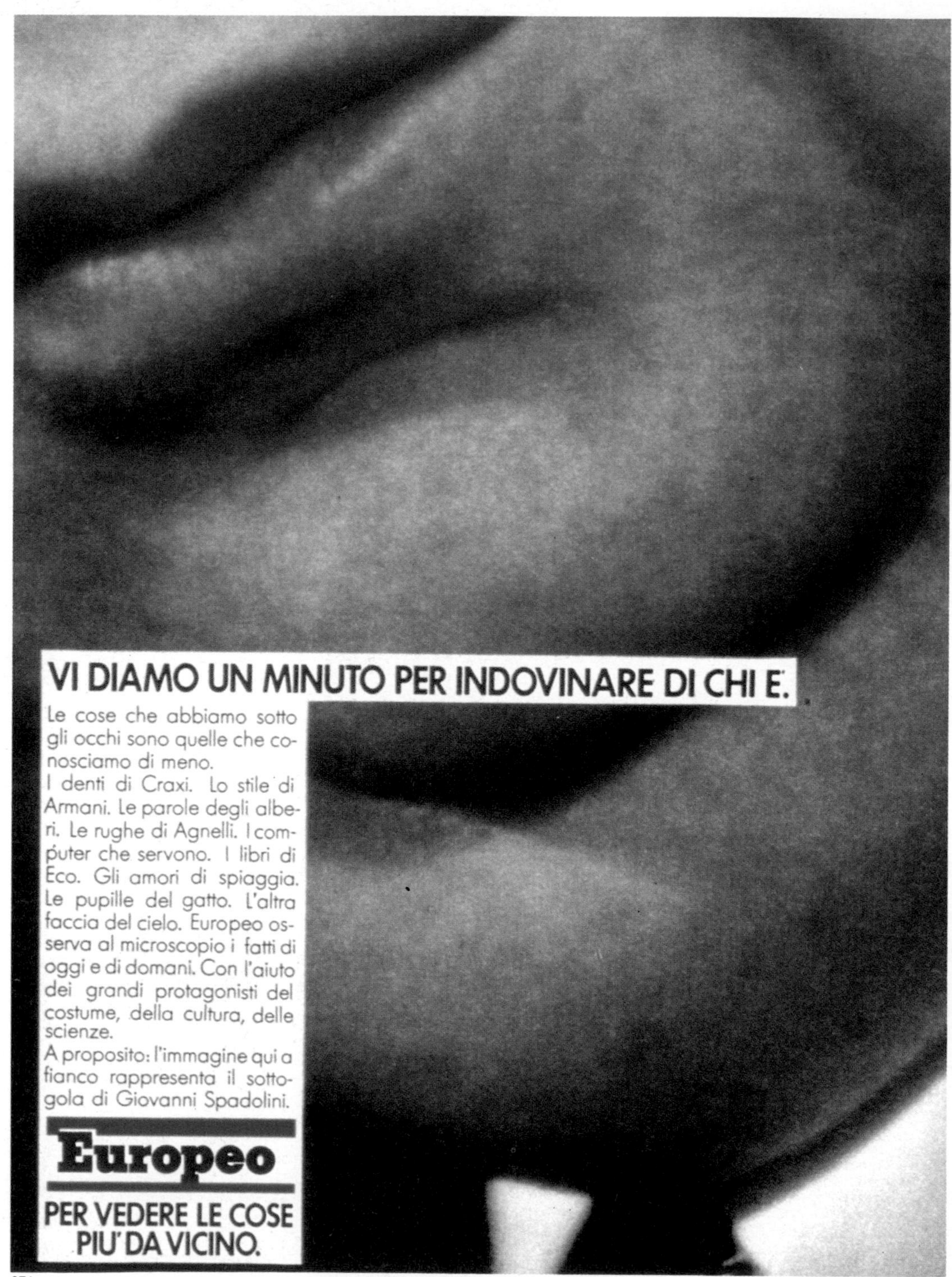

271

272
City & Country Home magazine
Canada
Agency: McCann-Erickson, Toronto

One of a series of beautiful images intended to match the stylishness of the magazine itself. It is an ad addressed to advertisers, telling them that readers of *Home* are trendsetters through whom they can influence a wider audience.

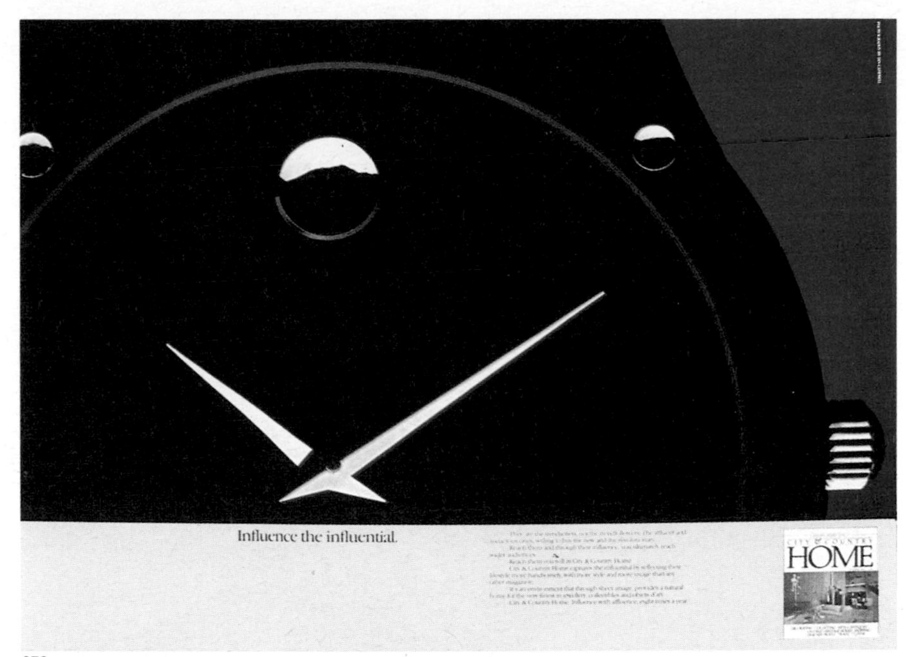

272

273
The Daily Mail
United Kingdom
Agency: Saatchi & Saatchi Compton, London

The newspaper, stablemate of the *Mail on Sunday,* has a high proportion of women readers. That provides the excuse for this eye-catching picture in the advertising trade press.

273

274
Kodansha paperbacks
Japan
Agency: Dentsu, Tokyo

The funny side of murder, depicted here as part of a campaign to promote the reading of thrillers.

275
Bonnier book publishing
Sweden
Agency: Young & Rubicam, Stockholm

The Bonnier group is, among other things, one of Europe's biggest book publishers, and this ad details the extent of its activities in publishing both original works in Swedish and translations (under various imprints). Recalling the founding of the firm 150 years ago, it says the manuscript is what all of Bonnier's operations are based on. Headline: 'To spread great ideas'.

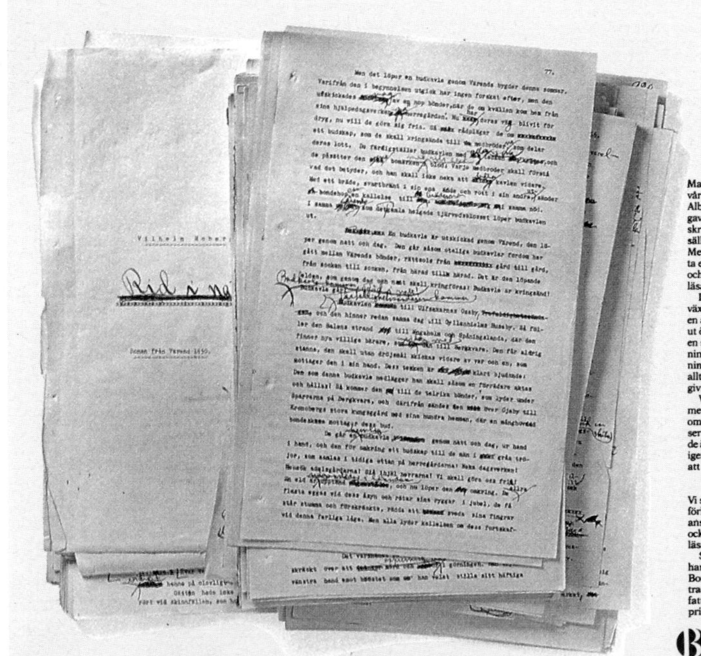

Att sprida de stora idéerna.
Manuskriptet är den grund som hela vår stora verksamhet vilar på. När Albert Bonnier för snart 150 år sen gav ut sin första bok fick han en handskriven text. Idag kommer texten inte sällan ur en ordbehandlingsmaskin. Men hela tiden har vårt jobb varit att ta emot manuskript av bra författare och sprida dem till så många svenska läsare som möjligt.
Den unge Alberts lilla vågspel har växt till Nordens största förlagsgrupp, en av de stora i Europa. Varje år ger vi ut över 500 titlar och svarar idag för en sjättedel av den svenska bokutgivningen, men en tredjedel av försäljningen. En bok från Bonniers säljer alltså dubbelt så bra som böcker utgivna av andra.
Vår filosofi är att tidigt få kontakt med lovande unga författare på olika områden. Tack vare våra stora resurser kan vi stödja och hjälpa dem när de är nya och okända. Och när de slagit igenom har vi ojämförliga möjligheter att föra deras böcker ut till läsarna.
ATT KÄNNA ANSVAR.
Vi som arbetar i den Bonnierska bokförlagsgruppen känner ett stort ansvar, inte bara mot företaget utan också mot litteraturen, författarna och läsarna.
Svenska romaner och svensk lyrik har alltid varit en huvudlinje hos Bonniers. Men vi har också en stark tradition när det gäller utländska författare. Hittills har vi givit ut 51 nobelpristagare. Många av världens mest lästa underhållningsförfattare har också kommit hos oss.
Och vi arbetar också på många andra områden. De olika förlagen i bokförlagsgruppen ger ut uppslagsböcker och andra stora verk, som kräver lång planering och investeringar på många miljoner. Ett av våra förlag, Bonnier Fakta, har hand om alla slag av facklitteratur, från de största böckerna till de minsta. Många barnboksklassiker har kommit hos Bonniers och vårt Juniorförlag fortsätter den linjen som en av de ledande utgivarna i landet.
ATT FÖLJA TIDENS KRAV
Vi sprider våra böcker på många sätt, allt efter tidens krav. Bokhandeln har alltid varit en hörnsten i vår distribution. Vi har också bokklubbar med många hundra tusen medlemmar, som gör att våra böcker av alla slag kan nå ut till nya läsare, allt efter deras smak och önskemål. Dit levererar också de andra företagen i vår bokförlagsgrupp, som alla har sina specialiteter; Forum, Alba, Viva och det delägda Wahlström & Widstrand.
ATT TRO PÅ DET MAN GÖR
Vi tror inte på böcker därför att vi lever på att ge ut dem. Tvärtom. Vi är i bokbranschen därför att vi tror på böcker. Vår tro på bokläsningens möjligheter och framtid är i dag starkare än någonsin och vi strävar efter att i många år framåt stå till tjänst för författarna och läsarna.
Att fortsätta sprida de stora idéerna.
BONNIERFÖRETAGEN

275

276, 277
Central Television
United Kingdom
Agency: Benton & Bowles, London

The sphere is the emblem of Central, the commercial TV station for the English Midlands. The ads aim to communicate to advertisers the size of the region and its suitability for test marketing as being representative of the country as a whole.

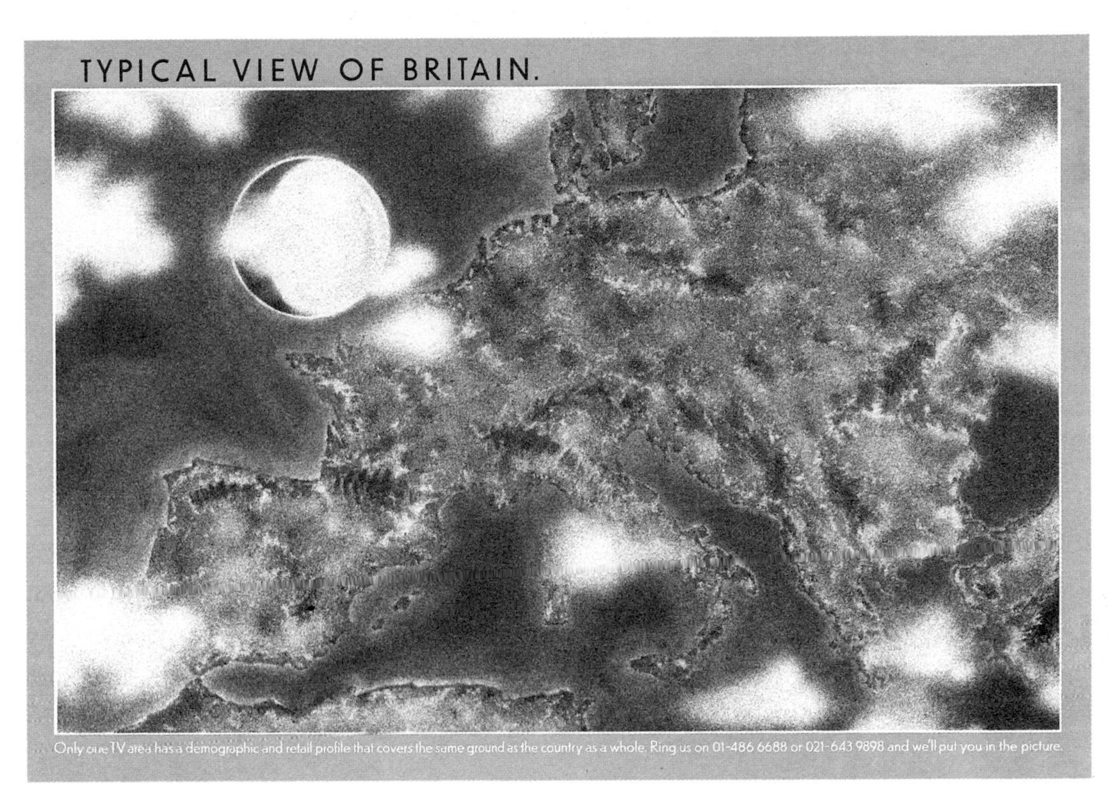

276

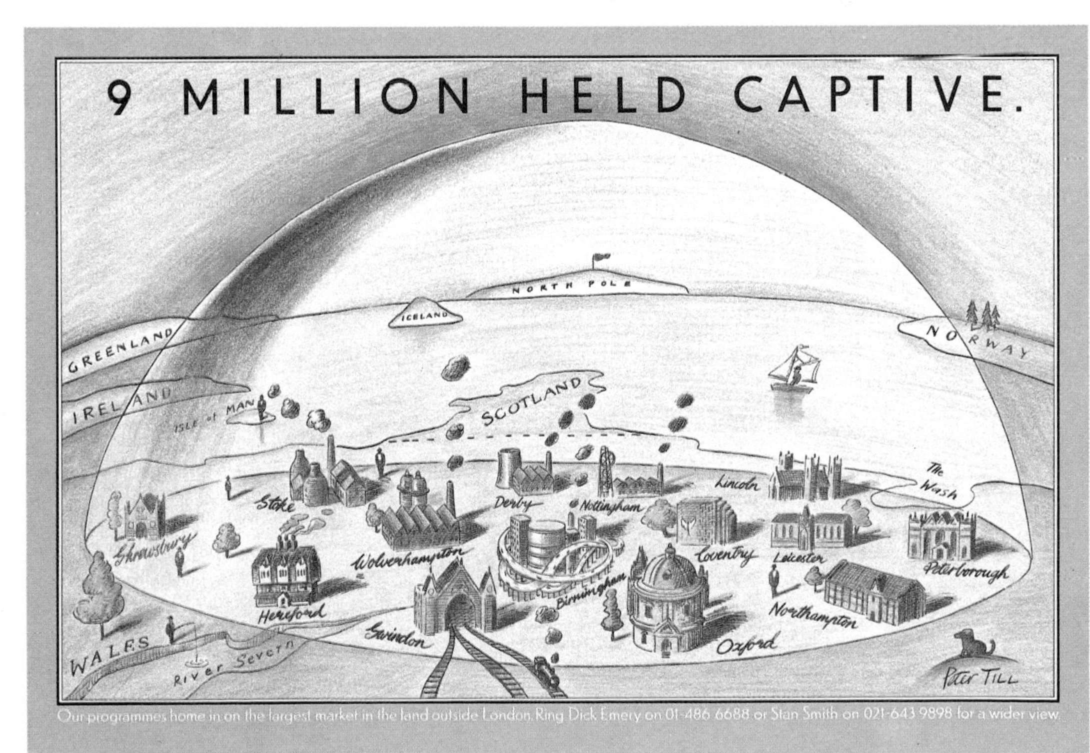

277

278
CKFM Radio, Toronto
Canada
Agency: McCann-Erickson, Toronto

The station has used 'The sound of our Toronto' as an on-air promotional theme for years. The agency's job was to translate that theme into print, which it did with a series of magazine spreads with headlines like 'Hooray' (over pictures of a parade), 'Whee' (the roller coaster in an amusement park) or, as here, 'Clickety-Clack'.

279
Olympic Games on TV
Japan
Agency: Dentsu, Tokyo

The Federation of 102 Commercial Broadcasters paid for this ad which is headed 'Do nothing but watch TV'. The sparrows, animatedly discussing which programmes they intend to see, symbolize the preoccupation of most Japanese with the Olympics.

280
More O'Ferrall poster sites
United Kingdom
Agency: Saatchi & Saatchi Compton, London

A witty way of illustrating the flexibility of the poster medium. The four pictures refer respectively to an insurance company, a fly killer ('more effective than 10 Exocets') a car tyre and a fertiliser.

281
London Weekend Television
United Kingdom
Agency: Gold Greenlees Trott, London

This poster promotes viewing of a programme introducing new entertainers. Words and graphics speak for themselves.

278

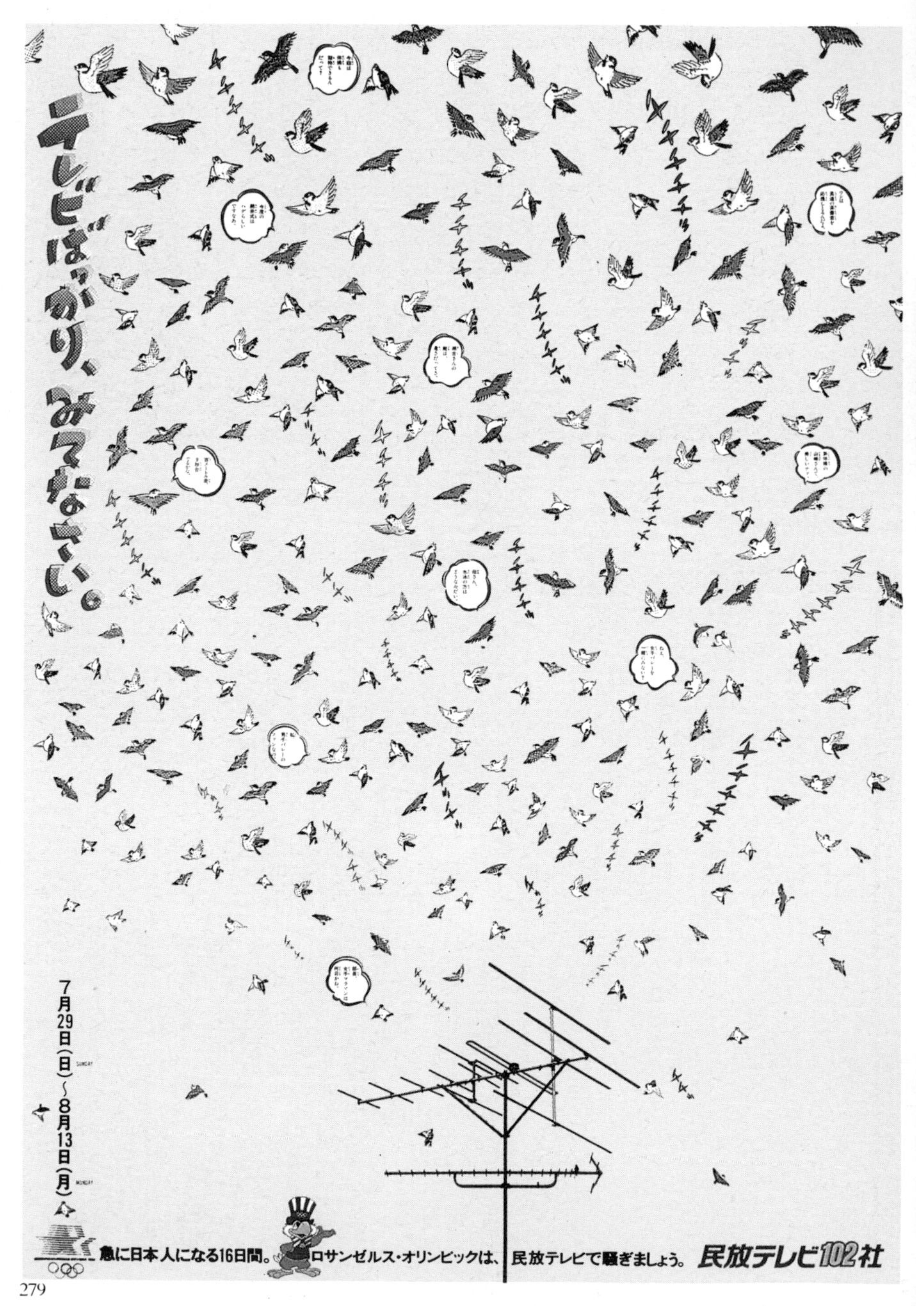

279

Long live the insane art director.

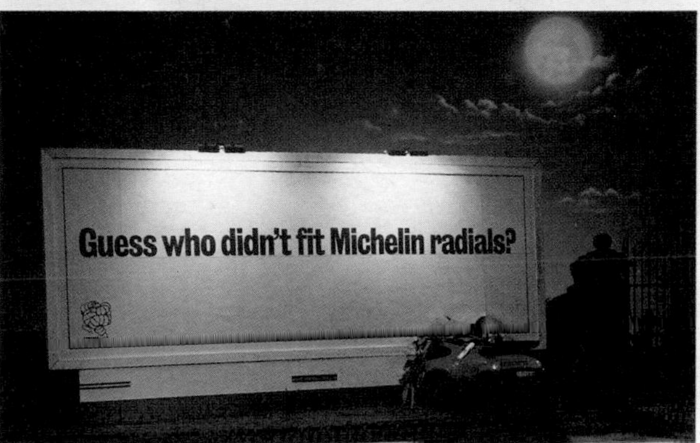

More flexibility. More impact. More O'Ferrall

280

A computer judges the talent
LWT Sat. 6·30pm. 'The Fame Game'.
LWT

281

282
Persil washing powder
United Kingdom
Agency: J. Walter Thompson, London

Continuation of a visually distinctive campaign sampled in last year's edition. The new series of posters illustrates the traditional whiteness claim with pictures of sportsmen.

283
Benfatto dishwashing liquid
Italy
Agency: CPV Kenyon & Eckhardt, Milan

An attempt to put a little glamour into an unglamorous product. 'Do you know what new thing we have here?' says the man. 'Of course', replies the woman, 'otherwise I'd not be here.' The product's name means 'well done'.

282

283

284
Coal for domestic fires
United Kingdom
Agency: Kirkwood & Partners, London

This poster, print back-up to a very effective TV commercial, majors on the emotional appeal of a real fire. Its magic, says the agency, cannot be rivalled by imitation fires, fuelled by gas or electricity.

284

285
Window glass
West Germany
Agency: J. Walter Thompson, Frankfurt

One of several unusual pictures of outdoor scenes viewed, we are given to understand, through glass. The message is that glass allows one to see the world outside in warmth and comfort. Headline: 'Breakfast in the open. Behind Flachglas glass.' Copy says Flachglas can cope with all kinds of demands, including provision of big windows through which nature can be seen and enjoyed without hindrance.

285

286
Gardena garden equipment
Norway
Agency: McCann-Erickson, Oslo

'The grass is greener on the other side' says the headline. The visual concept is very similar to that of the Indian ad for Cera bathroom fittings (in the Furniture section) where use of the product puts colour into an indoor, instead of, as here, an outdoor, scene.

286

287
Glomesh handbags
Australia
Agency: Conaghan & May Ayer, Sydney

For years Glomesh has run testimonial ads featuring well-known Australian women. The agency says it was confronted with two problems: 'We had virtually exhausted local personalities and talent fees were becoming prohibitive.' The solution was to recruit Australian women with interesting lifestyles resident overseas. Dale Tryon is a businesswoman in London and wife of Lord Tryon. Endorsers in other ads are a writer in New York and a dancer in Paris.

287

288
Samsonite luggage
United Kingdom
Agency: TBWA, London

The 'classified ad' asks for a travelling companion with strength, endurance and good looks. A neat way of using advertising itself as a thematic source for ads.

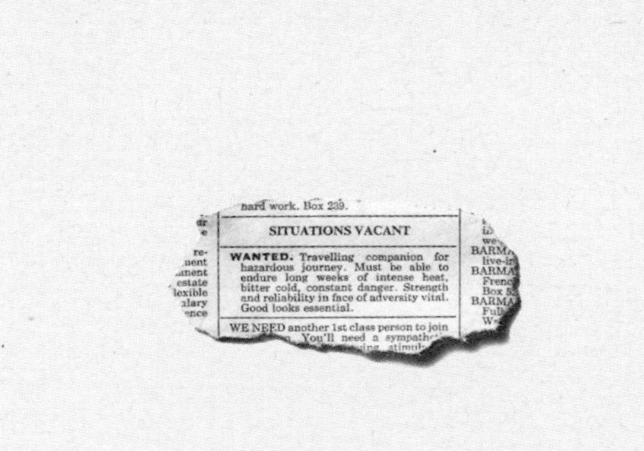

288

289

290

291

289
Post-it memo pads
Japan
Agency: Dentsu, Tokyo

To demonstrate how useful 3M Post-it memos are, the ad shows a message stuck to a microphone telling an announcer while he is on the air that his daughter has passed her examinations. Headline: 'Memos tell as much as the mouth.'

290
Hostmann-Steinberg printing inks
West Germany
Studio: Noth & Hauer, West Berlin

The theme of Noth & Hauer's 1985 calendar for this client is 'Wondrous Shadows'. Among other pictures in the calendar is one of a man holding a dead match, while his shadow holds a burning one.

291
Hostmann-Steinberg printing inks
West Germany
Studio: Noth & Hauer, West Berlin

'A fast black' is how the ad describes the product. The style is very different from that of the calendar (290) produced for the same advertiser.

292
Literary Guild
United States
Agency: Foote Cone & Belding, New York

It is common practice for book club ads to display a selection of titles available to subscribers. Usually, and boringly, they are stuck together in one part of the page. FCB has had the simple but visually effective idea of using such pictures to break up the copy and make it more interesting.

293
Teeny Weeny Itsy Bitsy Book Light
India
Agency: Enterprise Advertising, Bombay

Since a book light is most likely to be bought by book-lovers, reasoned the agency, the best way to advertise it is through well known characters from fiction. The humour of this Indian campaign (for example Sherlom Hoax instead of Sherlock Holmes) seems curiously English.

294
Schlage locks
United States
Agency: Doyle Dane Bernbach, San Francisco

The drama of the picture, showing the danger of insecure locks, almost makes one forgive the agency for the appalling pun.

292

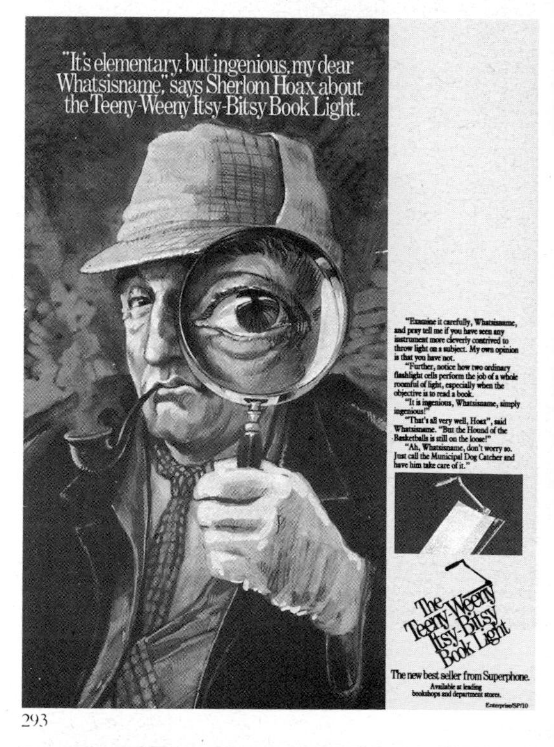

293

294

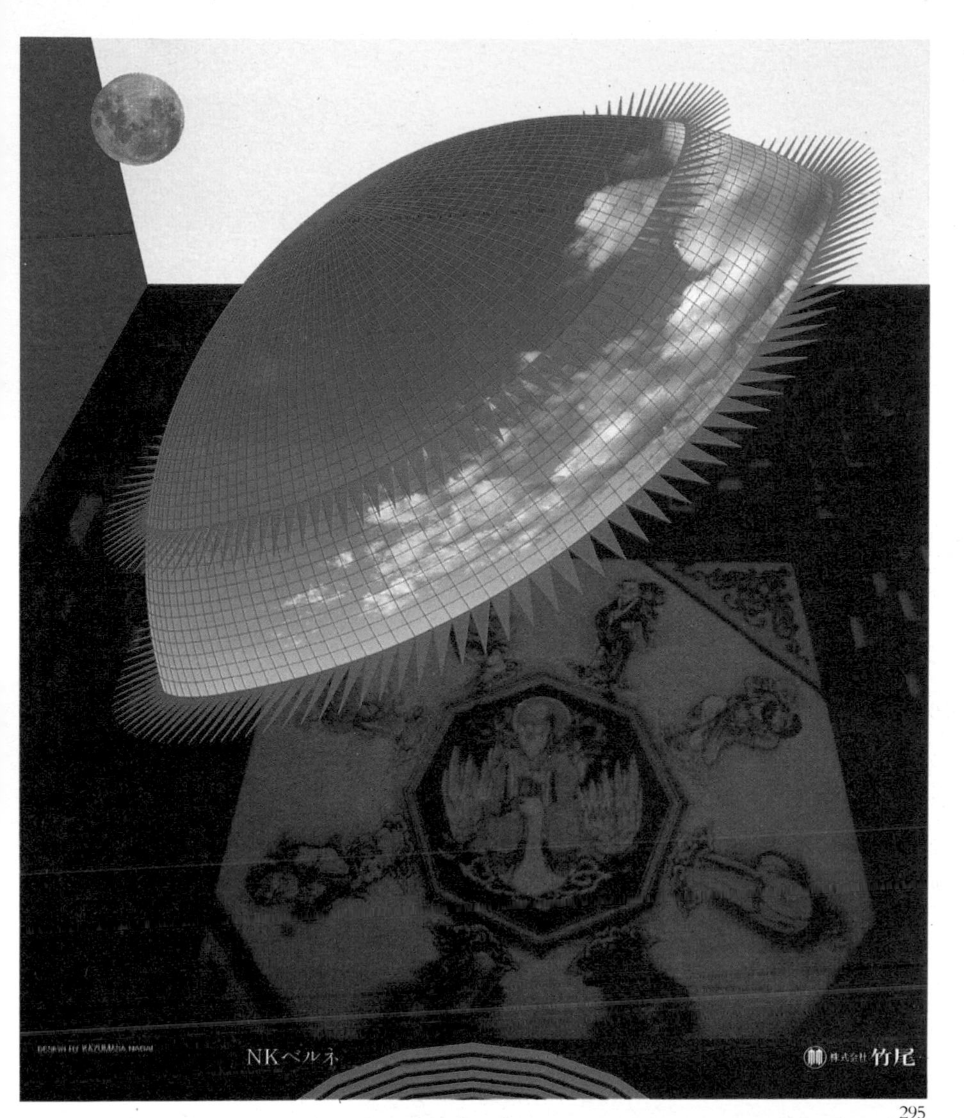

295

296

295, 296
Paper
Japan
Studio: Nippon Design Centre, Tokyo

Two in a series of magazine ads, with designs by Kazumasa Nagai, for the Takeo paper company. Each ad was printed on a different variety of paper.

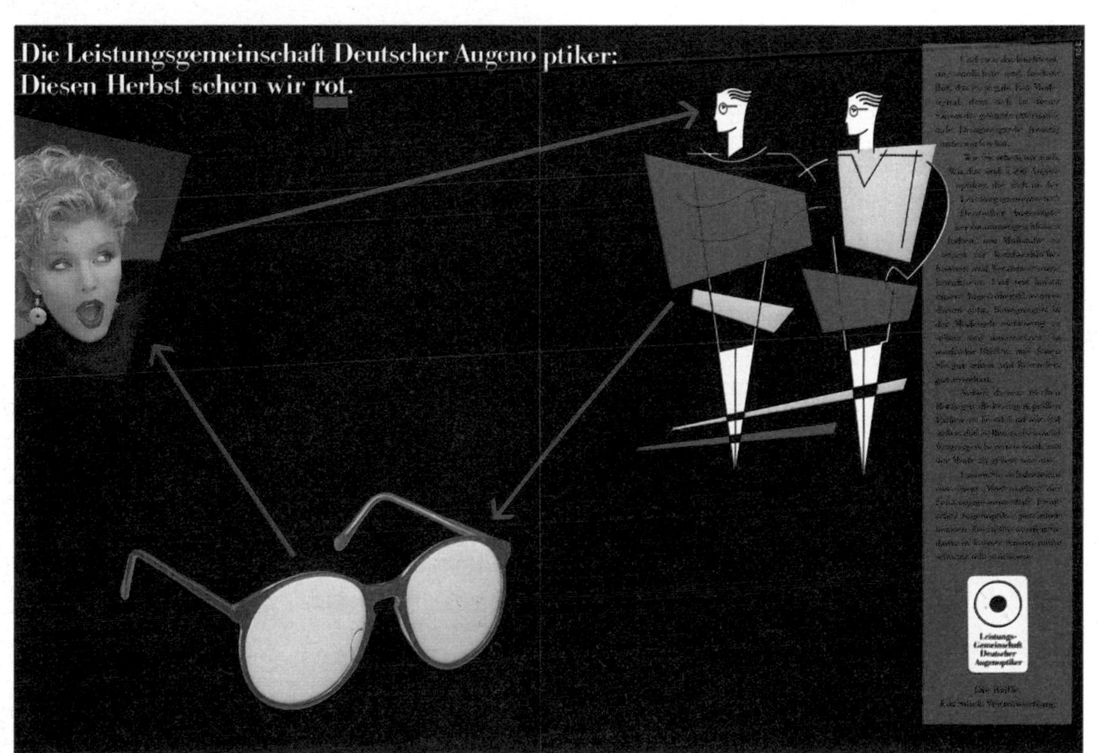

297

297
Spectacles
West Germany
Agency: Troost Campbell-Ewald, Düsseldorf

'This autumn we see red', says the message from the Association of German Opticians. Copy makes clear that they are concerned with supplying spectacles that are not only efficient but fashionable, and red is presented as the 'in' colour.

Whatever happens, minors will continue to pick it.

Brothers, what we're talking about is solidarity.
All out support from our comrades in the kindergartens, as well as nationwide advertising support from us.
(This year we're donating £3.5m to the cause.)
As usual, this powerful union will bring hundreds of people onto your shop-floor.
Not that we're calling a halt there. Next year, we'll be digging into even richer seams, with further additions to the range.
This will ensure that your business remains a goldmine for years to come.
On this matter, we are confident of achieving a unanimous agreement.

LEGO
The world's most popular toy.
©1984 LEGO GROUP ®LEGO is a registered trade mark.

298

CURVER
L'ART PLASTIQUE

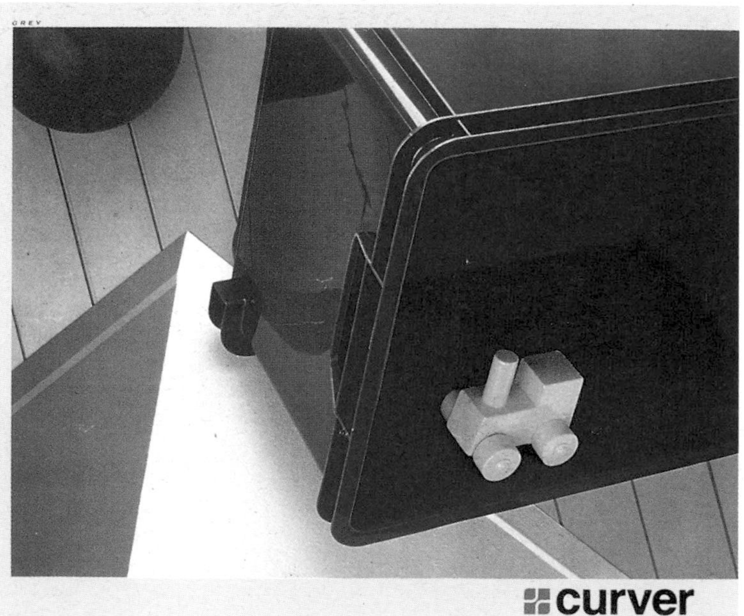
curver

299

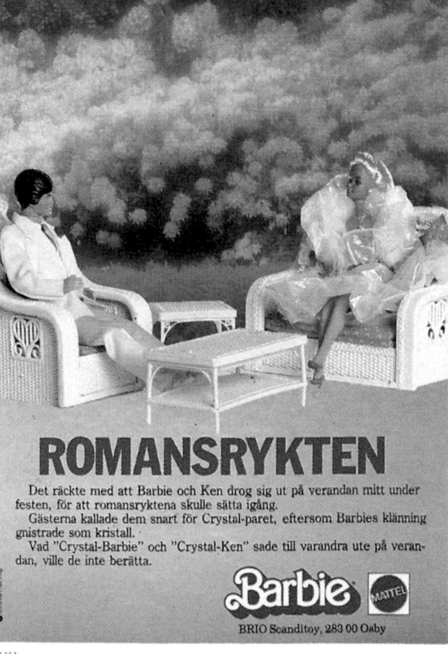
ROMANSRYKTEN
Det räckte med att Barbie och Ken drog sig ut på verandan mitt under festen, för att romansryktena skulle sätta igång.
Gästerna kallade dem snart för Crystal-paret, eftersom Barbies klänning gnistrade som kristall.
Vad "Crystal-Barbie" och "Crystal-Ken" sade till varandra ute på verandan, ville de inte berätta.
Barbie
MATTEL
BRIO Scanditoy, 283 00 Osby

300

298
Lego
United Kingdom
Agency: TBWA, London

This trade ad uses Lego building blocks to make a recognisable, and topical, portrait of Arthur Scargill, leader of the striking British coal-miners. The headline pun 'minors will continue to pick it' (miners will continue to picket) is not very sophisticated, but it probably went down well enough with the toy dealers who were being told about Lego's consumer advertising plans.

299
Curver plastic utensils
France
Agency: Grey, Paris

The products are bright and pretty, and so are the ads. Headline: 'Curver, plastic art.'

300
Barbie dolls
Sweden
Agency: Ted Bates, Helsingborg

The 1984 campaign for Barbie dolls set out to glamorize them in accord with what was seen as a shift in public taste. The heading on this ad is 'Rumour of romance', and copy refers to the tête-à-tête between Barbie and Ken on a verandah during a party. The two dolls are called 'the crystal couple' because of Barbie's dress, 'sparkling like crystal'.

301
Telephone service
Denmark
Agency: Young & Rubicam, Copenhagen

'Lunch meeting for five people' says the headline on this ad, which explains how cheap, as well as time-saving, a conference telephone hook-up can be.

302
Telephone service
Norway
Agency: Myres/Lintas, Oslo

Simple but relevant visual device draws attention to the different rates for directly dialled phone calls to other countries. Research had shown that people tended to overestimate the cost of such calls. Headline: 'Ring Christmas in.'

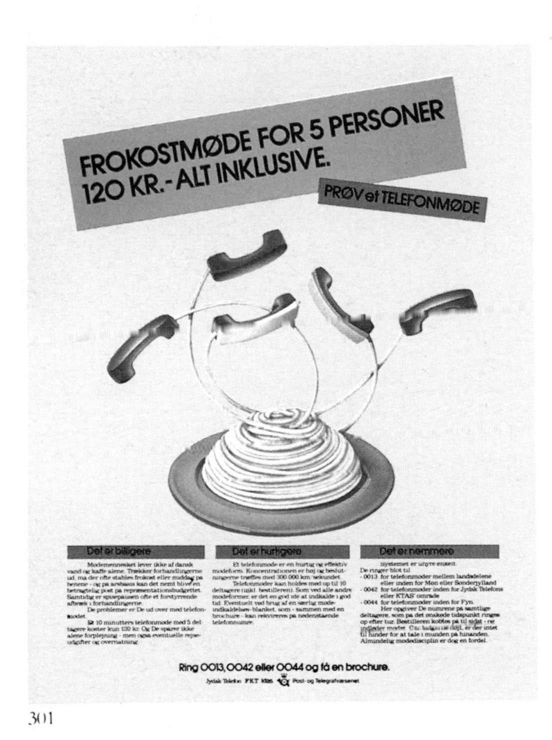

301

302

IF YOU HAD SORE, SWOLLEN BREASTS YOU WOULDN'T WANT TO BE CUDDLED EITHER.

HOW CAN I GO TO THE CUP FINAL WHEN MY HEAD'S THROBBING?

DON'T EXPECT ME TO SHAVE WITH THESE SPOTS ALL OVER MY CHIN.

I CAN'T POSSIBLY CLEAN THE CAR WITH THIS NAGGING BACKACHE.

MY STOMACH ACHES AND IT'S SO BLOATED MY BOSS ASKED IF I WAS PREGNANT.

I'LL NEVER CLIMB THE LADDER OF SUCCESS WITH LEGS THIS WOBBLY ONCE A MONTH.

Have you ever wondered how men would carry on if they had periods?

At the risk of sounding sexist, we must observe that men can be terrible babies when they're ill.

A cold so easily becomes 'flu.' A headache, 'migraine.' Indigestion, a 'suspected heart attack.'

If men had periods, the cry would go up for the 3-week month, never mind the 5-day week.

The fact is, it's women who have the periods. Month after month after month . . . for about 35 years.

And far from carrying on, women are busy, for the most part, soldiering on.

We like to think we're some help.

As the chart shows, there are 'Dr White's products designed to make your life a bit more bearable, whatever kind of periods you have to put up with.

And whatever your personal preferences might be.

Unlike most other sanitary protection manufacturers, we have no axe to grind in the tampons versus towels war: we make both. And we make both exceptionally well.

Dr White's Contour tampons have rounded end applicators, so insertion doesn't make you catch your breath…or anything.

Dr White's Panty Pads have a unique Tendasoft cover to keep you drier and more comfortable.

And Dr White's Maxi press-on has two widely-spaced adhesive strips running the length of the towel, so it stays securely put whether you're climbing a mountain or, indeed, the ladder of success.

After 104 years in the business, we aren't naive enough to imagine we could make your period a lot of laughs, exactly.

*But we're certain we can make it less of a (dare we say it?) bl**dy nuisance.*

WHICH DR. WHITE'S TOWELS AND TAMPONS WILL SUIT YOU BEST?

IF YOUR PERIOD IS:	Light	Medium	Heavy	Very Heavy
Looped Towel	Dr White's No. 1	Dr White's No. 1 or 2	Dr White's No. 2	Dr White's No. 2 or 3
Press-on Towel	Dr White's Panty Pads Regular	Dr White's Maxi or Panty Pads Super	Dr White's Maxi or Panty Pads Super	Dr White's Maxi
Press-on Mini Towel	Dr White's Fastidia			
Applicator Tampon	Dr White's Contour Regular	Dr White's Contour Super or Regular	Dr White's Contour Super	

Dr White's Towels and Tampons.

Help make your period less of a problem.

IF YOU'RE FINDING YOUR PERIOD A PROBLEM, PLEASE FEEL FREE TO WRITE TO SISTER MARION AT LILIA-WHITE LTD, ALUM ROCK ROAD, BIRMINGHAM B8 3DZ.

303

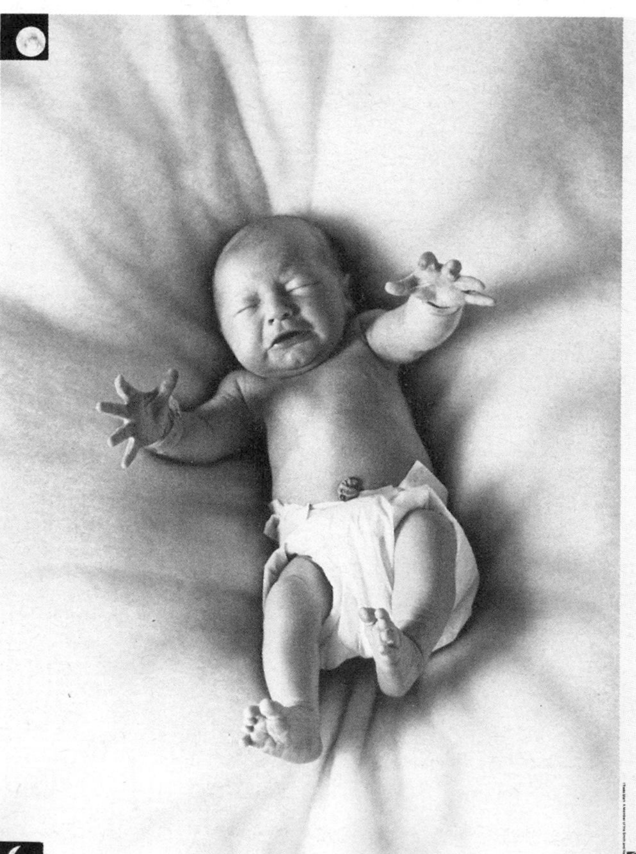

Having a baby will change your life. It could also change your method of sanitary protection.

After the sheer discomfort and seemingly endless waiting, you could be forgiven for asking if it is all worth it.

But the joy of seeing your new born baby for the first time erases any doubts.

Your only wish is to get back on your feet again.

Everyone from the doctor to your grandmother has given you advice on how to cope with the new arrival.

But rather less advice on how to cope with yourself. Such as dealing with up to four weeks heavy flow after nine months without a period.

Especially those of you who have never needed to wear a towel before.

All this at a time when you're already tired, emotionally drained and have plenty of better things on your mind.

We understand what you're going through and offer some practical advice.

A quick check of the chart shows that we make a number of products to cope with heavy flow.

For example, 'Dr White's Maxi Press-on Towel designed to handle the heaviest flow.

Dr White's Maxi has two widely-spaced, adhesive strips that run the length of the towel to keep it in place, and a polythene backing that extends up the sides and over the edge to eliminate the fear of leaking.

It's constructed to absorb evenly, keeping you drier and more comfortable at a time when you're particularly sensitive.

Because it's not enormously bulky it doesn't restrict your movements and allows you the freedom to get back into normal clothes again.

And when your periods return to normal, whether you prefer towels or tampons, we'll have the products to meet your needs.

In the meantime, Dr White's Maxi will help you get on with more important matters.

Like looking after your baby.

WHICH DR. WHITE'S TOWELS AND TAMPONS WILL SUIT YOU BEST?

IF YOUR PERIOD IS:	Light	Medium	Heavy	Very Heavy
Looped Towel	Dr White's No. 1	Dr White's No. 1 or 2	Dr White's No. 2	Dr White's No. 2 or 3
Press-on Towel	Dr White's Panty Pads Regular	Dr White's Maxi or Panty Pads Super	Dr White's Maxi or Panty Pads Super	Dr White's Maxi
Press-on Mini Towel	Dr White's Fastidia			
Applicator Tampon	Dr White's Contour Regular	Dr White's Contour Super or Regular	Dr White's Contour Super	

New Dr White's Maxi Press-On Towels.

Help make your period less of a problem.

SAMPLES? FOR A FREE TRIO OF DR WHITE'S MAXI, JUST WRITE TO DEPT M (WW1), LILIA-WHITE LTD, ALUM ROCK ROAD, BIRMINGHAM B8 3DZ.

304

303, 304
Dr White's sanitary towels and tampons
United Kingdom
Agency: Bartle Bogle Hegarty, London

Once upon a time the Saatchi & Saatchi ad agency got a lot of publicity for a poster showing a pregnant man. (It was designed to promote use of male contraceptives.) That kind of sex reversal joke goes down well with the British. It is employed here, again with a serious purpose, in a way very similar to that of the TBWA ad for New Balance women's sports shoes, in the Clothing & Footwear section. The other ad eschews humour but may be no less effective.

305
Valdispert tranquiliser
Netherlands
Agency: Young & Rubicam, Amsterdam

The message of the headline and of the picture is that 'Some remedies for slight nervousness are worse than the malady.' Copy details the harmful side-effects of which the product is claimed to be free.

306
Verecolene Complesso lassativo
Italy
Agency: CPV Kenyon & Eckhardt, Milan

'This is an advertisement which every doctor, if he has five minutes to spare, should read' says the headline. Copy refers to a survey on the causes of constipation. The ad has run in medical magazines.

Bij lichte nervositeit
kunnen sommige middelen
erger zijn dan de kwaal.

Lichte nervositeit vraagt om een licht middel. Valdispert bewijst z'n werkzaamheid keer op keer, zowel in onderzoeken als in de praktijk. Toch kent Valdispert totaal geen bijwerkingen. Valdispert versuft niet, beïnvloedt de rijvaardigheid niet en geeft geen gewenning. Valdispert, de natuurlijke rustgever.

305

Questo è un annuncio che ogni medico, se avesse cinque minuti di tempo, dovrebbe leggere.

Caro dottore, sappiamo che il suo tempo è prezioso e non vogliamo rubargliene troppo. Pensiamo però che possa farle piacere conoscere i risultati di un'indagine sulla stipsi, condotta fra i medici a cura dell'Istituto di ricerche Delfo.

Ecco le opinioni più diffuse tra gli intervistati:

1. La stipsi va assumendo, ogni giorno di più, il ruolo di "manifestazione ossessiva della nevrosi collettiva e sintomo di malessere sociale in aggravamento".

2. Le principali cause della stipsi non organica sono dovute:

a) Alla ingestione di alimenti poveri di scorie, molto raffinati;

b) All'inibizione volontaria dello stimolo durante le riunioni di lavoro, lo studio, gli impegni e le attività della vita contemporanea;

c) A fattori psichici come lo stress e l'ansietà, i quali possono indurre stipsi per contrazione spastica e stato ipertonico della muscolatura del colon. La stipsi cronica è piuttosto frequente nei soggetti troppo ansiosi e sotto stress;

d) Allo scarso esercizio fisico: la vita sedentaria può condurre, infatti, alla cosiddetta "stipsi atonica".

3. Il lassativo non andrebbe scelto su arbitrio del paziente, ma su consiglio del medico, che deve inquadrare la stitichezza in un contesto organico ben definito e proporre il prodotto più adatto.

Se queste sono anche le sue opinioni, le sarà certamente capitato di consigliare ai suoi pazienti Verecolene Complesso.

La specialità medicinale produce una equilibrante azione lassativa, grazie alla completezza della sua formulazione.
Si tratta, infatti, di un'associazione di sostanze ed estratti di note erbe naturali, che favoriscono il ripristino della funzionalità intestinale. E' un regolatore che, per la presenza del coleretico fencibutirolo, stimola anche le funzioni del fegato.

Come vede, ci sono molti buoni motivi per continuare a consigliare Verecolene ogni volta che le parrà utile integrare le cure con un regolatore intestinale.

Verecolene Complesso è un prodotto che si basa sulla esperienza etica della Maggioni Farmaceutici.

Verecolene Complesso. Per una delicata azione lassativa.

306

307, 308
Inderal and Inderal LA
United States
Agency: Sudler & Hennessey,
New York

Both these ads ran in American medical journals. The language of the body copy is technical, but the headlines and photographs are very much in the style of consumer advertising. Except, of course, that the heart shape, in ads addressed to cardiologists, is that of the real organ and not the cliché symbol used to promote so many products that have nothing to do with its functioning.

309
Epivax dog vaccines
United Kingdom
Agency: Fletcher Shelton Delaney,
London

This odd-looking animal is what the agency calls a multi-dog. Both picture and copy convey the message that the new range of Epivax vaccines protects any kind of dog against a variety of maladies. The ad is targeted at vets.

310
Colac laxative
Japan
Agency: McCann-Erickson Hakuhodo,
Tokyo

'Pink-coloured salad' is how these pills are labelled in the headline. Colac, brand leader with more than a third of its market, features vegetables in its advertising to project the image of a natural product. It is, of course, no such thing.

311
Solprin soluble aspirin
New Zealand
Agency: Ward & Grey, Auckland

A neat use of the Scrabble theme, though this, like chess or snakes and ladders, has become a standby of creative departments in many countries.

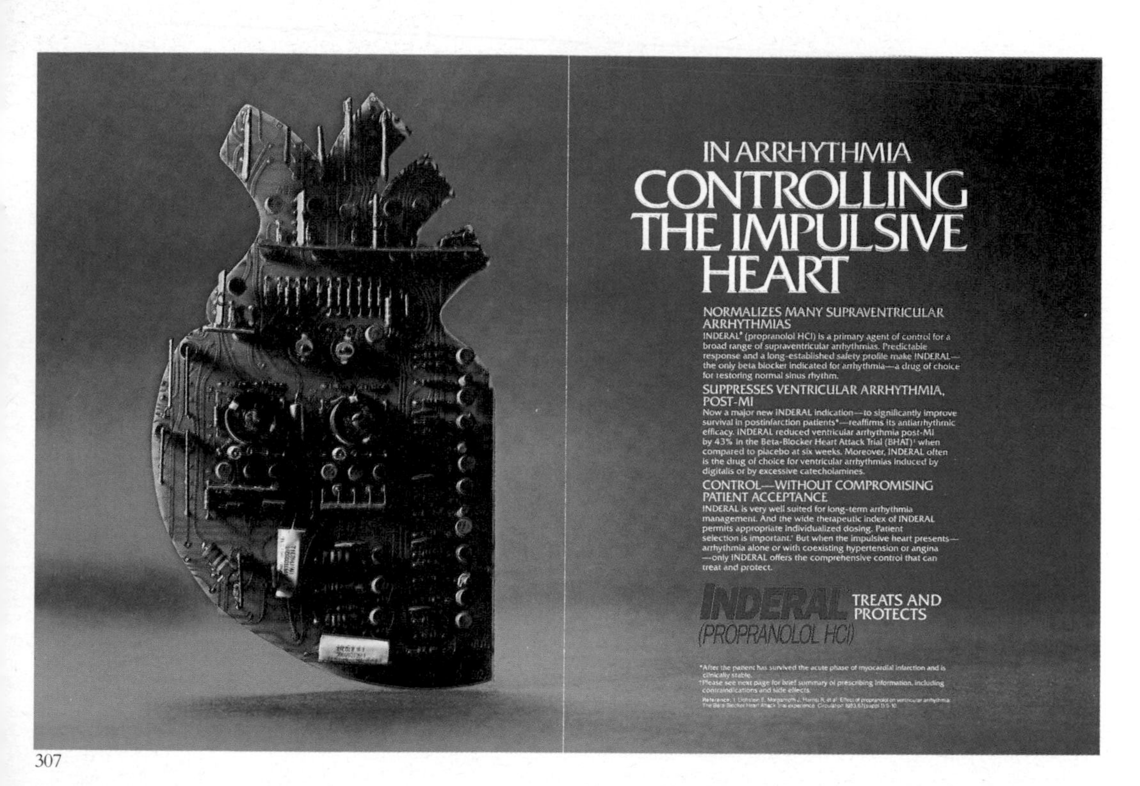

307

308

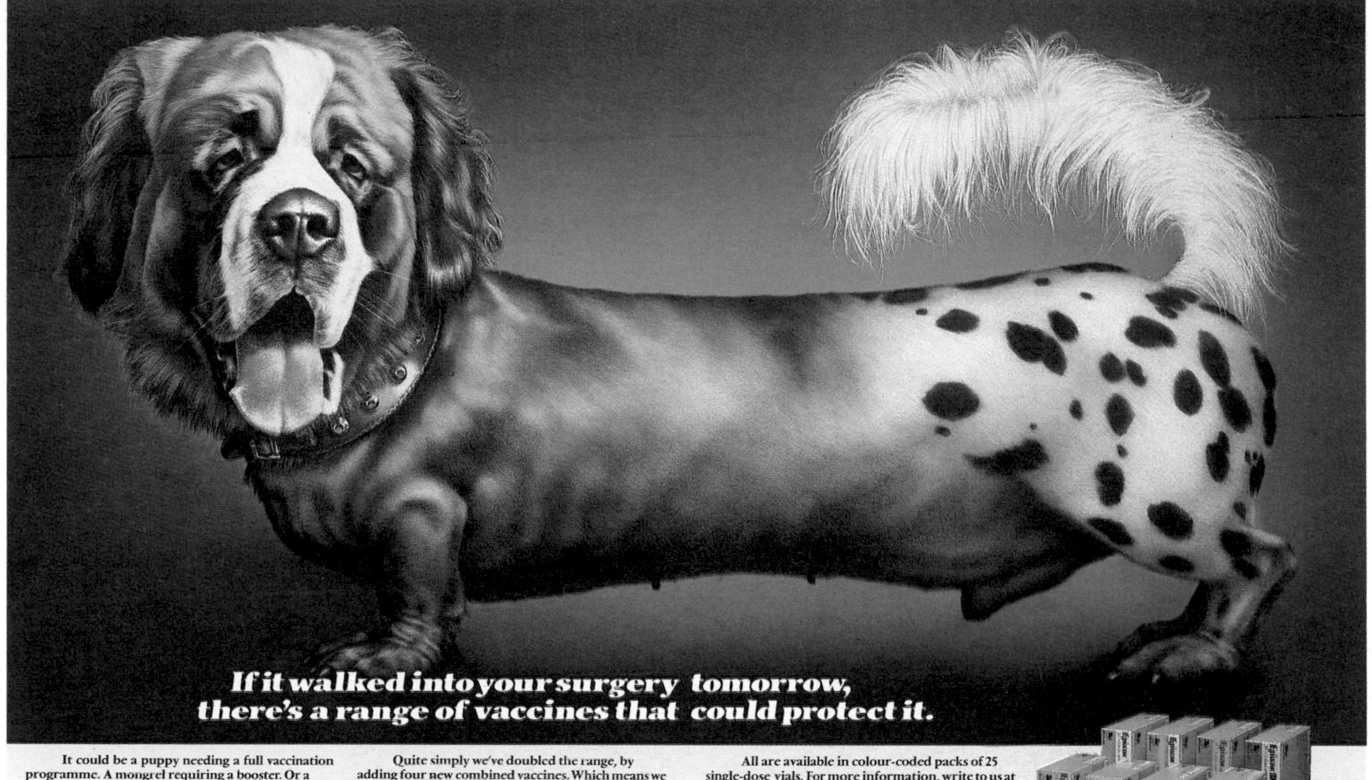

If it walked into your surgery tomorrow,
there's a range of vaccines that could protect it.

It could be a puppy needing a full vaccination programme. A mongrel requiring a booster. Or a pedigree St. Bernard about to enter Crufts.

Whatever dog confronts you, our new extended range of Epivax* vaccines gives you the flexibility to protect it against distemper, hepatitis, parvovirus and leptospirosis in whatever way you think best.

Quite simply we've doubled the range, by adding four new combined vaccines. Which means we can now give you every possible permutation.

Inactivated, live, single or multi-component. For administration alone or together.

The four additions are Epivax PL, Epivax kHL, Epivax kHPL and Epivax DH_2.

All are available in colour-coded packs of 25 single-dose vials. For more information, write to us at The Wellcome Foundation Ltd, Crewe Hall, Crewe, Cheshire CW1 1UB. Or ring us on Crewe (0270) 583151.

You'll soon see why Epivax could prove to be a vet's best friend.

Epivax from Wellcome

Wellcome

EPIVAX D CANINE DISTEMPER VACCINE (LIVING) B VET C (1970) CONTAINS NOT LESS THAN 10^3 $TCID_{50}$ OF CANINE DISTEMPER VIRUS PER DOSE. **EPIVAX DH** COMBINED CANINE DISTEMPER AND CONTAGIOUS HEPATITIS VACCINE (LIVING) CONTAINS NOT LESS THAN 10^3 $TCID_{50}$ OF CANINE DISTEMPER VIRUS AND 300 $TCID_{50}$ OF CONTAGIOUS HEPATITIS VIRUS PER DOSE. **EPIVAX DH_2** COMBINED CANINE DISTEMPER AND $ADENOVIRUS_2$ VACCINE (LIVING) CONTAINS NOT LESS THAN 10^3 $TCID_{50}$ OF CANINE DISTEMPER VIRUS AND NOT LESS THAN $10^{4.1}$ $TCID_{50}$ OF CANINE $ADENOVIRUS_2$ (CAV_2) PER DOSE. **EPIVAX P** CANINE PARVOVIRUS VACCINE (INACTIVATED) CONTAINS HOMOLOGOUS CANINE PARVOVIRUS. **EPIVAX PL** COMBINED CANINE PARVOVIRUS AND LEPTOSPIRA VACCINE (INACTIVATED) CONTAINS HOMOLOGOUS CANINE PARVOVIRUS AND COMBINED LEPTOSPIRA VACCINE PREPARED FROM CULTURES OF *L. INTERROGANS* SEROTYPES *CANICOLA* AND *HAEMORRHAGIAE*. **EPIVAX kHL** COMBINED CANINE CONTAGIOUS HEPATITIS AND LEPTOSPIRA VACCINE (INACTIVATED) CONTAINS CANINE CONTAGIOUS HEPATITIS VIRUS AND COMBINED LEPTOSPIRA VACCINE PREPARED FROM CULTURES OF *L. INTERROGANS* SEROTYPES *CANICOLA* AND *HAEMORRHAGIAE*. **EPIVAX kHPL** COMBINED CANINE CONTAGIOUS HEPATITIS, PARVOVIRUS AND LEPTOSPIRA VACCINE (INACTIVATED) CONTAINS CANINE CONTAGIOUS HEPATITIS VIRUS, HOMOLOGOUS CANINE PARVOVIRUS AND COMBINED LEPTOSPIRA VACCINE PREPARED FROM CULTURES OF *L. INTERROGANS* SEROTYPES *CANICOLA* AND *HAEMORRHAGIAE*. **LEPTOVAX* PLUS L** CONTAINS COMBINED LEPTOSPIRA VACCINE (VETERINARY) PH EUR. **DOSE:** (EPIVAX D, DH, DH_2:) THE RECONSTITUTED CONTENTS OF ONE VIAL (SEE DATA SHEETS FOR RECONSTITUTION PROCEDURE) BY S.C. INJECTION; (EPIVAX P, PL, kHL, kHPL, LEPTOVAX PLUS L:) THE CONTENTS OF ONE VIAL BY S.C. INJECTION. SEE DATA SHEETS FOR RECOMMENDED PRIMARY AND BOOSTER VACCINATION SCHEDULES. **CONTRA-INDICATIONS** DO NOT VACCINATE PUPPIES UNDER 6 MONTHS OLD WITH EPIVAX DH_2, PL, kHL OR kHPL; NOR WITH EPIVAX D IF RECONSTITUTED WITH EPIVAX kHL OR kHPL, OR EPIVAX DH IF RECONSTITUTED WITH EPIVAX PL. **WARNINGS** (LEPTOVAX PLUS L:) NIL; (ALL EPIVAX VACCINES:) DO NOT VACCINATE UNHEALTHY DOGS. DO NOT EXPOSE DOGS TO THE RISK OF INFECTION FOR AT LEAST 2 WEEKS (OR, WITH EPIVAX DH, 1 WEEK) AFTER THE FIRST DOSE. **SIDE-EFFECTS** OCCASIONAL HYPERSENSITIVITY REACTIONS; (EPIVAX DH:) CORNEAL OPACITY, USUALLY TEMPORARY, MAY VERY OCCASIONALLY OCCUR SOON AFTER VACCINATION AGAINST CONTAGIOUS HEPATITIS. ADDITIONAL INFORMATION IS AVAILABLE. **VETERINARY & AGRICULTURAL DIVISION,** THE WELLCOME FOUNDATION LTD, CREWE, CHESHIRE

*TRADE MARK.

309

310

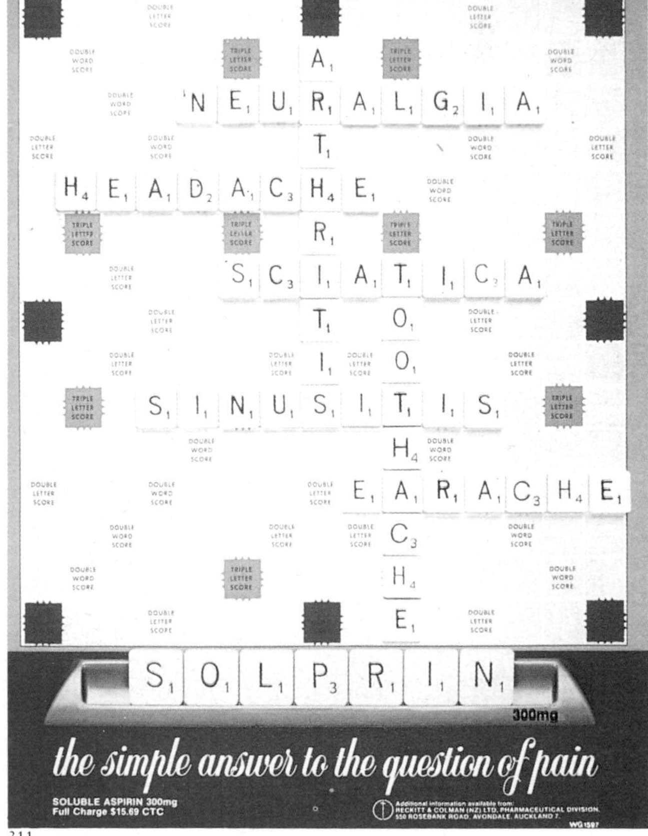

311

312
Novalucol indigestion remedy
Sweden
Agency: Young & Rubicam, Stockholm

Novalucol, says the headline, 'helps you on the job'. It does so by reducing excess stomach acid, not by putting a third arm in an unlikely place, but nobody is likely to be misled.

312

313
Kleenex toilet paper
Australia
Agency: SSC&B: Lintas, Sydney

A less revolutionary approach than in the Swedish ad for Vita Lamm, but visually elegant. Because Kleenex is positioned as the decorative brand of bathroom tissues, great attention is paid to the specially built sets used in this campaign. The ads appear as double-page spreads in women's magazines.

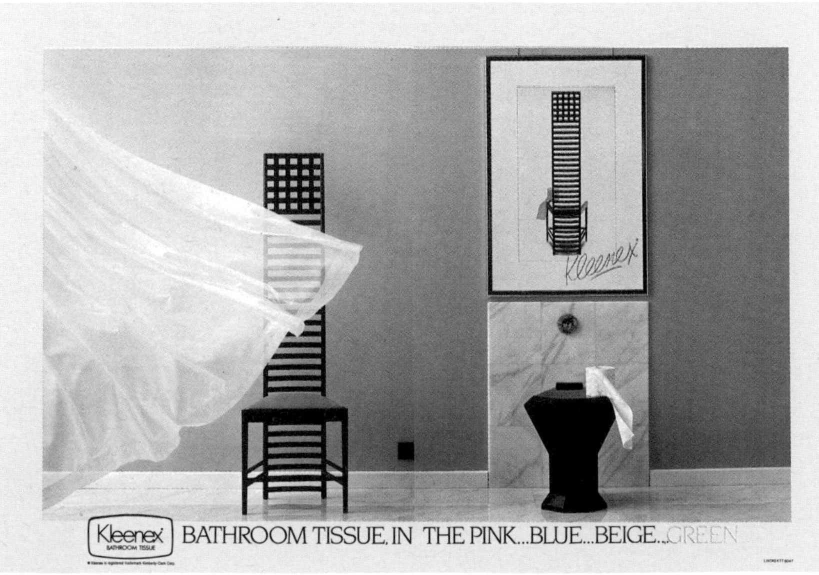

313

314, 315
Vita Lamm toilet paper
Sweden
Agency: Ted Bates 1, Stockholm

This campaign is unprecedented in Sweden, if not in the world, for showing people actually sitting on the toilet. The aim is to bring a touch of surprise to a normally low-interest product. The heading says 'Everyone does it'. Pay-off line: 'Vita Lamm. There's nothing softer.'

314

315

OLYMPUS OM4 DIE ENTSCHEIDUNG FÜR DAS PROFI-BILD.
OLYMPUS
Erleben Sie die modernste Art kreativer Bildgestaltung! Mit der neuen Olympus OM-4 – der ersten Spiegelreflexcamera mit Multi-Spotmessung Der professionelle Vorteil zu bisherigen Systemen: Sie können jetzt selektiv bis zu 8 beliebige Motivpunkte
messen. Die OM-4 speichert diese Spot-Werte. Der Cameracomputer ermittelt daraus das Belichtungs-Optimum automatisch. Entscheiden Sie jetzt selbst, welche Bildqualität in Ihren Motiven steckt! Mit der Spitzencamera im OM-System: Olympus OM-4.
Informationen beim Fachhandel. Oder direkt von Olympus, Postfach 10 49 08, 2000 Hamburg 1. Schweiz: R. Bopp AG, Zürich. Österreich: Olympus, Wien.
OLYMPUS

316

316
Olympus OM4 camera
West Germany
Agency: William Wilkens, Hamburg

You cannot get more delightfully colourful than this portrait by photographer Uwe Ommer. The heading says the Olympus is the camera to pick for professional-quality pictures.

317
Pentax Super A camera
United Kingdom
Agency: KMP Partnership, London

The average adult male brain weighs the same as the Super A with motordrive, says the copy. That provides the justification for the striking visual juxtaposition, as also does the camera's electronic sophistication, with six operating modes.

318
Pentax PC35AFM camera
United Kingdom
Agency: KMP Partnership, London

Very simple, very effective idea. The copy itself makes the visual point. As the headline says, only the few words printed in red refer to what the users of this foolproof automatic camera have to do for themselves.

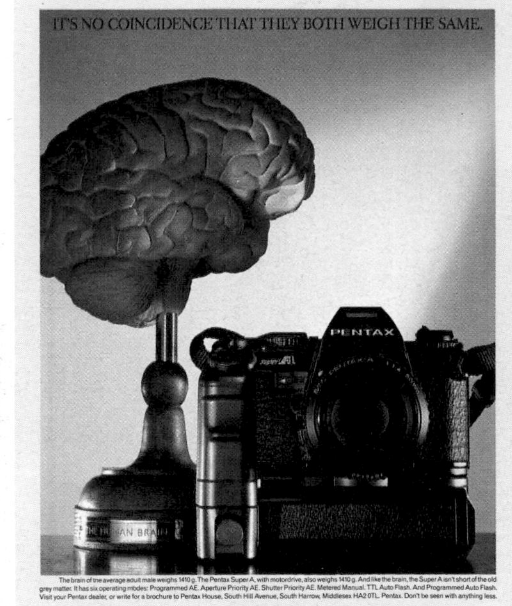

317

IF IT'S BLACK, THE CAMERA DOES IT FOR YOU. IF IT'S RED, YOU DO IT.

Is our new camera a highly sophisticated beast?

Or basically a simple one?

Read the following step-by-step instructions (printed in red) then decide.

Slide the red catch, to open the lens cover.

This releases a safety device in the camera that stops you taking pictures by accident. (No more moody shots of the inside of your pocket or handbag.)

If you've just put in a new film, you can forget the old routine of continually pressing the button and winding-on till a '1' appears.

The film automatically winds on to '1' when you close the camera back. You'll know it's winding-on properly by looking at an indicator.

And you'll know there's film in the camera because you'll see it there, through a window.

If you're using the new DX film, by the way, the camera will have automatically set the film speed for you. It can read this information electronically, from a code on the film cassette.

Clever, eh?

But now it's time for you to do some work.

Press the red button, to take the picture.

As you lightly press the button, a photo-electric sensor measures the amount of light.

The camera then automatically sets itself to the right shutter speed and lens aperture.

But not before it's told you what it's doing, via a coloured lamp in the viewfinder.

Green means 'ok to shoot,' red means 'hold on a minute.'

While all this is going on, the camera is busy focusing itself.

Using its pair of piercing auto focus eyes.

The left eye sends out a fine infra-red beam that bounces off the subject, and is then reflected back to the right eye.

Sensors in the camera then measure the angle between the outward and inward beam and set the lens to the right focusing range.

All in less than one second.

And all regardless of whether it's light or dark. (Infra-red beams can't tell the difference.)

Keep on pressing the button, and the camera will take the picture, then automatically wind on the film ready for the next shot.

The end of those "Have I wound on the film?" doubts.

So far, we've assumed that a green light flashed in the viewfinder and gave you the ok to shoot. What if you see a red light?

Along with a 'beep-beep' sound, this tells you that there's not enough light to take the picture without flash.

And thus presents you with yet another arduous task.

Press down the red lever, to use flash.

The built-in pop-up flash will now pop up.

The unit charges itself in about six seconds. When the 'flash ready' lamp glows amber, go ahead and shoot.

If you want to be in the picture yourself, use the self-timer lever.

With or without flash, this delays the shutter release by about ten seconds.

When you hear a 'beep-beep,' and see a red lamp flicker, pose, and put on your best smile.

Three seconds later, the camera will take the picture.

By now, you may be wondering if there's anything else the camera can do for itself.

There is. When you've taken the last picture, a motor will rewind the film for you.

You'll then have to take the film to be developed.

If you can manage that, all on your own.

See the new PC35 AF-M at your Pentax dealer or write for a brochure to this address:

Pentax House, South Hill Avenue, South Harrow, Middlesex HA2 0LT.

Pentax. Don't be seen with anything less.

IT'S NO COINCIDENCE THAT THEY BOTH WEIGH THE SAME.
PENTAX

318

319

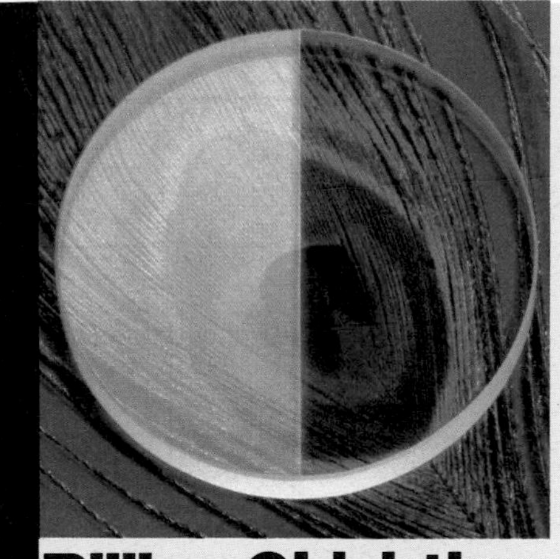

320

321

322

319
Yashica TAF camera
West Germany
Agency: Segmenta, Hamburg

A Kodacolor ad by Young & Rubicam, Frankfurt, in last year's selection, used the owl's piercing eye as an image of photographic efficiency. Here it is the eagle's eye which is compared with the Carl Zeiss lens in the camera.

320, 321
Nikon cameras
West Germany
Agency: Hildmann Simon Rempen & Schmitz/SMS, Düsseldorf

Two of a series of beautifully laid-out ads for Nikon combining strong visuals with clear, explanatory copy. 'Cheap lenses have their price' says one headline. It is implied, though not actually stated, that the right side of the peacock feather is being viewed through a Nikon lens, but not the left side. The other ad, featuring the camera-toting tourist with the flowery shirt, says 'Foolproof. And from Nikon.'

322
Agfachrome CT200 film
France
Agency: Ecom, Paris

'The colours of achievement' says the headline on this ad which claims Agfa has developed a film which can accurately reproduce 'the true colours of life'.

323
Fujicolor HR1600 film
West Germany
Agency: Lintas, Hamburg

The product, claimed to be the world's fastest colour film, enables clear pictures to be taken of high-speed action or in poor light. The image of the champagne cork popping out, therefore, makes a relevant selling point as well as symbolising the advent of something to celebrate. The headline says 'To better times'.

324
Ilford HR film
United Kingdom
Agency: Aspect Advertising, London

The artist Peter Blake apparently is in the habit of painting from photographs rather than from life. This ad is raised above the level of a mere endorsement by its attractive composition, including the wall shadow of Blake at work.

325
Tamron lenses
United Kingdom
Agency: Doyle Dane Bernbach, London

The lens described in the copy is one with a zoom range of 35mm to 210mm. Its versatility is conveyed by means of the five different-sized, interlocking pictures of the same nude sunbathing scene. Note the coyness with which the genitals are concealed while the women's breasts are well exposed. This is sexual titillation trying to look respectable.

326
Ilford Multigrade II paper
United Kingdom
Agency: Aspect Advertising, London

The 'tough guys' and 'softies' are reproduced in harder and softer tones on Ilford's versatile photographic paper.

323

324

325

IT ONLY TAKES A MOMENT TO TU RN TOUGH GUYS INTO SOFTIES.

With Ilford's new Multigrade II system, you get every contrast grade on a single sheet of paper.

And you can change grades in a matter of moments. Because instead of fumbling around for the right paper, you simply change a filter in your enlarger.

(For the ultimate in contrast range, the system includes half-grade filters as well as all six whole grades.)

If you're the type who likes a bit of adventure in the darkroom, you can even make prints which combine several different grades.

Just as we've done here, with the muscle men, under the masterful eye of Terence Donovan.

What you gain in flexibility, you don't lose in terms of quality either.

Multigrade II goes from a base white which is pure white, to a maximum black which is rich and solid.

Surprisingly, it costs no more than ordinary photographic paper. And it comes in gloss, pearl and matt finishes.

As for the filters, you'll find that your Ilford stockist is now offering them at a very special introductory price.

And once you've made a saving on the filters, think what you're going to save on paper. Because with Multigrade II, you need never have a single sheet lying around and going to waste.

ILFORD MULTIGRADE II

THE PAPER THAT MAKES EVERY GRADE.

326

327
Kodacolor VR film
France
Agency: Young & Rubicam, Paris

'Accurate enough to fool you' is the caption. The kitten with its paw in a photographed pool is reminiscent of the Kenyon & Eckhardt campaign for Kodak in Thailand, sampled in last year's edition, where one ad had a cat looking longingly at a lifelike photograph of a fish.

328
Kodak Vericolor film
Spain
Agency: McCann-Erickson, Madrid

This ad tells professional photographers of the accuracy with which Vericolor reproduces colours of all kinds, those of natural skin as well as those of a mask. Headline: 'Cold, Heat'. The doubling of the picture is to illustrate the claim that nothing is lost when enlargements are made.

329
Kodacolor VR
Denmark
Agency: Young & Rubicam, Copenhagen

'Kodak captures more small details than any other colour film' is the claim here. That may or may not be true, but the picture is certainly detailed in its sensuality.

327

328

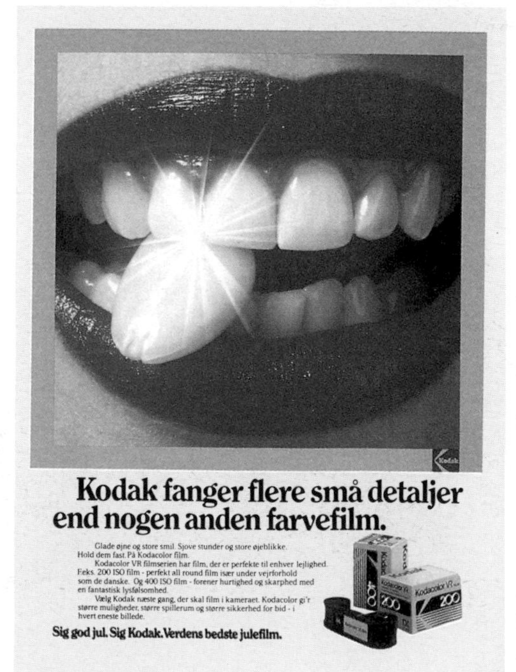

329

330, 331
Kodachrome 64
West Germany
Agency: Young & Rubicam, Frankfurt

This campaign exhibits the work of various photographers together with their tributes to the quality of the film. In one ad Osamu Hayasaki of Japan says 'This film guarantees the finest distinctions, even in white. That's fantastic.' In the other Alberto dell'Orto of Italy boasts of achieving 'more dramatic' effects.

330

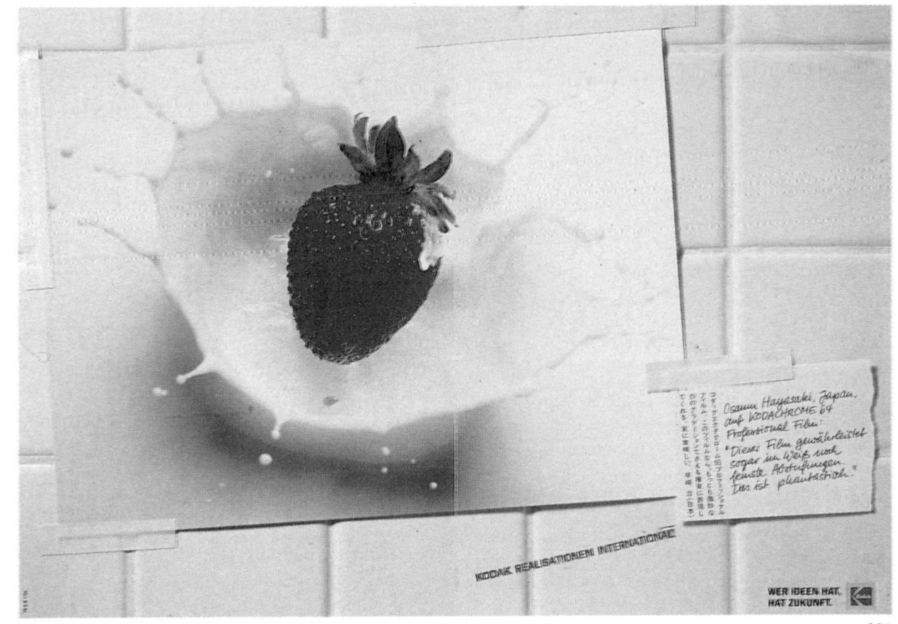

331

332
Kodacolor VR film
United Kingdom
Agency: McCann-Erickson, London

One of a series of photographs by David Montgomery which mimic famous paintings. Some of the pictures are so similar to the canvases which inspired them that some readers have been misled into believing they were looking at photos *of* the paintings.

332

333, 334
The Spastics Society
United Kingdom
Agency: Benton & Bowles, London

The background to this campaign is a high degree of public ignorance about cerebral palsy. It is aimed both at remedying this situation and at raising awareness of the Society.

"Just because I couldn't speak, they thought I had nothing to say."
MY NAME IS JENNY.
I HAVE CEREBRAL PALSY.
BUT THANKS TO THIS WORD
PROCESSOR, I'VE NOW GOT
A SAY IN MY FUTURE.
It's not that people don't care, it's just that they don't think. THE SPASTICS SOCIETY

333

"They only ever see the chair, not the person sitting in it."

JOB APPLICANTS
Please wait here

It's not that people don't care, it's just that they don't think. THE SPASTICS SOCIETY

334

THE NUMBER OF CHILDREN
WHO DIE THROUGH
HUNGER IS
EQUIVALENT TO
THREE HIROSHIMAS
EVERY WEEK

We all live in fear of a potential nuclear war. But millions of people in developing countries are part of another holocaust.

A silent holocaust. Hunger.

The statistics are grim. 500 million people go hungry every day. (That's the size of the entire population of Europe.) And 40,000 children will die from hunger-related diseases between now and tomorrow.

Yet the world produces enough grain to give every person on earth a nourishing 3,000 calories a day. Which is why Oxfam has launched a new campaign of hope.

We've called it 'Hungry for Change.' And it stems from a conviction that change is not beyond our reach. But we cannot act alone. We need you.

First, arm yourself with the facts. (You'll find them in our free information pack). When you're fully informed, spread the word. We'll tell you how you can campaign for the changes the poor so urgently need.

Please give us your support. Get your pen and fill in the coupon. Because only by working together can we turn back the tide of hunger.

OXFAM

I AGREE THAT HUNGER IN THE WORLD IN 1984 IS AN OUTRAGE. I'D LIKE TO JOIN THE 'HUNGRY FOR CHANGE' CAMPAIGN. PLEASE SEND ME YOUR FREE INFORMATION PACK. SEND TO: GUY STRINGER, OXFAM ROOM CP1, FREEPOST, OXFORD OX2 7BR. MEANWHILE, I ENCLOSE A DONATION OF £______ FOR CREDIT CARD DONATIONS, RING 0865 56916.

NAME______ ADDRESS______ POSTCODE______

335

335, 336, 337
Oxfam
United Kingdom
Agency: Fletcher Shelton Delaney, London

The macabre illustrations, by Peter Till and Peter Brookes, are quite appropriate to the theme of this campaign to educate public opinion about the extent of hunger in the Third World. Because the campaign, which focuses on the economic imbalance between rich and poor nations, is not aimed at direct fund-raising for the charity, it was decided to adopt a 'political/editorial' style.

SOARING INTEREST RATES: WHO REALLY PAYS?

For the poor in the Third World, the debt crisis is not something to read about in the newspapers. It is a matter of survival.

Hunger has always been rife; but it is now reaching an inconceivable scale. We have all seen the horrifying pictures of Ethiopia today, but severe hunger is not confined to that one corner of Africa; 500 million go hungry every day. (That's the size of the entire population of Europe.) And the figures are on the increase. Yet a look at the past decade's economic policies shows that the rich countries of the North have much to answer for.

Financial Collapse

In 1973, the price of oil doubled twice. The poorer nations had no alternative but to borrow heavily from the banks of the industrialised world. The banks were eager to oblige; they were enjoying large surplus funds from the oil-producing countries who had raised the price in the first place.

Then in 1979 the unthinkable happened: interest rates charged by the major banks started to soar and the price of oil doubled again.

Already hopelessly in debt, and now in the shadow of world recession, many developing nations were brought to the brink of financial [illegible]

Trapped

Fearing the impact such a collapse would have on the world monetary system, the rich banks brought in the IMF and jointly agreed new loans. But as these loans only covered the interest payments they were mere paper transactions.

Furthermore, the loans came on condition that Third World governments cut back on spending and build up exports. In some countries these harsh policies have eased the debt problem for the banks. But the sacrifices in human terms have been severe. Land that should be feeding people is producing food for European and North American consumers. Thousands of acres are being devoted to raising crops for European livestock, whose milk and butter end up as part of the rich world's food mountains. Health care, already basic, is now seriously threatened. And government projects such as irrigation schemes have been abandoned.

Such austerity measures have had a drastic effect on the poor. They are scarcely able to feed themselves. They are trapped in an economy where inflation soars. And they face a daily struggle to survive. Many don't.

In fact 40,000 children die through hunger every day. Which is why Oxfam has launched a new campaign.

Hungry for Change

We've called it 'Hungry for Change'. And it stems from a conviction that change is not beyond our reach. Because by publicising the injustice of world hunger, we can attempt to penetrate the barrier of the developed world's indifference. But we need your support.

How You Can Help

It may seem like an impossible task. But there are many ways you can help. They may only be small steps, but eventually they can lead to change.

First, arm yourself with the facts. (You'll find them in our information pack shown below.) When you're informed, [illegible]

Talk to your friends, family and colleagues.

We'll be inviting you to campaign with us. And we'll tell you how you can raise funds for projects designed to help the poorer people help themselves. Please give us your support. And please fill in the coupon. Because every one of us has it within our power to help. But only together can we turn back the tide of hunger.

OXFAM

I AGREE THAT HUNGER IN THE WORLD IN 1984 IS AN OUTRAGE. I'D LIKE TO JOIN THE 'HUNGRY FOR CHANGE' CAMPAIGN. PLEASE SEND ME YOUR FREE INFORMATION PACK.
Send to: Guy Stringer, Oxfam Room PE03 Freepost, Oxford OX2 7BR.

NAME______ ADDRESS______
______ POSTCODE______ MEANWHILE I ENCLOSE A DONATION OF £______ FOR CREDIT CARD DONATIONS, RING 0865 56916

336

WHO'S GETTING FAT ON THE LAND THAT SHOULD BE FEEDING THE HUNGRY?

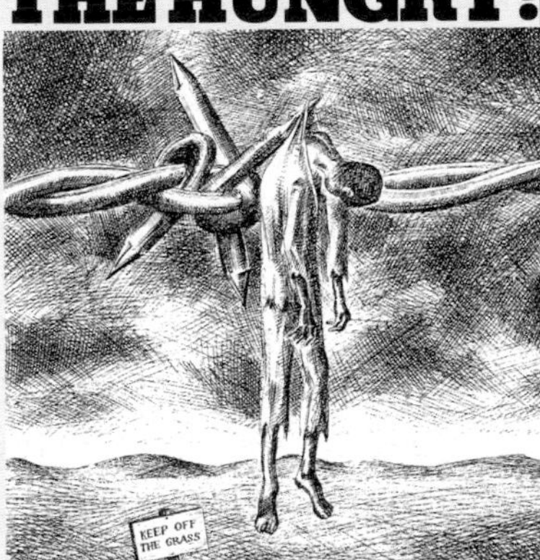
KEEP OFF
THE GRASS

Every day, thousands of Latin Americans go hungry while vast acres of their land produce crops for the rich world's consumers. The policy is called 'export cropping'. And it isn't confined to Latin America. It happens in Africa and much of Asia too.

In fact, export cropping is now practised so widely that it takes up more than a quarter of cultivated land in the Third World. Land that could be used by hungry families to grow their own food.

This lack of land leads to untold hunger and deprivation for literally millions. But what is equally disturbing is the role the economically developed world plays in encouraging this practice.

GREED

First comes greed. The rich nations, comprising 30% of the world's population, consume over 80% of its resources. (Not because they need to; the UK alone swallows over £500 million worth of slimming aids every year.*) But there is another kind of greed, equally unpalatable, that promotes increased export cropping.

Financial greed.

CRIPPLED

In 1973, the price of oil doubled twice. The poorer nations had no option but to borrow heavily from the banks of the industrialised world. These banks, overwhelmed with surplus funds from the oil-producing countries, channelled massive loans to Third World countries, and saddled them with floating interest rates.

These interest rates have since soared so high, they have crippled many of the poorer nations.

Today, the debt crisis continues. And in an attempt to stem the problem, Third World governments have been forced to step up export cropping.

In human terms, the sacrifices have been severe. The poor are scarcely able to feed themselves. They are trapped in an economy where inflation soars. And they face a daily struggle to survive.

Many don't. Every single day, 40,000 children die through hunger. Which is why Oxfam has launched its campaign.

HUNGRY FOR CHANGE

We've called it 'Hungry for Change'. And it stems from a conviction that change is not beyond our reach. Because by publicising the injustice of world hunger, we can attempt to penetrate the barrier of the rich world's indifference.

But we need your support.

HOW YOU CAN HELP

It may seem like an impossible task. But there are many ways you can help. They may only be small steps, but eventually they can lead to change.

First, arm yourself with the facts. (You'll find them in our information pack shown below.) When you're informed, spread the word. Talk to your friends, family and colleagues. We'll be inviting you to campaign with us. And we'll tell you how you can raise funds for projects designed to help the poorer people help themselves. Please give us your support. And please fill in the coupon. Because every one of us has it within our power to help. But only together can we turn back the tide of hunger.

OXFAM

*Euromonitor Slimming Products Report 1982.

I AGREE THAT HUNGER IN THE WORLD IN 1984 IS AN OUTRAGE. I'D LIKE TO JOIN THE 'HUNGRY FOR CHANGE' CAMPAIGN. PLEASE SEND ME YOUR FREE INFORMATION PACK.
Send to: Guy Stringer, Oxfam Room SP07 Freepost, Oxford OX2 7BR.

NAME______ ADDRESS______
______ POSTCODE______ MEANWHILE I ENCLOSE A DONATION OF £______ FOR CREDIT CARD DONATIONS, RING 0865 56916.

337

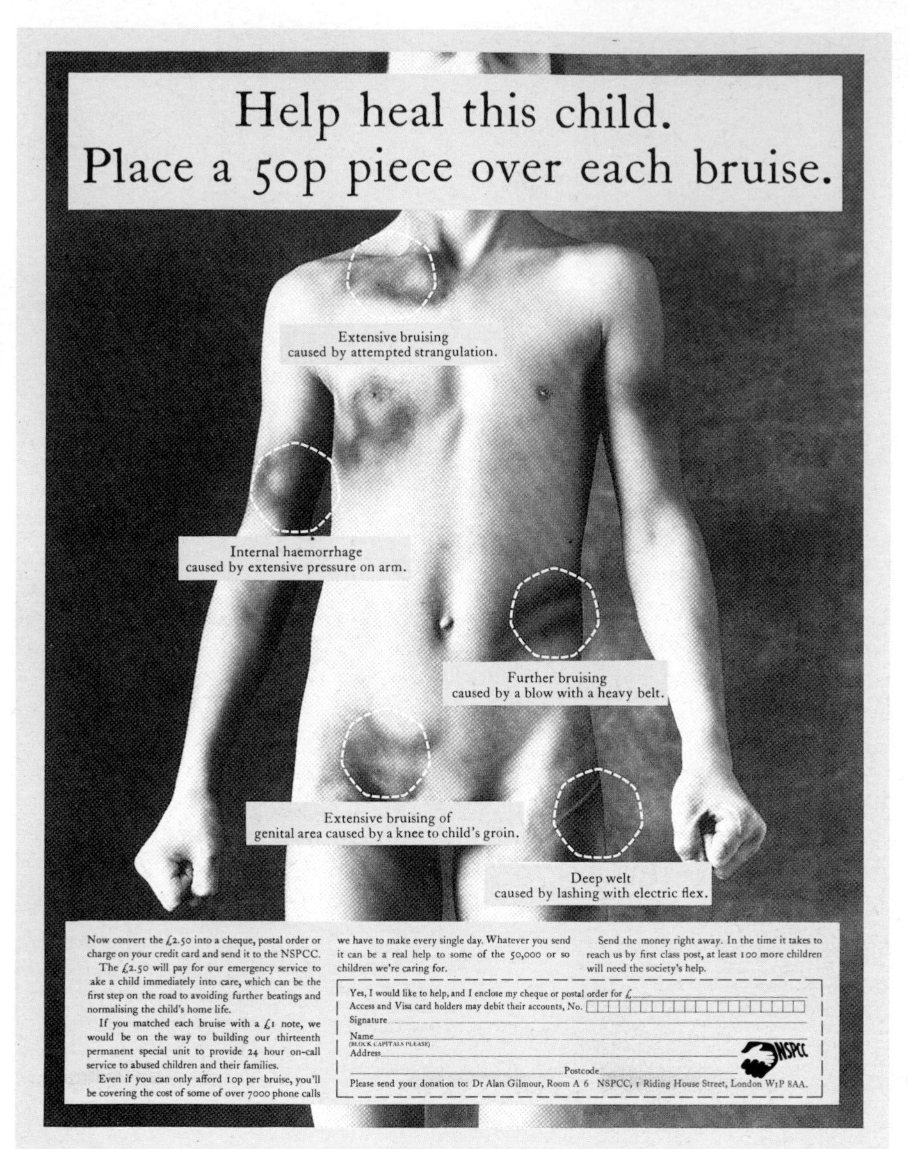

338

No sense, no feelings?
They may not think as fast but they feel as deeply.

340

340
Mencap (Royal Society for Mentally Handicapped Children and Adults)
United Kingdom
Agency: Young & Rubicam, London

Rather similar in approach to the Spastics Society campaign, this also attempts to confront the reader with the facts about handicapped people instead of common misconceptions.

338, 339
National Society for the Prevention of Cruelty to Children
United Kingdom
Agency: Saatchi & Saatchi Compton, London

Strong, provocative ads which recall some of those, for the Health Education Council, with which Charles Saatchi made his reputation years ago, though the copywriter here is not him but John Bacon. With their invitations to perform immediate actions, the headlines are involving in a way rare in advertising. The ads were inspired by reports of actual events.

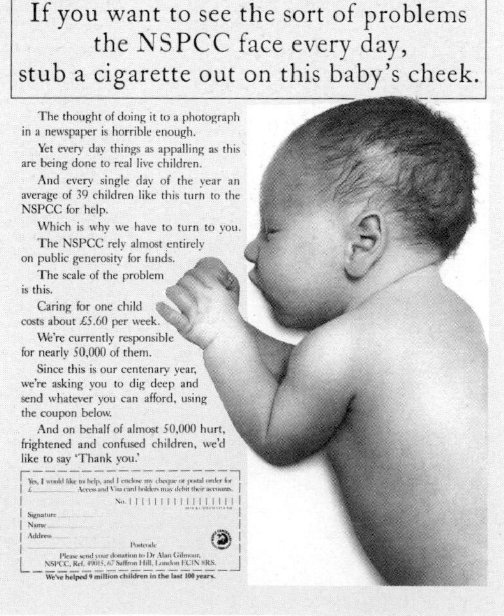

If you want to see the sort of problems
the NSPCC face every day,
stub a cigarette out on this baby's cheek.
The thought of doing it to a photograph in a newspaper is horrible enough.
Yet every day things as appalling as this are being done to real live children.
And every single day of the year an average of 39 children like this turn to the NSPCC for help.
Which is why we have to turn to you.
The NSPCC rely almost entirely on public generosity for funds.
The scale of the problem is this.
Caring for one child costs about £5.60 per week.
We're currently responsible for nearly 50,000 of them.
Since this is our centenary year, we're asking you to dig deep and send whatever you can afford, using the coupon below.
And on behalf of almost 50,000 hurt, frightened and confused children, we'd like to say 'Thank you.'
Help heal this child.
Place a 50p piece over each bruise.
Extensive bruising
caused by attempted strangulation.
Internal haemorrhage
caused by extensive pressure on arm.
Further bruising
caused by a blow with a heavy belt.
Extensive bruising of
genital area caused by a knee to child's groin.
Deep welt
caused by lashing with electric flex.
Now convert the £2.50 into a cheque, postal order or charge on your credit card and send it to the NSPCC.
The £2.50 will pay for our emergency service to ake a child immediately into care, which can be the first step on the road to avoiding further beatings and normalising the child's home life.
If you matched each bruise with a £1 note, we would be on the way to building our thirteenth permanent special unit to provide 24 hour on-call service to abused children and their families.
Even if you can only afford 10p per bruise, you'll be covering the cost of some of over 7000 phone calls we have to make every single day. Whatever you send it can be a real help to some of the 50,000 or so children we're caring for.
Send the money right away. In the time it takes to reach us by first class post, at least 100 more children will need the society's help.
Yes, I would like to help, and I enclose my cheque or postal order for £
Access and Visa card holders may debit their accounts.
No.
Signature
Name
(BLOCK CAPITALS PLEASE)
Address
Postcode
Please send your donation to Dr Alan Gilmour,
NSPCC, Ref. 49015, 67 Saffron Hill, London EC1N 8RS.
We've helped 9 million children in the last 100 years.

339

341
Alcoholics Anonymous
Brazil
Agency: MPM, Rio de Janeiro

A man crucified on a wine glass – the image says it all. Caption: 'Alcoholics Anonymous can be his salvation.'

342
Alcohol age limit legislation
United States
Agency: Young & Rubicam, New York

Remarkably the advertiser behind this grim message in support of a Bill to raise the minimum age for purchasing alcohol is an insurance company, Metropolitan Life. No doubt the ad was also intended to promote favourable opinions of the company, but that is not what the copy is about. Note the visual resemblance to the AEG ad by Y&R, London in the Industrial section.

343
American Cancer Society
United States
Agency: Young & Rubicam, New York

An interesting attempt to marry self-interest and altruism. Explaining the visual, copy says: 'If you could look into the eyes of generations yet to come you would be there. Because immortality lies not in the things you leave behind but in the people your life has touched.'

342

341

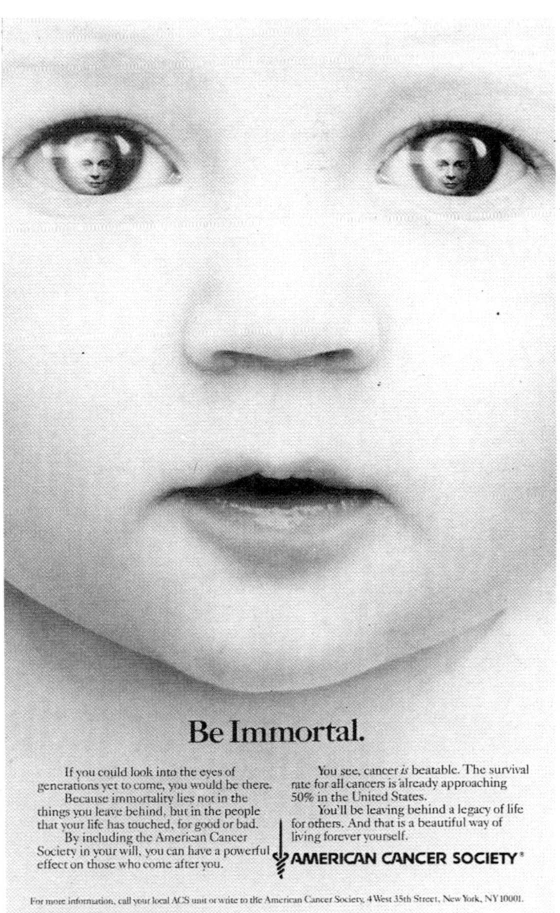

343

344
Nursing recruitment
United Kingdom
Agency: TBWA, London

The anatomical jokes are the sugar on a serious pill, namely the message that nursing takes brain as well as emotion.

345
Anti-jaundice campaign
India
Agency: Shilpi Advertising, Ahmedabad

The syringe-cum-gun symbolises the danger of injections with unsterilised syringes. The ad ran during a severe outbreak of hepatitis B in Ahmedabad, partly caused by the use of unsterilised syringes.

346, 347
Health information
Norway
Agency: Ogilvy & Mather, Oslo

These menacing distortions of everyday objects – the snake-like vacuum cleaner and the shark-toothed chair – illustrate a campaign by the Norwegian Government Information Service to make people pay more attention to keeping fit. The vacuum cleaner ad warns of the physical stresses which can be incurred through heavy housework. It is headed 'Housework is no joke.' The other ad, headed 'Important message to those who sit a lot at work,' talks of the aches and pains caused by a sedentary life. Both invite readers to send away for a book on 'The body's sore points'.

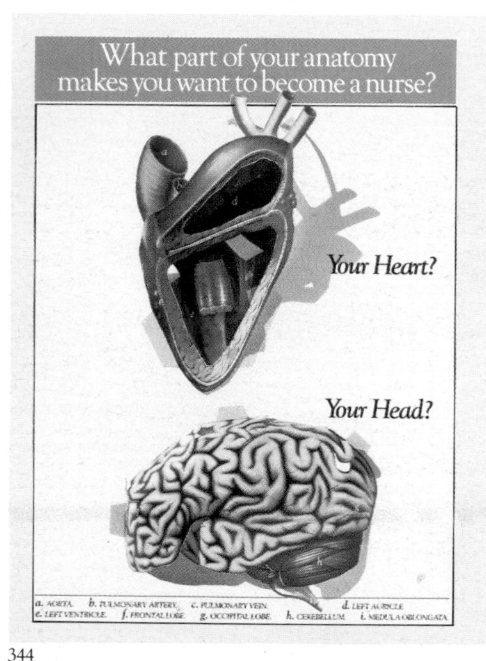

Deep-down, your heart may be hinting that you've got what it takes to become a nurse.
Before noble stirrings nudge you any further, be sure you have fixed firmly in your head exactly what kind of nurse you have in mind.
There's more than one kind of nurse. Some wear uniform, others don't. Many don't find themselves near a hospital from one week to the next.
All are equally important. All with their own separate training. All requiring different skills.
Uppermost, all demand that you have a head on your shoulders and a brain between your ears.

RMN

The letters stand for Registered Mental Nurse.
Anyone, at anytime, can become mentally ill. It can happen when normal things, like stress or depression, prevent you from living life normally.
But like appendicitis or a heart complaint, mental illness can be effectively treated. Over half the people who actually need to be admitted to psychiatric hospitals are home within a month.
An RMN is perhaps more mature. You can't help a person cope with their problems if you've never had to face up to problems of your own.
Certainly an RMN doesn't expect fast returns. A lifetime can't be pieced together in a day. And because sheltering someone from the outside world may not be the best way for him to come to terms with it, some RMNs work in the community, rather than in hospitals.
To qualify takes three years of ward and community experience, practical assessment and studying for written exams.

RNMH

Whereas mental illness occurs when a normal mind ceases to function normally, mental handicap is usually present at birth, or from an early age.
A Registered Nurse for the Mentally Handicapped is a key member of a highly trained team of professionals that includes psychologists, therapists and social workers.
Their objective: to help mentally handicapped people reach their full potential. To help them become as independent as possible.
It can take many months to teach a mentally handicapped person to put his socks and shoes on by himself. Or to tell the difference between a 10p and a £1 coin. But away from institutional care, out in the community, unless he can understand this he can't buy himself a tea and sandwich in a café. Or chocolate from a slot machine.
A mentally handicapped person *can* learn. It simply takes longer, demanding enormous patience, intelligence and intuition on behalf of the nurse.
There will be times when you feel you're getting nowhere. But although progress is slow and rewards small, results are great.
Most mentally handicapped people are now able to live outside hospitals.
Many holding down jobs.
Something they might never have achieved on their own.

RGN

Like an RMN, and an RNMH, to qualify as a Registered General Nurse takes three long, hard years' training.
During this time, the image of the uniformed angel of mercy flitting from bed to bed fades dramatically.
As the only person in continuous day-to-day contact with patients, an RGN has to constantly assess the condition of each patient on the ward, plan how best to care for them, put the plan into operation and keep a close record of all steps taken.
Wherever RGNs are based, the situations they find themselves in can vary enormously.
For example, a 19 year old girl has severe facial lacerations. She went head-first through a windscreen. She's worried about what her fiancé will think when he sees her. This is not helping her recovery.
How would you prepare *him* before he walks into the ward?
Needless to say, as part of the training to become an RGN, an RNMH or an RMN, you'll learn to cope. You'll also study the human body.
Long before that, at the interview, you'll be expected to demonstrate where your head is in relation to your heart.
For further information, write to the Chief Nursing Officer, PO Box 702 (3R/121), London SW20 8SZ.

Nursing

344

The injection that can cure you can give you a killer disease

Contaminated syringes and needles are spreading Hepatitis type B, a disease that can be fatal. So take an injection only when it is absolutely essential. When you take one, make sure that the syringe and needle have been autoclaved or sterilized by boiling for atleast 15 minutes. Dabbing the instrument with spirit does not kill the virus. Only a duly authorised doctor can give injections.

Guard against jaundice.

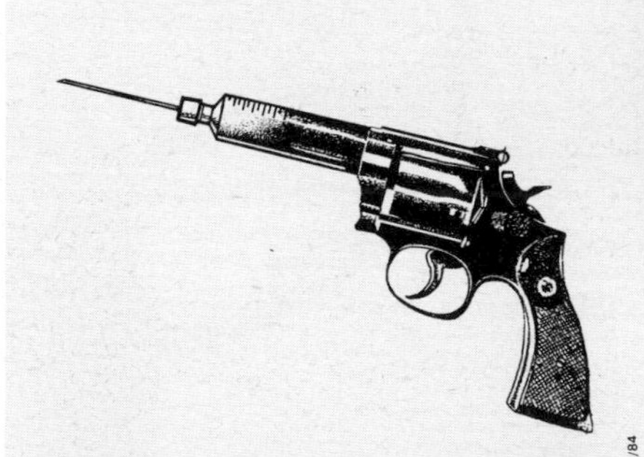

Ahmedabad Municipal Corporation

AMC 31/84

345

Husarbeid er ingen spøk

Det har du kanskje allerede erfart. Ryggsmerter hører til de vanligste plager som forekommer. Plager som rammer store deler av befolkningen – før eller senere.

Til tross for at mye nytt utstyr letter husarbeidet betraktelig, blir heller ikke du som jobber hjemme spart for disse plagene. Husarbeidet kan utsette deg for belastningssykdommer. Hos de aller fleste kommer uhumskhetene av langvarige og for store påkjenninger. Strekk ut kroppen og ta en pust i bakken. Det hjelper med forandring og variasjon. Hjelpemidlene du bruker er dessuten ofte dårlig tilpasset kroppen din. En støvsuger med for kort skaft kan ta knekken på selv den sterkeste rygg. Og hvordan er det med høyden på kjøkkenbenken din, eller på arbeidsbordet? Sjansen er dessuten stor for at dine hverdagsløft er gale.

Gjør ditt for å beskytte kroppen

Belastningssykdommene er blitt vår folkesykdom nr. 1. Skal vi stanse denne utviklingen, må vi gjøre noe med problemet. Vi må bli mer oppmerksomme på farene, både på arbeidsplassen og hjemme.

Sender du inn kupongen til høyre, vil du få tilsendt en bok som forteller deg mer om belastningssykdommer, hvorfor vi får dem og hvordan de kan forebygges.

Boka gir gode tips om hvordan løfteteknikk, arbeidsstillinger og riktig tilrettelegging og organisering av arbeidet kan verne kroppen din.

Tungt husarbeid utsetter deg for belastningssykdommer. Mange blir angrepet i nakke, skuldre eller rygg.

Husarbeid er ingen spøk. Sørg for at utstyret er tilpasset deg slik at du unngår uheldige arbeidsstillinger. Unngå for mange og tunge løft.

Send meg boka «Kroppens ømme punkter».
Navn: ______
Adresse: ______
Postnr./-sted: ______
Ant. bokmål: ___ Ant. nynorsk: ___
Boka vil bli tilsendt sammen med et innbetalingskort på kr 39,– + porto.
Kupongen sendes til Statens informasjonstjeneste, Postboks 8026, Dep. 0030 Oslo 1.
Holdningskampanjen for kroppen din
Kommunal- og arbeidsdepartementet/Sosialdepartementet/ Statens informasjonstjeneste 3E/84

346

Viktig melding til deg som sitter mye på jobben

90% av den norske befolkning får plager i rygg/nakke/skuldre i løpet av sitt liv. Og du som sitter mye på jobben er spesielt utsatt.

Det finnes utallige måter å sitte på, og vi har lett for å innta stillinger som virker behagelige i øyeblikket. Men, selv om du sitter riktig fra starten av, bør du ikke sitte for lenge i samme stilling. Reis deg opp, beveg deg litt og varier i gode sittestillinger.

Riktig utstyr på arbeidsplassen

Arbeidsgiveren har et spesielt ansvar for å legge forholdene til rette slik at du unngår uheldige belastninger på jobben. At utstyret skal være tilpasset den enkelte er en selvfølge.

Gjør ditt for å beskytte kroppen

Belastningssykdommene er blitt vår folkesykdom nr. 1. Skal vi stanse denne utviklingen, må vi gjøre noe med problemet. Vi må bli mer oppmerksomme på farene, både på arbeidsplassen og hjemme, og lære mer om hvordan vi kan unngå disse sykdommene.

Sender du inn kupongen til høyre, vil du få tilsendt en bok som forteller deg mer om belastningssykdommer, hvorfor vi får dem og hvordan de kan forebygges.

Boka gir gode tips om hvordan løfteteknikk, arbeidsstillinger og riktig tilrettelegging og organisering av arbeidet kan verne kroppen din.

Det å sitte kan være farligere enn du tror. Visste du at ryggen din er utsatt for større belastning når du sitter enn når du står? Reis deg opp og beveg deg litt av og til.

Send meg boka «Kroppens ømme punkter».
Navn: ______
Adresse: ______
Postnr./-sted: ______
Ant. bokmål: ___ Ant. nynorsk: ___
Boka vil bli tilsendt sammen med et innbetalingskort på kr 39,– + porto.
Kupongen sendes til Statens informasjonstjeneste, Postboks 8026, Dep. 0030 Oslo 1.
Holdningskampanjen for kroppen din
Kommunal- og arbeidsdepartementet/Sosialdepartementet/ Statens informasjonstjeneste 3G/84

347

348
Road safety
Norway
Agency: Heltberg Creative Service, Oslo

One of a dramatic series of ads with the pay-off line 'Don't let children pay for your negligence.' This one tells of a six-year-old boy whose parents failed to teach him how to use his bicycle properly. Headline: 'Kare got a bike on his sixth birthday.'

348

349
Crime prevention
Norway
Agency: Heltberg Creative Service, Oslo

This lively scene, like a still from a feature film, comes from a campaign by the Norwegian Crime Prevention Council. The headline says 'Put the thief out of work', and copy urges readers not to buy stolen goods and thus encourage crime.

349

350
Army recruitment
United States
Agency: N.W. Ayer, New York

This ad presents the US Army as a high-tech organisation, with the aim of attracting high school graduates. Hence the picture showing how 'thermal imaging' enables soldiers to see at night.

350

351
The Engineering Council
United Kingdom
Agency: Wight Collins Rutherford Scott, London

The Engineering Council was set up to promote the education of engineers in Britain, regarded as urgent because, as copy says, 'Japan produces 10 times as many engineering graduates.' The picture is of a set built specially for the ad but bearing a close resemblance to Westminster Abbey's Poets' Corner, with the addition of engineering symbols.

352
Army officer recruitment
United Kingdom
Agency: Collett Dickenson Pearce & Partners, London

Both pictures and story – concerned with the experiences of a young Army lieutenant in the British contingent of the multinational force in Beirut – are fascinating. Whether they would convince anyone that the Army was a satisfying career is another question. In retrospect the multinational force was a waste of effort, and the copy does not really hide that.

352

351

353

353
London police recruitment
United Kingdom
Agency: Collett Dickenson Pearce & Partners, London

The visual gimmick here is the series of watch-faces showing times in the evening and through the night. Next to each is a note detailing an incident, each in a different part of London, in which police were involved.

354, 355
GLC (Greater London Council)
United Kingdom
Agency: Boase Massimi Pollitt Partnership, London

A much admired – and politically controversial – campaign by the GLC, controlled by the Labour Party, to resist Conservative Government legislation to abolish it. Both the poster wrapped in red tape and the one showing a wall-faced bureaucrat symbolise the alleged unconcern of central government about Londoners' problems.

354

355

356
Conservatives in Europe
United Kingdom
Agency: Saatchi & Saatchi Compton, London

This election poster talks of the need for Britain to have strong representation in the European Parliament but, unusually, implies rather than declares that electors should vote Conservative. However, the most interesting feature is the typography, by Roger Kennedy, which the agency says 'breaks all the conventional rules to compel you to read the words.'

ADVERTISEMENT

AT LEAST THESE DAYS WE'RE ONLY FIGHTING OVER BEEF AND LAMB.

Shell-shocked after two world wars, the nations of Europe started to pick up the pieces.

With factories and economies in ruins, rebuilding Europe's prosperity was a most pressing need.

The solution was to unite the economies of Western Europe within the European Community.

This has created the world's largest trading market – larger than even the United States.

ADVERTISEMENT

It has also made war between our European countries inconceivable. Today we fight our battles in the European Parliament.

That's why it's so important we have strong representatives there, who will push to ensure a fair deal from our European partners.

Through the European Parliament we can press for money to help our inner cities – and to train our unemployed youngsters.

We can slash the red tape that hinders our trade with Europe – and thereby safeguard the $2\frac{1}{2}$ million jobs involved.

And we can demand a reasonable reduction in our contribution to the budget, to the benefit of the taxpayer.

On June 14th, you can have a say in the future of Europe, by electing someone who will represent you in the European Parliament. Someone who will stand up for British interests.

We're in Europe for good now. Just how good it will be depends upon your support.

BRITAIN NEEDS A STRONG VOICE IN EUROPE.

Conservatives in the European Parliament.

356

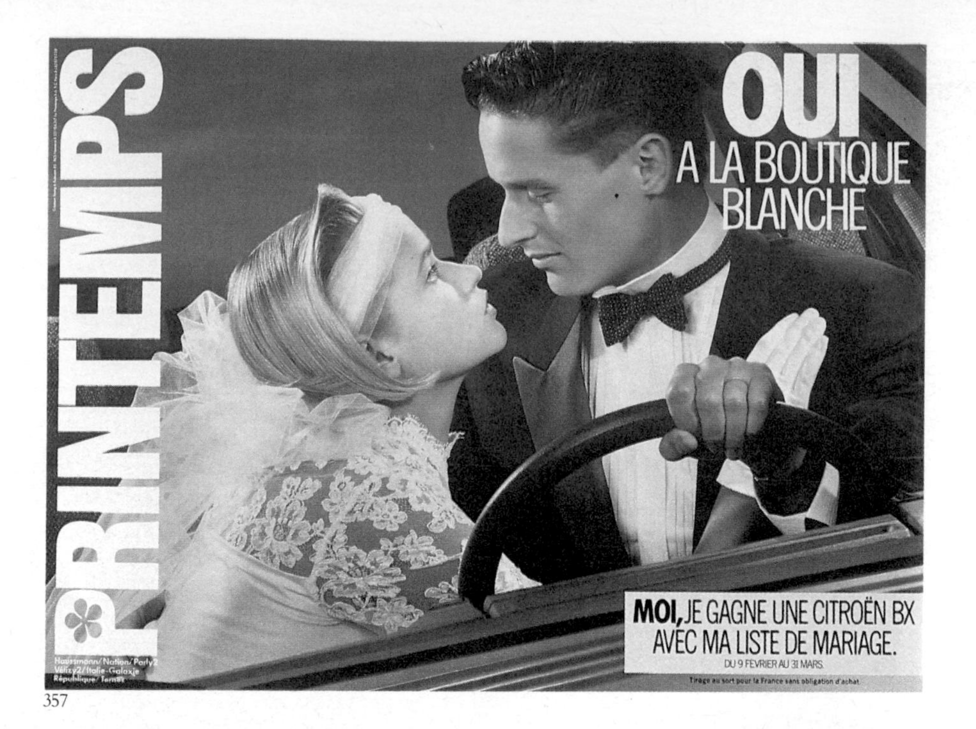

357

358

357, 358, 359
Printemps department store
France
Agency: Young & Rubicam, Paris

Three stylish posters. One, for a special 'Blue Exhibition', has the heading 'My eyes are full of blue'. Another, for the store's bridal gowns, is headed 'Yes to the white boutique'. The third is for tourists to read.

359

360

361

362

363

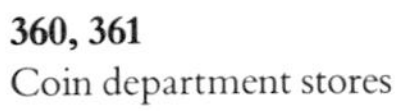

360, 361
Coin department stores
Italy
Agency: ATA Univas, Milan

The accent in this campaign is on fun. It is also designed to make clear the correct pronunciation of the client's name, which many Italians get wrong, saying it like the English word coin instead of separating the vowels. TV commercials are lively with a catchy tune to the campaign slogan 'Coin is in' ('in' being the English word). In each press ad the letter *i* is replaced with a person.

362
Coin department stores
Italy
Agency: B Communications, Milan

The agency lost the account to ATA in 1984, though it had produced some elegant advertising. This example presents ski clothes for men with the pay-off line 'Coin, quality is in fashion.'

363
Bijenkorf department store
Netherlands
Agency: Young & Rubicam, Amsterdam

'Tomorrow morning we unveil the silliest department store in the Netherlands' says the headline. The three 'silly' days to which copy refers are the days of a sale with many price reductions.

364a, 364b, 364c
Dickins and Jones department stores
United Kingdom
Agency: Saatchi & Saatchi Compton, London

An amusing way of getting over the problem that manufacturers contribute to the cost of stores advertising and, of course, want their products mentioned. Instead of showing a catalogue of fashions Saatchis simply put the manufacturers' labels on a naked body. The most striking thing about the ad, however, is that it occupies three consecutive double-page spreads.

365
Sunchain
Japan
Agency: McCann-Erickson Hakuhodo, Tokyo

A spring promotion for this 24-hour store's 'sandwich parade'. Copy says: 'Sunchain has so many delicious sandwiches you won't be able to make up your mind.' The headline is 'The dilemma of love.'

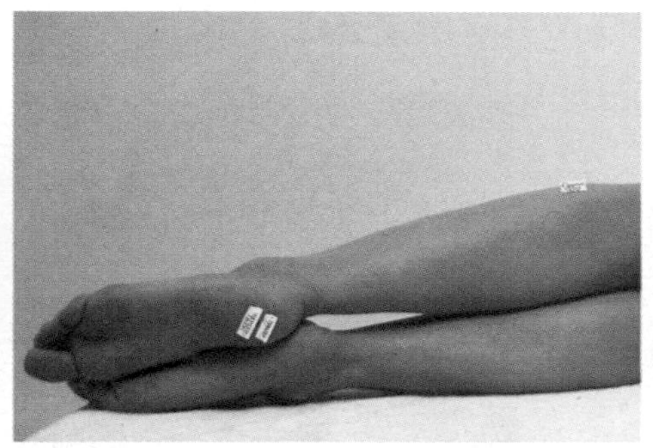
364a

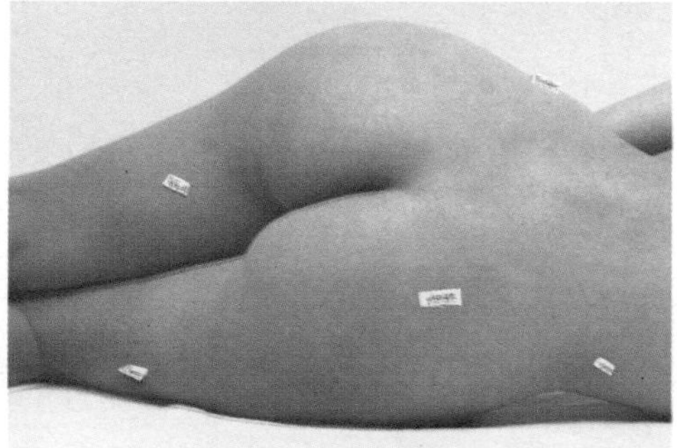
364b

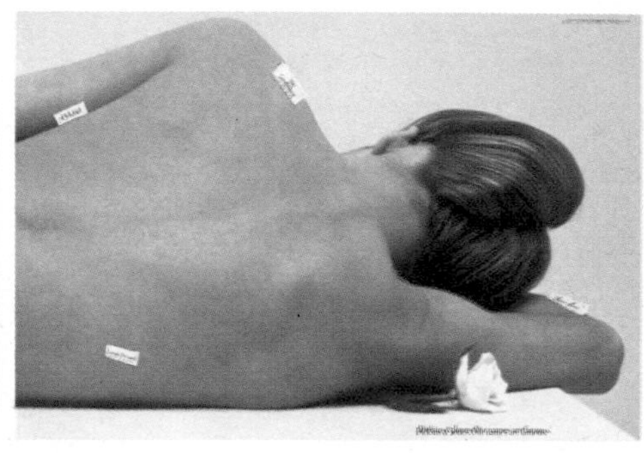
364c

365

La littérature est vaste comme le monde. Tous les voyages sont possibles. Ici, chacun fait escale où bon lui semble.
fnac
La fnac. L'oxygène de la tête.

366

367

368

369

366
FNAC stores
France
Agency: Publicis, Paris

FNAC sells a range of leisure products including books. Here the store is called 'The oxygen of the head', and the copy says 'Literature is as vast as the world. All journeys are possible. Here everyone stops where he pleases.'

367
Wienerwald restaurants
West Germany
Agency: Leonhardt & Kern, Stuttgart

The jolly, appetising picture reflects the headline claim that Wienerwald restaurants are for sweet-toothed revellers. The standard of an eating house's desserts and ice-creams, says copy, is a measure of its general quality.

368, 369
Denny's restaurants
United States
Agency: Foote Cone & Belding/Honig, Los Angeles

Two first-rate bits of humorous imagination. The poster with the sun as a plate of food is particularly pleasing.

370
Silk Cut cigarettes
United Kingdom
Agency: Saatchi & Saatchi Compton, London

The silk is cut. A simple yet stylish way of complying with the restrictive rules on tobacco advertising without showing a pack at all. Not just a visual pun, the picture lends a touch of elegance to a mild and bland cigarette.

371, 372
Benson & Hedges Longer Length Cigarettes
United Kingdom
Agency: Collett Dickenson Pearce & Partners, London

How to press home the message that these cigarettes really are longer? Here are two ways. Another used in the campaign is a picture of a poster with a strip torn off because the cigarette was too long to fit.

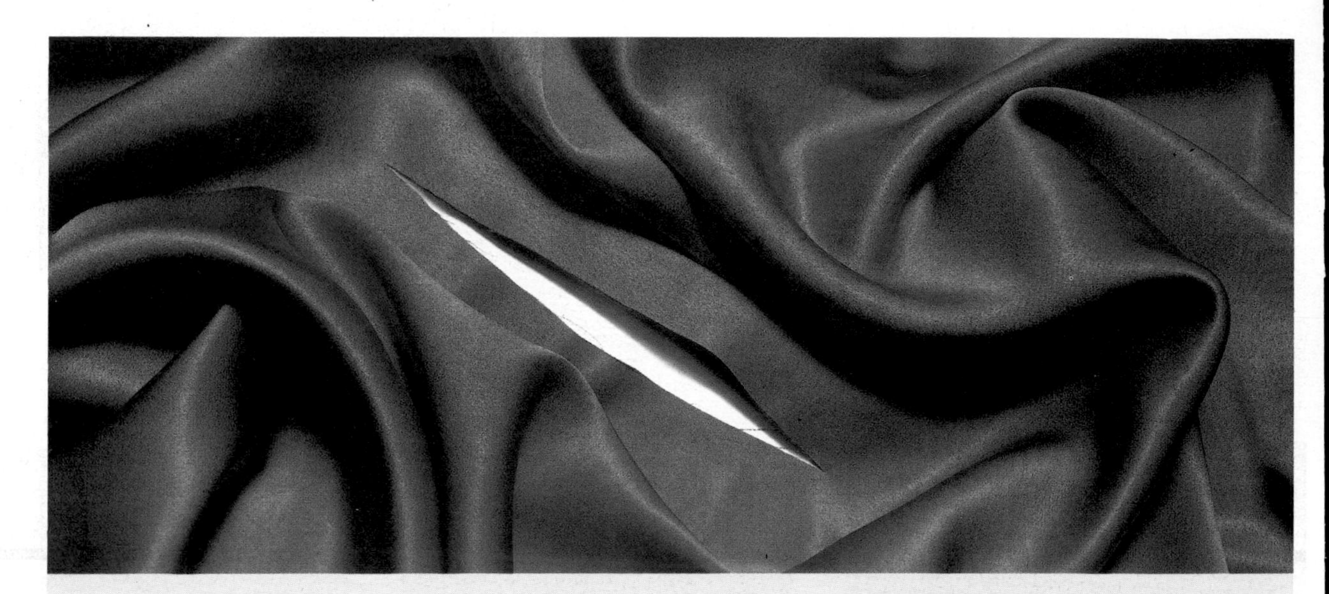
LOW TAR As defined by H.M. Government DANGER: Government Health WARNING: CIGARETTES CAN SERIOUSLY DAMAGE YOUR HEALTH

370

Benson and Hedges

LOW TO MIDDLE TAR Manufacturer's Estimate
DANGER: Government Health WARNING: CIGARETTES CAN SERIOUSLY DAMAGE YOUR HEALTH

371

Benson and
Hedges longer
length.
LOW TO MIDDLE TAR As defined by H.M. Government
DANGER: Government Health WARNING:
CIGARETTES CAN SERIOUSLY DAMAGE YOUR HEALTH

372

SUPERKINGS

BEYOND THE KING SIZE

LOW TO MIDDLE TAR As defined by H.M. Government
DANGER: Government Health WARNING:
CIGARETTES CAN SERIOUSLY DAMAGE YOUR HEALTH

373

PLAZA
EXTRA SUAVE

PLAZA
EXTRA SUAVE
Slims

Uma classe a mais.

Qualidade Souza Cruz

374

373
John Player Superkings cigarettes
United Kingdom
Agency: Ogilvy & Mather, London

The wall is supposed to represent the world of ordinary king-size cigarettes, and the image painted on it that of the new bigger-than-king-size category. Playing visual games with packs is one of the few creative ways of complying with the UK's strict rules on cigarette advertising.

374
Plaza cigarettes
Brazil
Agency: MPM, Rio de Janeiro

The object of this campaign is to show the king-size and slim versions of the brand as being of the same quality or 'one class'. In other ads other games are played with the packs, for example representing them as coffee cups.

375, 376, 377
Benson & Hedges Special Filter cigarettes
United Kingdom
Agency: Collett Dickenson Pearce & Partners, London

Still going strong after many years, this campaign continually comes up with new visual gimmicks. Even when the brand name has been shaved off the pack, the advertiser is, to UK consumers, instantly identifiable.

MIDDLE TAR As defined by H.M.Government
DANGER: Government Health WARNING: CIGARETTES CAN SERIOUSLY DAMAGE YOUR HEALTH

375

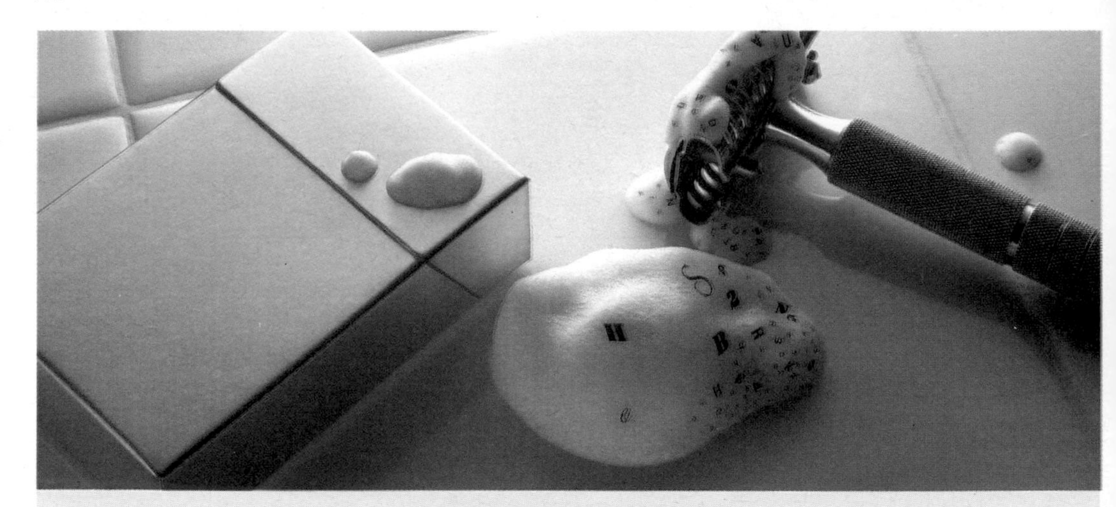
MIDDLE TAR As defined by H.M.Government
DANGER: Government Health WARNING: CIGARETTES CAN SERIOUSLY DAMAGE YOUR HEALTH

376

MIDDLE TAR As defined by H.M.Government
DANGER: Government Health WARNING: CIGARETTES CAN SERIOUSLY DAMAGE YOUR HEALTH

377

378

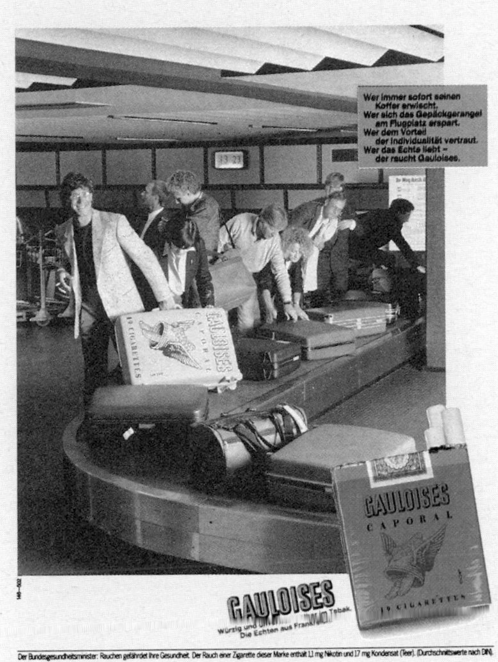

379

378, 379
Gauloises cigarettes
West Germany
Agency: Heye Needham & Partner, Hamburg

An individual (and long-running) campaign addressed to people who fancy themselves as individuals. 'The one who loves what is genuine is the one who smokes Gauloises' says copy. In one ad the woman is identified as 'liking to be sometimes naked without being uncovered'. The other identifies the Gauloises smoker as the person 'who recovers his suitcase immediately' and 'stays out of the airport luggage hassle'.

380
Blend cigarettes
Sweden
Agency: McCann-Erickson, Stockholm

Sweden has even stricter rules than Britain on what may be shown in ads for cigarettes. Only a single pack against a neutral background is allowed. This campaign depends on strong headlines such as, here, 'The truth and nothing but the truth.' Copy asks why buy Blend? The answer given is 'The taste, the taste, the taste, the taste.'

380

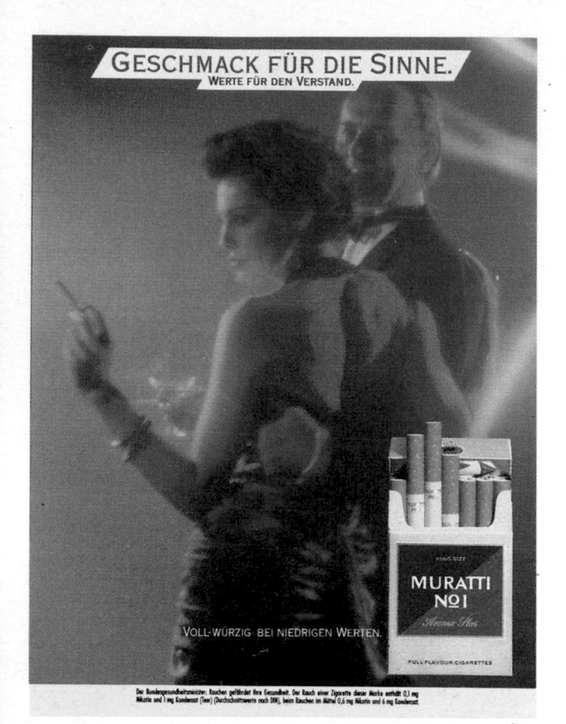

381

381
Muratti No. 1 cigarettes
West Germany
Agency: Young & Rubicam, Frankfurt

UK rules forbid cigarette advertisers, among other things, to associate their products pictorially with social success. That obviously does not apply to this campaign. The colour scheme is distinctive. Headline: 'Taste for the senses, prices for the intellect.'

382

383

382, 383
Gallant cigarettes
Switzerland
Agency: Young & Rubicam, Bern

Two pictures, two languages, but the same theme and the same copy line, 'A new taste lights up.' Women lighting cigarettes for men makes an interesting change from the opposite, and conventional, image. Of course, this kind of human interest advertising is not allowed as far as cigarette-makers in some other European countries are concerned.

384, 385
Falstaff cigars
United Kingdom
Agency: Collett Dickenson Pearce & Partners, London

English whimsy at its best. This campaign bears a family resemblance to the Plymouth Gin campaign by another London agency, Lowe Howard-Spink Campbell-Ewald, whose directors originally worked for CDP.

386
Hollywood cigarettes
Brazil
Agency: MPM, Rio de Janeiro

This ad urges smokers to buy the ten-pack carton. Each of the ten crumpled packs has a different caption such as 'Darling, did you smoke all my cigarettes?' and 'Oh God, it's raining and I've no cigarettes left.' The carton at the bottom is captioned 'Without comment.' This ad marked the first time the client, Souza Cruz, the biggest cigarette advertiser in Brazil, allowed crumpled packs to be pictured.

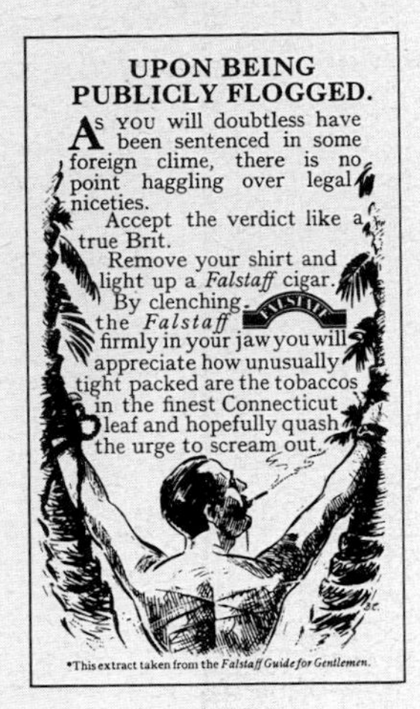

385

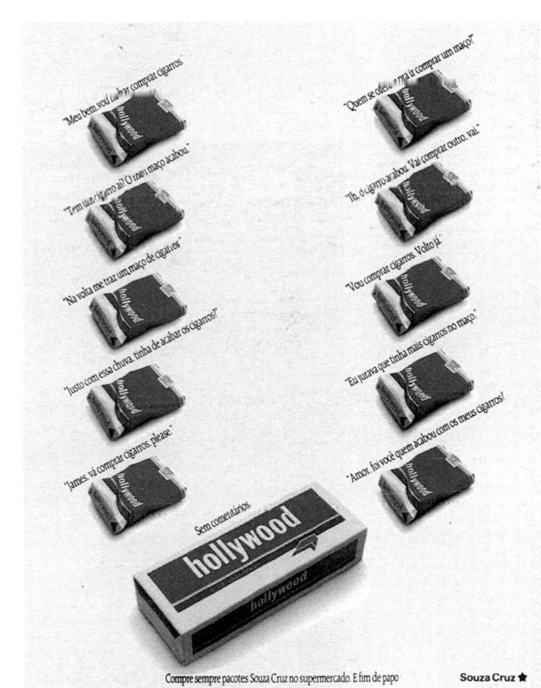

386

UPON BEING ARRESTED.

Do not break down cursing your luck.

Compliment the detective upon his efficiency. Let him know he has landed a rare bird indeed by producing a *Falstaff* cigar.

Do not attempt a bribe, but savour for yourself the unusually firm texture and richness of the tobaccos wrapped in Connecticut leaf.

Take a generous supply with you, as snout barons are considered to be the élite within Her Majesty's establishments.

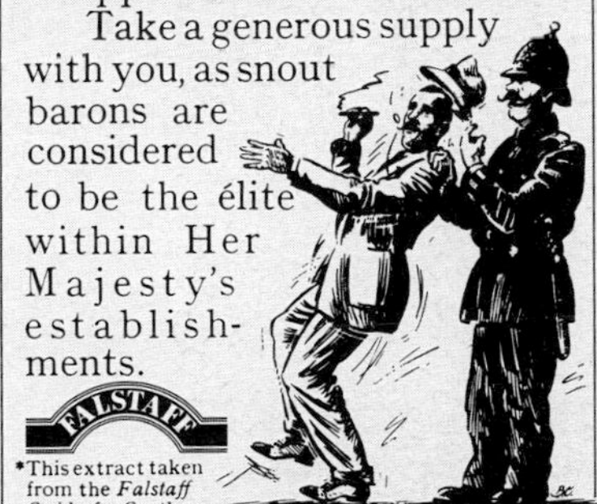

FALSTAFF

*This extract taken from the *Falstaff Guide for Gentlemen*.

384

WE THINK YOU SHOULD TREAT OUR CLEANSER SERIOUSLY...
USE Nº7 SPECIAL CREAM CLEANSER
EVERY MORNING
USE Nº7 SPECIAL CREAM CLEANSER
EVERY NIGHT
USE Nº7 SPECIAL CREAM CLEANSER
365 DAYS A YEAR
CLEANSING IS VITAL TO ANY SKIN.
HOWEVER, THE BOOTS SKIN CARE RESEARCH LABORATORIES HAVE DISCOVERED THAT DIFFERENT TYPES OF SKIN NEED DIFFERENT TYPES OF CLEANSER. HENCE Nº7 SPECIAL CREAM CLEANSER FOR DRY SKIN.
IT'S A MUCH RICHER FORMULATION THAN MOST. BUT IT LIQUEFIES ON CONTACT WITH YOUR WARM SKIN, DRAWING OUT THE IMPURITIES. WIPE IT OFF AND YOUR FACE FEELS SUPER-CLEAN YET SOFT. IN OTHER WORDS, THE BEST OF BOTH WORLDS. JUST WHAT YOU EXPECT FROM Nº7.
FOR MORE ADVICE ABOUT YOUR SKIN CARE, TALK TO THE Nº7 CONSULTANT AT LARGER BRANCHES OF BOOTS.
Nº7
FORMULATED EXCLUSIVELY BY
BOOTS SKIN CARE RESEARCH LABORATORIES, NOTTINGHAM
AVAILABLE AT MOST BRANCHES OF BOOTS
SUBJECT TO STOCK AVAILABILITY

387

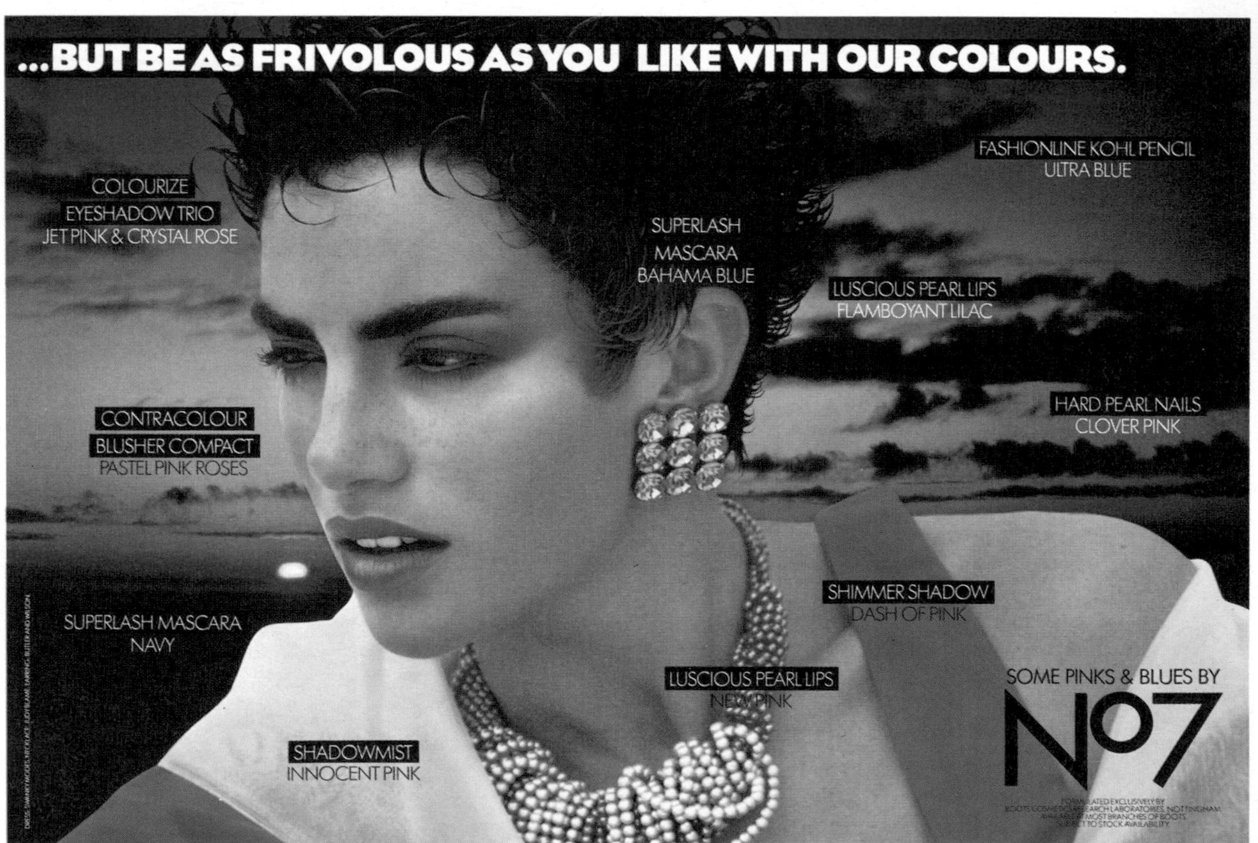
...BUT BE AS FRIVOLOUS AS YOU LIKE WITH OUR COLOURS.
COLOURIZE
EYESHADOW TRIO
JET PINK & CRYSTAL ROSE
SUPERLASH
MASCARA
BAHAMA BLUE
FASHIONLINE KOHL PENCIL
ULTRA BLUE
LUSCIOUS PEARL LIPS
FLAMBOYANT LILAC
HARD PEARL NAILS
CLOVER PINK
CONTRACOLOUR
BLUSHER COMPACT
PASTEL PINK ROSES
SHIMMER SHADOW
DASH OF PINK
SUPERLASH MASCARA
NAVY
LUSCIOUS PEARL LIPS
NEW PINK
SHADOWMIST
INNOCENT PINK
SOME PINKS & BLUES BY
Nº7

388

RIMMEL
75 colours for lips (including browns)
BROWNS

389

387, 388
Boots No. 7 cosmetics
United Kingdom
Agency: McCormick Publicis, London

An effective combination of two ads dealing separately with 'serious' and 'frivolous' products in the Boots range. Would it be rude to say that the model looked much more attractive before she was tarted up for the second ad of the pair?

389
Rimmel cosmetics
United Kingdom
Agency: Foote Cone & Belding, London

Beautifully composed ad from an elegant series. Note that the girl is photographed in black and white with the exception of her lips.

390
Corolle eye-shadows
Italy
Agency: Publicis, Milan

The pink glove is what makes this ad for a new range of eye-shadow from L'Oréal. Headline: 'Special effects. The new silky eye-shadows.'

EFFETTI SPECIALI.
I NUOVI OMBRETTI-SETA.
Per un effetto così leggero e lucente.
Li senti al tocco,
scorrono leggeri sotto le tue dita.
I nuovi ombretti Corolle,
morbidi come la seta, diventano più intensi
se applicati bagnati.

390

391
Revlon Fleurs de Jontue fragrances
United States
Agency: Grey Advertising, New York

Very pretty – and feminine in the old-fashioned sense of the word. The picture is artfully composed, with attention focused on flowers, hand and lips. It would have lost impact if the whole of the woman's face had been shown.

391

392
L'Oréal cosmetics
United States
Agency: McCann-Erickson, New York

Model as big game huntress who will 'live dangerously this summer'. Yes, of course it's silly, but no doubt the picture was unusual enough to make many women look at it.

392

393
Wella Recrin shampoos
Italy
Agency: Benton & Bowles, Milan

'Wella has made a discovery as great as the sea: Recrin'. That's what it says. Recrin, whatever it may be, is apparently derived from a substance found on the sea bed. Hence the copy line and the picture. Pretty, but you could object that most people would not choose to wash their hair in sea water.

WELLA HA FATTO UNA SCOPERTA GRANDE COME IL MARE: RECRIN.
WELLA

393

EVEN NINE TO FIVE HAS ITS HIGHLIGHTS.
When everything around you pales, Harmony highlights the natural colour of your hair. With seven subtle shades that are as easy to use as shampoo, you'll feel your best because you'll look your best. Head and shoulders above the rest. HARMONY HIGHLIGHTS YOUR HAIR.
POISON
CONDITIONING COLOUR
Harmony
AS EASY AS SHAMPOOING
JWT072.P.840

394

The Standard
GLOOMY FORECAST
GETTING TO WORK: SLOW GOING?
ENGLAND WINS
IT'S ALL HERE IN BLACK
IT ALL LOOKS THE SAME
EVEN COMMUTING HAS ITS HIGHLIGHTS.
When everything around you pales, Harmony highlights the natural colour of your hair. With seven subtle shades that are as easy to use as shampoo, you'll feel your best because you'll look your best. No matter where you're going. HARMONY HIGHLIGHTS YOUR HAIR.
Harmony

395

394, 395
Harmony hair colorants
Australia
Agency: J. Walter Thompson, Sydney

Clever visual tricks not only draw attention to the model and the brand but communicate, more effectively than the copy, the message that use of Harmony will lend brightness to an otherwise drab existence.

396
Esprit shampoo
Canada
Agency: Foote Cone & Belding, Toronto

A nice, unpretentious, sexy picture. And, since it's a shampoo ad, who wants to see the model's face anyway?

397
Clear anti-dandruff shampoo
Italy
Agency: J. Walter Thompson, Milan

One of an unusual series of comic-style ads, this cartoon strip is entitled 'I had to get her out of my hair.' The 'her' turns out to refer to dandruff, not to the girl, but of course the ambiguity is untranslatable into English, which normally does not refer to inanimate objects by gender. The ambiguity is maintained throughout the strip until the last bubble of speech in which the hero says 'But what did you think? I was talking about dandruff.' Youngsters are likely to find it funny.

398
Johnson's Baby Shampoo
Netherlands
Agency: Young & Rubicam, Amsterdam

'Nine out of ten Dutch babies are crying about another shampoo' is the knocking headline. However, copy qualifies this by admitting that nine out of ten mothers are quite satisfied with other brands than Johnson's even though they know the latter is milder and less irritating for a baby's eyes.

399
Egg-Melk soap
Norway
Agency: Heltberg Creative Service, Oslo

The product contains fresh egg and milk extracts, as copy says. It is 'extra kind to your skin. Its aroma mild and gentle. The way a family soap should be.'

396

397

Negen van de tien Nederlandse baby's schreeuwen om een andere shampoo.

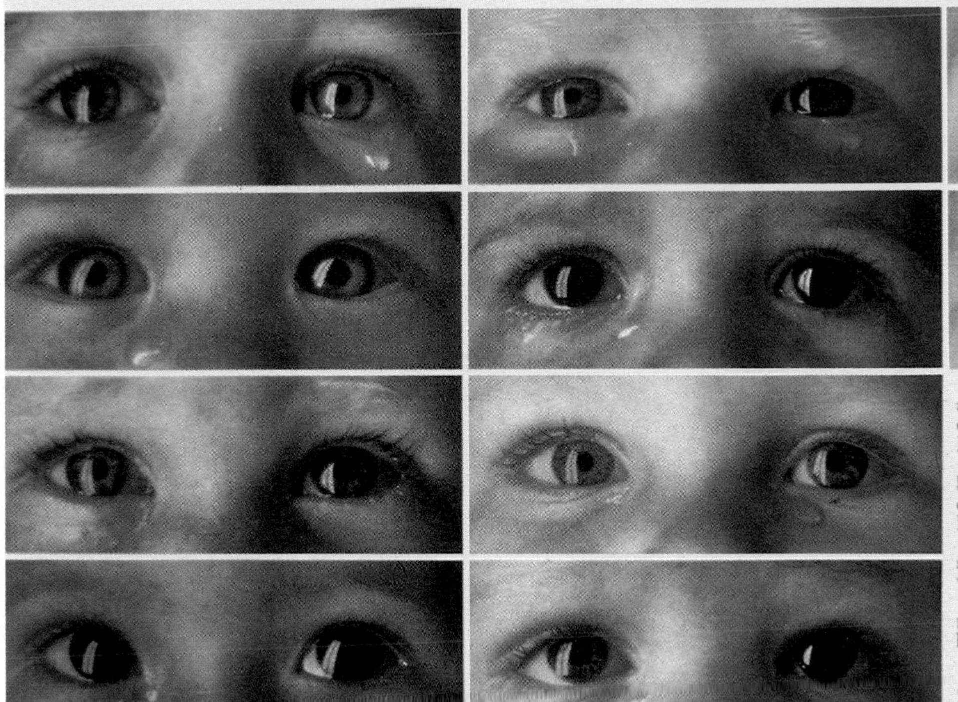

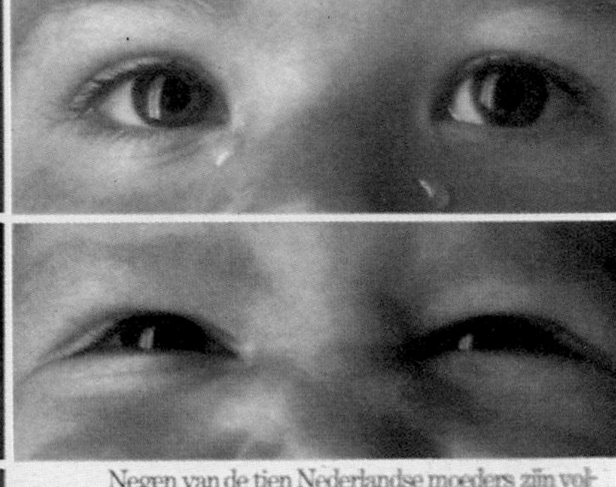

Negen van de tien Nederlandse moeders zijn volstrekt tevreden over 'hun' merk, zonder te beseffen dat er een shampoo bestaat die aanzienlijk milder is. Die van Johnson & Johnson.

Johnson's babyshampoo is mild voor baby's haartjes, mild voor baby's huidje en veel minder irritant voor baby's oogjes. Dat kan heel wat traantjes schelen.

Geen wonder dat Johnson's babyshampoo door moeders over de hele wereld verreweg 't meest gebruikt wordt.

Een niet gering compliment, want moeders willen uitsluitend 't beste voor hun baby. U toch ook? Johnson & Johnson

Johnson's babyshampoo. Geen traantje te veel.

EGG-MELK
SEPE
EGG-MELK
SEPE
Egg-Melk Sepe er tilsatt friske egg og melkestoff.
For at den skal være ekstra snill mot huden. Og dufte mildt og
behagelig. Slik skal en såpe for hele familien være.
NORDSTRØM & DUE

400
Close-up toothpaste
Canada
Agency: J. Walter Thompson, Toronto

The image of the toothpaste tube in the dentist's chair is not just a joke. Close-up, which had traditionally sold on a cosmetic (whiter teeth, fresher breath) platform, was relaunched with fluoride in 1983, but many people remained unconvinced of its medical (dental protection) qualities. This campaign was designed to persuade them that the brand was as effective medically as Crest and Colgate while continuing to help with social 'close encounters' as well as ones with the dentist.

401a, 401b
Aim toothpaste
United States
Agency: Sudler & Hennessey, New York

From a campaign mailed to dentists. The posters were pinned up by many of them in their surgeries as aids to educating children about dental hygiene.

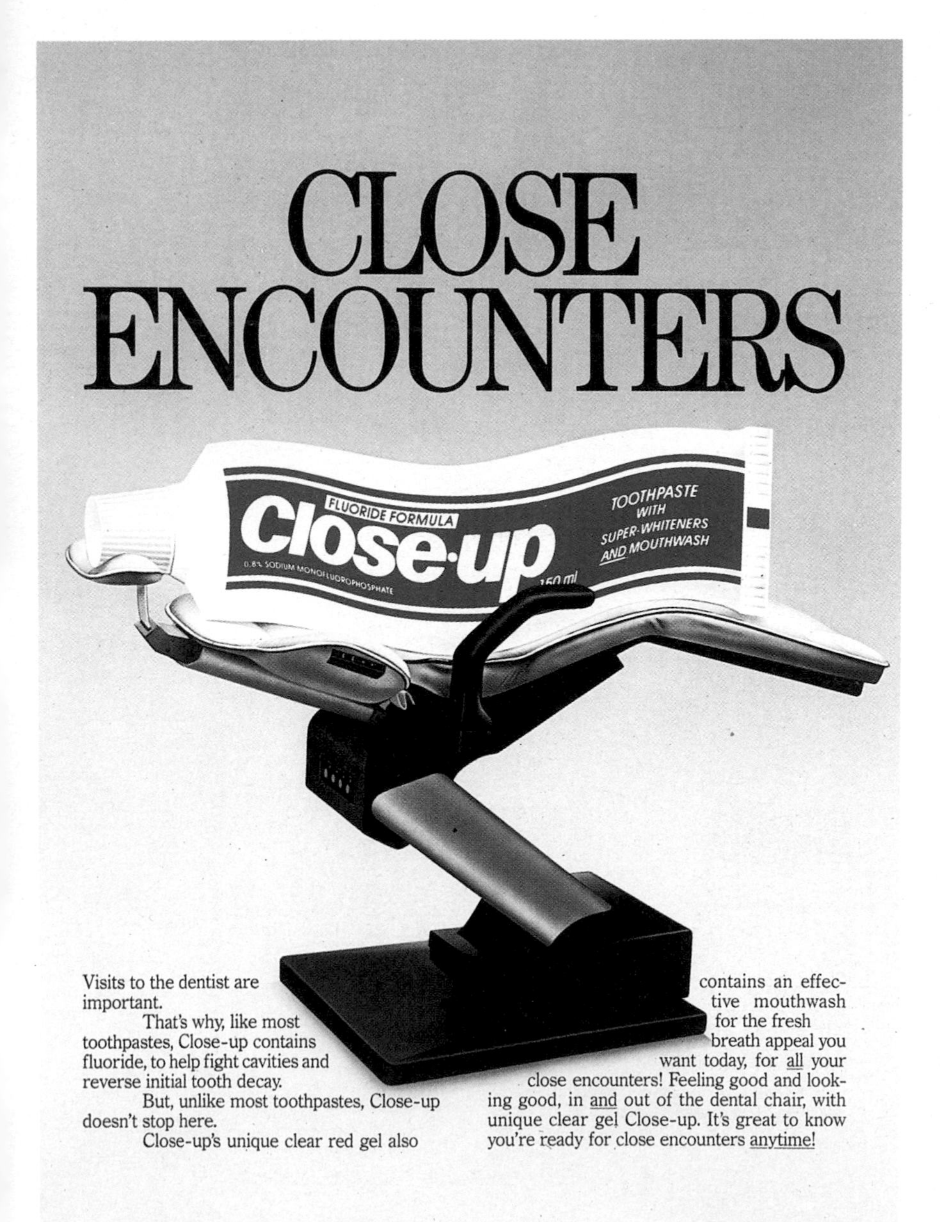

CLOSE
ENCOUNTERS
FLUORIDE FORMULA
Close-up
TOOTHPASTE WITH SUPER-WHITENERS AND MOUTHWASH
150 ml
Visits to the dentist are important.
That's why, like most toothpastes, Close-up contains fluoride, to help fight cavities and reverse initial tooth decay.
But, unlike most toothpastes, Close-up doesn't stop here.
Close-up's unique clear red gel also contains an effective mouthwash for the fresh breath appeal you want today, for all your close encounters! Feeling good and looking good, in and out of the dental chair, with unique clear gel Close-up. It's great to know you're ready for close encounters anytime!

400

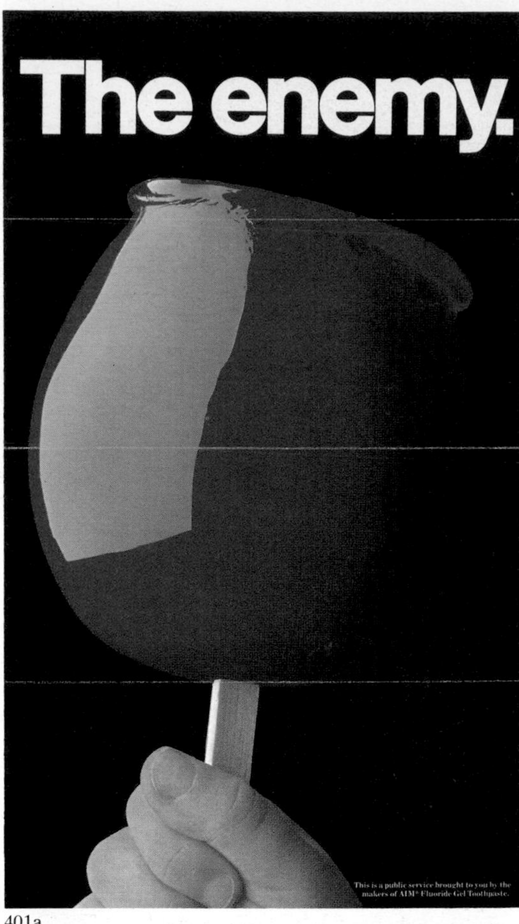

401a

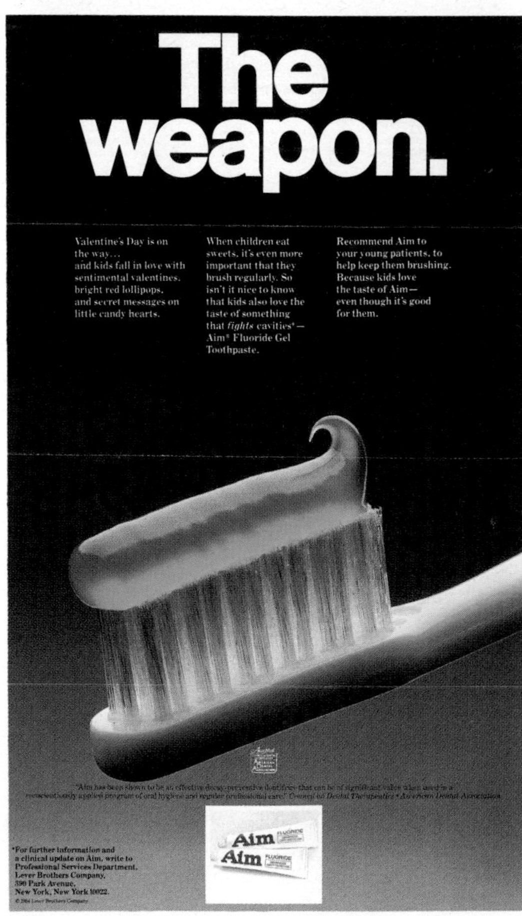

401b

402

402
Patrichs aftershave and cologne
India
Agency: Lintas, Bombay

Feminine charms well to the fore in this ad for men's toiletries made by Pond's India. The Spanish caption, 'The Patrichs moment', is intended, like other foreign-language captions in the campaign, to add exotic allure to an Indian-made product.

403

403
Chanel No. 5 bath products
United Kingdom
Agency: Ayer Barker, London

The aim is to convey an impression of luxury and sensual self-indulgence. The agency entitles this ad 'Splash'.

404

404
Chanel aftershave
United Kingdom
Agency: Ayer Barker, London

The image the agency seeks to create with this campaign is of traditional masculine sophistication, exploiting the trend to what it calls the 'new conservatism'. Another aim is to correct any impression that, after Chanel's launch of the Antaeus brand, the 'Gentleman's' range is a poor relation.

LAISSEZ-VOUS PRENDRE PAR LE TRAIN.

TGV.

TRAITEZ VOS AFFAIRES
A LA VITESSE
DES ORDINATEURS.

PARIS 7 H 35. LE JOUR SE LÈVE. CONFORT, CALME, AMBIANCE FEUTRÉE, IL TRAVAILLE. COUPS D'ŒIL RAPIDES PAR LA FENÊTRE : HORIZON, CROISEMENT DE LIGNES, PAGES BLANCHES, FRAPPE MACHINE S'INTERFÈRENT. PARIS EST DÉJÀ LOIN. SA PENSÉE EST PORTÉE, ACCÉLÉRÉE PAR LA VITESSE DU TRAIN. CERTITUDE, CONVICTION, SON DOSSIER EST PRÊT. 11 H 06 LE TGV ARRIVE À GENÈVE. RETOUR PRÉVU 16 H 44, OU, SI SA RÉUNION SE PROLONGE, 19 H 29.

Voyages d'affaires
SNCF

405

LAISSEZ-VOUS PRENDRE PAR LE TRAIN.

TRAIN DE NUIT

ARRIVEZ EN TRAIN
A VOS RÉUNIONS.

PARIS 22 H 00. LE CONDUCTEUR DE LA VOITURE-LIT L'ACCOMPAGNE À SA CABINE PARTICULIÈRE. ESPACE CONFORTABLE, INTIMITÉ, TRANQUILLITÉ. UNE NUIT DE REPOS AVANT MILAN. IL S'INSTALLE: CINTRE, CABINET DE TOILETTE, DRAPS DOUX ET FRAIS, UN DERNIER VERRE EN RELISANT LES NOUVELLES DU SOIR. IL EST BERCÉ PAR LE RYTHME DU TRAIN. MUSIQUE QUI PEU À PEU L'ENTRAÎNE VERS LE SOMMEIL. RÉVEIL EN DOUCEUR. PETIT-DÉJEUNER SERVI DANS SA CABINE PEU APRÈS L'ARRÊT À TURIN. 8 H 55 IL ARRIVE EN PLEINE FORME AU CŒUR DE MILAN. PRÊT POUR SON RENDEZ-VOUS PIAZZA DEGLI AFFARI.

Voyages d'affaires
SNCF

406

405, 406
French Railways
France
Agency: Boulet Dru Dupuy Petit, Paris

Two examples of an eye-catching magazine campaign aimed at business travellers. The slogan is 'Let yourself be taken by (or 'give yourself up to') the train.' One ad says the high speed train (TGV) allows you to do business at the speed of computers. The landscape seen through the train window is in the style of computer graphics. The other ad says the night train will get you to your morning meeting in Italy after a good night's sleep. And a gigantic moon fills the sleeping businessman's window.

407
French Railways
France
Agency: Boulet Dru Dupuy Petit, Paris

This small-space newspaper ad, run in conjunction with the same agency's magazine campaign, describes breakfast on the early morning train journey from Paris to Lille as 'First business of the day'.

408
French Railways
France
Agency: Young & Rubicam, Paris

A neat visual device reminds winter holiday-makers of the convenience of rail travel. Heading: 'Compact prices.' Y & R lost the account to Boulet Dru Dupuy Petit (see ads 405, 406, 408), a new agency founded by Y & R's own former bosses, Jean-Claude Boulet and Jean-Marie Dru.

PARIS 7H27 - LILLE 9H28.
LA PREMIÈRE AFFAIRE DE LA JOURNÉE.
LAISSEZ-VOUS PRENDRE PAR LE TRAIN
EN PARTANT PAR LE TRAIN, GAGNEZ DU TEMPS SUR VOTRE JOURNÉE. TRANQUILLEMENT, DEVANT UN BON PETIT DÉJEUNER, METTEZ NOIR SUR BLANC VOS DERNIÈRES IDÉES POUR VOTRE RÉUNION DU JOUR. ARRIVEZ FRAIS ET DISPOS, LES IDÉES CLAIRES.
VOTRE JOURNÉE COMMENCE BIEN.

407

Prix Compacts SNCF
Cette année, prenez un bon départ pour la neige et fartez S.N.C.F. à prix compacts. En choisissant bien la date de votre départ, si vous partez en famille, en couple ou en séjour d'au moins 5 jours, vous pouvez bénéficier de réductions importantes. Si vous allez skier en Savoie, vous profiterez également de ces prix compacts, sur les nouveaux trains "Corail" de jour. En partant les vendredi et samedi après-midi, vous arriverez le soir à votre station. En partant le matin, vous serez dès l'après-midi au pied des pistes. Renseignez-vous dans les gares et les agences de voyages. La neige, allez-y tout schuss à prix compacts.
Profitez des Tarifs 50
SNCF

408

409
Netherlands Railways
Netherlands
Agency: KVH/GGK, Amsterdam

'Inflated between Deventer and Zandvoort, cost 3.1 cents per kilometre', says the headline. The ad draws attention to the cheap price of rail travel especially with family excursion tickets. Deventer is a town in the middle of the country, Zandvoort a seaside resort. The inflatable swan obviously symbolises a seaside holiday with children.

410
Railway freight service
West Germany
Agency: Lintas, Frankfurt

'The newest star in the night sky', announces the headline, is the goods train Intercargo service. Freight sent in the late afternoon will arrive at its destination early the next morning.

411, 412
German Federal Railways
West Germany
Agency: McCann-Erickson, Frankfurt

The sex sell for railway travel? Yes indeed, or something very like it. The headline over the romantic scene in the train is 'Railway travel is like the cinema, only quicker.' Copy says many people get to know each other in trains and advises those who do not believe in such romantic encounters to go more often to the cinema. The other ad, of a more customary type, illustrates the drawbacks of road travel under the headline 'The road to your holiday is paved with surprises.'

409

410

BAHNFAHREN IST WIE KINO, NUR SCHNELLER.
Abgesehen von allen unseren Vorteilen – bekannt aus den Veröffentlichungen – hier nun ein zusätzlicher, besonders menschlicher. Mit der Bahn kommt man nicht nur schnell und sicher an, sondern sich auch näher. Statistisch gesehen lernen sich jedenfalls hier eine ganze Menge Leute kennen und schätzen. Was vielleicht nicht zuletzt auch mit der angenehmen Art zu reisen zusammenhängt, wie wir vermuten. Wie eng diese Bindungen dann werden, bleibt den Beteiligten überlassen. Wem solche Happy-Ends nun zu schnell und zu unwahrscheinlich erscheinen, dem empfehlen wir, öfters ins Kino zu gehen. Oder – noch besser – mit der Bahn zu fahren. Schließlich ist nichts im Leben und erst recht nichts bei der Bahn auszuschließen, wie man sieht.

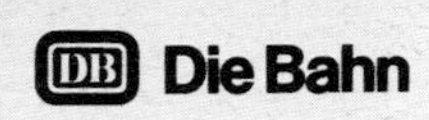
DB Die Bahn

411

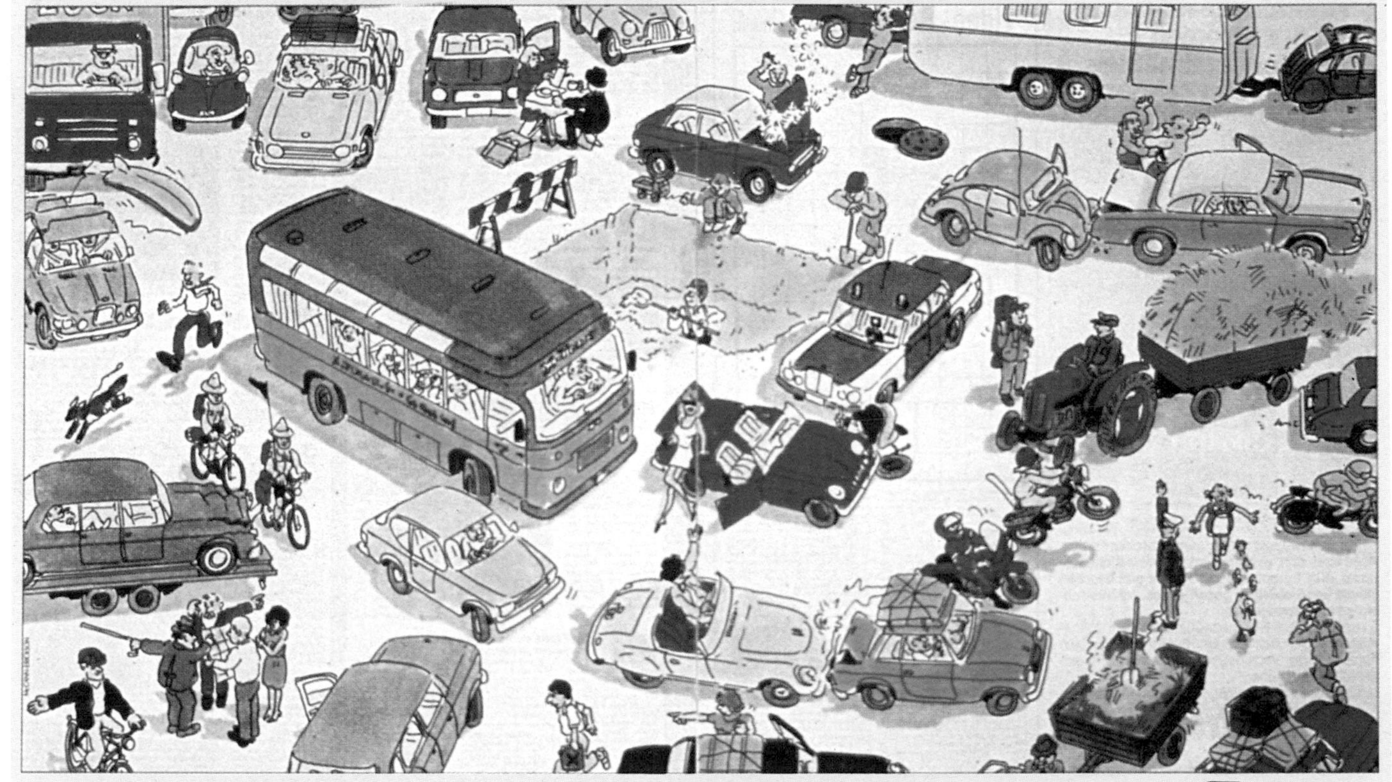
DER WEG IN DEN URLAUB IST MIT ÜBERRASC HUNGEN GEPFLASTERT.
DB Die Bahn

412

413
Austrian Railways
Austria
Agency: McCann-Erickson, Vienna

This, too, advertises freight services. Unlike the German ad by Lintas which attempts to symbolise the speed of the service, the Austrian campaign shows examples of the goods carried. Here 'The egg goes by train.'

414, 415
UTA
France
Agency: Doyle Dane Bernbach, Paris

UTA's business (or Galaxy) class has only two seats to a row. That is the justification for the unusual picture of an aircraft cabin looking like a real restaurant. It's a piece of poetic exaggeration, which you may or may not consider legitimate. The headline, 'For your business lunches we've put the little seats in the big ones', refers to the introduction of new, bigger seats. The other ad says 'It is wise to book your table several days in advance.'

414

415

413

416

416, 417
RATP (Paris public transport)
France
Agency: Ecom, Paris

These amusing pictures parody ads for other products. Take a look at the Lois jeans ad in the Clothing section and the Printemps store ad featuring a bridal couple in the Retail section. Yellow and brown are the colours of the ticket used on both buses and Metro trains in Paris. Hence 'On her skin was marked Ticket' and 'Yes to the Ticket'.

417

Iberia flies to Madrid from 21 European cities: Amsterdam, Athens, Brussels, Copenhaguen, Dublin, Dusseldorf, Frankfurt, Geneva, Lisbon, London, Lyon, Manchester, Marseilles, Milan, Munich, Nice, Porto, Paris. Rome, Vienna and Zurich.

Iberia also flies you to Barcelona from Brussels, Amsterdam, Athens, Copenhaguen, Frankfurt, Geneva, Lisbon, London, Lyon, Manchester, Milan, Munich, Nice, Paris, Rome, Vienna and Zurich.

And to Palma de Mallorca from Brussels, Amsterdam, Geneva, London, Lyon, Marseilles, Milan, Nice, Paris and Rome; to Malaga from Brussels, Amsterdam, Copenhaguen, Dublin, Frankfurt, Geneva, London, Manchester, Paris and Zurich; and to Santiago de Compostela, in the Northwest of Spain, from Frankfurt, Amsterdam, Geneva, London, Paris and Zurich. That means an average of 298 flights every week.

And if you need to go to other places in Spain, we also have flights from Brussels, Amsterdam, Frankfurt, London and Paris to Alicante; from Frankfurt, London and Paris to Valencia; from Frankfurt and London to Sevilla; from London to Bilbao, Las Palmas, Tenerife and Mahón; and from Geneva, Zurich, London, Brussels and Paris to Ibiza.

And with three classes: First, Preference or Economy. Always in comfort. Always with convenient departures.

Now Iberia makes more than 255 stops daily throughout Europe.

That's why, in Spain, we call Iberia the "Gran Vía". And in Europe, the European Highway.

And both merge into Iberia's American Highway when crossing the Atlantic.

Iberia: Spain's Highway to the world.

418

418
Iberia
International
Agency: NCK, Madrid

One of several different 'highways' featured in this campaign. There are Spanish and American ones also to communicate graphically the number of cities Iberia flies to. In Europe it has services to 21 cities outside Spain.

DÉCOLLEZ
POUR VOS WEEK-ENDS
par IBERIA
Escapade en Espagne
Echappez-vous, le temps d'un week-end, en pays de lumière. Madrid, Barcelone, Séville et Malaga vous ouvrent leurs portes les plus secrètes.
Au rendez-vous, ballades dans l'histoire, découvertes artistiques, culturelles, flâneries au soleil de nos provinces, sports et détente.
Nos tarifs Amigo* qui reflètent, eux aussi, la douceur de vivre, vous invitent à passer le week-end en Espagne avec Iberia.
*Conditions spéciales d'application : consultez votre agence de voyages ou téléphonez à Inforiberia (1) 720.41.41.
IBERIA

419

419
Iberia
France
Agency: Coutau-Thibaud, Paris

Putting the landscape in the belly of the plane makes a change from the usual ways of representing aircraft desti-nations. It contrasts interestingly with NCK's approach (418).

The widest seat in the air.

Our Super Club business class offers you the widest seats in the air. In fact they are so wide that we could only fit them into the cabin in rows of six. This means that you are never more than one seat away from the aisle.

But though there are fewer seats than before, there are still just as many cabin attendants. So you will now receive more individual care and attention than ever.

And that is not all. There is more to Super Club than extra space, extra comfort and extra special service. You get extra baggage allowance too. (Now increased to 30 kg.)

Super Club. The business class where all the extras are standard.

BRITISH AIRWAYS Super Club
The world's favourite airline.

420

420
British Airways
United Kingdom
Agency: Saatchi & Saatchi Compton, London

This is the press version of a very expensive TV commercial for BA's Super Club business class. One of those ideas which make a stronger impression on the screen than on the page.

421
Western Airlines
United States
Agency: Doyle Dane Bernbach, Los Angeles

What you are looking at, in case you're not sure, is a whale's tail. The aim of the ad is to promote holiday travel to Alaska, using the whale as a symbol of the State's uniqueness.

422
British Airways
United Kingdom
Agency: Saatchi & Saatchi Compton, London

Now this poster, with its two-in-one symbol of rain and sunshine, owes nothing to television. It makes full and ingenious use of the print medium.

423
Air Canada
United Kingdom
Agency: Ogilvy & Mather, London

The 'dragon plane', with its Chinese associations, was used to launch Air Canada's London-Bombay-Singapore service in January, 1985, with 96-sheet posters a major element in the campaign.

421

Manchester to Nice in two hours.

Direct flights from Manchester to ten European destinations.

The world's favourite airline. British airways

422

423

424, 425
Package holidays
West Germany
Agency: Ogilvy & Mather, Frankfurt

A campaign paid for by a group of holiday tour operators. The headline over the picture of the little girl and the drawing of a car in the sand is 'A car holiday is fine. A package holiday by air is finer.' The other ad says: 'Recreation. When, where and how you want.'

Erholung.
Wann, wo und
wie Sie wollen.
Ihre Flug-
Pauschalreise.

Wie wär's: Nahtlos bräunen, mit dem Jeep durch die Wüste, Orientierungstour durch die Antike? Eine Flug-Pauschalreise bietet so viele Möglichkeiten, wie Sie Ideen haben. Alles, was lästig ist, nimmt Ihnen Ihr Reisebüro ab: Flug buchen, Versicherungen abschließen, Bus bestellen, Zimmer reservieren.

So, jetzt liegen zwischen Alltag und Urlaub nur noch ein paar Flugstunden. Am Ziel: Koffer auspacken, rein in den Pool, rauf auf den Tennisplatz, ab in die Bar – die Reihenfolge bestimmen Sie. Auch, ob Sie im Hotelrestaurant essen oder lieber mit dem Lunchpaket losziehen. Bei einer Flug-Pauschalreise gehen Sie Ihre eigenen Wege. Läuft mal was quer – kein Problem: Mit Ihrer Reiseleitung können Sie deutsch reden. Auch über Ihre vielen Urlaubsideen.

Ihre TUI,
NUR, ITS, LTU,
Hapag-Lloyd
und Condor.

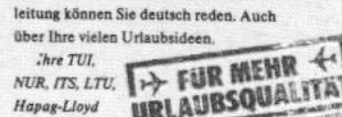

424

Auto-Urlaub
ist schön.
Eine Flug-
Pauschalreise
ist schöner.

Auto-Urlaub oder Flug-Pauschalreise? Ist das denn so ein großer Unterschied? Und ob. Da können Sie nämlich Straßenkarte, Keilriemen und Stau vergessen.

Statt dessen genießen Sie schon den Hinflug. Gemütlich zurücklehnen, ausspannen. Möchten Sie ein Glas Sekt? Bitte anschnallen, wir landen in wenigen Minuten. Bus oder Taxi kutschieren Sie ins Hotel, die Reiseleitung gibt Tips, Koffer auspacken und schon paddeln Sie im Pool und machen dabei Pläne. Für Verpflegung ist gesorgt: Frühstück, Vollpension oder Ausflugs-Lunchpaket. Kaputt von der Reise? Nicht die Bohne. Also abends mal schnell in Pedro's Bar, oder Mondscheinspaziergang unter Palmen. Ohne Muskelkater vom langen Fahren.

Kurz: Urlaub von der ersten bis zur letzten Minute. Lust bekommen? Na, dann los.

Ihre TUI,
NUR, ITS.
Hapag-Lloyd
und Condor.

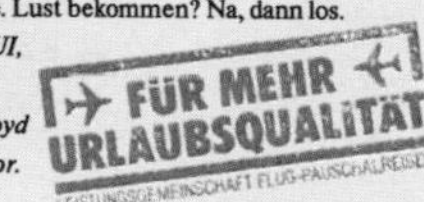

425

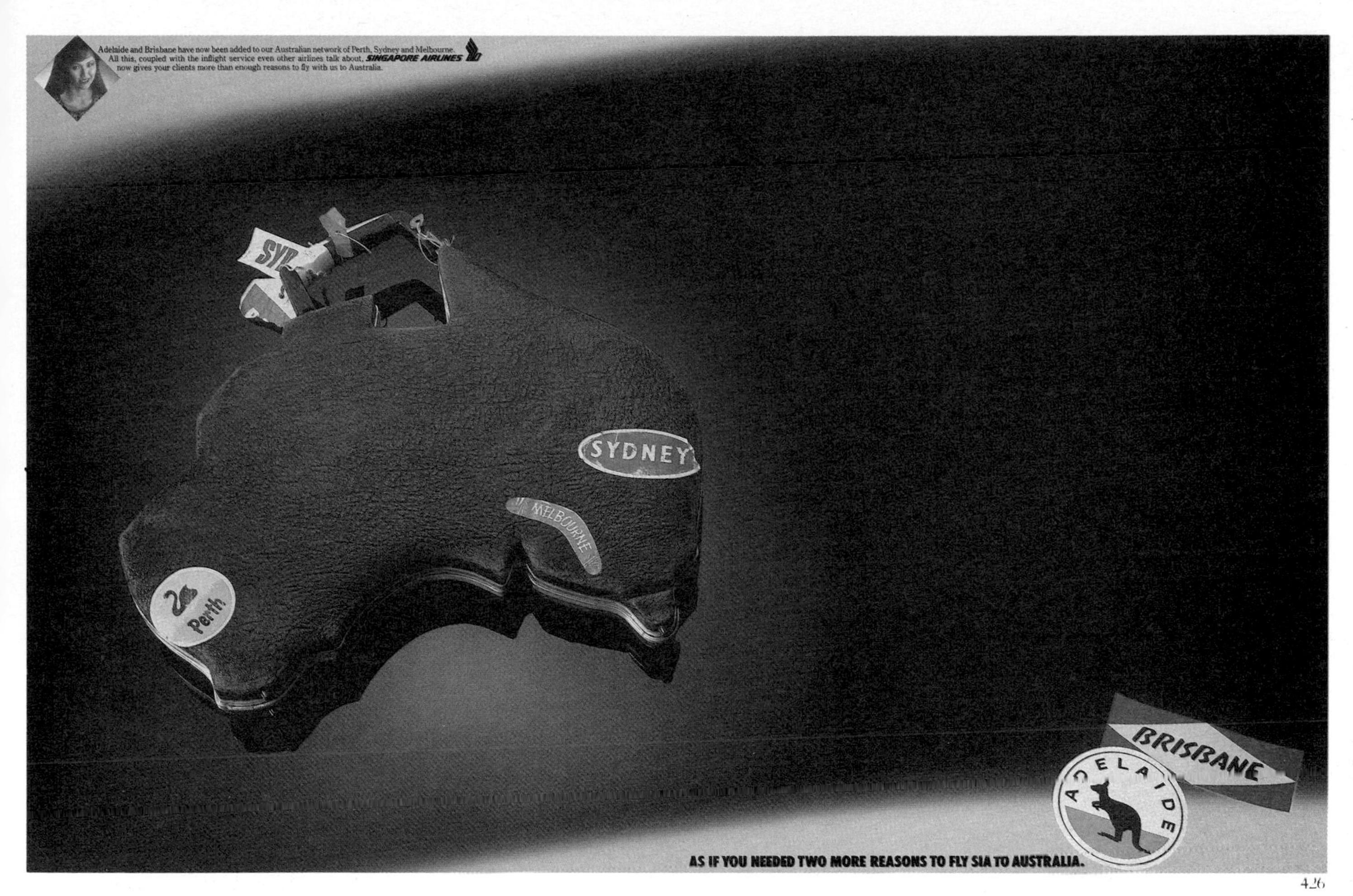

AS IF YOU NEEDED TWO MORE REASONS TO FLY SIA TO AUSTRALIA.

426

426
Singapore Airlines
United Kingdom
Agency: TBWA, London

A witty visual device – Australia represented as a suitcase – serves the serious purpose of showing which Australian cities SIA already serves. The ad announces the addition of two more destinations, Adelaide and Brisbane.

427
SAS International Hotels
Norway
Agency: Foote Cone & Belding, Oslo

From a campaign of full-page newspaper ads aimed at frequent business travellers and pointing out the advantages of staying in hotels owned by the Scandinavian Airlines System. The headline says 'In SAS hotels you can check in your luggage and get your boarding card at reception.' The visual amalgamation of hotel and airplane backs up the message.

SCANDINAVIAN
På SAS-hotellene
kan du sjekke inn kofferten
og få boarding-kortet
i resepsjonen*
På SAS-hotellene har vi ikke bare gjort det lettere for forretningsfolk å bo og arbeide. Vi har gjort det lettere å reise.
Glem slepingen på tunge kofferter.
Glem køen foran skranken på flyplassen. Hos oss ordner du alt i resepsjonen på hotellet. Der leverer du koffertene og får boarding-kortet. På flyplassen går du bare direkte på flyet.
På SAS-hotellene har ordet service fått mening. Kom skal du se.
SAS
INTERNATIONAL HOTELS
*SAS Airline Check-in er tilgjengelig på de fleste av våre hoteller for passasjerer med SAS First Class, First Business Class, Business Class eller EuroClass billetter, og for fullt betalende innenlands passasjerer.

427

428, 429
Japan Air Lines
United Kingdom
Agency: SSC&B:Lintas, London

Traditional Japanese imagery is called upon to help assure the executive class traveller that JAL pays special attention to comfort and hospitality.

430
Townsend Thoresen ferries
Netherlands
Agency: Marketwinning Ayer, Wierden

Speed is the theme here. The headline suggests you may be drinking tea in England before you've had time to get round to coffee on the boat.

431
DFDS Seaways
Norway
Agency: Ogilvy & Mather, Oslo

'Spring comes earlier in Copenhagen', says the caption, which is true, of course, as far as Norwegians are concerned. But the shipping line is not promising to supply the romance.

432
Bermuda tourism
Canada
Agency: Foote Cone & Belding, Toronto

One of a series promoting Bermuda as a holiday resort during the autumn months. For once a pun seems to be justified.

428

429

430

431

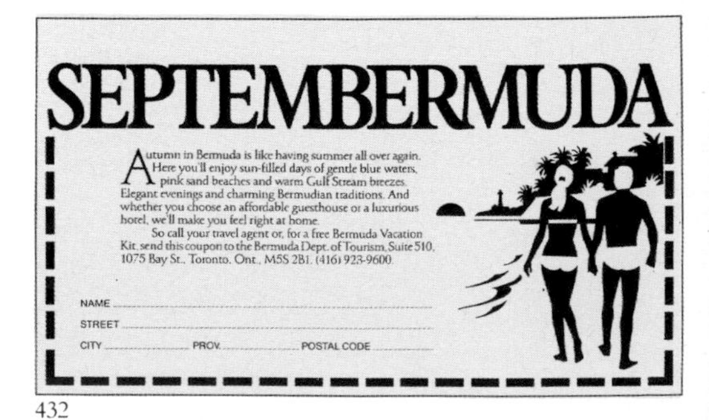

432

433, 434, 435
Hapag-Lloyd sea cruises
West Germany
Agency: Leonhardt & Kern, Stuttgart

These ads depict life on the cruise ship Europa, described in one headline as a 'Grand hotel with sea view'. Among the many advantages listed is the fact that it stores caviar in a special cold room. If the temperature there varies by as little as 1.1 degrees centigrade, an electronic warning system produces a 'Caviar alarm on the bridge', where three sailors can be seen receiving orders on how to cope with it. Europa cruises cater for a wide variety of people, and some are shown in the ad headed 'What does a typical cruise holidaymaker look like?'

Grand-Hotel mit Meerblick.

Es ist schneeweiß, 200 m lang, 28 m breit, 13 Etagen hoch… Es hat Reception, Salons, Bars, Restaurants, Nachtclubs, Kino, Friseur, Bank, Reisebüro, Bibliothek, Konditorei, Weinkeller, Fitness Center, Sauna, 3 Swimmingpools…

Es hat Zimmer, die 21 qm groß und schön komfortabel mit Baderaum, Klimaanlage, Teppichboden, Sitzgruppe, Telefon, Farbfernseher etc. ausgestattet sind…

Es hat 300 Mann und Frau Personal für 600 Gäste.

Es ist ein Grand-Hotel, das Europa heißt und zauberhafte Eigenschaften hat:

Während Sie im Restaurant frischen Hummer genießen oder auf dem Lidodeck Golf trainieren oder im Kino einen Krimi angucken oder im Hallenbad um die Wette kraulen oder sich im Club Belvedere mit Rotariern treffen oder morgens um sieben mit dem Frühsport beginnen oder beim Captains Dinner heftig flirten oder sich im Liegestuhl sonnen oder beim tea for two cheek to cheek tanzen oder einen Dia-Vortrag anhören oder sich den Rücken massieren lassen oder ein Telegramm aufgeben oder einfach aufs Meer blicken… während Sie all dies tun (oder all dies bleiben lassen) bringt Sie das Grand-Hotel Europa mit steten 21 Knoten zu den schönsten Plätzen der Welt!

Wenn Sie mehr über die ms Europa und Genaueres über ihr Kreuzfahrten-Programm und Interessantes über die großen Kabinen wissen wollen, dann gehen Sie doch mal bei Ihrem Reisebüro vorbei.

Oder schreiben Sie an Hapag-Lloyd AG, Kreuzfahrten, Postfach 107947, D-2800 Bremen 1.

Schauen Sie mal auf die 13 Decks der ms Europa:
DECK 1 *(Signaldeck)*: *Hier werden die Flaggen gesetzt, hier sind die Antennen, die uns mit der ganzen Welt verbinden.*
DECK 2 *(Columbusdeck)*: *Einerseits mit aussichtsreicher Sicht, andererseits mit einem versteckten Plätzchen für FKK-Anhänger.*
DECK 3 *(Lidodeck)*: *Schwimmbad mit gläsernem Schiebedach, Lido Bar, Club Belvedere, Sonnendeck mit Liegestühlen, Golftraining, Shuffleboard.*
DECK 4 *(Sportdeck)*: *Auf diesem und auf anderen Decks ist viel Platz für Sport: Tischtennis, Gymnastik, Tennis…, auch mal Shuffleboard, Deckschach etc.*
DECK 5 *(Sonnendeck)*: *Swimmingpool unterm freien Himmel, Liegedeck, Clipper Bar mit offenen Promenaden.*
DECK 6 *(Oberdeck)*: *Europa Salon, Delfter Krug, Bibliothek, Boutique, Juwelier, Frisiersalon, Stand zum Tontaubenschießen.*
DECK 7 *(Hauptdeck)*: *Europa Restaurant, Information, Zahlmeister, Touristikbüro, Casino.*
DECK 8 *(Atlantikdeck)*: *Riesige Küche, duftende Bäckerei, feine Konditorei.*
DECK 9 *(Pazifikdeck)*: *In großen Kühl- und Lagerräumen werden hier Weine und eine Menge sonstiger Vorräte untergebracht.*
DECK 10 *(A-Deck)*: *Theater, das je nach Bedarf auch Konferenzraum und Kino ist. Hausdruckerei, Hospital.*
DECK 11 *(B-Deck)*: *Foto-Labor, Schneiderei.*
DECK 12 *(C-Deck)*: *Fitness Center mit topfiten Geräten, Hallenbad mit Gegenstromanlage, Sauna, Massage-Raum, Solarium, Ruheraum und, nicht zu vergessen, der Nachtclub Kajüte.*
DECK 13 *(D-Deck)*: *Ganz unten liegt das Herz der Europa mit den beiden Hauptmaschinen.*

P.S. Auf der Europa gibt es allein 3870 qm Liegefläche!

ms Europa — Hapag-Lloyd AG

433

Kaviar-Alarm auf der Kommandobrücke!

Es waren einmal zwei deutsche Reedereien. Die eine hieß »Hamburg - Amerikanische Packetfahrt-Actien-Gesellschaft«, kürzer Hapag. Die andere war der »Norddeutsche Lloyd« in Bremen. Beide taten sich 1970 als Hapag-Lloyd zusammen; doch jede Reederei hatte bereits vorher mit über 1300 Schiffen in über 100 Jahren jede Menge Erfahrung auf den sieben Meeren gesammelt. Und das spüren Sie, wenn Sie auf das Hapag-Lloyd-Kreuzfahrtenschiff ms Europa kommen. Hier geht's ganz schön gründlich, pünktlich und perfekt zu.

Beispielsweise die Landausflüge: Sie werden ein Jahr im voraus organisiert. Wenn wir am Mittwoch, dem 26. Dezember 1984, einen [illegible] findet der auch statt.

Oder die Betreuung: Auf 600 Kreuzfahrer kommen 300 Mann und Frau Besatzung, um Sie rundrum zu verwöhnen.

Oder das himmlische Essen: Da fliegen wir zur Spargelzeit gut und gern mal 350 Kilo frischen Schwetzinger Stangenspargel von Frankfurt nach Montego Bay/Jamaika, wenn dort gerade die Europa kreuzt.

Perfekt sind auch die 21 qm großen Kabinen und das Kinoprogramm und die Gymnastiklehrerin und die Liederabende und das Fitness Center und der Nachtclub und der Tango-Unterricht und die Lagerräume…

A propos Lagerräume, nur ein kleines Beispiel: Wir lagern unseren russischen Kaviar in einem besonders gesicherten Kühlraum, der elektronisch bewacht wird. Schwankt die Temperatur im Kaviarraum auch nur um 1,1 Grad C, gibt es Kaviar-Alarm auf der Kommandobrücke!

Daß wir bei all dem Perfektionismus ganz schön gemütlich sein können, möchten wir Ihnen nebenbei auch sagen.

Wollen Sie mehr über die Europa wissen? Dann kreuzen Sie doch mal bei Ihrem Reisebüro auf. Oder schreiben Sie uns: Hapag-Lloyd AG, Kreuzfahrten, Postfach 107947, D 2800 Bremen 1.

ms Europa — Hapag-Lloyd AG

434

Wie sieht ein typischer Kreuzfahrer aus?

Eines sind sie alle, die Kreuzfahrer auf der ms Europa: verschieden! Da sind zum Beispiel abgeklärte Abenteurer und frische Hochzeitspärchen dabei, oder Manager, Hausfrauen, Akademiker, Privatiers, Handwerker, Angestellte, Freiberufler, ganze Familien, einzelne Damen, Bekannte und Unbekannte, welche mit 1 Dutzend Koffern und andere mit 1 Reisetasche.

Alle Altersgruppen kreuzen auf: Das Ergebnis von 2 Reisen, die wir kürzlich machten, wird jene überraschen, die meinen, das Kreuzfahren setze ein ziemlich gestandenes Alter voraus. 7% sind bis 19 Jahre, 5% sind 20–29 Jahre, 19% sind 30–44 Jahre, 35% sind 45–59 und 34% sind darüber.

Das Interessante an Bord der Europa: Jeder ist aufgeschlossen, jeder akzeptiert den anderen, so wie er ist. Man macht zusammen Landausflüge, Malkurse, Tanzstunden; dreht Jogging-Runden auf den endlosen Decks; spielt Schach und Bridge, Golf und Tennis; geht gemeinsam in den Nachtclub, ins Kino, zur Frühgymnastik, zum Captains Dinner, zum Kostümball, ins Fitness Center. Oder man geht sich einfach aus dem Weg… denn alles ist auf der Europa möglich!

Wenn Sie ganz genau wissen wollen, wie ein typischer Kreuzfahrer aussieht, dann kommen Sie doch mal an Bord! Unsere Reisen bringen Sie zu den schönsten Plätzen, fernsten Inseln, weißesten Stränden und fremdesten Menschen. Sie dauern 7 bis 99 Tage und kosten von 2.310,– bis 94.510,– DM. Ihr Reisebüro sagt Ihnen gerne, wo wir in diesem Jahr noch aufkreuzen. Oder schreiben Sie uns. Hapag-Lloyd AG, Kreuzfahrten, Postfach 107947, D-2800 Bremen 1.

ms Europa — Hapag-Lloyd AG

435

436
Thomson Holidays
United Kingdom
Agency: J. Walter Thompson, London

For this winter sports ad the agency had the bright idea of putting two headlines on the same picture. Turn it upside down and you'll see that the skier does indeed need the 'full course of lessons' which the upside-down headline offers.

436

437
Berlin tourism
West Germany
Agency: Uniconsult, West Berlin

'Have a look for once at Berliners behind the façade', says the head. The picture is of a mural, 'the biggest zip fastener in the world', and copy says murals are ubiquitous in the city.

437

438, 439
Club Méditerranée
Italy
Agency: CPV Kenyon & Eckhardt, Milan

The picture of the footprint bears the caption 'Sometimes what is written on sand makes an impression for the whole of your life'. It's a subtle way of suggesting that a Club Med holiday will leave you with lasting memories. The 'guitar' ad, placed by the business incentives division of the Club, says 'Our proposal to give more rhythm to your managers.' Firms are invited to send their best staff on a Club Med holiday.

440
Bahamas tourism
United States
Agency: N.W. Ayer, New York

From a campaign aimed at sports enthusiasts and based on the wide range of sporting facilities in the islands. The campaign was designed to run in specific sports publications, such as golfing or sailing magazines, as well as general ones.

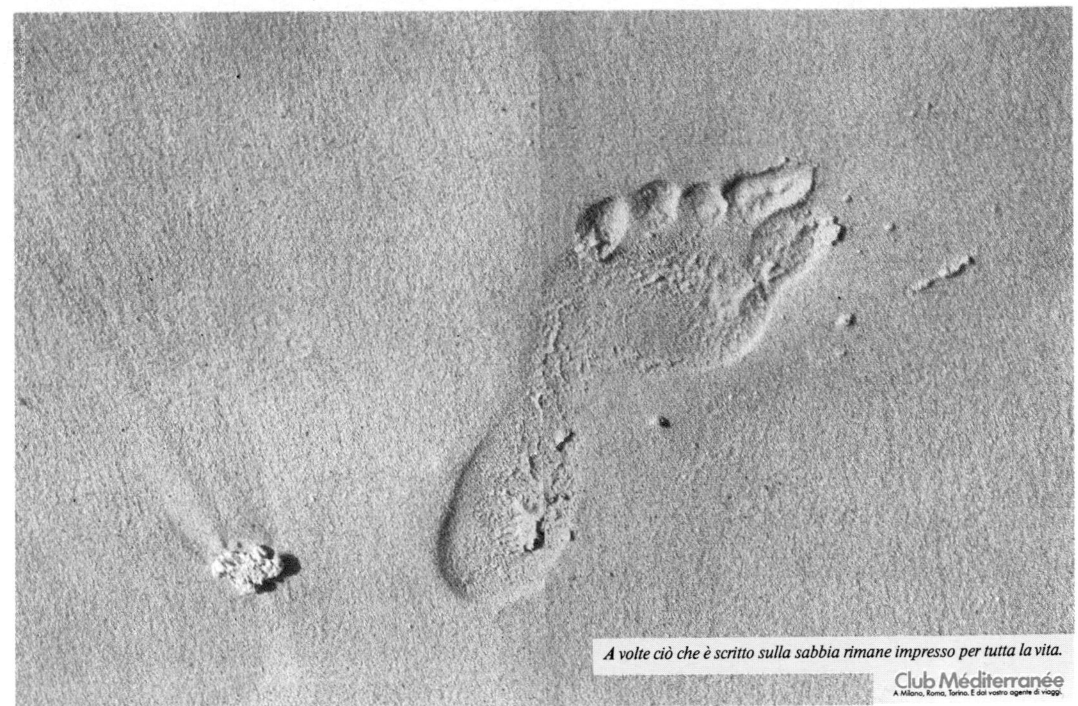

A volte ciò che è scritto sulla sabbia rimane impresso per tutta la vita.
Club Méditerranée
A Milano, Roma, Torino. E dal vostro agente di viaggi.

438

La nostra proposta per dare ancora più ritmo ai vostri manager.
Club Méditerranée
Divisione Incentive. Tel. 77861.

439

221
32 SPORTS MAKE IT BETTER IN THE BAHAMAS.
The sports paradise known as The Bahamas is the perfect adult playground. Where you can fish, snorkel, sail, golf, dive, play tennis, or just drift with the tide. Nature blessed The Bahamas with a warm sun. Sugar-fine beaches.
And crystal-clear waters. All we did was dress it up with more sports than you could possibly cover in one vacation.
For more sports information, call 800-32-SPORT. For reservations on Nassau/Paradise Island, Freeport/Grand Bahama or the Family Islands, see your travel agent or call toll free 800-327-0787. In Dade County, 433-3821.

440

list of credits

1, 2, 3
Agency self-promotion
United Kingdom
Advertiser: Ogilvy & Mather, London
Account director: Alec Worster
Creative director: Don Arlett
(Cave dwellers:)
Art director: Derrick Hass
Copywriter: Rowan Dean
Photographer: Barney Edwards
(Screwed-up ad:)
Art director: Garry Horner
Copywriter: Indra Sinha
Photographer: Martin Thompson
(Boot:)
Art director: Martyn Wlsh
Copywriter: Malcolm Gluck
Photographer: Jimmy Wormser

4, 5
Agency self-promotion
Japan
Advertiser: Kasugai, Nagoya City
Creative director: Shozo Murase
Art director: Shozo Murase
Copywriter: Shozo Murase
Designers: Jun Yoshida, Toshinori Nozaki
Illustrator: Masahiko Fujii

6, 7
Agency self-promotion
Spain
Agency: McCann-Erickson, Madrid
Creative director: Angel del Pino
Art director: Antonio Mosquera
Copywriter: Chelo Hernandez
Photographer: Miguel Martinez

8
Agency self-promotion
Netherlands
Advertiser: Ted Bates, Amsterdam
Account director: W.J.C. Kau
Creative director: Roger Hale
Art director: Roger Hale
Copywriter: Donald Lopez Cardoso
Photographer: Hans Kroeskamp

9
Agency self-promotion
United Kingdom
Advertiser: Young & Rubicam, London
Creative director: Chris Wilkins
Art director: Peter Ibbitson
Copywriter: Chris Wilkins
Designer: Peter Ibbitson
Photographer: Frank Farrelly

10
Agency self-promotion
USA
Advertiser: Hutchins/Young & Rubicam, Rochester, New York
Account director: Jim Morey
Creative director: Bob Haefner
Art director: Dave Clar
Copywriter: Jim Morey
Photographer: George Kamper

11
Agency self-promotion
Italy
Advertiser: Young & Rubicam, Milan
Creative director: Gavino Sanna
Art director: Gavino Sanna
Copywriter: Andrea Concato

12
Agency self-promotion
Netherlands
Advertiser: Marketwinning Ayer, Wierden
Account director: Hans Horneman
Creative director: Erno Reuvekamp
Art directors: Charles Riviere, Fred ten Tusscher
Copywriter: Erno Reuvekamp
Photographer: Paul Haverkort

13
Agency self-promotion
Italy
Advertiser: FCA/Sabbatini Baldoni
Creative directors: Sandro Baldoni, Lele Panzeri
Art director: Lele Panzeri
Copywriter: Sandro Baldoni
Photographer: Joe Oppedisano

14
Haig whisky
Japan
Advertiser: Suntory
Agency: Dentsu, Tokyo
Creative director: Masahiro Nakamura
Art director: Masahisa Nakamura
Copywriter: Hiroshi Ichikura
Photographers: Kishin Shimoyama, Masayuki Motomiya

15
Cuty Sark whisky
France
Advertiser: Cusenier
Marketing director: Christian Boulard
Brand manager: Gérard Vignacq
Agency: Young & Rubicam, Paris
Account director: Claude Faucher
Account supervisor: Philippe Hamache
Creative directors: Jean-Paul Bacquer, Gérard Monot
Art director: Pascal Midavaine
Copywriter: Claude Drouilhat
Illustrator: Pascal Midavaine

16
Doble-V whisky
Spain
Advertiser: Commercial Domecq/ Hiram Walker
Agency: McCann-Erickson, Madrid
Art director: Luis Solero
Copywriter: Rosa Villasante
Photographer: Miguel Martinez

17
Seagram's V.O. Canadian whisky
United States
Advertiser: Seagram Distillers
Executive vice-president, marketing: T. McInerny
Marketing director: R. McCarthy
Agency: Ogilvy & Mather, New York
Account director: Michael Newbrand
Account manager: Adam Sunderland
Creative director: Tom Rost
Art director: Saskia Mossel
Copywriter: Steve Baer
Photographer: George Hausman

18
Johnnie Walker whisky
Switzerland
Advertiser: Siegenthaler
Client executive: Harry Siegenthaler
Agency: Young & Rubicam, Bern
Account director: Ingrid Gfeller
Creative director: H.J. Zürcher
Art director: Mathias Babst
Copywriter: H.J. Zürcher
Photographer: R. Spengler

19
Johnnie Walker Red Label whisky
United Kingdom
Advertiser: The Distillers Company
Marketing director: David McNair
Group product manager: Peter Clarke
Product manager: Ged Buffee
Agency: Young & Rubicam, London
Account director: Charles Hare
Account manager: Sam Mitchell-Innes
Creative director: Chris Wilkins
Art director: Peter Ibbitson
Copywriter: Chris Wilkins
Photographer: Max Forsythe

20
Hennessy Cognac
United Kingdom
Advertiser: International Distillers & Vintners
Marketing director: Tony Scouller
Agency: Leagas Delaney Partnership, London
Account director: Simon Jones
Creative director: Tim Delaney
Art director: Graeme Norways
Copywriters: Patrick Woodward, Tim Delaney
Illustrator: François Gillet
Photographer: François Gillet

21
Hine Cognac
United Kingdom
Advertiser: The Distillers Company
Marketing director: David McNair
Brand manager: Therese Baker
Agency: Dorland Advertising, London
Account director: John Browell
Creative director: David McGrath
Art director: Tony Whetton
Copywriter: Honor Whetton
Photographer: Rolph Gobits

22
Rémy Martin VSOP Cognac
United Kingdom
Advertiser: Rémy Martin
Managing director: John Mangiacapra
Agency: SSC&B:Lintas, London
Account director: Tim Isaac
Account manager: Ben Mackintosh
Creative director: Terry Coombes
Copywriter: Mavis Cain
Photographer: Derek Seagrim

23
Plymouth Gin
United Kingdom
Advertiser: Long John International – Plymouth Gin
Marketing director: Malcolm Burr
Agency: Lowe Howard-Spink Campbell-Ewald, London
Account director: David Jones
Creative director: Alfredo Marcantonio
Art director: Alan Waldie
Copywriter: Adrian Holmes
Illustrator: Roy Knipe

24
Gordon's Gin
United States
Advertises: Renfield Importers
Agency: Grey Advertising, New York
Account director: Stewart Hegleman
Account manager: Arthur Ostrob
Creative director: Richard Karp
Art director: Louis Hernandez
Copywriter: Judy Frisch
Photographers: Michael Gray, Tony Baroza, Larry Silver

25
Gordon's Gin
United Kingdom
Advertiser: Tanqueray, Gordon & Company
Marketing director: Peter Goodchild
Brand manager: Derek Long
Agency: Foote, Cone & Belding, London
Account director: Robert Ballin
Account supervisor: Kevin Green
Account executive: Douglas Chirnside
Creative director: Barry Smith
Art director: Bob Gill
Copywriter: Peter Cayless
Photographer: Mick Dean
Illustrator: Alan Adler
Typographer: Mark Smith

26
Smirnoff vodka
United Kingdom
Advertiser: International Distillers & Vintners
Marketing director: Anthony Scouller
Product Group Head: Chris Nadin
Brand manager: Richard Allaway
Agency: Young & Rubicam, London
Account director: Alistair Delves
Account manager: Tom Bury
Creative director: Chris Wilkins
Art director: Colin Morris
Copywriter: Peter Townsend
Photographer: Brian Griffin

27
Vladivar Vodka
United Kingdom
Advertiser: G. & J. Greenall
Marketing director: Peter Clarke
Advertising director: Michael Lloyd-Davies
Agency: Kirkwood & Partners, London
Account director: Martin Mason
Account manager: Carolyn Ashton
Creative director: Ken Mullen
Art director: Paul Franks
Copywriter: Mike O'Brien
Illustrator: Phil Green
Photographer: Ian Giles
Typographer: Valerie Buckler

28, 29
Martini
West Germany
Advertiser: Martini & Rossi
Marketing manager: Helmut Engelbrecht
Product manager: Hans-Wilhelm Lahr
Agency: McCann-Erickson, Frankfurt
Account director: Ingeborg von Fürstenberg
Art director: Gert Mayr-Steinmentz
Copywriter: Frank Leithäuser
Photographer: Heinz Wuchner

30
Martini Extra Dry
United Kingdom
Advertiser: Martini & Rossi
Communications director: Tony Hill
Advertising manager: Wendy Plim
Product and brand manager: Robert Berry
Agency: McCann-Erickson, London
Group director: John Bradbury
Account director: Andrew Shingleton
Account manager: Nick Steyn
Executive creative director: Don White
Creative director: Martin Mayhew
Art director: Martin Mayhew
Copywriter: Martin Mayhew
Photographer: John Gladwin

31
Campari
International
Advertiser: Davide Campari, Milan
Marketing director: Marco Perelli Cippo
Agency: B Communications, Milan
Account director: Gigi Bertani
Creative director: Titti Fabiani
Art director: Vittoria Cattaneo
Copywriter: Federico Mola
Photographer: Dennis Manarchy

32
Suntory Twilight: Cocktails Book
Japan
Advertiser: Suntory
Agency: Dentsu, Tokyo
Creative director: Masahisa Nakamura
Art director: Masahisa Nakamura
Copywriter: Michiaki Taguchi
Illustrators: Masahisa Nakamura, Zenpaku Suzuki

33a, 33b
Amaretto di Saronno
France
Advertiser: Illva
Marketing director: Giorgio Stanzani
Agency: Roux Séguéla Cayzac & Goudard, Paris
Account director: Jean-Claude Rassat
Creative director: Thierry Granier Deferre
Art director: Eric de la Hosseraye
Copywriter: Hugo Veuillet
Photographer: Jeremy Bailey

34
Taranagi Kiwi-Fruit Cocktail
South Africa
Advertiser: Gilbeys Distillers & Vintners
Marketing director: Peter Fleck
Advertising director: Hentie Engelbrecht
Product manager: Chris Weedon
Brand manager: Don Ball
Agency: Campbell-Ewald, Cape Town
Account director: Joe Sievers
Creative director: Peter Southworth
Copywriter: Greg Burke
Photographer: Jac de Villiers
Typographer: Mary Henry
Repro: Hirt & Carter

35
Banks's Ale
United Kingdom
Advertiser: Wolverhampton and Dudley Breweries
Agency: TBWA, London
Creative directors: Neil Patterson, Malcolm Gaskin
Art director: John Knight
Copywriter: David O'Connor Thompson
Illustrator: Larry Franklin

36
Tetley Bitter Beer
United Kingdom
Advertiser: Joshua Tetley
Brand manager: Paul Weilgus
Agency: Kirkwood & Partners London
Account director: Robert Deighton
Account manager: Martin Mason
Creative director: Ken Mullen
Art director: Tony Muranka
Copywriter: Ken Mullen
Illustrator: Chris Moore

37
Long Life beer
United Kingdom
Advertiser: Allied Breweries
Marketing director: Ian Hannah
Advertising director: Alan Mason
Agency: Kirkwood & Partners, London
Account director: Robert Deighton
Account manager: Martin Mason
Creative director: Ken Mullen
Art director: Tony Muranka
Copywriter: Ken Mullen
Illustrator: Ted Hammond
Typographer: Valerie Buckler

38
Loburg beer
Belgium
Advertiser: Stella Artois
Marketing team: Michel Uyttendael, Michael Kuypers, Tony Brutsaert
Agency: McCann-Erickson, Brussels
Account executive: Xavier Jadoul
Creative team: Paul Beal, Stu Thorpe, André Wij
Photographer: Roy Stiles, London

39
Allied Breweries take-home beers
United Kingdom
Advertiser: Allied Breweries
Marketing director: Robin Stotter
Advertising manager: Terry Watkins
Agency: Kirkwood & Partners, London
Account director: Martin Mason
Creative director: Ken Mullen
Art director: Colin Underhay
Copywriter: Alex Pearl
Illustrator: Paul Davies
Typographer: Valerie Buckler

40
Kirin beer
Hong Kong
Advertiser: Kirin Brewery Company
Agency: SSC&B:Lintas, Hong Kong
Account manager: Tony Perone
Creative director: Tony Perone
Art director: Benny Cheng

41
Kirin beer
Japan
Advertiser: Kirin Brewery Company
Advertising director: Tushio Takamatsu
Agency: Dentsu, Tokyo
Account manager: Koichi Suzuki
Creative director: Akira Odagiri
Art director: Tetsu Goto
Designer: Shigenobu Yamamoto
Copywriter: Akira Kagami
Photographer: Masayuki Motomiya

42
Babycham
United Kingdom
Advertiser: Showerings
Managing director: David Gwyther
Product manager: Kevin Lannigan
Agency: Saatchi & Saatchi Compton, London
Account director: Sue Coupland
Account manager: Chris Edwards
Creative director: Jeremy Sinclair
Art director: Jonathan Iles
Copywriter: Maxine Baker
Photographer: Jem Grischotti

43
Cockburn's Special Reserve Port
United Kingdom
Advertiser: John Harvey & Sons
Marketing director: Walter Caldwell
Marketing manager: Ann Stewart
Product and brand manager: Phil Taylor
Agency: J. Walter Thompson, London
Account director: David Baker
Account manager: William Eccleshare
Executive creative director: Allen Thomas
Creative director: Rick Cook
Art director: Tom Moult
Copywriter: Simon Collins
Illustrator: Paul Slater

44
French wines
Denmark
Advertiser: Sopexa
Agency: McCann-Erickson Copenhagen
Art director: Pernille Kjaer
Copywriter: Hanne Ingwersen

45
Sanraku wines
Japan
Advertiser: Sanraku
Agency: Dentsu, Tokyo
Account director: Atsushi Yamashita
Creative director: Masamichi Yoshino
Art directors: Masamichi Yoshino, Hiroyuki Itoh
Copywriter: Reiko Negishi
Photographer: Masayoshi Sukita

46
Veuve de Vernay wine
United Kingdom
Advertiser: Colman's of Norwich
Marketing director: Roger Munby
Brand manager: Steve Duncan
Agency: Foote Cone & Belding, London
Account director: Les Stern
Account supervisor: Hugh Salmon
Account executive: Nick Mustoe
Creative director: Barry Smith
Art director: Gerard Stamp
Copywriter: Loz Simpson
Photographer: Ian Giles
Typographer: Mark Smith

47
French wines
United Kingdom
Advertiser: Food & Wine from France
Marketing director: Michel Gérard
Advertising manager: Janice Wilson
Agency: Aspect Advertising, London
Account director: Jeremy Prescot
Account manager: Patricia Hodgins
Creative directors: John Davis, Malachy Quinn
Art director: John Davis
Copywriter: Malachy Quinn
Photographer: Jimmy Wormser

48
Audi Quattro
West Germany
Advertiser: Audi, Ingolstadt
Sales director: Dr Wischenbarth
Advertising director: Helmut Maasen
Advertising manager: Dieter Eichelmann
Brand manager: Hartmut Plamböck
Agency: Team/BBDO, Düsseldorf
Management supervisor: Klaus-Jürgen Schulte
Account executive: Horst Krapohl
Executive creative director: Michael Hausberger
Creative directors: Eckhardt Rössler, Jürgen Heymen
Art director: Wolfgang Groffy
Copywriters: Eckhardt Rössler, Dirk Driesen
Photographer: Manfred Rieker Studio, Magstadt

49
Audi 100
United Kingdom
Advertiser: Volkswagen
Marketing manager: John Meszaros
Agency: Bartle Bogle Hegarty, London
Account director: Jerry Judge
Creative director: John Hegarty
Art directors: Gary Denham, Brian Morrow
Copywriter: David Watkinson
Photographer: Jerry Oke

50
Audi Quattro
United Kingdom
Advertiser: Volkswagen
Marketing manager: John Meszaros
Agency: Bartle Bogle Hegarty, London
Account director: Jerry Judge
Creative director: John Hegarty
Art director: Gary Walton
Copywriter: Phil Wiggins
Illustrator: Susan Akantarilla

51a, 51b
Renault 5 TSE
Advertiser: Renault
Marketing executives: J.-Claude Muller, Véronique Lefebvre
Agency: Publicis, Paris
Account managers: Jacques-François Martin, Philippe Senejoux
Art director: Jean-Marie Moisan
Copywriter: Laurent Forlani
Illustrator: Gilbert Mas

52, 53
Fiat Panda
Italy
Advertiser: Fiat
Agency: Benton & Bowles, Milan
Account director: Rick Ray
Account manager: Ivano Pavarin
Creative director: Gavino Sanna
Art director: Roberto Fiamenghi
Copywriter: Andrea Concato
Illustrator: Studio Plagio

54
Volvo 740
United Kingdom
Advertiser: Volvo Concessionaires
Marketing director: Bill Phelan
Marketing manager: Martin Runnacles
Agency: Abbott Mead Vickers/SMS, London
Account director: Paul Tredwell
Account manager: Jane Loxley-Hughes
Creative director: David Abbott
Art director: Ron Brown
Copywriter: David Abbott
Photographer: Martin Thompson

55
Opel Corsa TR
Spain
Advertiser: Opel-General Motors
Agency: McCann-Erickson, Madrid
Creative director: Angel del Pino
Creative group head: Roberto de Gracia
Art director: Fernando Soto
Copywriter: Charo Sanchez
Photographer: Miguel Martinez

56
Volkswagen Polo
United Kingdom
Advertiser: VAG (UK)
Marketing director: Brian Bowler
Advertising manager: John Meszaros
Product manager: Dominique Burnell
Agency: Doyle Dane Bernbach, London
Account director: Keith Shingfield
Account manager: Andrew Crosthwaite
Creative director: Tony Brignull
Art director: Rob Morris
Copywriter: Stuart Blake
Photograph: Brighton Evening Argus

57
Volkswagen Golf GTi
United Kingdom
Advertiser: VAG (UK)
Marketing director: Brian Bowler
Advertising manager: John Meszaros
Product manager: Lucy Cooper
Agency: Doyle Dane Bernbach, London
Account director: Keith Shingfield
Account manager: Andrew Crosthwaite
Creative director: Tony Brignull
Art director: Alan Dunbreck
Copywriter: Peter Gunn
Photographer: Max Forsythe

58a, 58b
Citroën CX GTI
France
Advertiser: Citroën
Marketing director: Christian Bailly
Agency: Roux Séguéla Cayzac & Goudard, Paris
Account director: Jean-Luc Lenoir
Creative director: Dominique Chevalier
Art director: Pierre Gautronet
Copywriter: Michel Clairon
Photographer: Jean-Paul Goude

59
Ford cars
United Kingdom
Advertiser: Ford Motor Company
Marketing director: W. E. Camplisson
Advertising manager: Graham Smith
Agency: Ogilvy & Mather, London
Account director: Angus Grieve
Account manager: Jeremy Holmes
Creative director: Don Arlett
Art director: Terry Holben
Copywriter: Peter Sugden

60
Ford Mercury Lynx
United States
Advertiser: Lincoln-Mercury
General manager: Robert Rewey
Advertising manager: John Vanderzee
General marketing manager: Ross Roberts
Agency: Young & Rubicam, Detroit
Group director: Chuck Riley
Account supervisor: Tim Hart
Group creative director: John Nieman
Art director: Mike Schell
Copywriter: Mark Fenske

61
BSL tankers
France
Advertiser: BSL
Marketing manager: Hélène Tarral
Agency: GMC/Brains Ayer
Account director: Jérôme Camus
Creative director: Michel Dufaux
Art director: Guy-Noël Pelé
Illustration: Studio Bahamas

62
Pirelli tyres
United Kingdom
Advertiser: Pirelli
Marketing director: Martin Wood
Advertising director: Peter Roberts
Product manager: Peter Tyson
Agency: McCormick Publicis, London
Account director: James Flammiger
Account manager: Paul Jackson
Creative director: Gerry Moira
Art director: John Aldred
Copywriter: Gerry Moira
Illustrator: Bob Carlos Clark

63
Goodyear Grand Prix-S
United Kingdom
Advertiser: Goodyear Tyre & Rubber Co
Marketing director: Mike Powell
Agency: Lowe Howard-Spink Campbell-Ewald, London
Account director: David Jones
Creative director: Alfredo Marcantonio
Art director: Trevor Kennedy
Copywriter: Steve Spence
Photographer: Jimmy Wormser

64
Honda CBX motorcycle
Netherlands
Advertiser: Honda
Marketing manager: Rien Koster
Agency: Team, Rotterdam
Concept/copywriter: Jan van Buuren
Photographer: Klaas Bant

65, 66, 67
Hertz car-hire
France
Advertiser: Hertz
Marketing director: Michel Reynaud
Agency: Boulet Dru Dupuy Petit, Paris
Account director: Marie-Christine Dax
Creative director: Marie-Catherine Dupuy
Art director: Richard Claverie
Copywriter: Sylvie Ducourant
Photographer: Marty Evans

68
Shell petrol
France
Advertiser: Shell
Marketing director: Henri Lombard
Agency: Publicis, Paris
Account director: Marie-Thérèse Lombard
Art director: J.-Marie Moisan
Copywriter: Laurent Forlani
Illustrator: J.-Marie Moisan

69
Shell Top Motor Oil
Netherlands
Advertiser: Shell, Netherlands
Advertising director: H. A. Hokke
Product manager: R. Kroll
Brand manager: F. Wijnen
Agency: Ogilvy & Mather, Amsterdam
Account director: K. Krielen-Berkhout
Account manager: Jan Oldenburger
Creative director: Reinier Bresser
Art director: Emile Pater
Copywriter: Reinier Bresser
Illustrator: John Harwood
Photographer: Rob van Uchelen

70
Shell Super Diesel T motor oil
Norway
Advertiser: Shell, Norway
Marketing director: Odd Borge
Agency: Ogilvy & Mather, Oslo
Account director: Jon Vangsøy
Creative director: Bjørn Aune
Art director: Bjørn Aune
Copywriter: Tom Dahl
Photographer: Rune Venjar

71
Europ Assistance
France
Advertiser: Europ Assistance
Marketing director: Guy Morvan
Agency: Publicis, Paris
Account director: Christine Sauvalle
Art director: J.-Marie Moisan
Copywriter: Laurent Forlani
Illustrator: Romain Slocombe

72, 73, 74
Alexon women's clothes
United Kingdom
Advertiser: Steinberg Ltd
Marketing director: Anthony Stanbury
Agency: Saatchi & Saatchi Compton, London
Account director: Tony Cator
Account manager: Lavinia Guy
Creative director: Jeremy Sinclair
Art director: Paul Arden
Copywriter: Tim Mellors
Photographers: Richard Avedon (African Collection), Terence Donovan (Nude), Barry Lategan ('Less is More')

75
Sistiene women's clothes
Japan
Advertiser: Sistiene
Agency: Kasugai
Creative director: Shozo Murase
Art director: Shozo Murase
Designers: Jun Yoshida, Toshinori Nozaki
Illustrator: Koichi Inakoshi

76
Gloria Vanderbilt women's clothes
United States
Advertiser: Murjani
Agency: Doyle Dane Bernbach, New York
Account director: Arie Kopelman
Account manager: Milton Harkrader
Creative director: Mike Mangano
Art director: Bill Yamada
Copywriter: Ira Silver
Photographer: Jean Pagliuso

77
Rodier women's clothes
France
Advertiser: La Lainière de Roubaix
Marketing director: Pierre Santelli
Advertising manager: Geneviève Oulmi
Agency: Boulet Dru Dupuy Petit, Paris
Account director: Dominique Reinhard
Account executive: Anne Vaisière
Creative director: Marie-Catherine Dupuy
Art director: Richard Claverie
Copywriter: Sylvie Ducourant
Photographer: Peter Lindberg

78
New Man clothes
United Kingdom
Advertiser: New Man
Marketing director: Gilles Humbert
Advertising manager: Bernard Masson
Agency: Aspect Advertising, London
Account director: Mark Robinson
Creative directors: John Davis, Malachy Quinn
Art director: John Davis
Copywriter: John Davis
Illustrator: John Davis

79
Wrangler jeans
United Kingdom
Advertiser: Wrangler
Advertising manager: Robin Dilley
Agency: Collett Dickenson Pearce, London
Account director: Jonathan White
Creative director: David Brown
Art director: Rodger Williams
Copywriter: Paul Gayter
Illustrator: Charles Settrington

80
Lois jeans
France
Advertiser: Lois
Managing director: Jean-Pierre Emden
Agency: Grey, Paris
Account director: Jan van Aal
Creative director: Jean-Paul Lichtenberg
Art director: Michel Prestat
Copywriter: Pascal Maury
Photographer: Jacques Olivar

81
Maverick jeans
Argentina
Advertiser: Induswheel Saic
Marketing director: Osvaldo Datino
Agency: SSC&B:Lintas, Buenos Aires
Account director: Roberto Presas
Account manager: Rolando Fernandez
Creative director: Hector Mas
Art director: Eduardo Harvey
Copywriter: Carlos Panichelli

82
Fu's jeans and baggy trousers
India
Advertiser: Intercraft
Marketing directors: Vijay Mehta, Purshottam Dhir
Agency: Enterprise Advertising, Bombay
Account director: Rajiv Agarwal
Account manager: Alban Mendonca
Creative director: Mohammed Khan
Art director: Elsie Nanji
Copywriter: Rajan Nair
Photographer: Nadirsh Naoroji

83
Woollen garments
Netherlands
Advertiser: International Wool Secretariat
Agency: Young & Rubicam, Amsterdam
Account director: Malcolm Parker Brady
Account manager: Pedro Stempels
Creative directors: Hans Born, Duncan Mackintosh
Art director: Wim de Boer
Copywriter: Joris Bergsma
Photographer: Chris Lewis

84
Welcomme knitting wool
France
Advertiser: La Lainière de Roubaix
Marketing director: Michel Uytterhaegen
Product manager: Baudouin Prové
Agency: Boulet Dru Dupuy Petit, Paris
Account director: Sylvie Vinçon
Account executive: Cecile Ascola
Creative director: Marie-Catherine Dupuy
Art director: Marie-Christine Boissier
Copywriter: Alain Jalabert
Photographer: Elgort

85, 86
Woollen garments
France
Advertiser: International Wool Secretariat
Advertising manager: Marie-Laure Novel
Agency: Publicis, Paris
Account directors: Marie-Claude Mayer, Martine Pont
Art director: Marie Brazier
Copywriter: Béatrice Dallies-Labourdette
Photographer: Paolo Roversi

87, 88
Eiser tights
Finland
Advertiser: Eiser
Advertising manager: Satu Lindroos
Agency: Liikemainonta-McCann, Helsinki
Creative director: Jarl Lagercrantz
Art directors: Tuula Kauppinen, Anne Virtanen
Copywriters: Tuula Kauppinen, Eva Tietavainen
Photographer: Lasse Wuori

89
Pingouin tights
France
Advertiser: La Lainière de Roubaix
Marketing director: Michel Leonard
Product manager: Jean-Louis Dierickx
Agency: Boulet Dru Dupuy Petit, Paris
Account director: Dominique Reinhard
Account executive: François Michels
Creative director: Marie-Catherine Dupuy
Art director: Richard Claverie
Copywriter: Sylvie Ducourant
Photographer: Olivier Rotoscani

90
Jim underpants
Spain
Advertiser: Fabrilmalla
Agency: Tandem DDB Campmany Guasch, Barcelona
Account director: Jordi Prats
Creative director: Toni Guasch
Art director: Salvatore Adduci
Copywriter: Toni Guasch
Photographer: José-Luis Mendez

91
Romano shoes
India
Advertiser: Sterling Shoes
Marketing director: Rafik Tejani
Agency: Enterprise Advertising, Bombay
Account director: Rajiv Agarwal
Creative director: Mohammed Khan
Art directors: Mohammed Khan, Elsie Nanji
Copywriter: Mohammed Khan
Photographer: Shantanu Sheorey
Illustrator: Javed Choudhary

92
K Shoes
United Kingdom
Advertiser: K Shoemakers
Marketing director: John Reeves
Marketing manager: Ian Kell
Agency: Abbott Mead Vickers/SMS, London
Account director: Hamish Pringle
Account manager: Moira Tweddle
Creative director: David Abbott
Art director: Ron Brown
Copywriter: David Abbott
Photographer: Barney Edwards

93, 94
Training shoes
United Kingdom
Advertiser: New Balance
Agency: TBWA, London
Creative directors: Neil Patterson, Malcolm Gaskin
Art director: Logan Wilmont
Copywriter: David O'Connor Thompson
Photographers: Stak, Ian Giles

95
Adidas sports shoes
Norway
Advertiser: Adinor, Norway
Marketing director: Knut Arve Grønvold
Agency: Myres/Lintas, Oslo
Account manager: Jan Bay
Creative director: Arve Bjerke
Art directors: Per Hanevik, Mads Due-Tønnesen
Copywriter: Espen Hansen
Photographer: Harald Førland

96
Adidas sports shoes
Spain
Advertiser: Adidas
Agency: Bassat Ogilvy & Mather, Barcelona
Account director: Eva Tabah
Creative director: Luis Bassat
Art director: Pepe Rosas
Copywriter: Esther Vicente
Photographer: Michel Malka

97
Nordica ski boots
Italy
Advertiser: Nordica, Italy
General manager: Piero Pianca
Agency: Publinter Ayer, Milan
Account director: Annibale Pagliarin (Publinter Ayer, Padua)
Creative director: Vito Nuzzi
Art director: Gianni Lalli
Copywriter: Antonio Briguori
Photographer: Orlando Zambarbieri

98
Rank Xerox Ladylike electronic typewriter
West Germany
Advertiser: Rank Xerox
Advertising manager: Werner Rott
Agency: Heye Needham & Partner, Düsseldorf
Account director: Dieter Hoever
Creative director: Partho Gosh
Art director: Klaus Appel
Copywriter: Jörg Wolfgram
Photographer: David Bailey

99
IBM typewriters
United States
Advertiser: IBM
Agency: Doyle Dane Bernbach, New York
Account director: Lloyd Highbloom
Account manager: Joe Dell Aquila
Creative director: Irwin Warren
Art director: Gary Goldsmith
Copywriter: Irwin Warren

100, 101
Commodore Computers
West Germany
Advertiser: Commodore
Marketing communications manager: Josef Hüchtebrock
Agency: J. Walter Thompson, Frankfurt
Account director: Heinz-Detlef Gericke
Account manager: Götz Turowski
Art director: Irene Rudolph
Copywriter: Hans-Georg Vogel
Photographer: P. Greul

102, 103
IBM computers
West Germany
Advertiser: IBM, West Germany
Advertising manager: Herbert Herz
Product manager: Hans Alex Bauer
Agency: GGK, Düsseldorf
Account manager: Peter Bury
Creative director: Michael Schirner
Art director: Michael Preiswerk
Copywriter: Franz Brauer
Illustrator: René Fehr

104
Digital Computers
Most European Countries
Advertiser: Digital Equipment Corporation
Marketing director: Bruno D'Avonso
Advertising manager: Wolf Dittmair
Product manager: Jorgen Helervsen
Agency: Benton & Bowles, London
Account director: Ted Aves
Account manager: David Mayers
Creative director: David Mitchell
Art director: David Mitchell
Copywriter: Mike Gough
Photographer: Adrian Flowers
Art buyer: Rita Pulford
Typographer: Ian Dillon

105
NCR computers
West Germany
Advertiser: NCR
Marketing manager: Günter Klein
Agency: Die Crew, Stuttgart
Account director: Holger Bungert
Creative director: Alfred Benz
Art director: Alfred Benz
Copywriter: Dieter Blum
Photographer: Horst Wackerbart

106
IBM small computers
United States
Advertiser: IBM, USA
Agency: Doyle Dane Bernbach, New York
Account director: Lloyd Highbloom
Account manger: Joe Dell Aquila
Creative director: Irwin Warren
Art director: Amy Levitan
Copywriter: Richard Middendorf
Illustrator: A. B. Silverman Inc.

107
Nelco Corona personal computer
India
Advertiser: Nelco Office Products Division
Marketing director: Raju Bhinge
Agency: Enterprise Advertising, Bombay
Account manager: M. Raghunath
Creative director: Mohammed Khan
Art director: Sunil Mahadik
Copywriter: Rajan Nair

108
Honeywell computers
Italy
Advertiser: Honeywell
Advertising director: Enrico Guidotti
Agency: RSCG Mezzano Costantini Mignani, Milan
Account director: Dario Mezzano
Creative director: Marco Mignani
Art director: Gianpiero Vigorelli
Copywriter: Salvo Scibilia
Illustrator: Spikich

109
Honeywell computers
United Kingdom
Advertiser: Honeywell
Marketing director: Barry Francis
Agency: Gold Greenlees Trott, London
Account director: Steve Greenstead
Account manager: Mike Perry
Creative director: Dave Trott
Art director: Dave Waters
Copywriter: Jan van Mesdag
Photographer: Ian Giles

110
BBC Micro computer
United Kingdom
Advertiser: Acorn Computers
Marketing director: Chris Curry
Advertising director: John Caswell
Agency: Aspect Advertising, London
Account director: Eric Wilton
Account manager: Anthony Ray
Creative director: Malachy Quinn
Art director: Derek Rangecroft
Copywriter: Robin Murtough
Photographer: Bob Miller

111
Sharp PC5000 personal computer
United Kingdom
Advertiser: Sharp
Marketing services manager: Peter Maltby
Agency: Ayer Barker, London
Account director: Jonathan Hill
Creative director: Terry Howard
Art director: Cyril Vickers
Copywriter: Terry Howard
Photographer: Gary Bryan
Typographer: Mac McAloon

112
Philips Elephant Computer
Singapore
Advertiser: Philips, Singapore
Marketing manager: Thomas Lim
Advertising manager: Chua Seng Chwee
Agency: SSC&B:Lintas, Singapore
Account manager: Lawrence Seah
Creative director: Peter Wharton
Art director: John Yap
Copywriter: Rachel Wong
Illustrator: John Yap

113
ICL Distributed Computer Systems
United Kingdom
Advertiser: ICL
Marketing director: Roger Hill
Advertising manager: Terry Ward
Agency: J. Walter Thompson, London
Account director: David Rousell
Creative director: Max Henry
Art directors: Peter Celiz, Guy Moore
Copywriter: Kevin Ovard
Illustrator: Mick Brownfield

114
Alice children's computer
France
Advertiser: Matra Data Systems
Managing director: Philippe d'Argent
Agency: Boulet Dru Dupuy Petit, Paris
Account director: Marie-Christine Dax
Creative director: Marie-Catherine Dupuy
Art director: Philippe Pollet-Villard
Copywriter: Olivier Dorangeon
Photography and illustration: Philippe Cauquil, Robert Petersen

115
Data General computer systems
United States
Advertiser: Data General
Manager: Dennis Byron
Agency: Foote Cone & Belding, New York
Account director: Anne Lynn
Creative directors: Tedd Littleford, Hector Robledo
Art director: Bob Funk
Copywriter: Kim Olson
Photographers: Mitchell Funk & Arthur Meyerson, Woodfin/Camp

116
Apricot Communiqué service
United Kingdom
Advertiser: ACT
Marketing director: John Leftwitch
Agency: Collett Dickenson Pearce & Partners, London
Account director: David McLaren
Creative director: David Brown
Art director: Garry Horner
Copywriter: Indra Sinha
Photographer: Stak

117
Acornsoft computer games
United Kingdom
Advertiser: Acornsoft
Agency: Aspect Advertising, London
Account director: Eric Wilton
Account manager: Anthony Ray
Creative director: Malachy Quinn
Art director: Ian Sishton
Copywriter: David Pickles
Photographer: Angus Forbes
Model maker: David Hayes

118
Burroughs Linc
France
Advertiser: Burroughs
Marketing director: Michel Prudhomme
Agency: Boulet Dru Dupuy Petit, Paris
Account director: Hervé Brunette
Account executive: Alain Margerit
Creative director: Marie-Catherine Dupuy
Art director: Pascal Midavaine
Copywriter: Alain Jalabert
Photographer: Peter Knaup

119
Comshare System W software
United Kingdom
Advertiser: Comshare
Marketing director: Glyn Read
Advertising director: Glyn Read
Agency: The Leagas Delaney Partnership, London
Account director: Simon Jones
Account manager: Susan Holiday
Creative director: Tim Delaney
Art director: Graeme Norways
Copywriters: Tim Delaney, John Bedford
Photographer: Nick Tucker

120
British Telecom telex service
United Kingdom
Advertiser: British Telecom
Marketing director: M. Ford
Advertising manager: C. Royal
Product manager: P. Ashby
Brand manager: E. Smith
Agency: KMP Partnership, London
Account director: David Barraclough
Account manager: Niki Smith
Creative director: John Wood
Art director: Ken Grimshaw
Copywriter: John Donnelly
Photographer: Nic Tompkin

121
Xerox 3890 copier
Japan
Advertiser: Fuji Xerox
Agency: Dentsu, Tokyo
Account director: Ryuji Hattori
Creative director: Shunmei Takahashi
Art directors: Masamichi Yoshino, Hiroyuki Itoh
Copywriter: Ryoichi Akiba
Photographer: Ikko Narahara
Illustrator: Tamotsu Tomizawa

122
IBM copier
United States
Advertiser: IBM
Agency: Doyle Dane Bernbach, New York
Account director: Lloyd Highbloom
Account manager: Joe Dell Aquila
Creative director: Irwin Warren
Art director: Rick Elkins
Copywriter: Rhonda Peck
Photographer: Larry Robins

123
Rank Xerox Marathon copier
Netherlands
Advertiser: Rank Xerox
Marketing director: V. C. J. Zoetmulder
Advertising director: A. van Dijk
Agency: Young & Rubicam, Amsterdam
Account director: Nick van Loendersloot
Account manager: Simon Werkendam
Creative directors: Hans Born, Duncan Mackintosh
Art director: Richard Wagner
Copywriter: Michael Levisson
Photographer: Chris Steffens

124
Rank Xerox 1055 copier
France
Advertiser: Rank Xerox
Marketing director: Jean-Pierre Senemaud
Director of external relations: Daniel Bordes
Advertising director: Mathieu Mollet
Agency: Young & Rubicam, Paris
Account director: Francis Meyer
Account supervisor: Michel Maître
Creative directors: Jean-Paul Bacquer, Gérard Monot
Art director: Christian Vince
Copywriter: Philippe Chatiliez
Photographer: Rob Pederson

125
Sony
Netherlands
Advertiser: Brandsteder Electronics
Agency: KSM, Haarlem
Account director: Robert Poll
Art director: Aad Booman
Copywriter: Willem Mudde
Illustrator: Henk Mittendorf

126
IBM
Netherlands
Agency: KVH/GGK, Amsterdam
Account director: Ad van Vuuren
Art director: Morton Kirschner
Copywriter: Hans Kroese
Photographer: Ruud Posthuma

127
Thomson-Electronic
West Germany
Marketing director: Klaus Härtenstein
Agency: Heye Needham & Partner, Düsseldorf
Account director: Rudolf Jahns
Art director: Jean Lessenich
Copywriter: Partho Gosh
Illustrator: Kadanji

128
Northern Telecom
United States
Marketing director: Roy Cottier
Agency: J. Walter Thompson, Chicago
Account director: William Howard
Account manager: Don Peterson
Creative directors: Tom DeMint, Derek Norman
Art director: Derek Norman
Copywriter: Bernadette Doran
Illustrator: Guy Billout

129
Siemens India
India
Marketing director: A. K. Srivastava
Advertising manager: R. Kharwa
Agency: Lintas, Bombay
Account director: Stanley Pinto
Account supervisor: Rajesh Pant
Creative director: Madhu Gadakari
Art director: B. R. Kumawat
Copywriter: Gautam Bose
Photographer: Hari Mahidhar

130a, 130b, 130c
Volvo
International
Agency: TBWA, London
Creative directors: Chris Martin, Neil Patterson, Malcolm Gaskin
Art director: John Knight
Copywriter: Chris Martin
Illustrator: David Hockney

131
Tinplate manufacturers
West Germany
Advertiser: IZW (Tinplate Information Centre)
Advertising manager: Elke Herzog
Agency: Lintas, Hamburg
Account managers: Christel Heher, Kurt Martens
Art director: Jürgen Assmann
Copywriter: Eckart Totzeck
Photographer: Brigitte Richter

132
RAG
West Germany
Advertiser: Ruhrkohle AG, Essen
Advertising director: Hans Karlisch
Client executives: Dr Klaus Kocks, Thomas Chusit
Agency: Team/BBDO, Düsseldorf
Account manager: Horst Stephan
Creative director: Michael Hausberger
Art directors: Rolf Lange, Jürgen van Soest
Copywriter: Michael Hausberger
Photographer: Peter Godry

133
International Paper
United States
Marketing director: Joe Robinson
Advertising manager: Robert Lauterborn
Agency: Ogilvy & Mather, New York
Account manager: Peter Craighead
Creative directors: Malcolm End, Billings Fuess
Art director: Tracy Wong
Designer: Tracy Wong
Copywriter: Billings Fuess
Photographer: Harold Krieger

134
Atlantic Richfield Company
United States
Advertiser: Atlantic Richfield Co. (Arco)
Marketing director: Nancy Budd
Brand manager: Bill Grieg
Corporate managers: Lew Angelos, Larry Baschon, Frank Laudonio, Don Anderson
Agency: Foote Cone & Belding/Honig, Los Angeles
Creative director: Michael Wagman
Art director: Larry Corby
Copywriter: Michael Wagman

135
Borg-Warner
United States
Advertiser: Borg-Warner Corporation
Vice-president, communications: Robert Morris
Advertising manager: Kathleen Nelson
Agency: Foote Cone & Belding, Chicago
Account director: Tom Marti
Account executive: Donna Noonan
Creative directors: Rick Steinman, Bert Hoddinott
Art director: Jim Fansler
Copywriter: Rick Steinman
Photographer: Charlie Westerman
Print production: Ron Russell

136
Findus
Sweden
General manager: Christer Denrell
Agency: Ted Bates, Helsingborg
Account director: Kjell Cronert
Creative directors: Kjell Cronert, Ola Hallberg, Dündar Ünal
Art director: Dündar Ünal
Copywriter: Ola Hallberg
Illustrator: Dündar Ünal

137
Drug manufacturers
India
Advertiser: Indian Drug Manufacturers' Association
President: H. F. Khorakiwala
Client executive: I. A. Alva
Agency: Jaisons Advertising
Account director: Prakash Jain
Art director: Ashok Karnik
Copywriters: copy department, Jaisons
Illustrator: Ashok Karnik

138
American Telephone & Telegraph
United States
Advertising manager: Dave Shaver
Agency: N.W. Ayer, New York
Account director: Howard Stoner
Creative director: James Murphy
Art director: Robert Needleman
Copywriter: James Murphy
Photographer: Steve Steigman

139a, 139b, 139c
Skandia Insurance Company
Sweden
Information manager: Carl Borgenstierna
Advertising manager: Gunnar Lundkvist
Agency: SSC&B: Lintas, Stockholm
Account director: Gunnar Schlyter
Account manager: Eva Malm
Creative director: Berndt Johansson

140
Shell
United Kingdom
Advertising director: Hugh Wickham
Brand manager: John Collyer
Agency: Ogilvy & Mather, London
Account director: Mike King
Account manager: Lynne Woolmer
Creative director: Don Arlett
Art director: Derrick Hass
Copywriter: Rowan Dean
Photographer: Max Forsythe

141
Design New Wave '84 exhibition
Japan
Advertiser: Japan Design Committee
Director: Yusaku Kamekura
Advertising director: Kaoru Obata
Studio: Nippon Design Centre, Tokyo
Account director: Masayasu Inomata
Account manager: Makoto Takahashi
Creative director: Kazumasa Nagai
Art director: Kazumasa Nagai

142
1985 World Cup Marathon
Japan
Advertiser: World Cup Marathon Organising Committee
Marketing director: Hanji Aoki
Agency: Dentsu, Tokyo
Account director: Susumu Kochi
Account manager: Yoshinobu Takeuchi
Creative director: Kyoji Okura
Art directors: Kyoji Okura, Hirotoshi Seki
Copywriter: Masaki Tsuruho
Illustrator: Shintaro Ajioka

143
Sankai Juku dance troupe
International
Advertiser: Mitsubishi Motors, Overseas division
Marketing director: Akira Kondo
Advertising manager: Takashi Morimoto
Studio: Takayuki Itoh Design Office, Tokyo
Creative director: Takayuki Itoh
Art directors: Takayuki Itoh, Nobuko Kamakura
Designer: Nobuko Kamakura

144
London Theatres
United Kingdom
Advertiser: Society of West End Theatres
Development officer: Penny Owens
Agency: Saatchi & Saatchi Compton, London
Account director: Daniel Clare
Creative director: Jeremy Sinclair
Copywriter: Simon Carbery
Typographers: Roger Kennedy, Roger Pearce

145
Ninth Festival of Asian Arts
Hong Kong
Advertiser: The Urban Council, Hong Kong
Studio: SS Design, Hong Kong
Art director: Kan Tai-keung
Designers: Freeman Lau, Eddy Yu, Kan Tai-keung
Photographer: Fotostudio

146
New York Philharmonic concert
India
Advertiser: VST Industries
Marketing director: B. P. Singh
Product manager: K. Kumaramangalam
Agency: Enterprise Advertising, Bombay
Account director: Rajiv Agarnal
Creative director: Mohammed Khan
Art director: Elsie Nanji
Copywriter: Rajan Nair
Illustrator: Javed Choudhary

147
Guys and Dolls
West Berlin
Advertiser: Theater des Westens
Studio: Noth & Hauer, Berlin
Account managers: Volker Noth, Cordes Hauer, Peter Sodemann
Art directors and copywriters: Volker Noth, Cordes Hauer, Peter Sodemann

148
Berlin Film Festival
West Germany
Studio: Noth & Hauer, Berlin
Account managers: Volker Noth, Cordes Hauer, Peter Sodemann
Art directors and copywriters: Volker Noth, Cordes Hauer, Peter Sodemann

149
Government Building Agency exhibition
Netherlands
Advertiser: Government Building Agency
Studio: Samenwerkende Ontwerpers (Co-operative Designers), Amsterdam
Designer: André Toet
Photographer: Maarten van de Velde

150
Götabanken
Sweden
Advertiser: Götabanken
Marketing director: Ulf Lundahl
Advertising manager: Lars Wigart
Agency: Ted Bates 3, Stockholm
Account director: Michael Hoffman
Creative director: Jerker Belvert
Copywriter: Svante Malmström
Illustrator: Magnus Andersson

151, 152, 153
Norddeutsche Landesbank
West Germany
Advertiser: Norddeutsche Landesbank
Agency: Grey, Düsseldorf
Account director: Michael Hundt
Account manager: Rainer Barth
Creative director: Wolfgang Berger
Art director: Jean Lessenich
Copywriter: Volkar Nienhoff
Illustrators: Goffin (spectacles), André François (others)
Photographer: Lothar Mader

154
Amro Bank
Netherlands
Advertiser: Amro Bank
Agency: FHV/BBDO, Amsterdam
Account director: Alan Parfitt
Art director: Pim van der Meer
Copywriter: Ton van den Bos
Photographer: Dirkjan Nijhuis

155
Sparebanken
Norway
Advertiser: Sparebanken
Marketing director: Aase Gudding Gresvig
Brand manager: Arild Drolsum
Agency: Foote Cone & Belding, Oslo
Account director: William Richter
Creative director: Trygve Engebraaten
Art director: Trygve Engebraaten
Copywriter: Hans Christian Bøler
Photographer & Illustrator: Angus Forbes, Dirty Tricks Department

156
NatWest Bonus Saver Account
United Kingdom
Advertiser: National Westminster Bank
Advertising director: Danielle Barr
Agency: J. Walter Thompson, London
Account director: David Baker
Creative director: Allen Thomas
Art director: Tom Moult
Copywriter: Simon Collins
Photographer: John Bantim

157
National Westminster Bank
United Kingdom
Advertiser: National Westminster Bank
Marketing manager: Dick Williams
Advertising director: Danielle Barr
Campaign manager: Sue Green
Agency: J. Walter Thompson, London
Account director: David Baker
Creative director: Richard Phillips
Art director: Richard Patterson
Copywriter: John Platt
Photographer: Graham Ford

158
First Interstate Bancorp
United States
Advertiser: First Interstate Bank
Marketing director: Paul Minch
Brand manager: Steve Tabussi
Agency: Foote Cone & Belding, Los Angeles
Creative director: Michael Wagman
Art director: Ann King
Copywriters: Debbie Most, Phyllis Vernick

159
Banco Exterior de España
Spain
Advertiser: Banco Exterior de España
Agency: McCann-Erickson, Madrid
Creative director: Angel del Pino
Art director: Jose Antonio Bocanegra
Copywriter: Roberto de Gracia
Photographer: Luis Dominguez
Illustrator: Eugenio Ramos

160
Alliance Building Society
United Kingdom
Advertiser: Alliance Building Society
Advertising manager: David Gillard
Agency: TBWA, London
Account director: Mike Davis
Creative directors: Neil Patterson, Malcolm Gaskin
Art director: Malcolm Gaskin
Copywriter: Neil Patterson
Illustration: Neville Graphics

161
Chase Lincoln First
United States
Advertiser: Chase Lincoln First
Marketing director: John McNeil
Advertising manager: Kathy Tighe
Agency: Hutchins/Y&R, Rochester, New York State
Account director: Joan Edelstein
Account manager: Tracy Ladd
Creative director: Mike Fountain
Art director: Mike Fountain
Copywriter: John Connelly
Illustrator: Richard Wehrman

162
Investors In Industry Group
United Kingdom
Advertiser: 3i
Advertising manager: Sue Palmer
Agency: Doyle Dane Bernbach, London
Account director: Peter Brock
Account manager: Nigel Beard
Creative director: Tony Brignull
Art director: John Dodson
Copywriter: Peter Neeves
Illustrator: Jeff Fisher

163
ICFC
United Kingdom
Advertiser: 3i
Advertising manager: Sue Palmer
Agency: Doyle Dane Bernbach, London
Account director: Peter Brock
Account manager: Nigel Beard
Creative director: Tony Brignull
Art director: Zoe Atkins
Copywriter: Pip Ledger
Illustrator: Louise Voce

164
Alex Lawrie
United Kingdom
Advertiser: Alex Lawrie Factors
Marketing directors: Malcolm Smith, Barry Birch
Marketing manager: Steve Gibbons
Agency: Gold Greenlees Trott, London
Account director: Brian Crook
Creative director: Dave Trott
Art director: Dave Cook
Copywriter: Chris Bardsley
Photographer: John Claridge

165
Diners Club
Hong Kong
Advertiser: Diners Club International
Agency: SSC&B:Lintas, Hong Kong
Account manager: Tony Perone
Creative director: Tony Perone
Art director: Benny Cheng
Illustrator: Kevin Orpin

166
Eurocard
West Germany
Advertiser: Eurocard, Germany
Client executive: Michael Neese
Marketing director: Michael Neese
Marketing manager: Werner Euler
Product manager: Claudia Seel
Agency: Young & Rubicam, Frankfurt
Account director: Michael Richter
Account manager: Ulf Heuer
Creative director: Reinhard Lombacher
Art director: Manfred Schmitt
Copywriter: Bernd Fellinger
Photographer: Thomas Hoepker

167
Legal & General
United Kingdom
Advertiser: Legal & General
Marketing director: John Craddock
Advertising manager: Douglas Wright
Product manager: Barry Page
Agency: Kirkwood & Partners, London
Account director: Toby Sachs
Account supervisor: Carolyn Ashton
Creative director: Ken Mullen
Art director: Colin Underhay
Copywriter: Alex Pearl
Photocomposition: David Fitzgerald

168
Albany Life Assurance
United Kingdom
Advertiser: Albany Life Assurance
Marketing director: Peter Kelly
Agency: Lowe Howard-Spink Campbell-Ewald, London
Account director: Frank Lowe
Creative director: Alfredo Marcantonio
Art director: David Christensen
Copywriter: Chris O'Shea
Photographer: Jimmy Wormser

169
Connecticut General Life Insurance Company
United States
Advertiser: CIGNA
Agency: Doyle Dane Bernbach, New York
Account director: Lloyd Highbloom
Account manager: Bill Yankus
Creative director: Diane Rothschild
Art director: David Nathanson
Copywriter: Jane Talcott
Photographer: Larry Robbins

170
Bovril cubes
United Kingdom
Advertiser: Bovril
Marketing director: Jim Currie
Advertising manager: Christine Tebbot
Agency: Ogilvy & Mather, London
Account director: Richard Evans Thomas
Account manager: Stephen Fraser
Creative director: Don Arlett
Art director: Martyn Walsh
Copywriter: Malcolm Gluck
Illustrator: Mick Brownfield

171
Sharwood's sauces
United Kingdom
Advertiser: J. A. Sharwood
Marketing director: Mark Veit
Marketing manager: Gareth Jones
Agency: Wight Collins Rutherford Scott, London
Account director: Amanda Walsh
Creative director: Andrew Cracknell
Art director: Mick Devito-French
Copywriter: Derek Day
Photographer: Martin Thompson
Typographer: Keith Mackenzie

172
Heinz Tomato Ketchup
Belgium
Advertiser: H. J. Heinz
Marketing director: Jean-Claude Jamar
Agency: Young & Rubicam, Brussels
Account director: Nigel Bishop
Account executive: Hilde Ransschaert
Creative director: Roger Mader
Art director: Willy Coppens
Copywriter: Jo de Boeck
Producer: Marcel Vyncke
Photographer: Georges van Rijck

173
Birds Eye vegetables
United Kingdom
Advertiser: Birds Eye Wall's
Agency: McCann-Erickson, London
Creative director: Don White
Art director: Derek Smith
Copywriter: Alan Clark
Photographer: Tessa Traeger

174
Hettema Zonen potatoes
Netherlands
Advertiser: Hettema
Agency: Weda Erkend, Leeuwarden
Account director: Rob Loeff
Creative director: Theo de Witte
Art director: Theo de Witte
Copywriter: Jan Willem Renders
Designer: Theo de Witte
Photographer: Randall Scobie

175
Heinz Baked Beans
United Kingdom
Advertiser: H. J. Heinz
Marketing director: David Sculley
General manager, marketing: Matt McBride
Product manager: Iain Paton
Agency: Young & Rubicam, London
Account director: Jane Quelch
Account manager: Rachel Gaunt
Creative director: Chris Wilkins
Art director: Ian Batey
Copywriter: Owen Stevens
Photographer: Steve Cavalier

176
Eggs
Netherlands
Advertiser: Produktschap van Pluimvee & Eieren (Poultry & Egg Producers)
Agency: ACT, Amsterdam
Account director: J. Botter
Art director: B. Knipsel
Copywriter: T. Kranenburg
Photographer: Brian Morris

177, 178, 179
Voiello pasta
Italy
Advertiser: Voiello
Marketing director: Mario Nervegna
Agency: RSCG Mezzano Costantini Mignani, Milan
Account director: Lidia Roscelli
Creative director: Marco Mignani
Art director: Alfonso Costantini
Copywriter: Marco Mignani
Photographer: Paolo Gandola

180
Fyffes bananas
United Kingdom
Advertiser: Fyffes
Marketing director: Duncan Miller
Agency: Marsteller, Little & Strodl, London
Account director: Bill Lovelock
Creative director: David Little
Art director: Dan Strodl
Copywriter: David Little
Illustrator: Martin Gasgoine

181
Chiquita bananas
Belgium
Advertiser: United Brands Continental
Marketing director: Jean-Paul van Weverberghe
Agency: Young & Rubicam, Brussels
Account supervisor: Jean-Pierre Paris
Creative director: Roger Mader
Art director: Bill Good
Copywriter: Bill Good
Photographer: J. P. Vanderelst

182
Del Monte canned fruit and cream
Sweden
Advertisers: Del Monte, Arla dairies
Advertising director: Claes Fick
Agency: McCann-Erickson, Stockholm
Account director: Lennart Hogman
Account manager: Matts Karlsson
Creative director: Matts Karlsson
Copywriter: Sophie Slettengren

183
Calvé peanut butter
Netherlands
Advertiser Calvé-de Betuwe
Marketing director: Frits Offerhaus
Agency: J. Walter Thompson, Amsterdam
Account director: Michael Brockbank
Creative director: Ton Vergouw
Art director: Bart Hammer
Copywriter: Harry Obdeijn
Photographer: Jurriaan Eindhoven

184
Apéricube cheese
France
Advertiser: Fromageries Bel
Product manager: Jean-Marc Landriau
Agency: Young & Rubicam, Paris
Account director: Jacques Lévy
Creative directors: Jean-Paul Bacquer, Gérard Monot
Art director: Bruno Richard
Copywriter: Claude Drouilhat
Illustrator: Mike Savat

185
Jif peanut butter
United States
Advertiser: Procter & Gamble
Agency: Grey Advertising, New York
Account director: Neil Kreisberg
Account managers: William Heath, Joe Celia
Creative director: Robert Skollar
Art director: Lesley McCann
Copywriter: Janet Ammann
Photographer: Carl Fischer

186
Kiri cream cheese
France
Advertiser: Fromageries Bel
Product manager: Jean-Claude Landriau
Agency: Young & Rubicam, Paris
Account director: Jacques Lévy
Account supervisor: Patrice Clipez
Creative directors: Jean-Paul Bacquer, Gérard Monot
Art director: Christian Vince
Copywriter: Philippe Chatiliez
Photographer: Gilles Bouyer

187
Outline margarine
United Kingdom
Advertiser: Van den Berghs
Advertising director: Paul Clark
Agency: McCann-Erickson, London
Account director: Chris Kleanthous
Creative director: Keith Ravenscroft
Art director: Brian Maclaren
Copywriter: Keith Ravenscroft

188
Dutch cheeses
Canada
Agency: McCann-Erickson, Toronto
Creative director: Harrison Yates
Art director: Marcee Ruby
Copywriter: Herb Skelton
Photographer: Frank Angelone

189
Gervais petit suisse
France
Advertiser: Gervais Danone
Product managers: Marina Menu, Alain Degalle
Agency: Young & Rubicam, Paris
Account director: Patrice Clipez
Account supervisor: Pierre de Roualle
Creative directors: Jean-Paul Bacquer, Gérard Monot
Art director: Olivier Bersin
Copywriter: Annick Valla
Photographer: Catherine Caron

190
St Ivel Shape soft cheese
United Kingdom
Advertiser: St Ivel
Marketing director: David Merriot
Agency: Bartle Bogle Hegarty, London
Account director: Tim Lindsay
Creative director: John Hegarty
Art director: Gary Walton
Copywriter: Phil Wiggins
Illustrator: Chris Wormell
Photographer: Gary Bryan

191
Jordans Original Crunchy Bars
United Kingdom
Advertiser: Jordans
Agency: TBWA, London
Account director: Jeremy Warshaw
Creative directors: Neil Patterson, Malcolm Gaskin
Art director: Malcolm Gaskin
Copywriter: Neil Patterson
Photographer: Kevin Summers

192
Motta snacks
Italy
Advertiser: Sidalm
Marketing manager: Diego Basso
Brand manager: Stefano Nason
Agency: Foote Cone & Belding, Milan
Account director: Franco Bertolini
Account executive: Aurelia Cazzani
Creative director: Gabriele Zarotti
Art director: Marina Mapelli
Copywriter: Luisa Riva
Illustrator: Daniele Morini

193
Kit Kat chocolate bar
United Kingdom
Advertiser: Rowntree-Mackintosh
Marketing director: Clive Snowden
Advertising manager: David Lamb
Product manager: Bill Williams
Brand manager: David Rowlands
Agency: J. Walter Thompson, London
Account director: Miles Colebrook
Account manager: John Williams
Creative director: Max Henry
Art director: Luciana Carta
Copywriter: Geoff Weedon
Photographer: Max Forsythe

194
Penguin chocolate bars
United Kingdom
Advertiser: United Biscuits
Marketing director: Terry Stannard
Product manager: Hugh Fletcher
Agency: Saatchi & Saatchi Compton, London
Account director: Paul Bainsfair
Account manager: Nick Kerr
Creative director: Jeremy Sinclair
Art director: Jonathan Iles
Copywriter: Jonathan Iles
Photographer: Martin Thompson

195
Smarties
United Kingdom
Advertiser: Rowntree Mackintosh
Marketing director: Clive Snowden
Advertising manager: David Lamb
Product manager: John Short
Brand manager: Susan Scrimgeour
Agency: J. Walter Thompson, London
Account director: Miles Colebrook
Account manager: John Williams
Creative director: Max Henry
Art director: Billy Mawhinney
Copywriter: Nick Welch
Illustrator: Martin Lambie Nairn
Photographer: Jack Bankhead

196
Reese's Pieces
United States
Advertiser: Hershey
Agency: Doyle Dane Bernbach, New York
Account director: Peter Falcone
Account manager: Bob Jeffrey
Creative director: Mick Mangano
Art Director: Sharon Occhipinti
Copywriter: Helen Miller
Illustrator: Todd Schorr

197
Nescafé (Gold Label)
Norway
Advertiser: Nestle-Findus
Marketing director: Bredo Holmsen
Product manager: Tore Schjøth
Agency: Heltberg Creative Service
Account director: Arne Dahl
Creative director: Egil Jabobsen
Art director: Egil Jacobsen
Copywriter: Arne Dahl
Photographer: Jhon Kevern, London

198
Kanis & Gunnink coffee
Netherlands
Advertiser: Kanis & Gunnink
Agency: PPGH Moussault, Amsterdam
Account director: P. Bär
Art director: D. Koekkoek
Copywriter: H. Kramp

199
Colombian coffee
United States
Advertiser: National Federation of Coffee Growers of Colombia
Agency: Doyle Dane Bernbach, New York
Account director: Peter Falcone
Account manager: Peter le Comte
Creative director: John Noble
Art director: Ron Lovie
Copywriter: Patty Volk
Photographer: Harry De Zitter

200
Milk
Sweden
Advertiser: Arla
Advertising director: Jan Olof Bengtsson
Agency: Ted Bates 1, Stockholm
Account director: Johan Bohlin
Creative director: Peter Molin
Copywriter: Susanne Glemme
Illustrator: Holger Edström

201
Nescafé (Gold Label)
Netherlands
Advertiser: Nestlé
Marketing director: Jacques Krielen
Agency: J. Walter Thompson, Amsterdam
Account director: Fred de Boer
Creative director: Ton Vergouw
Art director: Ton Vergouw
Copywriter: Peter ten Hoopen
Photographer: Dirk Karsten

202
Milk
United Kingdom
Advertiser: Dairy Council for Northern Ireland
Chief executive: Doreen Francis
Agency: Harrison McCann, London
Account director: Iain Wodehouse-Easton
Creative director: John Crankshaw
Art director: Deniz Yesilirmak
Copywriter: Susanne Dunlap
Photographer: Dudley Reid

203
Ferrarelle mineral water
Italy
Advertiser: Sangemini Industrie e Servizi
Agency: Michele Rizzi e Associati, Milan
Art directors: Pierpaolo Cornieti (stork), Lele Panzeri (married couple)
Copywriter: Michele Rizzi
Illustrator: Martiradonna Paolo (stork)
Photographer: Claudio Gaiaschi (married couple)

204
Evian mineral water
United Kingdom
Advertiser: Evian (Agencies)
Managing director: Richard Foulsham
Agency: TBWA, London
Account director: Kate Marber
Creative directors: Neil Patterson, Malcolm Gaskin
Art director: John Knight
Copywriter: Chris Martin
Illustrator: Connie Jude

205
Lucozade
United Kingdom
Advertiser: Beecham Foods
Marketing director: Mike Fensome
Product manager: Frank Auton
Brand manager: Trudy Reynolds
Agency: Ogilvy & Mather, London
Account director: Miles Young
Account manager: Jonathan Little
Creative director: Don Arlett
Art director: Nick Evans
Copywriter: Nick Evans
Photographer: David Fairman

206
Sunkist lemon drink
France
Advertisers: Sunkist/Dunand & Compagnie
Agency: DDB2, Paris
Account directors: Alain Garnier, Michel Simonot
Creative director: Martine Collet
Art director: Jean-Luc Collard
Copywriter: Jean-Claude Davallan
Photographer: André Berg

207
Coca-Cola
Japan
Advertiser: Coca-Cola, Japan
Marketing director: Akira Ueno
Advertising director: Gen Omma
Agency: Dentsu, Tokyo
Account director: Takuo Sada
Account manager: Tasuku Iyou
Creative director: Tatsuo Miyake
Art director: Osamu Asano
Copywriter: Komatsu
Illustrator: Hiroshige Ando

208, 209
Schweppes
West Germany
Advertiser: Schweppes
Marketing director: Karl-Ludwig Haug
Product manager: Ulrich Frebel
Agency: GGK, Düsseldorf
Account manager: Peter Hessel
Creative director: Michael Schirner
Art director: Michael Preiswerk
Copywriter: Franz Brauer
Illustrator: Uwe von Afferton
Photographer: Frank Exner

210
Karastan carpets
United States
Advertiser: Karastan
Advertising director: Ronald Urich
Agency: Ally & Gargano, New York
Account executive: Martha Holland
Group creative head: Helayne Spivak
Art director: Tom Wolsey
Photographer: Henry Wolf

211
Sisal carpets
Italy
Advertiser: Sisal
Marketing director: Mr. Merli
Advertising director: Mr. Locardi
Agency: STZ, Milan
Account director: Hans-Rudolf Suter
Creative director: Fritz Tschirren
Art director: Fritz Tschirren
Copywriter: Cesare Casiraghi
Photographer: Jean-Pierre Maurer

212
Woollen carpets
Netherlands
Advertiser: International Wool Secretariat
Marketing director: P. A. J. Strijland
Advertising director: H. Spannet
Agency: Young & Rubicam, Amsterdam
Account director: Malcolm Parker Brady
Account manager: Pedro Stempels
Creative directors: Hans Born, Duncan Mackintosh
Art director: Richard Wagner
Copywriter: Joris Bergsma
Photographer: Paul Wensveen

213
Behr Headline furniture
West Germany
Advertiser: Behr
Advertising manager: Günter Habermann
Agency: Marsteller, Frankfurt
Account director: Bernd Pfeil
Creative director: Dieter Jaschkowitz
Art director: Dieter Jaschkowitz
Copywriter: Dieter Jaschkowitz
Photographer: Joop Greypink

214
Dunlopillo beds
United Kingdom
Advertiser: Dunlopillo
Marketing director: Vic Rosati
Agency: TBWA, London
Account director: Kate Marber
Creative directors: Neil Patterson, Malcolm Gaskin
Art director: Mike Hannett
Copywriter: Dave Buchanan
Illustrator: Brian Grimwood

215
Kaldewei baths
West Germany
Advertiser: Franz Kaldewei
Advertising manager: Karl Surmann
Agency: Hildmann Simon Rempen & Schmitz SMS, Düsseldorf
Account director: Hans-Peter Esser
Account executive: Tim Timm
Creative director: Rainer Held
Art director: Rainer Held
Copywriter: Evelyn Froh
Photographer: Alan Ginsbourg

216
Marazzi tiles
Italy
Advertiser: Marazzi
Marketing director: Severo Rainoni
Agency: Benton & Bowles, Milan
Account director: Giovanni Benini
Account manager: Roberta Silla
Creative director: Gavino Sanna
Art director: Roberto Fiaminghi
Copywriter: Giampaolo Melideo
Photographer: Raffaello Brà

217
Saraband bedroom furnishings
Australia
Advertiser: Saraband
Agency: Dalziell Harper & Grey, Melbourne
Account director: Russell Stephenson
Creative director: Greg Harper
Art director: Grahame Dingle
Copywriter: Greg Harper
Photographer: Louis Pettracelli

218
Shelman parquet flooring
Greece
Advertiser: Shelman
Marketing director: G. Mantzaris
Agency: Ted Bates, Athens
Account director: George Vlachopoulos
Account manager: Annamaria Stamatis
Creative director: Stavros Georgiades
Art director: Nicolas Kaliakatsos
Copywriter: Stavros Georgiades
Photographer: George Fafalis

219
Pressalit toilet seats
Denmark
Advertiser: Dansk Pressalit
Agency: NP/Grey, Arhus
Account director: Hans Prehn
Creative directors: Hans Prehn, Thomas Crandall
Art director: Thomas Crandall
Copywriter: Hans Prehn
Photographer: Paul Henriksen

220
Cera bathroom fittings
India
Advertiser: Madhusudan Ceramics
Agency: Shilpi Advertising, Bombay
Account director: Uday Mawani
Account manager: Aslesha Koppula
Creative director: Sunil Sen
Art director: Sunil Sen
Copywriter: Usha Rajan
Illustrator: Yogesh Bhavsar

221
Bidone vacuum cleaner
Italy
Advertiser: Alfatec
Marketing director: Angelo Maspero
Agency: STZ, Milan
Account director: Hans-Rudolf Suter
Creative director: Fritz Tschirren
Art director: Fritz Tschirren
Copywriter: Cesare Casiraghi
Illustrator: Roberto Molino
Film director: Massimo Magri

222
Bosch domestic appliances
France
Advertiser: Bosch
Marketing director: Yves Colin
Agency: Delrieu Duprat, Paris
Account director: Marino de Boni
Creative director: Alec Medintzeff
Art director: Hervé Galland
Copywriter: Brigitte Saint-Aroman
Photographer: Jeremy Bailey

223
Candy domestic appliances
Italy
Advertiser: Candy Elettrodomestici
Marketing director: Arrigo Arrigoni
Agency: B Communications, Milan
Account director: Federico Mola
Creative director: Titti Fabiani
Art directors: Titti Fabiani, Vittoria Cattaneo
Copywriter: Maria Grazia Boffi
Photographer: Orio Raffo

224
Vortice convector heater
Italy
Advertiser: Vortice
Marketing director: Alex Poggi
Advertising manager: Sergio Tortorella
Agency: STZ, Milan
Account director: Hans-Rudolf Suter
Creative director: Fritz Tschirren
Art director: Fritz Tschirren
Copywriter: Pasquale Barbella
Photographer: Jean-Pierre Maurer

225
New World Option 3 cooker
United Kingdom
Advertiser: TI New World
Marketing manager: Mike Noakes
Agency: TBWA, London
Account director: Jamie Birkmyre
Creative directors: Neil Patterson, Malcolm Gaskin
Art director: Malcolm Gaskin
Copywriter: Neil Patterson
Photographer: Hazel Digby

226
Seiko pocket colour T-V receiver
Japan
Advertiser: Hattori Seiko
Agency: Dentsu, Tokyo
Account director: Tsuyoshi Inoue
Creative director: Shunmei Takahashi
Art director: Masamichi Yoshino
Copywriter: Ryoichi Akiba
Photographer: Bishin Jumonji

227
JVC VideoMovie
United Kingdom
Advertiser: JVC
Marketing director: Stephanie Lowy
Agency: Lowe Howard-Spink Campbell-Ewald, London
Account director: David Jones
Creative director: Alfredo Marcantonio
Art director: Kevin Jones
Copywriter: Paul Hodgkinson
Photographers: Gavin Cottrell, Jack Bankhead

228
Sony Trinitron TV receiver
United Kingdom
Advertiser: Sony
Marketing director: Mike Brown
Agency: Boase Massimi Pollitt Partnership, London
Account director: John McKnight
Account executive: Peter Clay
Creative directors: Alan Tilby, Paul Leeves
Art director: Dennis Willison
Copywriter: Julian Dyer
Illustrator: Guy Gladwell

229
Technics hi-fi set
Netherlands
Product manager: F.v.d. Engel
Agency: Ted Bates, Amsterdam
Account director: W. J. C. Kau
Account manager: Vincent Mascini
Creative director: Roger Hale
Art director: Roger Hale
Copywriter: Donald Lopez Cardoso
Illustrator: Dick Prins
Photographer: Dirk Karsten

230
Panasonic portable videoset
Netherlands
Advertiser: Haagtechno
Product manager: F.v.d. Engel
Agency: Ted Bates, Netherlands
Account director: W. J. C. Kau
Account manager: Vincent Mascini
Creative director: Dick van Duijn
Art director: Dick van Duijn
Copywriter: Maarten van der Spoel
Photographer: Martin Woods

231
BASF video cassettes
Netherlands
Advertiser: BASF, Netherlands
Marketing director: W. J. L. van Workum
Advertising director: A. Matena
Agency: Young & Rubicam, Amsterdam
Account director: Ollo den Tex
Account manager: Mandy Savage
Creative directors: Hans Born, Duncan Mackintosh
Art director: Duncan Mackintosh
Copywriter: Hans Born
Photographer: Jurriaan Eindhoven

232
Wharfedale loudspeakers
United Kingdom
Advertiser: Wharfedale
Marketing director: Roger Fearn
Agency: Saatchi & Saatchi Compton, London
Account director: Robin Hiscock
Account manager: David Wheldon
Creative director: Jeremy Sinclair
Art director: Digby Atkinson
Copywriter: Peter Wallach
Photographer: Graham Ford

233
Polaroid video cassettes
United States
Advertiser: Polaroid
Advertising director: Carl Johnson
Agency: Ogilvy & Mather, New York
Account director: Michael Vaughn
Account manager: Elizabeth Stearns
Creative director: John Doig
Art directors: Carole Deitchman, Thom Higgins
Copywriter: John Doig
Photographer: Howard Berman

234
Sharp radio-cassette recorder
United Kingdom
Advertiser: Sharp
Marketing services manager: Peter Maltby
Agency: Ayer Barker, London
Account director: Jonathan Hill
Art director: Kearl Hollis
Copywriter: Trevor Beattie
Photographer: Jem Grishotti
Typography: Cavalry Studio

235
JVC car stereo
United Kingdom
Advertiser: JVC
Marketing director: Stephanie Lowy
Agency: Lowe Howard-Spink Campbell-Ewald, London
Account director: David Jones
Creative director: Alfredo Marcantonio
Art director: Kevin Jones
Copywriter: Paul Hodgkinson
Photographer: Gavin Cottrell

236
Sony UCX audio tapes
United Kingdom
Advertiser: Sony UK
Marketing director: T. Iwai
Product manager: Geoff Muge
Agency: Boase Massimi Pollitt Partnership, London
Account director: John McKnight
Account manager: Tony Hirsch
Creative directors: Alan Tilby, Paul Leeves
Art director: Peter Gatley
Copywriter: John Pallant
Artwork: Parkway Studio

237
Instapure water filter
United States
Advertiser: Teledyne Water Pik
Agency: Doyle Dane Bernbach, Los Angeles
Account supervisor: Martha Baker
Art director: Wade Davis
Copywriter: Brandt Irvine
Photographer: John Bilecky

238, 239
I Guzzini electric lighting
Italy
Advertiser: I Guzzini
Managing director: Adolfo Guzzini
Advertising director: Stefano Anconetani
Agency: STZ, Milan
Account director: Hans-Rudolf Suter
Creative director: Fritz Tschirren
Art director: Fritz Tschirren
Copywriter: Pasquale Barbella
Illustrator: Giovanni Mulazzani ('Let there be light')
Photography: Occhiomagico (cow's head)

240
Osram lighting
West Germany
Advertiser: Osram, Munich
Marketing director: Eberhart Zangemeister
Advertising director: Hans-Jorn Schenkat
Agency: GGK, Düsseldorf
Account director: Rainer Schumann
Account manager: Michael Sohn
Creative director: Michael Preiswerk
Art director: Willi Barczat
Copywriter: Franz Brauer

241
Eswa and Termostan underfloor heating
Norway
Advertiser: STK (ITT)
Marketing directors: Svein Lyseng, Einar Aunan
Agency: McCann-Erickson, Oslo
Account manager: Arne Martinsen
Creative director: Sverre Holmen
Art director: Bjørn Andreseb
Copywriter: Gunnar Johansen
Photographer: Rune Venjar

242
Bontempi electronic organ
Italy
Advertiser: Bontempi
Marketing director: Mr. Guzzini
Agency: Publicis, Milan
Account director: Daniela Greco
Creative director: Horst Blachian
Art director: Horst Blachian
Copywriter: Alessio Derobertis
Illustrator: Folon

243
Duracell Batteries
United Kingdom
Advertiser: Duracell
Marketing director: Roy Doughty
Marketing manager: David Whiting
Agency: Dorland Advertising, London
Account director: Michael Bungey
Creative director: David McGrath
Art director: Mike Murphy
Copywriter: Alice Kavounas
Photographer: Geoff Smith

244
Kimberly-Clark toilet tissues
United Kingdom
Advertiser: Kimberly-Clark
Marketing director: Trevor Hamilton
Advertising director: Terry Ridgewell
Product manager: Peter Jackson
Agency: Fletcher Shelton Delaney, London
Account director: Barry Bryant
Account manager: Rachel Dyson
Creative director: Mike Trumble
Art director: Jeff Suthons
Copywriter: Bridget Jenkins
Photographer: Angus Forbes

245
Castrol Syntilo R
United Kingdom
Advertiser: Burmah-Castrol Industrial
Agency: Dorland Advertising, London
Account director: Charles Wigginton
Creative director: David McGrath
Art director: Gaynor Moore
Copywriter: Mark Wilkins
Illustrator: Jean Christian Knaff

246
Vortice ventilation and heating
Italy
Advertiser: Vortice
Marketing director: Alex Poggi
Advertising director: Sergio Tortorella
Agency: STZ, Milan
Account director: Hans-Rudolf Suter
Creative director: Fritz Tschirren
Art director: Fritz Tschirren
Copywriter: Cesare Casiragli
Photographer: Andrea Zani

247
Swarttouw stevedores
International
Advertiser: Frans Swarttouw
Managing director, sales and marketing: Hans Portheine
Agency: McCann-Erickson, Amsterdam
Account director: Frans Boes
Art director: Henk Haselaar
Copywriter: Han van Wel
Photographer: Ken Griffiths

248
ESAB robot welders
Netherlands
Advertiser: Swedish Trade Office
Marketing director: E. Wallström
Agency: Young & Rubicam, Amsterdam
Account director: Malcolm Parker Brady
Account manager: Bea Werner
Creative directors: Hans Born, Duncan Mackintosh
Art director: Wim de Boer
Copywriter: Joris Bergsma
Photographer: Paul Wensveen

249
Unichema oleochemicals
Western Europe, Far East and Australasia
Advertiser: Unichema International
Marketing director: W.-J. Struyck
Advertising manager: H. F. Kramer
Agency: Ayer Barker, London
Account director: Colin Bull
Creative director: Rob Heesom
Art director: Terry Ross
Copywriter: Jonathan Shadbolt
Photographer: Peter Williams

250
Filter mask
Japan
Advertiser: Sumitomo 3M
Agency: Dentsu, Tokyo
Account director: Yasuo Yamamura
Creative director: Masamichi Yoshino
Art directors: Nobuo Yoshinari, Hiroyuki Itoh
Copywriter: Hiroshi Hasegawa
Photographer: Masao Torii

251
Portucel packaging
Portugal
Advertiser: Portucel
Advertising manager: Dr Monteiro Pinho
Agency: McCann-Erickson/Hora, Lisbon
Account supervisor: Nunes de Almeida
Account executive: Jaime Nascimento
Creative director: Sergio Vaz
Art director: Jose Neves
Copywriter: Sergio Vaz
Illustrator: Henrique Manuel, Joseph Franz

252
Gujarat industrial locations
India
Advertiser: Industrial Extension Bureau
Agency: Shilpi Advertising, Ahmedabad
Account director: Sharad Suchde
Account manager: Shrinivas Bhat
Art director: Rashida Contractor
Copywriters: Nandita Challam, Usha Rajan
Illustrator: Mohan Patel

253
Solel Boneh International
International
Advertiser: Solel Boneh International
Studio: Shosh & Yona, Tel Aviv
Art directors: Shosh, Yona
Illustrator: Yakis Kidron

254
OPPalyte packaging film
United States
Advertiser: Mobil
Product manager: Jim Rich
Agency: Hutchins/Y&R, Rochester, New York State
Account director: Harvey Bozzi
Account manager: Diane Carapella
Creative director: Dave Clar
Art director: Dave Clar
Copywriter: Bob Haefner
Photographer: Mark Kazlowski

255
Rotherham Enterprise Zone
United Kingdom
Advertiser: Rotherham Metropolitan Borough Council
Marketing director: Brian Moore
Advertising manager: Peter Fairholm
Product manager: Keith Kettell
Agency: Ayer Barker, London
Account director: John Samuel
Account manager: Tony Pearce
Creative director: Robert Heesom
Art director: Robert Heesom
Copywriter: Robert Heesom
Photographer: Steve Garforth
Model makers: Parallax Models

256
AEG power supply systems
United Kingdom
Advertiser: AEG-Telefunken (UK)
Division manager: Kurt Weidenhaupt
Marketing manager: Lisa Spaducci
Agency: Young & Rubicam, London
Account manager: Stephen Pickthall
Creative director: Chris Wilkins
Art director: Colin Morris
Copywriter: Steve Pickthall
Photographer: Dave Stewart

257, 258
Platinum jewellery
West Germany
Advertisers: Rustenburg Platinum Mines, International Platinum Guild
Marketing director: Ken Maxwell
Advertising director: David Cullen
Agency: J. Walter Thompson, Frankfurt
Account director: Tom Martens
Account manager: Renate Bosse
Creative director: Gerd Rickart
Art director: Margot Weidenbach-Ernst
Copywriter: Dieter Hochstätter
Illustrator: Mats Gustavson
Photographer: Mane Weigand

259
'Diamond Desires'
United States
Advertiser: DeBeers Consolidated Mines
Marketing director: Jeremy Pudney
Agency: N. W. Ayer, New York
Account director: Harkness Cram
Creative director: Jeffrey Odiorne
Art director: George Kurten
Copywriter: Carolyn Reider
Photographer: Albert Watson

260
Gold jewellery
United States
Advertiser: International Gold Corporation
Agency: Doyle Dane Bernbach, New York
Account director: Peter Tate
Account manager: Brian Threlfall
Creative director: John Noble
Art director: Ron Louie
Copywriter: Alan Jacobs
Photographers: Albert Watson, George Holz

261
Pearls
Japan
Advertiser: Tasaki Pearls
Advertising director: Minoru Hirahara
Agency: Dentsu, Tokyo
Account director: Naoe Wakita
Creative directors: Naoe Wakita, Yoshimi Takeuchi
Art director: Takayuki Soeda
Copywriter: Toshie Suzuki
Photographer: Kazumi Kurigami

262
Timex watches
France
Advertiser: Timex
Advertising manager: Michel Beaumont
Agency: DDB2 Paris
Account director: Jérôme Leclabart
Creative director: Martine Collet
Art director: Anahi Leclerc
Copywriter: Pascal Bancou
Photographer: Uwe Ommer

263
Diamonds for men
United States
Advertiser: DeBeers Consolidated Mines
Marketing director: Jeremy Pudney
Agency: N. W. Ayer, New York
Account director: Harkness Cram
Creative director: Jeffrey Odiorne
Art director: Donald Zimmerman
Copywriter: Michael Korvin
Photographer: Deborah Turbeville

264
Tissot watches
United Kingdom
Advertiser: Tissot
Marketing director: Roger Taylor
Agency: Travis Dale & Partners, London
Account director: Peter Travis
Art director: Graham Fink
Copywriter: Jeremy Clarke
Photographer: Spencer Rowell

265
Lamborghini watches
France
Advertiser: Lamborghini
Marketing director: Daniel Gueorguievsky
Advertising director: Elisabeth Nicole
Agency: Soprano, Paris
Account director: Pierre Passot
Creative director: Jean-Claude Goldberg
Illustrator: Alain Dercourt
Photographer: Bertrand Chazarenc

266
Swatch watches
International
Advertiser: Swatch
Marketing director: Jacques Irniger
Agency: McCann-Erickson, Zürich
Account director: Verena Joos
Creative directors: Beat Hefermehl, Andreas Fierz
Art directors: Andreas Fierz, Marco Tanner
Copywriters: Beat Hefermehl, Martin Denecke
Photographers: Jürgen Tapprich, Gaston Wicky

267, 268
Mail on Sunday
United Kingdom
Advertiser: Associated Newspapers
Advertising manager: Ian Pay
Agency: Saatchi & Saatchi Compton, London
Account director: Mike Parker
Account manager: Peter Russell
Creative director: Jeremy Sinclair
Art director: Fergus Fleming
Copywriter: Simon Dicketts
Photographer: Derek Seagrim
Retoucher: Terry Day Company

269a, 269b
Working Woman magazine
United Kingdom
Advertiser: Wintour Publications
Advertising manager: Debbie Gresty
Editor: Audrey Slaughter
Agency: Aspect Advertising, London
Account director: John Ward
Account manager: Pam Wakelin
Creative director: Malachy Quinn
Art director: John Mundy
Copywriter: Phyllis Block
Photographer: John Swannell

270
People magazine
United States
Advertiser: Time Inc.
Promotion director: Robert Kyle
Agency: Young & Rubicam, New York
Group director: John McGarry
Account supervisor: James Tyrrell
Creative director: Brian Dillon
Art director: Barbara Dibue
Copywriter: Ira Sitomer

271
Europeo
Italy
Advertiser: Rizzoli
Marketing director: Rubens Storti
Product manager: Roberto Bonamartini
Agency: CPV Kenyon & Eckhardt, Milan
Account director: Giancarlo Villa
Creative director: Pasquale Barbella
Art director: Roberto Pizzigoni
Copywriter: Pasquale Barbella
Stock photograph

272
City and Country Home magazine
Canada
Advertiser: Maclean-Hunter
Marketing manager: Roger Flawn
Agency: McCann-Erickson, Toronto
Creative director: Stu Eaton
Art director: Brian Harrod
Copywriter: Ian Merlin
Photographer: Ian Campbell

273
Daily Mail
United Kingdom
Advertiser: Associated Newspapers
Marketing manager: Alwin Robinson
Agency: Saatchi & Saatchi Compton, London
Account director: Mike Gold
Creative director: Jeremy Sinclair
Art director: Paul Arden
Copywriter: Tim Mellors
Photographer: Jimmy Wormser

274
Kodansha paperbacks
Japan
Advertiser: Kodansha
Advertising director: Toru Kanetomo
Agency: Dentsu, Tokyo
Account director: Shizuo Hidaka
Account manager: Isao Takeshita
Creative director: Masaaki Tsuruho
Art directors: Tetsu Goto, Shotaro Sakaguchi
Copywriter: Akira Kikuchi
Photographer: Tamotsu Fujii

275
Bonnier book publishing
Sweden
Advertiser: Bonnier
Agency: Young & Rubicam, Stockholm
Account director: Lars Lundberg
Art director: Christian Eklund
Copywriter: Ivar Klaeson
Photographer: Lars Ortegren

276, 277
Central Television
United Kingdom
Advertiser: Central TV
Marketing director: Barry Reeve
Agency: Benton & Bowles, London
Account director: Pam Ings
Account manager: Lesley Thompson
Creative director: David Mitchell
Art directors: Richard Haydon ('Typical view'), Ken Hodgson ('9 million')
Copywriters: Barry Whitehead ('Typical view'), Richard Haydon, Keith Valentine, Barry Whitehead ('9 million)
Photographer: David Fairman ('Typical view')
Illustrator: Peter Till ('9 million')
Art buyers: Gill Simmonds ('Typical view'), Rita Pulford ('9 million')
Typographer: Ian Dillon

278
CKFM Radio, Toronto
Canada
Agency: McCann-Erickson, Toronto
Creative director: Stu Eaton
Art director: Barry Chemel
Copywriter: Wayne Hilinski
Photographer: Gillean Proctor

279
Olympic Games on TV
Japan
Advertiser: Federation of 102 Commercial Broadcasters
Agency: Dentsu, Tokyo
Creative director: Akira Odagiri
Art directors: Masamichi Yoshino, Hiroyuki Itoh
Copywriter: Ryoichi Akiba
Illustrator: George Akiyama
Photographer: Juichi Eguchi

280
More O'Ferrall poster sites
United Kingdom
Advertiser: More O'Ferrall
Marketing director: Peter Kent
Advertising manager: Marian Pitman
Agency: Saatchi & Saatchi Compton, London
Account director: Mike Parker
Account manager: Mike Gold
Creative director: Jeremy Sinclair
Art director: Mike Shafron
Copywriters: Dave Edwards, Simon Carbery, Simon Dicketts
Photographer: Jerry Oke
Model maker: Simon Cautry

281
London Weekend Television
United Kingdom
Advertiser: LWT
Marketing director: Mike Bell
Agency: Gold Greenlees Trott, London
Account director: Paul Simons
Account manager: Ross Capon
Creative director: Dave Trott
Art directors: John Fisher, Mike Owen
Copywriters: Andy Archer, Nick Wray
Photographer: Ian Giles

282
Persil washing powder
United Kingdom
Advertiser: Lever Brothers
Marketing director: David Stevenson
Advertising manager: Jeremy Stubbs
Marketing manager: Mark Sherrington
Brand manager: Aidan Lisser
Agency: J. Walter Thompson, London
Account director: David Rousell
Account manager: Nick Burstin
Creative director: Nick Fordham
Art director: Annie Carlton
Copywriter: Sandra Leamon
Photographer: David Fairman

283
Benfatto dishwashing liquid
Italy
Advertiser: Brill
Marketing director: Dante Bossi
Marketing manager: Paolo Lampugnani
Agency: CPV Kenyon & Eckhardt, Milan
Account director: Giancarlo Villa
Account manager: Jolanda Lucheroni
Creative director: Pasquale Barbella
Art director: Francesco Rizzi
Copywriter: Aldo Cernuto
Photographer: Jean-Pierre Maurer

284
Coal for domestic fires
United Kingdom
Advertiser: Solid Fuel Advisory Service
Marketing director: L. V. Penzer
Advertising manager: John Nettleton
Product manager: Bob Perrin
Brand manager: Geoff Ellard
Agency: Kirkwood & Partners, London
Account director: John Josling
Account manager: Silas Woolley
Creative director: Ken Mullen
Art director: Tony Muranka
Copywriter: Ken Mullen
Photographer: Jerry Oke

285
Window glass
West Germany
Advertiser: Flachglas
Publicity director: Reinhard Holsten
Agency: J. Walter Thompson, Frankfurt
Account director: Werner Preuss
Account manager: Kornelia Wähling
Creative director: Hermann Geckeler
Art directors: Claus Steffen, Thomas Heuter
Copywriters: Hermann Geckeler, Michael Diekert
Photographer: Peter Simmons

286
Gardena garden equipment
Norway
Advertiser: Markt & Co
Agency: McCann-Erickson, Oslo
Account managers: Einar Wettergren, Arne Martinsen
Creative director: Sverre Holmen
Art director: Sverre Holmen
Copywriter: Jan Espelid
Artists: Ian Fleming and Associates, London

287
Glomesh handbags
Australia
Advertiser: Glo International
Marketing executive: Brian Harris
Agency: Conaghan & May, Ayer, Sydney
Account director: Ken Farrington
Creative director: Neil Shennen
Creative team: Greg Alder, Tony Wong-Hee
Photographer: Robert Monro

288
Samsonite luggage
United Kingdom
Advertiser: Samsonite
Agency: TBWA, London
Account director: Simon Fitch
Creative directors: Neil Patterson, Malcolm Gaskin
Art director: Gary Walton
Copywriter: Phil Wiggins
Photographer: Graham Ford
Typographer: Nigel Dawson

289
Post-it memo pads
Japan
Advertiser: Sumitomo 3M
Agency: Dentsu, Tokyo
Account director: Yasuo Yamamura
Creative director: Masamichi Yoshino
Art directors: Nobuo Yoshinari, Hiroyuki Itoh
Photographer: Masao Torii

290
Hostmann-Steinberg printing inks
West Germany
Advertiser: Hostmann-Steinberg
Studio: Noth & Hauer, West Berlin
Creative team: Volker Noth, Cordes Hauer, Peter Sodemann
Photographers: Hartwig Klappert, Isa Eisermann

291
Hostmann-Steinberg printing inks
West Germany
Advertiser: Hostmann-Steinberg
Studio: Noth & Hauer, West Berlin
Account managers: Volker Noth, Cordes Hauer, Peter Sodemann
Art directors: Volker Noth, Peter Sodemann
Photographers: Hartwig Klappert, Isa Eisermann

292
Literary Guild
United States
Advertiser: Doubleday & Company
Marketing manager: Susan Beecher
Agency: Foote Cone & Belding, New York
Account director: Fidel Plantilla
Executive creative director: Len Sugarman
Executive art director: Joel Weissman
Executive copy director: Peter Einstein
Photographer: Carl Fisher

293
Teeny Weeny Itsy Bitsy Book Light
India
Advertiser: Superphone (India)
Marketing director: Mahesh Makhija
Agency: Enterprise Advertising, Bombay
Account director: Rajiv Agarwal
Creative director: Mohammed Khan
Art director: Elsie Nanji
Copywriter: Rajan Nair
Illustrator: Vinayak Bhoeer

294
Schlage locks
United States
Advertiser: Schlage Lock Company
Advertising manager: Patrick Murphy
Agency: Doyle Dane Bernbach, San Francisco
Account director: John Neitzel
Creative director: John Mercer
Art director: Cathy Danzeisen
Copywriter: John Frazier
Photographer: Ed Zak

295, 296
Paper
Japan
Advertiser: Takeo Company
Advertising director: Kei Kido
Studio: Nippon Design Centre, Tokyo
Account director: Masaysu Inomata
Account manager: Makoto Takahashi
Creative director: Kazumasa Nagai
Designer: Kazumasa Nagai

297
Spectacles
West Germany
Advertiser: Zentralverband der Augenoptiker
Advertising director: Peter Schulze
Agency: Troost Campbell-Ewald, Düsseldorf
Account director: Cornelius Muth
Account manager: Thomas Harmstorf
Creative director: Bernd Kreutz
Copywriter: Barbara Roertgen
Photographer: Kleinsborg & Appelbaum

298
Lego
United Kingdom
Advertiser: Lego
Marketing manager: Clive Nicholls
Agency: TBWA, London
Account director: Kate Marber
Creative directors: Neil Patterson, Malcolm Gaskin
Art director: Nick George
Copywriter: Alex Ayuli
Model maker: John Duffield

299
Curver plastic utensils
France
Advertiser: Soupledur – Curver
Agency: Grey, Paris
Account director: Antoine Pecnard
Account manager: Michel Ventura
Creative director: Jean-Claude Landais
Art director: Catherine Théry
Copywriter: Emmanuel Darrasse
Photographer: Stéphane Baudo

300
Barbie dolls
Sweden
Advertiser: Brio Scanditoy
Marketing director: Hans Lindohf
Advertising manager: Karin Nilsson
Product manager: Gösta Svensson
Agency: Ted Bates, Helsingborg
Account director: Sven Jacobsson
Art director: Dan Axel Lindberg
Copywriter: Ola Hallberg
Photographer: Roger Berg

301
Telephone service
Denmark
Advertiser: Post & Telegrafvaesenet
Advertising manager: Preben Storm
Brand manager: Willy Hansen
Product manager: Preben Larsen
Agency: Young & Rubicam, Copenhagen
Account manager: Thomas Lassen
Art director: Sonja Rasmussen
Copywriter: Pia Lynnerup
Illustrator: Fred Preston

302
Telephone service
Norway
Advertiser: Norwegian Telecommunications Directorate
Product manager: Dag Loewe
Brand manager: Morten Nielsen
Agency: Myres/Lintas, Oslo
Account director: Egil Torstensen
Creative director: Arve Bjerke
Copywriter: Kaare Snekvik
Photographer: Harald Foerland
Retouching: Saether & Olesen

303, 304
Dr White's sanitary towels and tampons
United Kingdom
Advertiser: Lilia-White
Marketing controllers: Philip Barnes
Agency: Bartle Bogle Hegarty, London
Account director: Jerry Judge
Creative director: John Hegarty
Art director: John Hegarty
Copywriters: Barbara Nokes (Man in underwear), Chris Palmer (Baby)
Photographers: Stak Aivalotis (Man in underwear), Camilla Jessel (Baby)

305
Valdispert tranquilliser
Netherlands
Advertiser: Vemedia
Marketing manager: R. J. Piers
Product manager: C. H. P. Mooy
Agency: Young & Rubicam, Amsterdam
Account director: Just Donker
Account manager: Mandy Savage
Creative directors: Hans Born, Duncan Mackintosh
Art director: Duncan Mackintosh
Copywriter: Hans Born
Photographer: Paul Wensveen

306
Verecolene Complesso laxative
Italy
Advertiser: Maggioni Farmaceutici
Marketing director: Alberto Fioruzzi
Brand manager: Sergio Copello
Agency: CPV Kenyon & Eckhart, Milan
Account director: Riccardo Cicinelli
Account manager: Fabio Carniel
Creative director: Pasquale Barbella
Art director: Antonella Pollini
Copywriter: Pasquale Barbella
Photographer: Renzo Boscolo

307, 308
Inderal and Inderal LA
United States
Advertiser: Ayerst Laboratories
Marketing director: H. Mosesson
Group product director: S. Auerbach
Brand managers: Diane Zimmerman (Inderal), Andy Panagy (Inderal LA)
Agency: Sudler & Hennessey, New York
Account director: Vincent Trovati
Account manager: Ken Kaplan
Creative director: Pat Levy
Art director: Rudi Sanchez
Copywriters: Steve West (Inderal), Lydia Green (Inderal LA)
Photographer: Irv Bahrt

309
Epivax dog vaccines
United Kingdom
Advertiser: Wellcome Foundation
Marketing director: R. Grice
Advertising director: S. Lane
Product manager: M. Freeman
Agency: Fletcher Shelton Delaney, London
Account director: Barry Bryant
Account manager: Nick Kendall
Creative director: Mike Trumble
Art director: Jeff Suthons
Copywriter: Bridget Jenkins
Illustrator: Andy Farley

310
Colac laxative
Japan
Advertiser: Nippon Vicks
Marketing managers: Mineko Ando, Seiji Kanemoto
Agency: McCann-Erickson Hakuhodo, Tokyo
Creative director: Sakae Tabata
Art director: Akio Nagai
Copywriter: Takao Sakakura
Photographer: Tetsuo Takai

311
Solprin soluble aspirin
New Zealand
Advertiser: Reckitt & Colman
Agency: Ward & Grey, Auckland
Account director: Tony Ward
Account manager: Alan Houghton
Creative director: Paula Keenan
Art director: Scott Yule
Copywriter: Paula Keenan
Illustrator: Scott Yule
Photographer: Chris Lewis

312
Novalucol indigestion remedy
Sweden
Agency: Young & Rubicam, Stockholm
Account directors: Göran Widtfeldt, Kenneth Fredriksson
Art director: Göran Widtfeldt
Copywriter: Kenneth Fredriksson
Photographer: Ola Lager

313
Kleenex toilet paper
Australia
Advertiser: Kimberly-Clark Australia
Marketing director: Greg Griffiths
Advertising manager: Heather Brown
Product manager: Bob Davidson
Brand manager: Dennis Hickey
Agency: SSC&B: Lintas, Sydney
Account director: John Holloway
Account manager: Dawn Perry
Creative director: Faie Davis
Art director: Faie Davis
Copywriter: Allan Crew
Photographer: Peter Luxton

314, 315
Vita Lamm toilet paper
Sweden
Advertiser: Modo
Marketing director: Christer Martensson
Advertising manager: Mats Nyquist
Agency: Ted Bates 1, Stockholm
Account director: Allan Berefeldt
Creative director: Christina Lundquist
Copywriter: Susanne Glemme
Illustrator: Jan Olof Bengtsson

316
Olympus OM4 camera
West Germany
Advertiser: Olympus
Advertising manager: Christoph Kunheim
Agency: William Wilkens, Hamburg
Account director: Wolfgang von Schneider-Marientreu
Art director: Bernd Häussler
Copywriter: Knut Körner
Photographer: Uwe Ommer

317
Pentax Super A camera
United Kingdom
Advertiser: Pentax
Marketing director: John Raddon
Advertising manager: Laurie Moore
Product manager: Mike Josephs
Agency: KMP Partnership, London
Account director: David Barraclough
Account manager: Nicky Horner
Creative director: John Wood
Art director: Paul Simblett
Copywriter: Howard Fletcher
Photographer: Robert Golden

318
Pentax PC35AFM camera
United Kingdom
Advertiser: Pentax UK
Marketing director: John Raddon
Advertising manager: Laurie Moore
Product manager: Mike Josephs
Agency: KMP Partnership, London
Account director: David Barraclough
Account manager: Nicky Horner
Creative director: John Wood
Art director: Paul Simblett
Copywriter: Howard Fletcher
Photographer: Robert Golden

319
Yashica TAF camera
West Germany
Advertiser: Yashica Kyocera
Advertising director: Leo Stejskal
Agency: Segmenta, Hamburg
Account director: Antye Raun
Creative director: Axel Schempp
Art director: Günter Schulte
Copywriter: Henning Lorenz
Photographers: Kisshazy (eagle), Gerhard Linnekogel (camera)

320, 321
Nikon cameras
West Germany
Advertiser: Nikon, Düsseldorf
Advertising manager: Kristof Friebe
Agency: Hildmann Simon Rempen & Schmitz/SMS, Düsseldorf
Account director: Frank Bettzüge
Creative director: Thomas Rempen
Art director: Thomas Rempen
Copywriter: Helmut Schmitz
Photographer: Hans Hansen ('Fool proof')
Stock photograph: ('Cheap lenses')

322
Agfachrome CT200 film
France
Advertiser: Agfa
Marketing director: Gilles Révillon
Advertising manager: Emile Martin
Agency: Ecom, Paris
Account director: Michelle Ossard
Creative director: Michel Rogale
Art director: Sei Sekigushi
Copywriter: Isabelle Brun
Photographer: Yves Buclet

323
Fujicolor HR1600 film
West Germany
Advertiser: Fuji Photo Film
Distribution manager: Günther Fidyka
Advertising manager: Wolfgang Winterscheidt
Agency: Lintas, Hamburg
Account director: Manfred Kirschnick
Account manager: Ana Paula Harder
Creative director: Joachim Crasemann
Art directors: Jürgen Assmann, Gerd Wolf
Copywriter: Arend Buck
Photographer: Peter Knaup

324
Ilford HR film
United Kingdom
Advertiser: Ilford
Advertising manager: Eva Beagan
Agency: Aspect Advertising, London
Account director: Mark Robinson
Account manager: Paul Chichester-Constable
Creative director: Malachy Quinn
Art director: Derek Rangecroft
Copywriter: Robin Murtough
Photographer: Brian Griffin

325
Tamron lenses
United Kingdom
Advertiser: Johnsons of Hendon
Marketing director: Mike Cheadle
Agency: Doyle Dane Bernbach, London
Account director: Robert Donin
Account manager: Antony Remedios
Creative director: Tony Brignull
Art director: Steve Sanderson
Copywriter: Martin Siddle
Photographer: Peter Lavery

326
Ilford Multigrade II paper
United Kingdom
Advertiser: Ilford
Advertising director: Eva Beagan
Agency: Aspect Advertising, London
Account director: Mark Robinson
Account manager: Paul Chichester-Constable
Creative director: Malachy Quinn
Art director: Derek Rangecroft
Copywriter: Robin Murtough
Photographer: Donovan

327
Kodacolor VR film
France
Advertiser: Kodak Pathé
Advertising director: Claude Genin
Product manager: Claude Briant
Agency: Young & Rubicam, Paris
Account director: Patrice Clipez
Account supervisor: Etienne Boisrond
Creative directors: Jean-Paul Bacquer, Gérard Monot
Art director: Christian Vince
Copywriter: Philippe Chatiliez
Photographer: Adrian Flowers

328
Kodak Vericolor film
Spain
Advertiser: Kodak
Agency: McCann Erickson, Madrid
Creative director: Angel del Pino
Art director: Luis Solero
Copywriter: Rosa Villasante
Photographer: Antonio Molina

329
Kodacolor VR
Denmark
Advertiser: Kodak
Marketing director: Jess Lausen
Advertising director: Mark Petersen
Product manager: Jens Jørgensen
Agency: Young & Rubicam, Copenhagen
Account manager: Frits Bülow
Art director: Britta Westhausen
Copywriter: Kirsten Lindemark
Photographer: Eric Curry

330, 331
Kodachrome 64
West Germany
Advertiser: Kodak
Marketing director: Richard Hiel
Advertising director: Herbert Grundmeier
Advertising co-ordinator: Friedrich Müller
Agency: Young & Rubicam, Frankfurt
Account director: Georg Daniels
Account manager: Jens Hagström
Creative director: Reinhard Lombacher
Art director: Heribert Burkert
Copywriter: Susanne Pinter
Photographers: Osamu Hayasaki ('White'), Alberto dell'Orto ('Hitch-hiker')

332
Kodak VR film
United Kingdom
Advertiser: Kodak
Marketing director: Peter Block
Advertising manager: Roger Clark
Product manager: Len Capp
Agency: McCann-Erickson, London
Group director: John Boyes
Account director: Ken McCrea
Account manager: Mark Campbell
Creative director: Martin Mayhew
Art director: David Lindsay
Copywriter: David Lindsay
Photographer: David Montgomery

333, 334
The Spastics Society
United Kingdom
Advertiser: Spastics Society
Marketing director: Andrew Ross
Advertising manager: Anita Maunsell
Agency: Benton & Bowles, London
Account director: Pam Ings
Account managers: Lynn Stephen ('Just because I couldn't speak'), Lesley Thompson ('They only see the chair')
Creative director: David Mitchell
Art directors: Ken Hodgson, David Mitchell
Copywriters: Keith Valentine, Terry King
Photographers: Max Forsythe ('Just because I couldn't speak'), John Londei ('They only see the chair')
Art buyers: Rita Pulford ('Just because I couldn't speak'), Gill Simmonds ('They only see the chair')
Typographer: Ian Dillon

335, 336, 337
Oxfam
United Kingdom
Advertiser: Oxfam
Marketing director: Sam Clarke
Agency: Fletcher Shelton Delaney, London
Account director: Lionel Knight
Account manager: Rachel Dyson
Creative director: Len Weinreich
Art director: Jeff Suthons
Copywriter: Bridget Jenkins
Illustrators: Peter Till (Hiroshimas, Barbed wire); Peter Brookes (Interest rates)
Concept creators: Jeff Suthons, Bridget Jenkins, Neil Brothwell, Sue Vanner

338, 339
NSPCC (National Society for the Prevention of Cruelty to Children)
United Kingdom
Advertiser: NSPCC
Marketing director: Frederick Lawrence
Agency: Saatchi & Saatchi Compton, London
Account director: John French
Account manager: Chris Edwards
Creative director: Jeremy Sinclair
Art director: Alan Midgely
Copywriter: John Bacon
Photographers: Ian Giles ('Cigarette'); Barney Edwards ('Help heal')

340
Mencap (Royal Society for Mentally Handicapped Children and Adults)
United Kingdom
Advertiser: Mencap
Secretary general: Brian Rix
Advertising director: Alan Leighton
Advertising manager: Fergus Logan
Agency: Young & Rubicam, London
Account director: Hywel Davies
Account manager: Judith Netherwood
Creative director: Chris Wilkins
Art director: Sian Vickers
Copywriter: Jeanne Willis
Photographer: Chris Holland

341
Alcoholics Anonymous
Brazil
Advertiser: Alcoholics Anonymous
Agency: MPM Propaganda, Rio de Janeiro
Creative director: Álvaro Gabriel de Almeida
Art director: Adeir Rampazzo
Copywriter: Toninho Lima
Photographer: Humberto Madeiros

342
Alcohol age limit legislation
United States
Advertiser: Metropolitan Life Insurance
Marketing director: Richard Keough
Advertising director: Robert Weinstein
Product manager: Dorothy Kelly
Agency: Young & Rubicam, New York
Group director: John Hatheway
Account supervisor: Richard Jones
Account executive: Charles Elberson
Creative director: Brian Dillon
Art director: Jean-Marie Poisson
Copywriter: Richard Sinreich
Photographer: Larry Robins

343
American Cancer Society
United States
Advertiser: American Cancer Society
Advertising manager: Nanette Atlas
Agency: Young & Rubicam, New York
Account manager: Ben Machtiger
Art director: Gail Kennedy
Copywriter: Colleen Wainwright
Photographer: Carl Fischer

344
Nursing recruitment
United Kingdom
Advertiser: Central Office of Information
Agency: TBWA, London
Account director: Chris Guille-Marrett
Creative directors: Neil Patterson, Malcolm Gaskin
Art director: Malcolm Gaskin
Copywriter: Neil Patterson
Illustrator: David Pelham
Model maker: David Malarkey

345
Anti-jaundice campaign
India
Advertiser: Ahmedabad Municipal Corporation
Agency: Shilpi Advertising, Ahmedabad
Account manager: Aslesha Koppula
Art director: Rashida Contractor
Copywriter: Ingrid Monterio
Illustrators: Yogesh Bhavsar, Mohan Patel

346, 347
Health information
Norway
Advertiser: Government Information Service
Marketing director: Steinar Bosnes
Agency: Ogilvy & Mather, Oslo
Account director: Bjarne Wollmann
Creative director: Bjørn Aune
Art director: Bjørn Aune
Copywriter: Tom Dahl
Illustrators: Rune Venjar, Anders Henriksen

348
Road safety
Norway
Advertiser: Public Road administration Central Information Service
Marketing director: Steinar Bosnes
Advertising managers: Per Øivind Nielsen, Ragnar Lie
Agency: Heltberg Creative Service, Oslo
Account director: Steinar Hodne
Creative director: Egil Jacobsen
Art directors: Tor Egeli, Kåre Ulsrud
Copywriters: Roald Stensby, Axel Hellstenius
Photographer: Stein Thue

349
Crime prevention
Norway
Advertiser: Norwegian Crime Prevention Council Central Information Service
Marketing director: Steinar Bosnes
Advertising managers: Per Øivind Nielsen, Britt Vangen, Anne-Lise Bakken
Agency: Heltberg Creative Service, Oslo
Account director: Steinar Hodne
Creative director: Egil Jacobsen
Art director: Tor Egeli
Copywriter: Roald Stensby
Photographer: Stein Thue

350
Army recruitment
United States
Advertiser: US Army Recruiting Command
Marketing executive: Major General J. O. Bradshaw
Advertising director: Colonel D. Borden
Agency: N. W. Ayer, New York
Executive account director: George Eversman
Executive creator director: Theodore Regan
Creative director: Philip Peppis
Art director: Mark Nussbaum
Copywriter: Conrad Randall
Photographer: Michael Pateman

351
The Engineering Council
United Kingdom
Director General: Dr. Kenneth Miller
Director of public affairs: Ron Kirby
Agency: Wight Collins Rutherford Scott, London
Account director: Claude Keith
Creative director: Andrew Cracknell
Art director: Steve Grime
Copywriter: Andrew Rutherford
Photographer: Graham Ford
Typographer: Keith Mackenzie

352
Army officer recruitment
United Kingdom
Advertiser: Central Office of Information
Campaign manager: Noel Thistlethwayte
Agency: Collett Dickenson Pearce & Partners, London
Account director: Nigel Clark
Creative director: David Brown
Art director: Rod Waskett
Copywriter: Paul Weinberger
Stock photographs

353
London police recruitment
United Kingdom
Advertiser: Metropolitan Police
Head of publicity: Julian Bradley
Agency: Collett Dickenson Pearce & Partners, London
Account director: Nigel Clark
Creative director: David Brown
Art director: John Foster
Copywriter: Chris Street
Photographer: Alan Brooking

354, 355
GLC (Greater London Council)
United Kingdom
Advertiser: GLC
Advertising manager: Tony Wilson
Agency: Boase Massimi Pollitt Partnership, London
Account director: Peter Herd
Account manager: Nick Hough
Creative directors: Alan Tilby, Paul Leeves
Art director: Peter Gatley
Copywriter: John Pallant
Photographer: Derek Seagrim (wall-face)

356
Conservatives in Europe
United Kingdom
Advertiser: European Democratic Group
Client executives: Colin Hart, Anthony Shrimsley
Agency: Saatchi & Saatchi Compton, London
Account director: Michael Dobbs
Account manager: John Chetwood
Creative director: Jeremy Sinclair
Art director: Andrew Ross
Copywriter: Mark Williams
Typographer: Roger Kennedy
Stock photograph

357, 358, 359
Printemps department store
France
Advertiser: Le Printemps
Marketing director: Jean-Marc Gely
Advertising managers: Alain de Saint-Sauveur, Gabrielle Chêne
Agency: Young & Rubicam, Paris
Account director: Claude Faucher
Account supervisors: Nathalie Cogis (Blue, Bridal), Virginie Loizeau ('Most Parisian')
Creative directors: Jean-Paul Bacquer, Gérard Monot
Art directors: Maïté Winterheimer (Blue, 'Most Parisian'), Sophie Desmarez (Bridal)
Copywriter: Annick Valla
Illustrators: A. Audras (Blue), Tony Viramontez ('Most Parisian')
Photographer: Jean-Baptiste Mondino (Bridal)

360, 361
Coin department stores
Italy
Advertiser: Coin
Client executive: Silvio Pellizzoni
Agency: ATA Univas, Milan
Account director: Franco Antonini
Creative director: Maurizio d'Adda
Art director: Bruno Acierno
Copywriter: Maurizio d'Adda
Photographer: Andre Carrara

362
Coin department stores
Italy
Advertiser: Coin
Marketing director: Lando Maddalena
Advertising manager: Ferdinando Zamprotta
Product manager: Emilio Bosoni
Agency: B Communications, Milan
Account director: Federico Mola
Creative director: Titti Fabiani
Art directors: Titti Fabiani, Vittoria Cattaneo
Copywriter: Rio Raikes
Photographer: Orio Raffo

363
Bijenkorf department store
Netherlands
Advertiser: Bijenkorf
Marketing director: J. M. J. M. Kessels
Advertising director: J. S. A. Toscani
Agency: Young & Rubicam, Amsterdam
Account director: Tiemen Bosma
Account manager: Eugenie Bürer
Creative directors: Hans Born, Duncan Mackintosh
Art director: Gerard Prins
Copywriter: Frits Rijksbaron
Photographer: Paul Wensveen
Retouching: Ruud van Ritbergen, Tieke Molenaar

364a, 364b, 364c
Dickins and Jones department stores
United Kingdom
Advertiser: Dickins and Jones
Marketing director: Mike Wiseman
Agency: Saatchi & Saatchi Compton, London
Account director: Tony Cator
Account manager: Caroline MacPherson
Creative director: Paul Arden
Art director: Mike Wells
Copywriter: David Edwards
Photographer: Terence Donovan

365
Sunchain
Japan
Advertiser: Sunchain
Agency: McCann-Erickson Hakuhodo, Tokyo
Creative director: Toru Yasui
Group Head: Misao Takano
Art director: Michio Nakahara
Copywriter: Kenichi Okubo
Photographer: Yushiyuki Morita

366
FNAC stores
France
Marketing managers: Didier Lecat, Jacques Parent
Agency: Publicis, Paris
Account director: Géraud Rives
Account manager: Christine Dubuc
Art director: Philippe Pouzol
Copywriter: Sophie Blanchat
Photographer: Mary-Ann Parkinson

367
Wienerwald restaurants
West Germany
Advertiser: Wienerwald
Marketing director: Maximilian Erlmeier
Agency: Leonhardt & Kern, Stuttgart
Account managers: Waldemar Meister, Michael Friedrich
Art director: Waldemar Meister
Copywriter: Michael Friedrich
Photographer: Rolf Bader

368, 369
Denny's restaurants
United States
Advertiser: Denny's
Senior vice-president, marketing: Barry Krantz
Agency: Foote Cone & Belding/Honig, Los Angeles
Account director: Larry Jones
Account manager: Craig Silver
Creative director: Michael Wagman
Art director: Larry Corby
Copywriter: Jack Foster
Illustrator: Nob Yamashita

370
Silk Cut cigarettes
United Kingdom
Advertiser: Gallaher
Advertising director: Mike Perry
Product manager: Nigel Northridge
Agency: Saatchi & Saatchi Compton, London
Account director: Neil Chalmers
Account manager: John Bowen
Creative director: Jeremy Sinclair
Art director: Paul Arden
Photographer: Graham Ford

371, 372
Benson & Hedges Longer Length cigarettes
United Kingdom
Advertiser: Gallaher
Marketing manager: Paul Rutherford
Agency: Collett Dickenson Pearce & Partners, London
Account director: Tony Stansfield
Creative director: David Brown
Art directors: Graham Fink (Concertina), John Fisher (Cut-out)
Photographers: Adrian Flowers (Concertina), Ed White (Cut-out)
Copywriter: Andrew Bruck (Cut-out)

373
John Player Superkings cigarettes
United Kingdom
Advertiser: Imperial Tobacco
Marketing director: Peter Brotherton
Advertising manager: David Baird
Brand manager: Garry Bond
Agency: Ogilvy & Mather, London
Account director: Martin Phelps
Account manager: Soames Hines
Creative director: Don Arlett
Art directors: Colin Tout, Carl Le Blond
Copywriter: Fletcher Watkins
Photographer: John Hammond
Model makers: Shirtsleeve Studios

374
Plaza cigarettes
Brazil
Advertiser: Souza Cruz
Agency: MPM, Rio de Janeiro
Creative director: Álvaro Gabriel de Almeida
Art director: Adeir Rampazzo
Copywriter: Toninho Lima
Photographer: Humberto Medeiros

375, 376, 377
Benson & Hedges Special Filter cigarettes
United Kingdom
Advertiser: Gallaher
Marketing manager: Paul Rutherford
Agency: Collett Dickenson Pearce & Partners, London
Account director: Tony Stansfield
Creative director: David Brown
Art directors: Graham Fink (Wolves), Nigel Rose (Shaving soap, Banana skin)
Photographers: Ed White (Wolves), Kevin Summers (Shaving soap), Rolph Gobits (Banana skin)

378, 379
Gauloises cigarettes
West Germany
Advertiser: British American Tobacco
Product manager: Rolf Biele
Agency: Heye Needham & Partner, Hamburg
Account director: Herber Schaaf
Creative director: Herber Schaaf
Art director: Uwe Mai
Copywriter: Herbert Schaaf
Photographers: Karin Elmers (Girl), Jens König (Airport)

380
Blend cigarettes
Sweden
Advertiser: Svenska Tobak
Advertising director: Hakan Wallen
Agency: McCann-Erickson, Stockholm
Account manager: Matts Karlsson
Creative director: C.-G. Clausen
Copywriter: Owe Elvén
Illustrator: Hakan Johansson

381
Muratti No1 cigarettes
West Germany
Advertiser: Martin Brinkmann
Marketing director: Werner Klatten
Advertising manager: Dag Podeus
Product manager: Jörg Felstehausen
Brand manager: Wolfgang Imlau
Agency: Young & Rubicam, Frankfurt
Supervisor: Michael Richter
Account director: Joe Nutt
Account manager: Ulf Heuer
Creative director: Reinhard Lombacher
Art director: Maria Christina Sennefelder
Copywriter: Susanne Erdmann
Photographer: Boudewijn Neuteboom

382, 383
Gallant cigarettes
Switzerland
Advertiser: Burrus & Co.
Marketing director: A. Weber
Advertising director: P. Genoud
Brand manager: F. Didier
Agency: Young & Rubicam, Bern
Account director: Suzanne Frei
Account supervisor: Claude Bosset
Creative director: H. J. Zürcher
Art directors: Mathias Babst, Lulu Müller
Copywriter: J. J. Zürcher
Photographer: Werner Bokelsberg, Hamburg

384, 385
Falstaff cigars
United Kingdom
Advertiser: Gallaher
Marketing manager: M. J. Ashdown
Agency: Collett Dickenson Pearce & Partners, London
Account director: John Ritchie
Creative director: David Brown
Art director: Judy Smith
Copywriter: Pete Mathews
Illustrator: Barry Craddock

386
Hollywood cigarettes
Brazil
Advertiser: Souza Cruz
Agency: MPM, Rio de Janeiro
Creative director: Álvaro Gabriel de Almeida
Art director: Adeir Rampazzo
Copywriter: Toninho Lima
Photographer: Humberto Medeiros

387, 388
Boots No 7 cosmetics
United Kingdom
Advertiser: Boots
Marketing director: Bertie Pinchera
Advertising manager: Sheilagh Patterson
Product manager: Elaine Kent
Brand manager: Gary Cormack
Agency: McCormick Publicis, London
Account director: Terry Oakley
Account manager: Sarah Bellman
Creative director: Gerry Moira
Art director: Molly Godet
Copywriter: Eliza Parker
Photographer: John Swannell

389
Rimmel cosmetics
United Kingdom
Advertiser: Rimmel International
Marketing director: Mike McNamara
Brand managers: Ann Hunter, Kathy Henning
Agency: Foote Cone & Belding, London
Account director: David Cheek
Account supervisor: Ann Hobden
Account executive: Sally Heath
Creative director: Barry Smith
Art director: Joanna Dickerson
Copywriter: Ray Skellorn
Photographers: John Swannell, Charley Stebbins
Typographer: Joanna Dickerson

390
Corolle eye-shadows
Italy
Advertiser: L'Oréal
Marketing director: Mr Resuli
Agency: Publicis, Milan
Account director: Daniela Greco
Account manager: Loreta Rossi
Creative director: Horst Blachian
Art director: Nick Lamicella
Copywriter: Daniela Salina
Photographer: Bill King

391
Revlon Fleurs de Jontue fragrances
United States
Advertiser: Revlon
Agency: Grey Advertising, New York
Account manager: Tom James
Creative director: Trisha Scudder
Art director: Gery Onorato
Copywriter: Martha Marchese
Photographer: James Moore

392
L'Oréal cosmetics
United States
Advertiser: Cosmair division of L'Oréal
Marketing director: Beatrice Dautresme
Agency: McCann-Erickson, New York
Art director: George d'Amato
Copywriter: Herb Green
Photographer: Irving Penn
Stylist: Freddie Liebka

393
Wella Recrin shampoos
Italy
Advertiser: Wella
Marketing director: Roger Meadows
Agency: Benton & Bowles, Milan
Account director: Giovanni Benini
Account manager: Eugenia Bisesti
Creative director: Gavino Sanna
Art director: Giampiero Vinti
Copywriter: Alba Minadeo
Photographer: Mario Zappalà

394, 395
Harmony hair colorants
Australia
Advertiser: Rexona
Agency: J. Walter Thompson, Sydney
Account director: Russell Ward
Creative director: Paul Priday
Art director: Reg Buckland
Copywriter: Larry Pitts
Photographer: Billy Wrencher

396
Esprit shampoo
Canada
Advertiser: S. C. Johnson & Son
Marketing director: Frank Bryant
Brand manager: Peter Cosentino
Agency: Foote Cone & Belding, Toronto
Account director: Barbara Taylor
Account executive: Susan Lalingo
Creative director: Bobby Phillips
Art directors: Alan Gair, Brian Richards
Copywriter: Bobby Phillips
Production manager: Rose-Ella Morrison
Photographer: Gillian Proctor

397
Clear anti-dandruff shampoo
Italy
Advertiser: Elida Gibbs
Marketing director: Giorgio Maschietto
Advertising manager: Silvio Pacillo
Product manager: Paolo Ballardini
Agency: J. Walter Thompson, Milan
Account director: Giuseppe Andreutti
Creative director: Genevieve Bini
Art director: Chiara Calvi
Copywriter: Pasquale Diaferia
Illustrator: Milo Manara

398
Johnson's Baby Shampoo
Netherlands
Advertiser: Johnson & Johnson
Advertising director: J. C. Groenhuizen
Agency: Young & Rubicam, Amsterdam
Account director: Nick van Loendersloot
Account manager: Simon Werkendam
Creative directors: Hans Born, Duncan Mackintosh
Art directors: Duncan Mackintosh, Richard Wagner
Copywriter: Hans Born
Photographer: Dirk Karsten

399
Egg-Melk soap
Norway
Advertiser: Nordstrom & Due
Marketing directors: Truels Due, Sverre Wiig
Agency: Heltberg Creative Service, Oslo
Account director: Steinar Hodne
Creative director: Egil Jacobsen
Art director: Egil Jacobsen
Photographer: Tomas Yeh

400
Close-up toothpaste
Canada
Advertiser: Lever Detergents
Marketing director: Patrick Bourgeois
Product manager: Barbara Haire
Agency: J. Walter Thompson, Toronto
Account director: Sorab Mistry
Account manager: Ian Davey
Creative director: Richard Constantineau
Art director: Leo Malbeuf
Copywriter: Su Bundock
Illustration: Studio Bel-Art

401a, 401b
Aim toothpaste
United States
Advertiser: Lever Brothers
Marketing director: Eugene Marrotta
Group product manager: Rick Ginsberg
Brand manager: Susan Friedman
Agency: Sudler & Hennessey, New York
Account director: Robert Brancaccio
Account manager: Peter Christofer
Creative director: Ernie Smith
Art director: Jane Cullen
Copywriter: Karen Irland
Photographer: Brad Guice

402
Patrichs aftershave and cologne
India
Advertiser: Pond's India
Vice-president, marketing: C. B. N. Reddy
Product manager: S. Ramkumar
Brand manager: Atul Vohra
Agency: Lintas, Bombay
Account director: Stanley Pinto
Account manager: Chintamani Rao
Creative directors: Alyque Padamsee, Aubrey Sequeira
Art director: Arun Vaidya
Copywriter: Aubrey Sequeira
Photographer: Sudhir Ramachandra

403
Chanel No. 5 bath products
United Kingdom
Advertiser: Chanel
Marketing director: Tony Evans
Agency: Ayer Barker, London
Account director: Peter Finch
Creative director: Terry Howard
Art director: Cyril Vickers
Copywriter: Terry Howard
Photographer: Gary Bryan

404
Chanel aftershave
United Kingdom
Advertiser: Chanel
Marketing director: Tony Evans
Agency: Ayer Barker, London
Account director: Peter Finch
Creative director: Terry Howard
Art director: Paul Girardot
Copywriter: Steve Ward
Photographer: Gary Bryan

405, 406, 407
French Railways
France
Advertiser: SNCF (French Railways)
Advertising director: Alain Cahen
Agency: Boulet Dru Dupuy Petit, Paris
Account director: Dominque Reinhard
Account executive: François Michels
Creative director: Marie-Catherine Dupuy
Art directors: Richard Clavery (Landscape, Moon), Stéphane Bielikoff (Cup)
Copywriters: Sylvie Ducourant (Landscape, Moon), Olivier Dorangeon (Cup)
Photographers: Robert Petersen (Landscape, Moon), Olivier Cauquil (Cup)

408
French Railways
France
Advertiser: SNCF
Agency: Young & Rubicam, Paris
Creative directors: Jean-Paul Bacquer, Gérard Monot
Art director: Pascal Midavainè
Copywriter: Claude Drouilhat
Photographer: Phil Jude

409
Netherlands Railways
Netherlands
Advertiser: Netherlands Railways
Agency: KVH/GGK, Amsterdam
Account director: Ad van Vuuren
Account executive: Henriette Fauchey
Art director: André van Leeuwen
Copywriters: Wim Michels, Henk Roozendaal
Photographer: Boudewijn Smit

410
Railway freight service
West Germany
Advertiser: German Federal Railways
Advertising director: Heinz-Dieter Wagner
Agency: Lintas, Frankfurt
Account director: Axel Zähler
Design: Michael Gros, Wolfgang Strenge

411, 412
German Federal Railways
West Germany
Advertiser: Deutsche Bundesbahn
Marketing manager: Mr. Remmert
Agency: McCann-Erickson, Frankfurt
Account director: Klaus Reinhardt
Creative team: Feico Derschow, Matthias Kersten
Photographer: Rolph Gobits (Romance)
Illustrator: Klaus Leven (Traffic jam)

413
Austrian Railways
Austria
Advertiser: Austrian Railways
Marketing manager: Gerold Korherr
Agency: McCann-Erickson, Vienna
Creative director: Wolfgang Bayer
Art director: Simon North
Copywriter: Patrick Schierholz
Photographer: Christian Pfaff

414, 415
UTA
France
Advertiser: UTA
Advertising managers: Didier Fournier, Nicole Malaquin
Agency: Doyle Dane Bernbach, Paris
Account director: Françoise Monet
Creative directors: Laurent Daniel, Anne Jambert
Art director: Laurent Daniel
Copywriter: Anne Jambert
Photographer: Jean Larivière

416, 417
RATP (Paris public transport)
France
Marketing director: Michel Barjansky
Advertising managers: Jacques Banaszuk, Pierre Robert Tranie
Agency: Ecom, Paris
Account director: Claude Tourault
Account manager: Françoise Bellanne
Creative director: Christian Vince
Art director: Sei Sekiguchi
Copywriter: Arnaud Laffile
Illustrator: FUTURA 2000

418
Iberia
International
Advertiser: Iberia
Marketing director: Teodoro Marcos
Brand manager: Eduardo Ruíz
Agency: NCK, Madrid
Account director: Pedro Llop
Account executive: Susan Simons
Creative director: Xavier del Valle
Art director: Pedro Herrero
Copywriter: Xavier del Valle
Illustrator: Juan Aboli

419
Iberia
France
Advertiser: Iberia
Client executive: Jean-Pierre Sauvage
Agency: Coutau-Thibaud, Paris
Account director: Thérèse Cousança
Creative director: Dan Jacobson
Copywriter: Anne Vernier
Art director: Dominique Ladoge
Illustrator: Jacques Servais

420
British Airways
United Kingdom
Advertiser: British Airways
Marketing director: Jim Harris
Advertising manager: Derek Dear
Agency: Saatchi & Saatchi Compton, London
Account director: Bill Muirhead
Account manager: Peter Buchanan
Creative director: Jeremy Sinclair
Art director: Andy Rott
Copywriter: Mark Williams
Photographer: Martin Thompson

421
Western Airlines
United States
Advertiser: Western Airlines
Agency: Doyle Dane Bernbach, Los Angeles
Account supervisor: Candy Kaelin
Art director: Stan Jones
Copywriter: Steve Diamant

422
British Airways
United Kingdom
Advertiser: British Airways
Marketing director: Jim Harris
Advertising manager: Derek Dear
Agency: Saatchi & Saatchi Compton, London
Account director: Bill Muirhead
Account manager: Peter Buchanan
Creative director: Jeremy Sinclair
Art director: Roy Askew
Copywriter: Ian Green
Photographer: Derek Seagrim

423
Air Canada
United Kingdom
Advertiser: Air Canada
Marketing director: John Burghardt
Agency: Ogilvy & Mather, London
Account director: Colin Hearn
Account manager: Sharon Nuttall
Creative director: Don Arlett
Art director: Carl Le Blond
Copywriter: David Ryland
Photographer: Stak
Model makers: Shirtsleeve Studios

424, 425
Package holidays
West Germany
Advertiser: Flug-Pauschalreisen
Co-ordinator: Raimund Schekeler (Marketing director, Condor)
Agency: Ogilvy & Mather, Frankfurt
Account director: Frank Hegewald
Creative director: Wolfgang Schoenholz
Art director: Peter Gamper
Copywriter: Erich Eckert
Photographer: Karl Schuesmann (Parasol),
Wilfried Becker (Child on beach)

426
Singapore Airlines
United Kingdom
Advertiser: Singapore Airlines
Agency: TBWA, London
Account director: Simon Fitch
Creative directors: Neil Patterson, Malcolm Gaskin
Art director: Nick George
Copywriter: Alex Ayuli
Photographer: Hazel Digby

427
SAS International Hotels
Norway
Advertiser: SAS International Hotels
Marketing director: Christian Sinding
Agency: Foote Cone & Belding, Oslo
Account director: William Richter
Creative director: William Richter
Art director: Trygve Engebraaten
Copywriter: Hans-Christian Bøhler
Photographer: C. A. Calson (CA Studio)

428, 429
Japan Air Lines
United Kingdom
Advertiser: Japan Air Lines
Advertising manager: Ron Bruce
Agency: SSC&B:Lintas, London
Account manager: Stephen Woodford
Creative director: Bob McLaren
Art director: Terry Coombes
Copywriters: Tim Read, Ellie Bird
Illustrator: Tudor Arts

430
Townsend Thoresen ferries
Netherlands
Advertiser: Townsend Thoresen
Client executive: P. M. Holt
Agency: Marketwinning Ayer, Wierden
Account director: Hans Horneman
Creative directors: Fred ten Tusscher, Erno V. Reuvekamp
Art director: Fred ten Tusscher
Copywriter: Erno V. Reuvekamp

431
DFDS Seaways
Norway
Advertiser: DFDS Norge
Marketing director: Erik Prestmarken
Agency: Ogilvy & Mather, Oslo
Account manager: Bjarne Wollmann
Creative director: Bjørn Smørholm
Art director: Bjørn Smørholm
Copywriter: Ingebrigt Steen Jensen
Photographer: Kristoffer Owe

432
Bermuda tourism
Canada
Advertiser: Bermuda Department of Tourism
Marketing director: Ron Manke
Canadian manager: Peter Smith
Agency: Foote Cone & Belding, Toronto
Account executive: Audrey Lanigan
Creative director: Bobby Phillips
Art director: Bruce Jones
Copywriter: Kurt Hagan
Production manager: Rose-Ella Morrison
Illustrator: Gerry Sevier

433, 434, 435
Hapag-Lloyd sea cruises
West Germany
Advertiser: Hapag Lloyd
Marketing director: Wolfgang Matz
Advertising manager: Horst Rickmann
Agency: Leonhardt & Kern, Stuttgart
Creative directors: Brigitte Fussnegger, Uli Weber
Art director: Uli Weber
Copywriter: Brigitte Fussnegger
Illustrators: Heinz Berger ('Typical holiday-maker'), W. Grebhard ('Grand Hotel'), Heseler & Heseler ('Caviar alarm')

436
Thomson Holidays
United Kingdom
Advertiser: Thomson Holidays
Group Communications manager: Allan Lees
Advertising and promotions manager: Andrew Main Wilson
Agency: J. Walter Thompson, London
Account director: Andrew Brown
Creative director: Richard Phillips
Art director: Anita Davis
Copywriter: John Platt
Stock photograph from Image Bank

437
Berlin tourism
West Germany
Advertiser: Berlin Tourist Office
Director: Hans-Jürgen Binek
Advertising manager: Hans-Joachim Steybe
Agency: Uniconsult, West Berlin
Account director: Birgit Cooper
Account manager: Uwe-Jens Zimmermann
Creative director: Thomas Mielke
Art director: Barbara Schäfer
Copywriter: Rolf Liersch
Photographer: Tom Gläser

438, 439
Club Méditerranée
Italy
Advertiser: Club Méditerranée
General manager: Antonio Carrozzini
Public relations executive: Diella Cervellini
Agency: CPV Kenyon & Eckhardt, Milan
Account director: Gianpaolo Carrozza
Account manager: Paola Pescetelli
Creative director: Pasquale Barbella
Art director: Roberto Pizzigoni
Copywriter: Aldo Cernuto
Photographer: Chico Bialas

440
Bahamas tourism
United States
Advertiser: Bahamas Ministry of Tourism
Director general: Baltron Bethel
Agency: N. W. Ayer, New York
Account director: Desmond Slattery
Account supervisor: Ronald Ricca
Creative director: Frank DeFilippo
Art director: George Fassbinder
Copywriter: Milt Lowe
Illustrator: Dennis Ziemienski

index of agencies and studios

index of advertisers